computer programs in
BASIC

PAUL FRIEDMAN

has worked as a professional computer programmer for the United States government and for Rockwell International, a major aerospace corporation. His work has familiarized him with dozens of computer systems, from the simplest microcomputers to the large and complex full capability machines.

A SPECTRUM BOOK

PRENTICE-HALL INC., Englewood Cliffs, New Jersey 07632

Library of Congress Cataloging in Publication Data

Friedman, Paul.
     Computer programs in BASIC.

     (A Spectrum Book)
       1. Computer programs—Catalogs. 2. Basic (Computer
program language) I. Title.
QA76.6.F74   001.64'25'029473   81-1606
ISBN 0-13-165225-7   AACR2
ISBN 0-13-165217-6 (pbk.)

Editorial/production supervision and interior design
    by Louise M. Marcewicz
Cover design by Michael Aron
Manufacturing buyer: Barbara A. Frick

    Throughout this book, we mention a great many pieces of hardware
and software by name. Most of these names are registered trademarks.
Because we cannot always tell who owns what trademark, we have not added
the usual ® after such trademarked names. Nonetheless, please respect
the trademark rights of the various manufacturers.

    Although every precaution has been taken to assure the accuracy
of the material in this book, neither the author nor the publisher assumes
liability for errors or omissions. We have neither tested nor run programs
listed in this book; information in the reviews is derived solely from the program authors' descriptions. We cannot warrant that the programs will work
as described. Before purchasing any software, inspect it carefully
to determine its suitability for your needs and your computer system.

10 9 8 7 6 5 4 3 2

Printed in the United States of America

PRENTICE-HALL INTERNATIONAL, INC., *London*
PRENTICE-HALL OF AUSTRALIA PTY. LIMITED, *Sydney*
PRENTICE-HALL OF CANADA, LTD., *Toronto*
PRENTICE-HALL OF INDIA PRIVATE LIMITED, *New Delhi*
PRENTICE-HALL OF JAPAN, INC., *Tokyo*
PRENTICE-HALL OF SOUTHEAST ASIA PTE. LTD., *Singapore*
WHITEHALL BOOKS LIMITED, *Wellington, New Zealand*

CONTENTS

7
APPENDIXES

PREFACE

You paid hundreds or even thousands of dollars for your new microcomputer. By now it may be dawning on you that a $1,000 computer with no software is just *$1,000 worth of scrap metal!*

You need programs to make your computer go. But how do you get those programs for your system? Do you pay $9.95 a piece or even more, just to buy a few simple game programs? Do you spend hours and hours trying to write the programs yourself?

There's a better way to get the software you want. Over a dozen magazines now serve the personal computer market. Every month, the pages of these magazines are crammed with programs, just waiting to be entered into your computer. With these programs you can quickly and easily build your own program library for *peanuts!*

But how do you find out what programs are available? By checking the pages of *Computer Programs in BASIC!* This book is your complete reference guide to over 1,600 published computer programs—programs that you can type into your computer for free!

Each review in this book is complete—it lists everything you need to know about a program or program group. A brief title line encapsulates the review for quick reference. Source information shows you where the program can be found. Any updates or corrections are shown so that you know that the information is accurate and complete. The text of the review gives you a full description of what the program does. In addition, the review gives you detailed technical information about what hardware and software the program needs. Everything you need to know is right at your fingertips.

You don't have to be a computer wizard to use *Computer Programs in BASIC*. That's because this book lists only *finished, ready-to-run programs* in BASIC, the easy-to-use language enjoyed by millions.

Even if you're a master programmer, you'll appreciate *Computer Programs in BASIC*. Why slave away hours, days, or even weeks writing a program when someone else has probably already done the work for you? These programs are *working, documented, and ready to go.*

If you have a personal computer in your home or office, don't be without your copy of *Computer Programs in BASIC*.

INTRODUCTION

HOW TO USE
THIS BOOK

During the past decade, the number of personal computers in operation across the nation has grown from a handful to over half a million. With more and more computers being used in homes, schools, and businesses, there is a growing demand for good, inexpensive software to drive these systems. *Computer Programs in BASIC* is designed to fill this need.

A wide variety of magazines now serve the personal computer market. Many of the articles in these magazines include listings of programs of interest to users of small computer systems. These listings form a vast reservoir of programs available to anyone at little or no cost. Unfortunately, these programs are scattered and disorganized. Up until now, anyone trying to find a program to solve a specific problem has had to do a great deal of searching.

This is where *Computer Programs in BASIC* comes in. A quick glance through this book is all you need in order to see what programs are available and where you can find them. Since we list only programs in BASIC, you know that when you find the program you want, you'll be able to read and understand it.

ANSI MINIMAL BASIC

Before we get started, we should give you some background on the BASIC language. BASIC was developed at Dartmouth College in 1963. The original language was intended to be a tool for teaching students the fundamentals of programming. Since it was never designed to handle "real world" problems, the original version of BASIC was somewhat limited in the features and statements it had.

In spite of its limitations, though, BASIC did begin to grow in popularity. To overcome the limitations of the early versions of BASIC, various computer manufacturers began to add new statements and features to "extend" the language. Each manufacturer added its own special set of extended features.

Now, the whole idea of using a "high-level" language such as BASIC is to put programs in a form that can be run on many different computers. As long as you stick with the "core" statements of BASIC, you can move your programs from computer to computer with relative ease. But the moment you start to use any of the extended statements of a particular version of BASIC—the very features that give the language reasonable capabilities—you can no longer count on being able to run your program on more than one system.

To help straighten out this situation, the American National Standards Institute (ANSI) has set up standards for BASIC. ANSI has done a commendable job of standardizing such computer languages as FORTRAN and COBOL. What they have done for these languages, they should be able to accomplish for BASIC.

As is its custom, ANSI has set up a list of rudimentary features to form the nucleus of the language. The core for BASIC is called ANSI Minimal BASIC. On top of this, modules are added to handle such features as matrices and file operations.

ANSI Minimal BASIC is used in this book to provide a list of common statements and functions that have well-defined meanings. Table 1 summarizes these statements and functions.

If you wish to purchase a copy of the complete ANSI standard for ANSI Minimal BASIC (X3.60-1978), it is available for $7.00 (plus $2.00 shipping) from:

American National Standards Institute, Inc.
1430 Broadway
New York, N.Y. 10018

THE REVIEWING FORMAT

The reviews in this book are designed to help you locate and use published computer programs. Each review discusses a program or a closely related group of programs. The reviews have been organized around six major categories: Business/Finance, Games, Math, Personal Interest, Science/Education, and Utility. Within these major headings, the reviews are classified by individual topics. An individual review is placed in the category and topic to which it most closely relates. A program is listed only once, even if it could reasonably fall into more than one category. Therefore, if you don't immediately see the program you want, check other categories.

Many programs are based on games or other noncomputer systems. To distinguish computer program names from other kinds of names, we print program

Table 1. ANSI Minimal BASIC

Statements

DATA	data storage statement	NEXT	end of FOR loop
DEF	function definition	ON . . . GOTO	computed GOTO
DIM	array definition	OPTION BASE	set lowest array subscript
END	end of program	PRINT	output to terminal
FOR . . . TO . . . STEP	execution loop	RANDOMIZE	randomize RND function.
GOSUB	subroutine call	READ	read from DATA statement
GOTO	branch to new statement	REM	remark
IF . . . THEN	conditional branch	RESTORE	reset READ pointer
INPUT	input from terminal	RETURN	return from subroutine
LET	assignment statement	STOP	stop execution

Functions

ABS(X)	absolute value	RND	random number
ATN(X)	arctangent	SGN(X)	sign
COS(X)	cosine	SIN(X)	sine
EXP(X)	*e* to the X power	SQR(X)	square root
INT(X)	largest integer not greater than X	TAB(X)	print tabulation
LOG(X)	natural log	TAN(X)	tangent

names in all capital letters (e.g., CHESS is a program that lets you play the game of chess).

Reviews in this book follow the format given below:

Title line. The first line of each review is the title line. It lists the review number and the title of the review. The review number should be used to identify the review in any correspondence you may have with us.

Author. This is the author (or authors) of this version of the program. (Someone else may have written the original version of the program.) This is *not necessarily* the author of the article in which the program appears.

Source. This part of the review shows you where you can find the program. The first line lists the magazine that printed the program, the magazine's date of issue, and (in parentheses) its volume and issue number. The second line gives the title of the article that has the program, the pages of the article, and (in parentheses) the pages of the program itself. If the program is part of an article that spans several issues of a magazine, all the parts of the article are shown.

Updates (optional). If later corrections, updates, or reprints have been published, they are listed here.

Description. The body of the review provides a complete capsule description of the program and what it does. If any flowcharts, sample runs of the program, or description of program variables are provided, these are noted at the bottom of the review.

Lines. This is the *estimated* number of lines in the program (±10%), a good indication of how much memory the program will require in order to run. Also noted here are any patches to the program given in the article (a patch is a short, optional modification to a program).

Version. This is the version of BASIC in which the program is written. The version is the one the author has listed. Sometimes the author doesn't say which version of BASIC has been used. In these cases we've tried to give

you some sort of indication as to what the version probably is.

Hardware. This lists any special pieces of hardware the program requires. We assume that you have a computer, a terminal, a means to load and save programs, and an adequate amount of RAM memory to run the program. We also assume you have a printer or printing terminal if the purpose of the program is to print forms, etc. We list only equipment the program *requires* in order to run; it may, in fact, be able to make use of more devices. We don't list equipment that might be needed to get the program onto your system or to save it again (even if done by CHAINing). (A frequently used method to avoid using data files in a program is to have the user store his data in DATA statements and then reSAVE the program.) We also don't list any interfaces that you may need to attach peripheral equipment to your computer.

We refer to a data file device as a "sequential file device" or a "random-access file device." A sequential file device is one in which data must be stored in sequential order (such as a cassette recorder). A random-access file device is any device in which data can be accessed in random order (such as a disk drive). We use these general terms because other types of file storage other than tape and disk may be available in the future.

Software. This section lists any special, non-BASIC software the program may need. In particular, it lists any *independently loaded* machine language or assembly language routines that the program uses. (For our purposes, a routine is machine language if the instructions are given in octal or hexadecimal notation, and is assembly language if the instructions are given in mnemonics.) Not listed are any machine language routines that are stored in the BASIC program (usually in DATA statements).

Non-ANSI. If the program uses any statements or functions that are not part of ANSI Minimal BASIC, these statements are listed here. Functions are denoted by a pair of parentheses following the function name (e.g., INP()). This convention is used even if the function doesn't actually use parentheses. Arguments, if any, are not shown.

In addition to non-ANSI statements and functions, we have chosen to flag selected other nonstandard features. If the program uses several of the matrix (MAT) operations (e.g., MAT INPUT, MAT READ, or MAT . . . ZER()), *MAT operations* is specified. Programs which use variable names with two letters or more than two characters are flagged with *two-letter variables* and *multi-letter variables,* respectively. (We don't count the $ used to indicate strings or the % used to indicate integers).

IF statements are part of ANSI Minimal BASIC. However, ANSI only allows the following form of IF:

IF [expression] [relation] [expression]
THEN [line number]

Many BASICs allow ELSE clauses, AND-OR-NOT relations, and/or statements following the THEN. We flag occurrences of these "enhanced" forms of IF statements as *extended IF.*

If *strings* is specified, the program uses Digital Equipment Corporation (DEC) format strings. If *HP strings* is specified, the program uses Hewlett-Packard (HP) format strings. (See "Which of These Programs will Run on My Computer?" for a discussion of these two types of strings.) Programs flagged with *strings* may also include the functions LEFT$, RIGHT$, MID$, LEN, and CHR$. Programs flagged with *HP strings* may use LEN and CHR$. Some BASICs allow HP strings to "masquerade" as DEC strings by omitting the character array DIM. It's our policy to lump such cases with *strings.*

If, in our opinion, a program would be unreasonably difficult for the average programmer to translate to another dialect of BASIC, the program is marked *not translatable.* Among the reasons we may mark a program *not translatable* are: It uses many special graphics characters or commands, it uses many specialized file commands, or it depends heavily on accesses (via PEEK, POKE, CALL, USR, etc.) to the system area of a particular BASIC.

MORE ABOUT THE REVIEWS

Though we've tried to make the reviews as simple and straightforward as possible, the reviewing process is necessarily complex. We can't possibly describe every significant detail about a program. But as long as you stick to using the reviews as just a general guide and not as an absolute authority, you should be able to use them with a minimum of difficulty. There are, however, a few subtle points that you should probably be aware of.

Our guiding philosophy throughout this book might be summed up as, "What information does a reasonably experienced programmer need to know to use a particular program?" We assume you're not just an automaton, blindly copying programs just as they're written. If it's possible for you to adjust a program slightly to fit your particular computer or version of BASIC without

too much effort, we're not going to flag it as requiring special attention.

The ANSI standard for Minimal BASIC is an exhaustive one. It spells out in minute detail everything, from how statements will operate to the exact syntax of numerical constants. As a practical matter, it would be impossible for us to check over each program to see whether it precisely matches the ANSI standard in every detail. As a compromise, we limit ourselves to just listing those statements and functions that are not in ANSI Minimal BASIC. We don't attempt to determine whether a program conforms to the ANSI standard in smaller details. We also accept modest variations from standard ANSI syntax for the Minimal BASIC statements (things such as LET statements without the keyword LET or "prompting" strings in INPUT statements).

This same philosophy of "assumed programmer flexibility" spills over into the area of hardware. Printers are expensive; most people can't affford one. Many computer programs print out listings of data using such statements as LPRINT. In most such cases, the printer really isn't necessary . . . the author just used it because it was around. It doesn't seem fair to list a printer as a hardware requirement for a program when a person without a printer need only change the LPRINT statements to regular PRINT statements. So, as a result, we don't list a printer as a hardware requirement unless a special type of printer such as an extra wide (132-column) model of printer is required.

For both hardware and software requirements, it may be possible to substitute for a particular requirement. For example, if an 8080-based microcomputer is required, it's usually possible to substitute a Z80-based one, since the Z80 uses an instruction set very similar to that of the 8080. The same thing applies for software. If a review lists a program as *not translatable,* you may still be able to run the program with another BASIC if the BASIC you use is compatible with the original BASIC.

It may also be possible for you to work around the difficult-to-translate areas. The most common reason for our marking TRS-80 programs *not translatable* is because it uses PRINT @ statements to format the screen. If you don't care about having a "pretty" display, you can change these to regular PRINT statements.

Therefore, if there's a program you'd like to use, don't give up on it just because it's marked *not translatable* or because it uses statements your BASIC doesn't have. Look it up, anyway. You may find that it is still possible for you to run the program in some form.

USING THE REVIEWS

Computer Programs in BASIC is intended only to help you locate programs for your computer. *Never use a review in this book as your sole criterion for selecting or purchasing a piece of software.* There are many factors to take into account when selecting exactly which programs will be right for you and your computer. Avoid disappointment. Check the program over closely before you buy it or attempt to use it. Since we do not test or validate programs, we cannot guarantee that the software listed in this guide will work as the program authors describe. Our

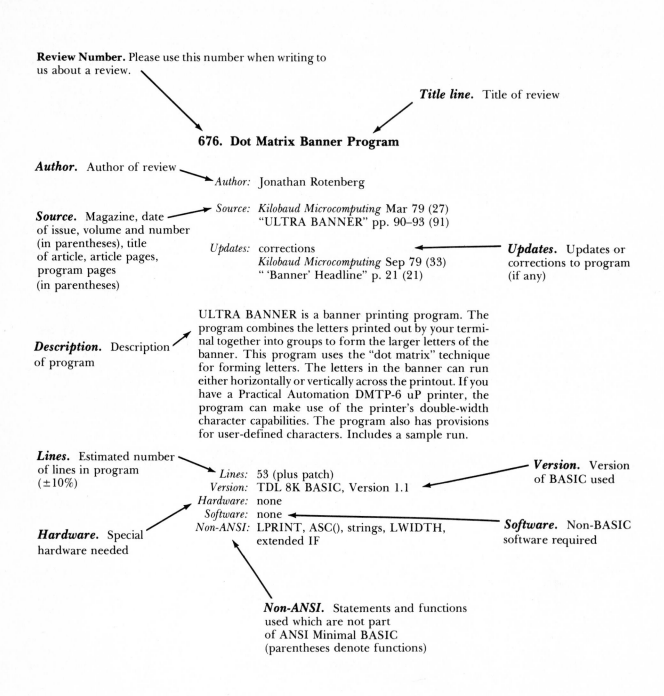

Review Number. Please use this number when writing to us about a review.

Title line. Title of review

676. Dot Matrix Banner Program

Author. Author of review

Author: Jonathan Rotenberg

Source. Magazine, date of issue, volume and number (in parentheses), title of article, article pages, program pages (in parentheses)

Source: *Kilobaud Microcomputing* Mar 79 (27) "ULTRA BANNER" pp. 90–93 (91)

Updates: corrections *Kilobaud Microcomputing* Sep 79 (33) " 'Banner' Headline" p. 21 (21)

Updates. Updates or corrections to program (if any)

Description. Description of program

ULTRA BANNER is a banner printing program. The program combines the letters printed out by your terminal together into groups to form the larger letters of the banner. This program uses the "dot matrix" technique for forming letters. The letters in the banner can run either horizontally or vertically across the printout. If you have a Practical Automation DMTP-6 uP printer, the program can make use of the printer's double-width character capabilities. The program also has provisions for user-defined characters. Includes a sample run.

Lines. Estimated number of lines in program (±10%)

Lines: 53 (plus patch)
Version: TDL 8K BASIC, Version 1.1
Hardware: none
Software: none
Non-ANSI: LPRINT, ASC(), strings, LWIDTH, extended IF

Version. Version of BASIC used

Software. Non-BASIC software required

Hardware. Special hardware needed

Non-ANSI. Statements and functions used which are not part of ANSI Minimal BASIC (parentheses denote functions)

Figure 1. Sample review.

information is based solely on the program listings and associated documentation.

WHERE CAN I GET THESE PROGRAMS?

Probably the most common question we're asked is, "Once I've located the programs I want in your book, where can I get the program listings?" Just because a program appears in an article published a few years back, don't think that you can't get a copy of it. There are many places you can go to find old program listings.

The first place you should look is, of course, your own bookshelf. How much did you pay for your microcomputer: $1,000, $2,000, more? With all that money tied up in hardware, doesn't it make sense for you to spend another $40 to $50 a year to keep yourself well supplied with computer information and software? At the very least, you should have subscriptions to *Byte* and *Kilobaud Microcomputing,* plus a magazine devoted to your particular type of computer. The more subscriptions you have, the better the inventory of software you'll have access to.

These subscriptions will keep you well informed about what's going on in the microcomputer field. The software listed on the pages of these magazines will more than pay for the subscriptions. Keeping a well-stocked supply of computer magazines is your best assurance that you'll be able to find the programs you want when you need them. You'll find a list of the various computer magazines serving the microcomputer market, their addresses, and their subscription rates listed in Appendix B in the back of this book.

Another good source of back issues is your local computer club. If you haven't joined one already, you should. Checking among other computer users, you're almost sure to find someone with the magazine you need who'll be willing to let you photocopy the material you want. Several of the computer magazines regularly run listings of computer clubs. You can check these listings to find one near you.

Also check out club-sponsored and other types of computer swap meets. With a little dickering, you can build up your back issue collection at bargain prices.

But let's say you can't find the issue you want in your own collection and no one you know has it. Does that mean that you have to do without? Fortunately, no. There are a variety of other places to go for program listings.

First, check a current issue of the magazine in question. Most of the computer magazines regularly run ads listing the back issues that they have for sale and their prices. In general, an issue will cost no more than the original cover price. Even if the magazine doesn't run ads, write to its editorial offices anyway and ask if they still have any copies of the issue you want. Enclose a check for the current cover price of the magazine. If the magazine still has any copies in stock, they'll send you one. Most magazines keep a supply of old issues going back two to three years from the current issue.

Also look for offers of magazine articles in book form. Some of the magazines take articles from their pages and combine the articles into books. A few magazines, such as *Dr. Dobb's Journal,* are available in complete form as books.

One of the most often overlooked sources of back issues is microform (microfilm rolls and microfiche cards). We find it amazing how quick most people are to turn up their noses at microfilm. You say you don't have a microfilm reader and, anyway, microfilm is too complicated to handle? Nonsense. Microfilm isn't just for James Bond types. Anyone can use it.

University Microfilms International is the national microfilming service. Its address and toll-free telephone number are:

University Microfilms International
300 North Zeeb Road
Ann Arbor, Michigan 48106
(800) 521-0600

They provide microfilm materials covering a vast range of subjects. UMI serves both libraries and the general public (you can order by phone—MasterCard and Visa are accepted).

The microcomputer magazines that currently are available in microform are noted in Appendix B. You'll have to call for a quote on the magazine you want, but the prices are nominal. A volume of a magazine on microfilm is usually substantially cheaper than the total of the original cover prices of the issues.

Besides computer magazines, you can select from UMI's huge collection of other magazines and documents on microfilm (over 10,000 different magazine titles alone). Want a copy of *Doc Savage Comics* (1941)? You can find it here! Be sure to write or phone for a free copy of the UMI catalog.

You say you don't have access to a microfilm reader? That's probably not true. Most libraries have them. In small libraries, the reader may be hidden away in a back room. In that case, you'll have to ask the librarian where it is and whether or not you can use it. If you've never used a microfilm viewer before, let the librarian show you how to operate it. Using a microfilm reader is really quite easy.

Getting the program listing you want from the microfilm into your computer is probably the most inconvenient part of using microfilm. You can, of course, simply copy down the listing onto paper. That's rather error-prone, though. A better way is to ask the librarian if you may plug your microcomputer in next to the reader. Then you can simply copy the program straight into your machine. At the larger libraries, you'll find microfilm readers with photocopy machines attached. Drop in a coin, and the photocopier will automatically make a copy of whatever is displayed on the screen.

Also remember that microfilm is just that: *film.* You can do anything with it that you can do with regular photographic film, including having your local photo lab blow up selected frames into 8- by 10-inch prints. But that gets kind of expensive if you're copying a long article. A better way is to clip the frames apart and mount them in regular 35 mm slide jackets. Then you can look at them using a slide projector or viewer.

There are two basic formats for microform materials: microfilm rolls and microfiche cards. Most microfilm readers use standard 35 mm, positive (black letters on a white background) film. Microfiche is the same stuff as microfilm, except that it is made up into 4- by 6-inch plastic cards. Microfiche is growing in popularity because the microfiche viewers are cheaper than conventional microfilm readers and are easier to use. Your choice of whether to use microfilm or microfiche will be dictated by what kind of reader your library has.

Even if you can't or don't wish to use a microform reader, you can still make use of UMI's collection. UMI will photocopy magazines in its microfilm library. The current charge is about $6.00 per article, or $0.10 per page for a complete issue. If your library has a microfilm photocopier, it's usually cheaper to buy the microfilm and do the photocopying yourself.

Speaking of libraries, more and more of them are becoming aware of the microcomputer field. Many now have regular subscriptions to *Byte, Kilobaud Microcomputing,* and the other major computer magazines. The best types of libraries in which to find these materials are university, college, city college, and technical school libraries. Unless you're a student, you probably won't be able to check materials out. However, such libraries almost always at least permit the general public to come in, browse around, and use the facilities.

Getting listings of old programs does sometimes take a bit of leg work. But with a little snooping around, you should be able to find copies of the programs you want.

WHICH OF THESE PROGRAMS WILL RUN ON MY COMPUTER?

After looking through this book, you may be wondering which of the listed programs will run on your type of computer. The answer is, "Most of them."

As you skim the various reviews, you'll probably notice that most of the programs were written in a version of BASIC other than the one which runs on your system. Does that mean that you're restricted to using just a small fraction of the programs that have been published? Of course not. One of the main advantages of programs written in a "high-level" language such as BASIC is that programs written for one computer can usually be used on another.

In general, you can take ANSI Minimal BASIC programs from one machine to the next with ease. The "core" statements of BASIC are very "portable"—they act the same on virtually all computers. However, most programs use at least a few nonstandard statements or functions.

Because the original Dartmouth BASIC was so limited in what it could do, manufacturers writing new versions of BASIC have each added on "extended" statements of one kind or another. Because there has been no standard from which to work, the different versions of BASIC have developed with different sets of extended statements. Still, all is not lost. Even without a formal standard, most manufacturers are starting to adopt a fairly uniform set of common extended statements and

functions. CHR$(X) means much the same thing in Radio Shack TRS-80 BASIC as it does in Commodore PET BASIC. Other statements such as PRINT USING (formatted print) have a commonly understood meaning, even if they're used slightly differently in different dialects of BASIC.

With the coming of ANSI Minimal BASIC and its extensions, we may expect much greater standardization of BASIC in the future. One factor helping this trend along is the dominance of Microsoft BASIC in the microcomputer field. Since Microsoft now supplies the BASIC interpreters for most of the major microcomputer companies, Microsoft BASIC has become a *de facto* standard.

PROGRAM TRANSLATABILITY

So much for the future of the BASIC language. But where does that leave you right now? For the time being, you're still stuck with the fact that a BASIC program written for one computer is usually going to require a few changes before it will run properly on another. In developing this book, we've tried to help you overcome this problem in two ways.

First, each review has a Non-ANSI section at the bottom of it. This section lists those statements and functions the program uses that are not part of ANSI Minimal BASIC. In addition, we have flagged occurrences of a few other nonstandard features such as two-letter variables.

Second, Appendix A lists the meanings of the assorted BASIC statements and functions found in this book. By checking the Non-ANSI section of a review to see what nonstandard language features the program uses, and then using Appendix A to determine the meanings of those statements and functions, you should be able to get a rough idea of whether or not you'll be able to adapt the program for your particular BASIC.

If the program uses statements or functions that your BASIC doesn't have, check the program listing. It may be that you can omit that part of the program without affecting the program too much. It may also be possible to write substitute statements that will perform the same function.

Occasionally, you'll see the notation "not translatable" listed in the Non-ANSI section. This means that, in our opinion, the program would require too much effort to translate to another dialect of BASIC. Among the reasons that this might be true are: the program uses special graphics characters or commands, the program accesses data or machine language subroutines in the system area of the computer's memory, or the program depends heavily on specialized, nonstandard statements (often true of programs that use random-access files).

Here we come to a very touchy point. Programmers come in all shapes and sizes. One user may be typing in his or her first program and can do little more than copy, character-for-character, what is printed on the page. The next may be a professional programmer, skilled enough to modify the BASIC interpreter, if that's what it takes to run the program. When we say "not translatable," what we mean is "not translatable without undue effort by a programmer with some, but not a lot, of knowledge of BASIC." Naturally, this determination is highly subjective.

We expect that you, the typical computer user, will have enough understanding of BASIC to make simple changes in a program as you type it in. If the program uses IF . . . THEN and your BASIC requires IF . . . GOTO, you should be able to make the change. If the program uses LPRINT statements (PRINT to printer) and you don't have a printer, you should be able to change the statements to regular PRINT statements. On the other hand, we don't expect you to start trying to simulate the functions of several complicated graphics commands. True, you might *in theory* be able to simulate these commands on your machine, but probably not without hours and hours of head scratching.

By the same token, we don't classify a program as not translatable just because it uses a few nonstandard facilities. Often a program will start off by POKEing a value into memory to set some system-dependent option. It doesn't seem reasonable to mark such a program as being not translatable. After all, if you're using a different BASIC, you can usually just omit the offending statement.

Clearly, if a program makes only trivial use of the special features of a particular BASIC, it should be translatable to another BASIC. If it makes very heavy use of such features, it must be considered not translatable. But what about the cases between these two extremes? Where do we draw the line? We emphasize that if you find a program you want, but it's marked not translatable, look it up anyway if you can. Even if you can't use the program as written, you may be able to follow its flow of logic in writing your own program.

TRANSLATION GUIDES

Besides the listings of BASIC statements and functions in Appendix A of this book, there are other useful aids for translating BASIC programs from one dialect to another. One of them is David Lien's book, *The BASIC Handbook*. This invaluable reference work catalogs the various BASIC statements and functions and explains how each of them is used. In addition, it provides alternative statements you can use if your BASIC doesn't support a particular feature. *The BASIC Handbook* is available by mail for $14.95 plus $1.35 postage and handling (California residents add 6% sales tax) from:

CompuSoft Publishing
8643 Navajo Road
San Diego, Calif. 92119

Another book that's mandatory reading for serious BASIC programmers is the *CONDUIT BASIC Guide*. This guide talks about the features found in different versions of BASIC. Though not as conveniently organized as *The BASIC Handbook*, the *CONDUIT BASIC Guide* goes into more detail about the differences among the various implementations of the BASIC statements. It also gives you guidelines to follow if you wish to make your programs "portable" for use on computer systems other than your own. You can order a copy of the *CONDUIT BASIC Guide* for $10.00 from:

CONDUIT
P.O. Box 388
Iowa City, Iowa 52244

PITFALLS IN BASIC

Okay. You've found the program you want. You've located the nonstandard statements and translated them. You've typed in the program and your BASIC interpreter has accepted the statements as being valid. Are you home free?

Not quite. Even in BASIC programs that seem otherwise straightfoward, there can still be a few pitfalls to trap the unwary. If your program seems to be correct, but still won't run properly, check it out for occurrences of the following special circumstances:

Hewlett-Packard versus Digital Equipment Corporation format strings. When strings were first introduced to BASIC by the major minicomputer manufacturers—Hewlett-Packard (HP), and Digital Equipment Corporation (DEC), each company chose to implement strings in a different way.

Hewlett-Packard chose what might be termed "character-array strings." These strings are stored as arrays of characters using DIM statements. Substrings (sections of strings) are extracted using a bracket or parentheses construct such as A$ = B$ (X,Y) (which sets A$ equal to characters X through Y of B$). Note that most implementations of HP format strings don't allow string arrays, because the parentheses are already used as the notation for substrings.

The Digital Equipment Corporation, on the other hand, chose what might be called "table strings." DEC strings are stored in a *string table,* an area of memory specifically set aside for strings. Versions of BASIC which use this format take substrings out of strings using functions such as LEFT$, RIGHT$, and MID$.

Most BASICs use strings which fall into one of these two camps. The leading users of HP strings are Hewlett-Packard, Data General, and North Star. DEC string users include DEC and Microsoft. Since Microsoft provides the BASIC interpreters for the vast majority of microcomputers (including PET, TRS-80, and others), DEC strings are the most commonly used type of strings on microcomputers. However, ANSI has lined itself up on the side of the HP format. ANSI's power to establish a standard is not to be underestimated. (Witness all the manufacturers touting how "ANSI compatible" their FORTRANs and COBOLs are.) It remains to be seen which form of strings will eventually win out.

RIGHT versus RIGHT$, MID$ versus SEG$. In DEC strings, beware. RIGHT$ (A$,3) means the right three characters of A$. RIGHT(A$,3), a function used in DEC BASIC-Plus, means the right-hand characters *starting at the third character* of A$. Also beware of the fact that some of the different substring functions do not act the same as MID$. MID$(A$,2,3) gets the three characters starting at the second character of A$. SEG$(A$,2,3,) returns the two characters from position 2 to position 3 of A$. (HP substrings act like this latter format.)

FOR statements. A few BASICSs (notably, TRS-80 Level II BASIC) use FOR statements that are slightly different from the standard ANSI FOR. In the normal ANSI FOR statement:

10 FOR I = 1 TO X

the value of X is checked against the starting value (1) the first time the FOR statement is reached. If X is less than 1, the FOR . . . NEXT loop never gets executed. But in the alternate form of FOR, the interpreter waits until the end of the loop before it checks. *Even if X is less than I initially, the loop will still be executed once!* This can also affect what value I has after the end of the FOR loop.

Multiple-statement IF statements. Some BASICs permit more than one statement on a line, using a colon or backslash to separate the statements. A problem occurs when you combine multistatement lines with IF statements:

10 IF X = Y THEN PRINT "#1": PRINT "#2"
20 REM

If the IF test fails (in this case, if X is not equal to Y), some BASICs will skip over the rest of the statements on the line (and go directly to line 20). Other BASICs skip over only the statement which directly follows the THEN (and thus in this case, would execute the second PRINT).

RND. The RND (random number) function acts differently in different versions of BASIC. The normal ANSI RND function is initialized with the RANDOMIZE statement. Each call to RND then returns to fractional value in the range of zero to one. In the ANSI form, RND doesn't take an argument. Some BASICs require a dummy argument that does nothing, such as RND (0). In other BASICs, the argument may have a meaning: RND(−1) is sometimes used in place of RANDOMIZE. RND(X) may return a value between zero and X. In integer-only BASICs, RND(X) may return an integer between one and X. There are other variations.

SGN. SGN(0) returns a zero in ANSI BASIC. In some BASICs it may return a value of one.

Recursive GOSUB. In some BASICs, GOSUB subroutines can call themselves. In others, this is not permitted.

Placement of END. Some BASICs require the END statement to be placed *only* on the last line of the program. If an END statement is placed anywhere in the middle of a program, the rest of the program may "disappear" from listings.

File operations. File operations such as OPEN, CLOSE, READ #, and WRITE are defined differently in the different versions of BASIC which have them. It's almost a sure bet that you'll have to modify any such statements if you want to use them on another machine.

PRINT USING. In the string which defines the format that a PRINT USING statement will use, different characters mean different things to the various dialects of BASIC. Again, it's almost a sure bet that you'll have to tinker with this type of statement if you wish to transfer it to another system.

Machine language. Any of the statements or func-

tions which directly access the computer's memory, either by manipulating data (PEEK and POKE), or by jumping to a machine language subroutine (CALL and USR), are going to be machine dependent. If you switch to a different BASIC, you'll probably have to change the memory addresses used. If you forget this, and accidently use the system area of your computer as a scratchpad for data, or try to jump to a system subroutine that doesn't exist in the new BASIC, you're going to make your computer *very* unhappy. If you're using your own machine language subroutines, remember that different BASICs use different protocols to return data, or even just to get back into the BASIC program.

Multiple meanings. Some nonstandard statements mean different things to different BASICs. In some BASICs, GET fetches a file record. In others it retrieves a single character from the keyboard. Depending on the BASIC used, SET can plot a point, set the display speed, specify a file device, or set a pointer into a file. Even if a statement is defined the same way in two different BASICs, it still may *act* slightly differently (remember the problem with FOR).

Trigonometric functions. Remember that trigonometric functions such as SIN and COS take arguments in *radians,* not degrees (usually).

Special-function characters. Some BASICs use special-function characters to do things like clear the screen or sound a beep. Not all BASICs use the same characters to do the same things.

Delayed-action statements. Some BASIC statements are like DIM and DEF in that they have a "delayed-action" effect. Initially, the BASIC interpreter just seems to jump over these statements. Only later do they appear to cause something to happen. Some BASICs allow functions with more than one statement, with everything between a DEFN and a FNEND being ignored until a function call is made. ON ERROR causes a jump to an error-handling routine *no matter where or when in the program the error occurs.* IF END is used in some BASICs to say "when you get to the end of an input file, jump to the specified statement." Note that you don't jump when you execute the IF END statement, but only when an INPUT or READ # finds an end-of-file. (In other BASICs, this is just a regular IF statement with the END being a function that returns a value indicating whether the end-of-file has already been found.)

Automatic zeroing. Some BASICs automatically set all variables to zero when a program starts up. Don't assume this is true for every version of BASIC.

AND, OR, and NOT. When used outside of an IF statement, the functions AND, OR, and NOT mean slightly different things to different versions of BASIC.

Round-off error. What is one divided by three in decimal? It is 0.33333333333 . . . , right? One third is a number that can't be expressed exactly in decimal form. This is called *round-off error.* The same thing happens in the binary number system that computers use, but it happens to different numbers. One tenth is a number that "goes on forever" and can't be expressed exactly in binary. You may find that some calculations involving numbers with fractional parts may become slightly inaccurate after awhile because of this problem. Depending on how good your BASIC interpreter is at covering up this inaccuracy, it may say that one tenth added to itself ten times is "0.99999999"! This problem can even affect such things as how many times a FOR loop executes when you use a STEP with a noninteger value.

Character sets. Not all computer systems use the ASCII character set. IBM computers use the EBCDIC character set. The ASCII value of a character may be different than the EBCDIC value. If you try to sort characters or do comparisons between characters based on their numerical character set values (using functions such as ASC), you may run into problems if you try to run your program on a computer that uses a different character set.

1

BUSINESS/FINANCE

BILLING

573. Computerized Billing Statement

Author: Lee Wilkinson

Source: *Kilobaud* Feb 77 (2)
"Computerized Statement" pp. 134–135
(134)

This is a program to produce computerized billing statements for a small business. Many small businesses have trouble collecting payments from their customers. This program helps to ease that problem by producing computer-typed statements. When customers receive a computer-printed statement they generally pay up faster because they don't want the computer company "doing the billing" to think they are tardy with their payments. The program does not use external files; all data is stored in memory in DATA statements. To save the data, you must resave the entire program. Includes a sample run.

Lines: 72
Version: MITS 8K BASIC
Hardware: none
Software: none
Non-ANSI: extended IF, LIST (used as a program statement), strings, two-letter variables, RUN (used as a program statement), ON . . . GOSUB

582. Simplified Billing System for a Transportation Company

Author: Carl Warren II

Source: *Kilobaud* Jun 77 (6)
"Simplifed Billing System" pp. 94–95 (95)

This is a simple billing system that does not require the use of external files. The billing data is entered, and then one or more copies of the billing report are produced. This program is, however, highly specialized for one par-

ticular firm. It does not show how such a billing system might be set up for other kinds of businesses. Includes a sample run.

Lines: 72
Version: MITS 8K 680 BASIC Version 1.0 Revision 3.2
Hardware: none
Software: none
Non-ANSI: NULL, extended IF, CLEAR, multi-letter variables, strings

944. Billing Statement

Author: O. Dial

Source: *Personal Computing* Apr 78 (2:4)
"Fishing the MOD Way" pp. 53–55 (54)

Updates: correction
Personal Computing Jul 78 (2:7)
"Catching a Mistake" p. 8 (8)

correction
Personal Computing Nov 78 (2:11)
"Fishing for Bugs" p. 6 (6)

This program accepts credit transactions and produces a statement of sales. The program stores account numbers, descriptions of the merchandise purchased, the amount of sales, and the dates of purchase. Includes a sample run.

Lines: 94
Version: Altair Extended Disk BASIC
Hardware: random-access file device
Software: none
Non-ANSI: not translatable

637. Billing for Hourly Services

Author: Bill Welborn

Source: *Kilobaud* Sep 78 (21)
"At Last: A Client Timekeeping System" pp. 32–39 (32–35)

Updates: correction to article
Kilobaud Oct 78 (22)
"Corrections" p. 100

Do you own a business where clients or customers are billed by the hour? This system can help you do your billing. Many businesses, especially professional services such as those of lawyers and accountants, bill by the hour. Large computer services charge a small fortune for doing billing for such businesses. With this system, you can use your personal computer to do the job. The system is made up of two programs. The first program is used to record the number of hours of service you provide for each client. The program can record what the hours are used for, so you can itemize your bill. The second program prints out the bills for each account. Includes sample runs and a list of program variables.

Lines: 34, 100
Version: IBM BASIC
Hardware: random-access file device
Software: none
Non-ANSI: strings, FILE, READ #, WRITE, END OF(), DATE(), IMAGE, ERASE, SPA(), PRINT USING, SKP()

1021. Electricity Billing

Author: David Whitehead

Source: *Personal Computing* May 79 (3:5)
"An Invoicing Program" pp. 64–65 (65)

This program produces invoices for electricity billing. Includes a sample run.

Lines: 75
Version: not given
Hardware: none
Software: none
Non-ANSI: STRING$(), strings, two-letter variables

1026. Rate-Setting and Billing for Small Utilities

Author: Stephen Smith

Source: *Personal Computing* Jan 79 (3:6)
"Rate-Setting and Billing for Small Utilities" pp. 43-52 (48-52)

When you mention water utilities, most people think of giant corporations serving millions of people. But thousands of communities across the land are served by small water and power companies. Each of these companies may serve just a few hundred or a few thousand people. With the advent of the microcomputer, even these small companies can now take advantage of the power and flexibility of computerized billing. The first of these two programs uses Monte Carlo simulations to determine what is the best rate to set for water usage. The second program is a billing program. It keeps track of water usage and generates bills for individual water users. Includes sample runs.

Lines: 121
Version: Microsoft BASIC
Hardware: two sequential file devices
Software: none
Non-ANSI: multi-letter variables, strings, extended IF, PEEK(), WAIT, POKE, ASC(), VAL()

1047. Invoice Printer

Author: Dan Obed

Source: *Personal Computing* Sep 79 (3:9)
"Small Business Invoicing" pp. 32–33 (32–33)

This program prints out invoices for small businesses. It does not store data, but it can automatically compute totals and sales tax for you. Includes sample output.

Lines: 47
Version: TRS-80 Level II BASIC
Hardware: none
Software: none
Non-ANSI: CLEAR, LPRINT, LPRINT USING, strings

BUDGETING

930. Budget Program

Author: O. Dial

Source: *Personal Computing* May–Jun 77 (1:3)
"Recursive Budgeting" pp. 54–59 (57–59)

Updates: commentary
Personal Computing Nov–Dec 77 (1:6)
untitled p. 4

uncorrected error
Personal Computing Oct 78 (2:10)
"Recursive Budgeting Bug" p. 12

Budgeting is a problem common to both business and personal finance. This program helps a person or group allocate a budget. The process used is an iterative one in which conflicts are gradually reduced one step at a time.

The program consists of three parts. In the first part, the program reads in the income available and deductions from income normally taken. From this, the program outputs a report of spendable income. The program then accepts input about variable expenses. If expenses exceed income (as they always do), the program uses an iterative dialog to resolve the conflicts. Upon conclusion of each iteration, a budget summary is printed to assist in the next iteration. At the end, the program prints out a final report of the budget showing both income and expenses. Includes sample output and a list of program variables.

Lines: 222
Version: MITS Extended BASIC
Hardware: none
Software: none
Non-ANSI: strings, extended IF, two-letter variables, CONSOLE, PRINT USING, SWAP, OUT

CONSTRUCTION

537. Lumber and Building Materials Calculations

Author: Jim Schreier

Source: *Interface Age* Jun 79 (4:6)
"LUMBER" pp. 80–83 (82–83)

Figuring how much a building job will cost is a complicated process. This program can take the sting out by doing all the calculations to show you how much the job should cost and which supplier is offering the best prices.

Lines: 183
Version: SWTPC 8K BASIC
Hardware: none
Software: none
Non-ANSI: strings, LINE, DIGITS, STRINGS, STR$( ), extended IF

719. Wallpaper-Paint-Paneling-Carpet Program for the PET

Author: Carol Ascolillo

Source: *Kilobaud Microcomputing* Aug 79 (32)
"COVER UP" pp. 26–37 (31–37)

COVER UP is a program designed to compute how much material you'll need to do wallpapering, painting, paneling, or carpeting jobs. The program works with a variety of room shapes. Using this program you can find out how much you'll need in the way of materials and how much they will cost. The program is broken into several parts

which automatically load themselves as needed off of a cassette.

Lines: 43, 154, 151, 140, 140
Version: PET BASIC
Hardware: PET
Software: none
Non-ANSI: not translatable

COSTS

966. Contract Labor Cost Program

Author: Karen Wolfe

Source: *Personal Computing* Aug 78 (2:8)
"Keeping Tabs on Contract Labor Costs" pp. 42–46 (45–46)

Do you own a job-oriented contracting business? If so, you will certainly need to keep track of your labor costs. Such records are vital, not only for computing sales tax, but also for maintaining the efficiency of your business. If you know exactly what your labor costs are, you can bid intelligently on new business. This program can help you maintain labor cost records. The program records labor costs and maintains a running record of these costs broken down by job and department. At any time, you can call up a report of what your labor costs are for each job. Includes a sample run.

Lines: 15, 92
Version: North Star BASIC
Hardware: sequential file device
Software: none
Non-ANSI: HP strings, OPEN, CLOSE, READ #, WRITE, %() (used to format printouts)

1054. Tracking Costs in a Service Business

Author: Clint Hentz

Source: *Personal Computing* Oct 79 (3:10)
"Tracking Costs in a Service Business" pp. 26–29 (27–29)

When operating a small service business, it's vital that you know how much it costs to deliver your services. Without this information you have no way of setting a realistic price for your services. This program helps you determine your costs by producing a variety of cost reports. You can use it to keep track of both labor and material costs. Includes a sample run.

Line: 147
Version: TRS-80 Level II BASIC
Hardware: sequential file device
Software: none
Non-ANSI: LPRINT, strings, extended IF, LPRINT USING, INPUT #, PRINT #

CREDIT

522. Credit Accounts

Author: Ray Vukcevich

Source: *Interface Age* Feb 79 (4:2)
"Managing Layaway Accounts" pp. 88–91 (90–91)

This program manages credit accounts for retail stores. You can use it to cut down on the paperwork involved in offering your customers a buy-now/pay-later option. The program has provisions for creating, updating, closing out, and reviewing credit accounts. It is self-prompting so it is quite easy to use. Information recorded includes customer name, address, item purchased, price, amount still owed, and date of purchase. Includes a sample run.

Lines: 202
Version: Micropolis Extended BASIC (ver. 2.0)
Hardware: random-access file device
Software: none
Non-ANSI: OPEN, CLOSE, GET, PUT, SCRATCH, strings, VAL( ), extended IF, FMT( ), CHAR$( )

DECISION ANALYSIS

585. Computer Decision-Maker Program

Author: Phil Feldman and Tom Rugg

Source: *Kilobaud* Jul 77 (7)
"Pass the Buck" pp. 90–96 (95)

Here is just the program for all of us indecisive, wishy-washy people: a computerized decision-making program. This program has the ability to explore relevant information you possess and to evaluate alternatives for you in a wide range of fields. The program is based on the concept of "utility." Utility is a way of assigning numerical values to various outcomes and/or alternatives in a decision model. By quizzing you on the relevant factors in a decision and asking you to rate the importance of each of these factors, the program can come up with a decision model for your problem. The final output of the program is an overall utility function of the basic alternatives under consideration. From this you should be able to reach a decision (maybe). Includes a sample run.

Lines: 82
Version: MITS BASIC
Hardware: none
Software: none
Non-ANSI: strings, CLEAR, extended IF

489. Business Risk Analysis

Author: Jon Prescott

Source: *Interface Age* Jan 78 (3:1)
"The Use of Microcomputers for Business Risk Analysis" pp. 88–92 (91–92)

This is a Monte Carlo simulation of business decision. Its purpose is to help a business person make business risk decisions. Includes a flowchart.

Lines: 148
Version: not given
Hardware: none
Software: none
Non-ANSI: strings, two-letter variables, extended IF, STR$( ), INP( ), OUT, FRE( )

935. Linear Programming for Decision Analysis

Author: Paul Whittington

Source: *Personal Computing* Jan 78 (2:1)
"Linear Programming: What's That?" pp. 67–71 (67–68)

Updates: correction
Personal Computing May 78 (2:5)
"Case In Point" p. 10 (10)

This is a program to assist you in solving problems by using linear programming methods. These methods are commonly used in business to find what levels of production, labor, or scheduling will produce the greatest profits. Typically, the various factors are graphed to find the solution or the point at which the greatest profit occurs. This program uses the computer to do the same job. Input to the program includes the decision variables, constraints, and objective function coefficients. The program outputs a table showing the opportunity costs of the decisions, as well as other information. Includes a sample run.

Lines: 264
Version: not given
Hardware: none
Software: none
Non-ANSI: none

539. Decision-Making Model

Author: Jack Spencer-Jones and David D. Blair

Source: *Interface Age* Jul 79 (4:7)
"A General Purpose Decision-Making Model for Small Business" pp. 68–73 (71–72)

Running a business is a nonstop round of decision making. Some decisions are easy to make. But when the decision involves a great many variables, you may wish to use your computer to help decide on the correct choice. This program uses a decision "trade-off matrix" to compare and rate possible options. You rate your various options according to factors you select. The computer then summarizes the data and arrives at a decision. You can also use the program to vary the decision factors, thus revealing how sensitive the result is to each of the individual factors. Includes a sample run.

Lines: 128
Version: North Star Disk BASIC
Hardware: none
Software: none
Non-ANSI: %( ) (used to format printouts), extended IF, HP strings

1045. Decision Evaluating Program

Author: Dick Straw

Source: *Personal Computing* Aug 79 (3?8)
"Evaluating Your Options" pp. 67–69 (69)

Most decisions are easy to make. You look over your choices and then select one. But when the choice involves considering many independent factors, you may have difficulty arriving at a reasonable conclusion. This program can help you by allowing you to rate each of your possible choices according to various factors you specify. For example, if you're trying to choose a new car, you might rate the cars according to looks, fuel economy, price, and features. The computer then uses this data to rank the possibilities.

Lines: 81
Version: TRS-80 Level II BASIC
Hardware: TRS-80
Software: none
Non-ANSI: not translatable

560. Weighted Decision Analysis

Author: C. P. Whaley

Source: *Interface Age* Nov 79 (4:11)
"Fuzzy Decision Making" pp. 87–91 (91)

Updates: modifications for North Star BASIC
Interface Age Feb 80 (5:2)
"The Micro-Mathematician" pp. 34–37 (34)

When faced with two distinct choices, most people can make a rational decision. But when the choice involves selecting among several fairly complex alternatives, most people have a tough time selecting the best choice. Usually, you randomly mull over the possibilities until one or another "seems the best." Fortunately, there's a more scientific way to arrive at a decision. This program uses weighted decision analysis to help you arrive at the best choice. You select categories to represent the various factors that will affect the decision. You also specify how much weight to give each factor. Finally, you go through your possible choices and rate each of your choices in each of the categories. The computer then puts all of this information together and comes up with a rating of the possible alternatives.

Lines: 88
Version: BASIC 8001 V12.8.76
Hardware: none
Software: none
Non-ANSI: strings, two-letter variables, extended IF, PLOT

DEPRECIATION

478. Depreciation Analysis

Author: Jim Huffman

Source: *Interface Age* Sep 77 (2:10)
"Depreciation Schedule Analysis Program—JHDSAP" pp. 143–149 (148–149)

The IRS allows depreciation to be calculated in a variety of ways for different tax purposes. This program can show you the best way to calculate depreciation on the things you own, to pay the least in taxes. The program starts out by accepting information about the object to be depreciated, such as its initial value, its useful life, and its scrap value. From this, the program generates tables showing what the depreciation would be using straight-line depreciation, sum-of-year's-digits depreciation, and declining-balance depreciation. The program can also compute the crossover point for switching depreciation methods. Includes a sample run and flowchart.

Lines: 101
Version: SWTPG 8K BASIC
Hardware: none
Software: none
Non-ANSI: DIGITS, extended IF, strings, ON . . . GOSUB

251. Depreciation Using Three Different Methods

Author: not given

Source: *Creative Computing* Nov–Dec 77 (3:6)
"Delving Into Depreciation" p. 132 (132)

This program computes a table of annual depreciation for a capital item using three different types of depreciation. The three types of depreciation considered are straight-line, sum-of-year's-digits, and double-declining-balance. The different methods are used for different tax-related purposes. Straight-line depreciation is used when a businessperson wishes to take the depreciation deductions for a piece of equipment or property late in its useful life. The other two methods are used when the depreciation deductions are to be taken early. The program takes into account the original cost of the item, the life of the item in years, and any scrap value the item might have. The output is a table showing the depreciation under the three depreciation methods. Includes a sample run.

Lines: 38
Version: not given
Hardware: none
Software: none
Non-ANSI: none

640. Depreciation Calculations

Author: John and Gordan Musgrove

Source: *Kilobaud* Oct 78 (22)
"Depreciation Calculations" pp. 40–42 (40–42)

Updates: commentary
Kilobaud Dec 78 (24)
"Adding to 'Depreciation' " p. 17

correction
Kilobaud Microcomputing Mar 79 (27)
"New Formula" p. 22

Depreciation is a way of accounting for the cost of large business expenses. When a business makes a large capital expenditure, the equipment purchased usually has a useful life of several years. It doesn't seem right to treat that expense as occurring totally in the year of purchase when the benefits last for many years. The way accountants

handle this problem is to "stretch out" the cost over several years. This is known as depreciation. These are two programs to compute depreciation and produce depreciation tables. One program uses straight-line depreciation. The other uses double-declining-balance depreciation. Includes sample runs and lists of program variables.

Lines: 29, 24
Version: Digital Group Maxi-BASIC
Hardware: none
Software: none
Non-ANSI: % () (used to format printouts)

683. Depreciation Tables

Author: Joe Ligori

Source: *Kilobaud Microcomputing* Apr 79 (28)
"Depreciation Analysis" pp. 82–83 (83)

Updates: improvement
Kilobaud Microcomputing Jun 79 (30)
"Simplifying 'Depreciation' " p. 23 (23)

improvement
Kilobaud Microcomputing Jul 79 (32)
" 'Depreciation Analysis' Mods" p. 22 (22)

Depreciation allows a business to spread the expense of a large capital purchase over several years. The IRS allows businesses to calculate depreciation in a variety of ways. The method you select can have a major effect on how much you will have to pay in taxes. This program can help you pick the type of depreciation that is best for your purposes. The program prints out depreciation tables showing what the depreciation would be on an asset using each of three different methods: straight-line, sum-of-year's-digits, and double-declining-balance. Includes a sample run and a list of program variables.

Lines: 89
Version: TRS-80 Level II BASIC
Hardware: none
Software: none
Non-ANSI: CLEAR, DEFDBL, DEFINT, STRING$(), strings, ' (used in place of REM), PRINT @, CLS, PRINT USING, extended IF, RUN (used as a program statement)

1018. Depreciation

Author: Karen Wolfe

Source: *Personal Computing* May 79 (3:5)
"Appreciating Depreciation" pp. 26–28 (27–28)

Updates: commentary
Personal Computing Sep 79 (3:9)
"Depreciation Update" p. 7

Depreciation calculations can give any businessperson nightmares. Not only are the calculations tedious and complicated, but there are all those weird IRS special rules to contend with. This program quizzes you about the depreciation calculations to be done. It can then grind out depreciation tables using declining balance, sum-of-year's-digits, or straight-line depreciation. The FILL statements are just used to switch output to a printer (if available). Includes a sample run.

> *Lines:* 142
> *Version:* North Star BASIC
> *Hardware:* none
> *Software:* none
> *Non-ANSI:* HP strings, FILL, %( ) (used to format printouts)

FINANCIAL ANALYSIS

252. Systematic Savings

> *Author:* not given

> *Source:* *Creative Computing* Nov–Dec 77 (3:6)
> "Systematic Savings" p. 132 (132)

This program computes the total amount of money which will accumulate under a systematic investment or savings program. The program asks how much you wish to invest per year, for how many years you wish to continue investing, and the annual rate of interest. From this, it computes and prints out a table showing how much you have invested and how much you have accumulated, including interest. You can use this program to find out how rich you'd be if you weren't investing all your money in home computer equipment. Includes a sample run.

> *Lines:* 11
> *Version:* not given
> *Hardware:* none
> *Software:* none
> *Non-ANSI:* none

497. Financial Analysis Program

> *Author:* Peter Burke

> *Source:* *Interface Age* Mar 78 (3:3)
> "A Financial Analysis Program" pp. 48–55 (55)

> *Updates:* correction
> *Interface Age* Nov 78 (3:11)
> untitled p. 14 (14)
>
> commentary
> *Interface Age* Apr 79 (4:4)
> "Some Thoughts on 'Financial Analysis' " p. 11

This financial analysis program solves problems in three areas: (1) annuities, (2) lump sums, and (3) bonds. The first section of the program deals with annuities. The program can deal with either present value annuities or future value annuities. An example of a present value annuity problem might be, "Given a bank loan of a certain value and interest rate, compute the monthly payments." A future value annuity problem would be one such as, "If I want to accumulate a certain amount of money at a certain interest rate, how much should my monthly deposits be?" The second area of the program deals with lump sum problems. Here, the program can compute number of periods, interest, present value, or future value when given the other three variables. The final section of the program deals with bonds and problems concerning bond values. Includes sample runs.

> *Lines:* 253
> *Version:* not given
> *Hardware:* none
> *Software:* none
> *Non-ANSI:* strings, extended IF, multiple-assignment

274. Systematic Savings

> *Author:* Stuart Denenberg

> *Source:* *Creative Computing* May–Jun 78 (4:3)
> "Systematic Savings Revisited" p. 131 (131)

If you were to put a certain amount of money into a savings account at a particular interest rate, how much would you have after several years? This program answers that question. Instead of using a fancy mathematic equation to solve the problem, the program simulates the compounding effect of interest on a "year-by-year" basis. The program prints out a table showing, by year, how much has been invested, and how much has been accumulated. A second program does the same thing, except that it does not assume that any money is being deposited after the initial deposit. Includes sample runs.

> *Lines:* 11, 9
> *Version:* not given
> *Hardware:* none
> *Software:* none
> *Non-ANSI:* none

622. Personal Annuity Program

> *Author:* Ken Barbier

> *Source:* *Kilobaud* May 78 (17)
> "Money Manipulations" pp. 90–92 (90)

This program assumes you have a sum of money that you wish to invest and then draw on. It takes into account inflation, the interest that you can earn on your money, and the amount you want to take out each month. Given this information, the program tells you how long the money will last. Its output is a table showing (by quarters) how much principal you have left, how much interest you have earned, and how much money you must draw to keep even with inflation. The table continues until the money runs out. If no money is drawn from the investment, the program becomes a straightforward compound-interest program. Includes sample runs.

> *Lines:* 43
> *Version:* Altair BASIC, 12K Extended, ver. 3.2
> *Hardware:* none
> *Software:* none
> *Non-ANSI:* strings, PRINT USING

634. Personal Finance Package

> *Author:* Lee Palenik

> *Source:* *Kilobaud* Aug 78 (20)
> "FINANC—A Home/Small-Business Financial Package" pp. 84–89 (86–89)

In these days of economic stress, it's getting more and more important to watch where your dollars are going. Here is a program that can help. It is a collection of personal finance routines called FINANC. FINANC can solve problems involving future value of a one-time investment, future value of regular deposits, depreciation rates, salvage value, cost of loans, remaining balance of loans, and many other problems relating to personal finance. Includes a sample run.

> *Lines:* 610
> *Version:* PET BASIC
> *Hardware:* none
> *Software:* none
> *Non-ANSI:* strings, STR$( ), extended IF, ON . . . GOSUB

656. Business Cycles Analysis for the TRS-80

> *Author:* Jim Wright

> *Source:* *Kilobaud* Dec 78 (24)
> "The Ups and Downs of Business" pp. 80–86 (84)

> *Updates:* commentary
> *Kilobaud Microcomputing* Apr 79 (28)
> "Wright On!" p. 18

Business, like everything else in life, has its ups and downs. Whether your interest is stock prices or retail sales, sometimes things will be going strong and other times they'll be hitting the skids. If you're going to keep on an even keel, you'll have to keep abreast of these changes. This program can help by recording and tracking business data. The program is designed to record, plot, and analyze a variety of kinds of data. Data storage is by cassette. The program can display data in either tabular or graph form. You can display the data in raw form. Or, you can have the program use moving averages to "smooth out" the minor fluctuations. Includes a sample run.

> *Lines:* 79
> *Version:* TRS-80 Level I BASIC
> *Hardware:* TRS-80
> *Software:* none
> *Non-ANSI:* not translatable

1012. Return on Investment

> *Author:* Kirtland Olson

> *Source:* *Personal Computing* Apr 79 (3:4)
> "Return on Investment" pp. 41–42 (40–41)

Return on Investment is one measure of an investment's desirability. This program computes the return on investment for a capital expenditure. Includes a list of program variables.

> *Lines:* 34
> *Version:* not given
> *Hardware:* none
> *Software:* none
> *Non-ANSI:* two-letter variables, ? (used in place of PRINT)

1013. Discounted Cash Flow Rate of Return

> *Author:* Kirtland Olson

> *Source:* *Personal Computing* Apr 79 (3:4)
> "Discounted Cash Flow Rate of Return" p. 43 (43)

> *Updates:* corrections
> *Personal Computing* Jul 79 (3:7)
> "Bugged By Bugs" p. 8 (8)

This program finds the interest rate at which discounted values of a future stream of capital exactly equal the initial investment. This rate is known as the discounted cash flow rate of return. It measures the profitability of an investment by taking into account both the money returned by the investment and the time at which the money becomes available. Includes a sample run.

Lines: 25
Version: not given
Hardware: none
Software: none
Non-ANSI: two-letter variables, GET, strings, extended IF, RUN (used as a program statement)

533. Analysis of Return on Investment

Author: Timothy Burke

Source: *Interface Age* May 79 (4:5)
"Microcomputer Analysis of Return on Investment" pp. 90–95 (94–95)

One of the most commonly overlooked factors in investment analysis is time. "Time is money" in a very real sense. Receiving $10,000 today is a different thing than receiving $10,000 next year. This is because if you get the $10,000 now, you can invest it and earn interest. Accountants and analysts use the term *present value* to denote the current value of a payment to be made in the future. Using the present value of all the money that an investment is likely to bring you, you can derive the *internal rate of return* (IRR) of the investment. This number is a good indication of how good the investment is. This program computes IRR of a potential investment, as well as other information. Includes a sample run.

Lines: 196
Version: Alpha BASIC 3.4, ver. 3.1
Hardware: addressable-cursor video display
Software: none
Non-ANSI: strings, SIGNIFICANCE, STRSIZ, PRINT USING

535. Accounts Payable Discounts/Average Collection Period

Author: Jim Schreier

Source: *Interface Age* May 79 (4:5)
"Two Views of Credit" pp. 100–101 (101)

These two programs answer two questions about your business. The first program answers the question, "How much is it costing me to pass up cash discounts?" The second program answers the question, "What is my average collection period on accounts receivable?"

Lines: 38, 30
Version: not given
Hardware: none
Software: none
Non-ANSI: LINE, DIGITS, extended IF, strings

714. Break-Even Calculations

Author: Ernie Brooner

Source: *Kilobaud Microcomputing* Jul 79 (31)
"Projecting Future Profits" p. 63 (63)

In any business, costs fall into two categories: fixed costs and variable costs. Fixed costs are those costs that (within a given range of production) stay the same no matter what your sales are. Building rent is an example of a fixed cost. On the other hand, variable costs vary according to how much you produce. At a low sales volume there isn't enough money to pay for the fixed costs. As sales rise, variable costs rise, but do so more slowly (we hope) than sales revenue. Break-even occurs when sales pay for both fixed and variable costs. This program calculates the break-even point for a business. Includes a sample run.

Lines: 33
Version: North Star BASIC
Hardware: none
Software: none
Non-ANSI: %() (used to format printouts)

1061. Economic Order Quantity

Author: Adrian Woods

Source: *Personal Computing* Nov 79 (3:11)
"Economic Order Quantity" pp. 28–33 (32–33)

A decision that most businesspeople must answer is, "When and how much should I reorder to keep my inventory in shape?" This program uses the technique known as Economic Order Quantity to determine the optimum order quantity and reorder point. The program has provisions for taking into account back orders, lead time, and stochastic (probabilistic) demand. Includes a sample run and a list of program variables.

Lines: 183
Version: PET BASIC
Hardware: none
Software: none
Non-ANSI: strings

1067. Break-Even Analysis

Author: Karen S. Wolfe

Source: *Personal Computing* Dec 79 (3:12)
"Breaking Even" pp. 33–36 (35–36)

In any manufacturing business there are two kinds of costs: fixed costs and variable costs. Fixed costs remain the same no matter how much you produce (building rent is generally a fixed cost). Variable costs, on the other hand, vary as your production level varies (raw materials are generally a variable cost). To find out how much you must produce to break even, you must take into account both kinds of costs. This program does this break-even analysis. It can compute your total cost, total revenue, and profit/loss at various production levels. It can also plot break-even graphs (no special graphics terminal is required). Includes a sample run.

Lines: 102
Version: North Star BASIC
Hardware: none
Software: none
Non-ANSI: HP strings, ! (used in place of PRINT), FILL, %() (used to format printouts)

GENERAL LEDGER

477. General Ledger Package

Author: Bud Shamburger

Source: Interface Age Sep 77 (2:10)
            "General Ledger Program" pp. 26–54

            sample runs
            Interface Age Oct 77 (2:11)
            "General Ledger Program" pp. 64–92

            listings
            Interface Age Nov 77 (2:12)
            "General Ledger Program" pp. 56–73
            (57–73)

Updates: commentary
            Interface Age Dec 79 (4:12)
            "More Shamburger" p. 20

The heart of any business accounting system is its general ledger package. This package of 14 programs is a complete general ledger system. The system handles all banking accounting including check transactions and bank statements. The system has complete facilities for producing all journals and ledgers. Reports that the system can generate include YTD budget, balance sheet, cash flow analysis, and monthly budget. Utilities provided include file back-up and record sorting. The system has a complete audit trail and back-up system. Includes flowcharts and sample runs. A Tarbell-format phonograph record with a machine-readable copy of the program is bound into the September 1977 issue.

Lines: 14 programs ranging from 36 to 482 lines
Version: MITS 12K Disk BASIC ver. 4.0
Hardware: random-access file device
Software: none
Non-ANSI: not translatable

434. Multi-Column Journal Balancing Program

Author: Charlie Pack

Source: Dr. Dobb's Journal of Computer Calisthenics & Orthodontia Oct 77 (2:9)
            "Multiple Column Accounting" pp. 36–41 (40–41)

The most common way of recording expenses in a small business is in a multi-column journal. The problem with this type of journal is that it requires quite a bit of bookkeeping arithmetic. Not only must all the columns be added correctly, but the entries in the journal along each line must be added (crossfooted). This program takes over these tasks. Once the journal entries are made, the program does all the addition and crossfooting. If there is an error in one of the entries, it can be corrected quickly and easily. The program also has provisions for special functions. The display commands allow all or part of the entries to be displayed. In addition, the program can do trial balances and can print out statements of cash receipts and disbursements. In fact, the program comes fairly close to being a complete general ledger system. Includes a sample run and list of program variables.

Lines: 312
Version: MITS Altair 8K BASIC
Hardware: none
Software: none
Non-ANSI: CLEAR, strings, STR$(), VAL(), extended IF, ON . . . GOSUB

606. Business Accounting Package

Author: Laurence McCaig

Source: Kilobaud Feb 78 (14)
            "Small Business Software" pp. 38–44 (40–44)

            Kilobaud Mar 78 (15)
            "Small Business Software" pp. 76–82 (77–82)

This series is intended to be a complete accounting package for a small business. The series appears to terminate abruptly with the second installment. No indication is given as to whether or not the series will be completed. The first two installments detail the accounts receivable portion of the system, and the file maintenance and active transaction programs. Includes flowcharts.

Lines: 14 programs ranging from 10 to 84 lines
Version: North Star BASIC
Hardware: random-access file device
Software: none
Non-ANSI: HP strings, ! (used in place of PRINT), OPEN, CLOSE, READ #, WRITE, CHAIN, extended IF, NOENDMARK( ), %( ) (used to format printouts)

968. Check Register Accounting System

Author: O. Dial

Source: *Personal Computing* Aug 78 (2:8)
"The Computer Checks into the Balancing Act" pp. 59–74 (66–74)

Personal Computing Oct 78 (2:10)
"The Computer Checks into the Balancing Act" pp. 43–53 (44–53)

Personal Computing Nov 78 (2:11)
"The Computer Checks into the Balancing Act" pp. 55, 72–82 (72–82)

This is a complete system for maintaining a checkbook-based accounting system. The system is fully integrated so that a single transaction entry is all that's required to produce a large array of specialized statements including Check Register, Check Register Notes, Accounts Distributions, Statements of Selected Accounts, Checkbook Reconciliation, and even the printed checks themselves! The programs are designed for naive users and lead you through the operations step by step. Even noncomputer-people should be able to use this system. Includes sample runs.

Lines: 12 programs ranging from 41 to 242 lines
Version: MITS Disk BASIC 4.0
Hardware: random-access file device, 132-column printer
Software: none
Non-ANSI: not translatable

704. Simple Bookkeeping Program

Author: Robert Marx

Source: *Kilobaud Microcomputing* Jun 79 (30)
"Keepbook" pp. 60–63 (61–62)

There are many accounting systems available for microcomputers. Most of them are large, complicated systems designed more for accountants than for ordinary folk. This bookkeeping system is quick and simple. All information for the system is written out on a source entry document. The document lists both expenses and income, giving dates, amounts, and descriptions. This data is entered into the computer. The computer can then type out monthly summaries showing, by account, current activity and activity for the year to date. Includes sample output.

Lines: 137
Version: North Star BASIC, release 4
Hardware: random-access file device
Software: none
Non-ANSI: not translatable

713. Revenue/Expense Recording System

Author: Forest E. Myers

Source: *Kilobaud Microcomputing* Jul 79 (31)
"A Data-File Creation Program for Small Business" pp. 44–46 (44–46)

Kilobaud Microcomputing Aug 79 (32)
"Report" pp. 78–79 (78–79)

These two programs record and print out revenue and expense data for your small business; in effect, they act as a mini general-ledger system. The first program records the revenue and expenses, classified by account and department. The second program uses this data to print out an Income and Expense Statement. Includes a sample run and a list of program variables.

Lines: 240 (plus patch), 128
Version: Micro Works Business BASIC
Hardware: random-access file device
Software: none
Non-ANSI: HP strings, # (used in place of PRINT), OPEN, CLOSE, GET, CONVERT, extended IF, EXIT, PUT, %() (used to format printouts)

INVENTORY

100. Inventory Pricing

Author: LeRoy Finkel

Source: *Calculators/Computers Magazine* May 77 (1:1)
"Inventory Pricing" pp. 53–56 (55)

Updates: correction to credits
Calculators/Computer Magazine Oct 77 (1:2)
untitled p. 91

Keeping track of inventories is a major headache for a small business. Here are three programs to help you keep track of your inventory. The programs accept various "batches" of goods at various prices. They then compute the total inventory, and keep track of the changing total as goods are added or removed. The first program accepts an inventory and keeps track of the total as goods are removed. The second program allows you to add goods to the inventory. Both programs are based on Last-In-First-Out (LIFO) accounting. The third program is created by making a one-line change to the second program. It changes the program to First-In-First-Out (FIFO) accounting. Includes sample runs.

Lines: 46, 64 (plus patch)
Version: none
Hardware: none
Software: none
Non-ANSI: HP strings

976. Inventory Program

Author: Ray Vukcevich

Source: *Personal Computing* Oct 78 (2:10)
"I'll Put You on Hold and Check" pp. 54–58
(56–58)

Updates: commentary
Personal Computing Jan 79 (3:1)
"Inventory Problems" p. 13

Do you really have your inventory under control? Does your secretary have to paw through endless chaotic records to find out what you've got (that is, if it can be found out at all)? This program can help you manage your inventory. INVENTORY is a program that does a variety of inventory functions. You can check whether an individual item is in stock, its unit cost, the estimated date of a new shipment, or what quantity you have on hand. If the part is ordered, the inventory records are adjusted immediately. You can also produce complete inventory reports. Includes a sample run.

Lines: 117
Version: Micropolis Extended BASIC ver. 2.0
Hardware: random-access file device
Software: none
Non-ANSI: OPEN, CLOSE, GET, PUT, GETSEEK, strings, CHAR$()

667. Inventory Control Using TRS-80 Level I BASIC

Author: John Yost, Jr.

Source: *Kilobaud Microcomputing* Feb 79 (26)
"Inventory Control with TRS-80" pp. 64–65
(65)

Keeping track of an inventory can be a major headache. A computer can make your task easier. But a large computer (even a large microcomputer) with disk drives and lots of memory costs lots of money. This inventory control system needs only an inexpensive TRS-80 Level I BASIC system. The program has provisions for creating and maintaining an inventory list. Data about the inventory is stored using the TRS-80's cassette drive. With 4K of memory, the system is limited to about 293 inventory items.

Lines: 84
Version: TRS-80 Level I BASIC
Hardware: sequential file device
Software: none
Non-ANSI: not translatable

559. Unit Inventory Control

Author: Chuck Atkinson

Source: *Interface Age* Nov 79 (4:11)
"Unit Inventory Control in Business" pp. 78–85 (82–85)

This inventory program is designed for businesses that handle relatively large-ticket items: boats, cars, computers, and such. Unlike businesses that handle a large number of very small articles, businesses which handle expensive merchandise generally need to keep track of each individual unit. This inventory program maintains such records. As written, the program creates inventory records for a boat business, but it can be easily modified for other businesses. The program records not only the various boats on hand, but also such information as the cost, location, and model identification of each boat. The program has complete provisions for editing and listing the inventory records. Note that the program requires files that seem to have a curious mixture of random-access and sequential characteristics. Includes a sample run.

Lines: 277
Version: BASIC-E
Hardware: random-access file device
Software: none
Non-ANSI: not translatable

LAW

956. Contract Forms Printer

Author: Charles Matz

Source: *Personal Computing* Jun 78 (2:6)
"Printing Contract Forms" pp. 39–42 (40–41)

This program prints out contract forms. You enter information such as your client's name and address, the amount of the contract, and the text of the contract, and the program types out one or more copies of the contract. The program has features for editing the text. The program is limited to a single format. Includes a sample run.

Lines: 175
Version: Computer Software Services Disk File BASIC
Hardware: none
Software: none
Non-ANSI: LINE, STRING, DIGITS, strings, VAL(), INPUT #, PRINT #, STR$(), extended IF

LOANS AND MORTGAGES

570. Declining Interest Loan Program

Author: Tom Rugg and Phil Feldman

Source: *Kilobaud* Feb 77 (2)
"A Useful Loan Payment Program" pp. 68–69 (68)

Updates: correction
Kilobaud Apr 77 (4)
"Typesetting Programs" p. 17 (17)

This program computes information about declining interest loans. You input the amount of the loan, the interest rate, and the length of the loan. The program then computes the monthly payments. It also gives a month-by-month breakdown of the remaining balance on the loan, the part of the payment going to reduce the principal, the part of the payment going for interest, and other information. If the user specifies a monthly payment rate, the program computes what the "balloon" payment at the end of the loan will be. Includes a sample run.

Lines: 42
Version: MITS 8K BASIC
Hardware: none
Software: none
Non-ANSI: strings

97. Home Mortgage Payments

Author: LeRoy Finkel

Source: *Calculators/Computers Magazine* May 77 (1:1)
"Home Mortgage" pp. 18–20 (20)

Updates: correction
Calculators/Computers Magazine Oct 77 (1:2)
untitled p. 91

This is a program to prepare a home mortgage amortization (pay-out) schedule. The program is based on a table of monthly payment rates. This table shows the rates for mortgages from 15 to 30 years in length, and with interest rates from 7% to 8½%. Given the number of years in the loan, the interest rate, and the mortgage amount, the program "looks up" the monthly payment, and then prints out the proper schedule. The schedule shows the amount of the monthly payment applied to the principal, the amount applied to interest, and the remaining balance of the loan. Includes a sample run.

Lines: 50
Version: not given
Hardware: none
Software: none
Non-ANSI: none

890. Mortgage Payments

Author: Tim Barry

Source: *People's Computers* May–Jun 77 (5:6)
"BASIC Mortgages" pp. 46–47 (47)

With the price of real estate going through the roof these days, it's getting harder and harder to afford a new home. This program can't help you make the payments on your dream house, but it can at least tell you what the payments will be. Knowing how much the payments will be for a house of any given size, you can accurately zero in on how large a home you can afford. The program inputs the price of the house, the interest rate, the mortgage term, and the down payment. From this, the program computes the monthly payments (not including tax or insurance). Includes a sample run.

Lines: 49
Version: IBM BASIC
Hardware: none
Software: none
Non-ANSI: strings

110. Home Mortgage Payment Table

Author: Bruce Staal

Source: *Calculators/Computers Magazine* Oct 77 (1:2)
untitled p. 92 (92)

This program produces a home mortgage payment table. You enter the amount of the mortgage, the length in years, and the interest rate. From this information, the program computes your monthly payments, and produces a table which lists how much of each payment goes to paying off the loan and how much goes to interest. This program is an improved version of a program which appeared in the previous issue of *CCM*. The old program computed the monthly payments by finding the amount in a table. This program computes the payments directly, providing for a much more flexible and powerful program. Includes a sample run.

Lines: 21
Version: not given
Hardware: none
Software: none
Non-ANSI: none

943. Loan Amortization Tables

Author: Charles DeLuca

Source: *Personal Computing* Apr 78 (2:4)
"Your Amortization Program" pp. 50–52 (50–51)

Updates: correction
Personal Computing Sep 78 (2:9)
"More Amortization" p. 8 (8)

This program generates loan amortization tables. The program inputs the total amount of the mortgage (or other loan), the interest rate, and either the duration of the loan or the monthly payment. If the duration is entered, the monthly payment is calculated, and vice-versa. The program then generates the tables. The tables show, on a month-by-month basis, the beginning balance, the amount of interest paid, the amount of the payment applied to the principal, the ending balance, the interest to date, and the principal paid to date. The program also shows year-end totals. Includes a sample run and a list of program variables.

Lines: 121
Version: Altair Extended Disk BASIC
Hardware: none
Software: none
Non-ANSI: strings, multi-letter variables, LPRINT USING, extended IF, PRINT USING, '(used in place of REM)

626. Simple Interest Loans

Author: Charles Carpenter

Source: *Kilobaud* Jun 78 (18)
"Tiny BASIC Shortcuts" pp. 42–44 (42–43)

This is a program to give information about simple interest loans. The input to the program is the principal of a loan, the interest rate, time in years, and payments in months. From this the program calculates how much interest you will pay, how much you will pay in total, and what the payments will be on the loan. This program is included in an article describing how to save memory space when programming in Tiny BASIC. Two versions of the program are given; one is in normal format, and the other is in a space-saving format. Includes a sample run.

Lines: 44, 29
Version: Tiny BASIC
Hardware: none
Software: none
Non-ANSI: PR

669. Loan Payment Table

Author: Rod Hallen

Source: *Kilobaud Microcomputing* Feb 79 (26)
"Simpler Interest" pp. 116–117 (116)

Updates: modifications to run on TRS-80
Kilobaud Microcomputing Apr 79 (28)
"Simple Conversion" p. 20 (20)

Do you know how much you have left to pay on your loans; how much you're paying out in interest; how much of your payments are going to pay off the principal? This program can answer these questions for you. Given information about a loan, it generates a table showing, by month, the portions of the loan payments going to principal and interest as well as how much of the loan remains to be repaid. Includes sample runs.

Lines: 27
Version: Processor Technology BASIC5
Hardware: none
Software: none
Non-ANSI: %() (used to format printouts), extended IF

543. Monthly Loan Payments

Author: Alfred Adler

Source: *Interface Age* Aug–Sep 79 (4:8)
"The Micro Mathematician" pp. 26–28 (28)

Updates: modifications
Interface Age Mar 80 (5:3)
"Comments on Mortgages" p. 13 (13)

This program computes what the monthly payments will be on a loan or mortgage. You specify the amount of the loan, its duration and what the rate of interest will be. The computer then figures out what the monthly payments will be. It also prints out a table showing, for each payment, how much will go for interest and how much will be used to retire the principal. The program also includes a provision for handling balloon payments. Includes a sample run.

Lines: 45
Version: PolyMorphic BASIC, Version A00
Hardware: none
Software: none
Non-ANSI: ! (used in place of PRINT), %() (used to format printouts)

406. Interest Accrued Between Two Dates

Author: Joe Ligori

Source: *Creative Computing* Nov 79 (5:11)
"Date Conversion" p. 141 (141)

As anyone who has let a loan drag on can testify, interest is not a static quantity—it grows with time. The amount of interest due on a loan is proportional to the term of the loan. This program computes the length of time between two dates. With this information, plus an interest rate you specify, the program computes how much interest would accrue on a loan between those dates. Includes a sample run.

Lines:	24
Version:	not given
Hardware:	none
Software:	none
Non-ANSI:	strings, VAL(), extended IF, PRINT USING, multi-letter variables

1120. Loan Payment Program

Author:	Milan Chepko
Source:	*Recreational Computing* Nov–Dec 79 (8:3) "TRS-80: Loan Payment" pp. 47, 57 (47)

Not all loans are fully "amortized" (paid off) over the course of the loan. Sometimes a loan involves a "balloon payment"; that is, a large, special payment at the end of the loan. This loan program calculates the payments for loans with balloon payments. You input the amount of the loan, the interest rate, the term of the loan, and the balloon payment. The computer then calculates the monthly payments, the total interest paid, etc. It also prints out a monthly breakdown of the payments. Includes a list of program variables.

Lines:	40
Version:	not given
Hardware:	none
Software:	none
Non-ANSI:	CLS, ' (used in place of REM), strings, extended IF

MAILING LISTS

1129. Mailing List Program

Author:	Robert Osband
Source:	*ROM* Feb 78 (1:8) "The Mailing List Program" pp. 24–28 (25–28)

Many organizations require mailing lists. This is a set of two programs for maintaining mailing lists. The programs store names, addresses, phone numbers, and user-defined information. There are provisions for adding, deleting, changing, and printing addresses. The programs are designed for use on video terminals. Includes a flowchart.

Lines:	48, 73
Version:	Altair Extended Disk BASIC
Hardware:	random-access file device, video display
Software:	none
Non-ANSI:	not translatable

498. Mailing List Program

Author:	Jim Huffman
Source:	*Interface Age* Apr 78 (3:4) "Mail Code Sort and Print Program" pp. 90–91 (91)

This is a program to sort and print mailing addresses for mailing lists. This program is suitable for small mailing lists. The mailing addresses are stored entirely in DATA statements so there is no need for external files. The mailing list it produces is sorted by zip code. As written, the program sorts the mailing addresses only by the first two digits of the zip codes. It can easily be modified to do a full five digit sort. Sample run is included.

Lines:	32
Version:	not given
Hardware:	none
Software:	none
Non-ANSI:	strings, VAL(), extended IF

765. Simple Mailing List Program

Author:	Richard Rosner
Source:	*Micro* Apr–May 78 (4) "The PET Vet Examines Some BASIC Idiosyncrasies" pp. 5–6 (5–6)

This simple mailing list program (designed to run on a Commodore PET computer) allows you to type in a list of names and addresses, and then store them on cassette. When you want a printout of the addresses, the progam can play them back for you.

Lines:	57
Version:	PET BASIC
Hardware:	sequential file device
Software:	none
Non-ANSI:	OPEN, CMD, LIST (used as a program statement), strings, two-letter variables, PRINT #, CLOSE, INPUT #, extended IF

500. Mailing List System

Author:	John Billing
Source:	*Interface Age* May 78 (3:5) "A Full Function Mailing List System" pp. 56–68 (59–66)

This is a package of programs that form a complete mailing list system. The various programs in the package are invoked by CHAIN calls. This is a very complete mailing system and has many features. Records may be added or deleted from the data base. The mailing addresses may be alphabetized. The output may be printed on single or quadruple width stock. There is a provision for the printing of form letters with individualized addresses. The unique feature of the system is that one mailing address may be included in up to 24 separate lists. If an address must be corrected, it need be corrected only once for all the lists that the address is on. Includes sample run. A machine readable copy of the program is bound in the magazine on a Kansas City format phonograph record.

Lines:	14 programs ranging from 26 to 156 lines
Version:	MSI BASIC-2C
Hardware:	random-access file device
Software:	none
Non-ANSI:	not translatable

621. Mailing List Programs for the Tarbell Cassette Drive and ASR-33

Author: Stephen Gibson

Source: *Kilobaud* (May 78 (17)
"A Simple Mailing System" pp. 78–82 (79–82)

Many small businesses and clubs would like to have the ability to print out mailing lists, but do not have a disk. This is a simple mailing list program for systems that do not have disks. Two versions of the program are included. The first version uses a Tarbell standard cassette drive to store the mailing addresses. The second version saves the addresses on papertape using an ASR-33 Teletype. Both versions print out addresses "three-up"—that is, the addresses come out in three side-by-side columns. Includes a sample run.

Lines:	128 (plus patches), 74
Version:	MITS 3.2 8K BASIC
Hardware:	Tarbell standard cassette or ASR-33 Teletype
Software:	none
Non-ANSI:	CLEAR, strings, two-letter variables, extended IF, POKE, OUT

507. Name and Address Storage System

Author: Gary Young

Source: *Interface Age* Aug 78 (3:8)
"Implementing Random Access for a Name and Address Retrieval System" pp. 103–105 (104–105)

Update:	correction
	Interface Age Dec 78 (3:12)
	"A Program Update" p. 10 (10)

This is a set of two programs to maintain an address list on a disk. The first program can add, delete, change, or search for records. The data that can be added to the data list include names, addresses, phone numbers, plus other user information as desired. Once entered, the CHANGE function can be used to update or correct information. Records can be deleted anywhere in the list using the DELETE function. Records can be found and printed out using the SEARCH function. The second program in the set is used to print out the data base. It has the ability to print all the information stored, or just part of it. Includes sample runs.

Lines:	215, 63
Version:	North Star BASIC
Hardware:	random-access file device
Software:	none
Non-ANSI:	HP strings, FREE(), OPEN, CLOSE, READ #, WRITE, NOENDMARK( ), extended IF

645. Address List Program

Author: Sherman Wantz and Brian Bateman

Source: *Kilobaud* Oct 78 (22)
"A Useful Address List Program" pp. 102–105 (104–105)

This program can store and retrieve an address list on cassette. The program has provisions for entering and selectively printing out the information stored. You can, for example, print out just people from one particular state. The program also stores other information such as birthdays and telephone numbers. Includes a list of program variables and a sample run.

Lines:	237
Version:	SWTPC 8K BASIC, ver. 2.0
Hardware:	sequential file device
Software:	none
Non-ANSI:	strings, LINE, VAL(), STR$(), PRINT #, extended IF

299. Newsletter Mailing List System

Author: Donald Williams, Sr.

Source: *Creative Computing* Nov–Dec 78 (4:6)
"Solving Those Mail List Problems—Mail List, Billing Program (and more) for Small Businesses" pp. 134–137, 140 (136–137)

This mailing list system was designed for use by newsletters or small magazines. The system provides for the printing of both mailing labels and billing notices. The mailing label part of the program has provisions for storing, updating, and printing mailing labels. The labels include names, addresses, zip codes, and expiration dates. When the list is printed out, the labels are segregated so that the newsletters can be bundled by zip code for the post office. The expiration dates provide the basis for the second part of the program. This section prints out billing notices for people whose subscriptions are about to expire. The program uses sequential files, but due to frequent file "rewinds," a random-access file device should probably be used. Includes a sample run (which was incorrectly placed on page 140 in another article).

Lines: 255
Version: SWTPC BASIC 8K (C), Flex disk version
Hardware: sequential file devices
Software: none
Non-ANSI: not translatable

300. Mailing List System

Author: Gary Young

Source: *Creative Computing* Nov–Dec 78 (4:6)
"Mailing List System" pp. 138–144 (142–144)

Updates: correction
Creative Computing Feb 79 (5:2)
"Our Face is Red Dept." p. 4 (4)

One of the most popular uses of computers in small businesses is generating and maintaining mailing lists. This is a two-part system to maintain and print mailing lists. The first program is used to create and update the lists. The second program prints out the lists. The lists can be in either zip code or alphabetical order. Includes a sample run. Ignore the printout on page 140; it belongs to another program.

Lines: 237
Version: North Star BASIC release 3
Hardware: random-access file device
Software: none
Non-ANSI: HP strings, extended IF, OPEN, CLOSE, READ #, WRITE, TYP(), EXIT

40. Mailing List Programs for Amateur Radio

Author: Thomas Doyle

Source: *Byte* Jan 79 (4:1)
"A Computerized Mailing List" pp. 84–89 (86–89)

Updates: commentary
Byte Jul 79 (4:7)
"A Faster Mailing List" pp. 6, 98

This is a collection of short programs which, together, form a complete mailing list system. This particular system has been adapted to serve the needs of amateur radio clubs. There are programs for creating, updating, and printing mailing labels. The mailing labels can be printed out in either single- or double-column format. Information stored includes names, addresses, phone numbers, and amateur radio call signs.

Lines: 15, 14, 24, 23, 20, 27, 20
Version: BASIC-E
Hardware: random-access file device
Software: none
Non-ANSI: not translatable

659. Address List Editor

Author: Brian Bateman and Sherman Wantz

Source: *Kilobaud Microcomputing* Jan 79 (25)
"Address List Editor" pp. 44–50 (49–50)

This program is an address list editor. It is designed to be used in conjunction with the address list program that appeared in the October 1978 ssue of *Kilobaud* ("A Useful Address List Program," p. 102). This program allows you to create and update address lists. The lists can then be printed out with the address list program. Includes a sample run.

Lines: 197
Version: SWTPC 8K BASIC 2.0
Hardware: sequential file device
Software: none
Non-ANSI: LINE, strings, extended IF

1002. Simple Mailing List Programs

Author: Bruce Showalter

Source: *Personal Computing* Mar 79 (3:3)
"Pseudo File Processing in BASIC" pp. 30–31 (30–31)

These two programs each print out a mailing list that has been stored in DATA statements. The first program just types out the entire list. The second program prints the addresses corresponding to record numbers you type in.

Lines: 14, 20
Version: not given
Hardware: none
Software: none
Non-ANSI: strings

1147. Simple Mailing List Program

Author: Paul Phelps

Source: '68' Micro Journal Nov–Dec 79 (1:9)
untitled pp. 26–27 (27)

This is a simple mailing list program for creating, updating, and printing address labels. The program is billed as a Christmas card address list program, but the program can actually be used for any type of mailing list. The first 20 names on the address list can be used as a separate list for special addresses.

Lines: 103
Version: Percom SuperBASIC
Hardware: random-access file device
Software: none
Non-ANSI: OPEN, CLOSE, READ #, PRINT #, RESTORE #, LINE, PORT, strings, extended IF

PAYROLL

101. Pay Computing Programs

Author: Peter Sessions

Source: Calculators/Computers Magazine May 77 (1:1)
"Payroll" pp. 63–74 (70–74)

Updates: correction to credits
Calculators/Computers Magazine Oct 77 (1:2)
untitled p. 91

This is a collection of short programs to compute how much to pay your employees. The programs demonstrate the various ways that pay may be computed. Some of the types of pay considered are straight pay, overtime pay, commissions, piece work, and stratified piece work. Includes sample runs.

Lines: 16 programs ranging from 9 to 61 lines
Version: not given
Hardware: none
Software: none
Non-ANSI: none

102. Stratified Piece-Rate Pay Program

Author: LeRoy Finkel

Source: Calculators/Computers Magazine May 77 (1:1)
"BASIC Test Units" pp. 76–81 (78)

This program computes pay for work done under a stratified piece-rate pay system. The program shows how much a worker would be paid if his or her pay was based on a flat rate for a fixed number of units produced, plus escalating rates for greater production. Includes a sample run.

Lines: 18
Version: not given
Hardware: none
Software: none
Non-ANSI: none

468. General Payroll Package

Author: Bud Shamburger

Soruce: Interface Age Jul 79 (4:7)
"General Payroll Package" pp. 96–120
(108–120)

This general payroll package is part of a series of business application programs. This article in the series covers the subject of payroll software. The payroll package provided is a set of six programs. The payroll package can perform a variety of payroll functions. It can maintain payroll records, keep track of hours worked, and record FICA deductions. There are four disk utility programs also provided. Included are a flowchart and sample runs.

Lines: 95, 523, 315, 102, 54, 40, 63, 61, 41, 190
Version: MITS BASIC ver. 4.0
Hardware: random-access file device
Software: none
Non-ANSI: not translatable

1124. Small Business Payroll System

Author: Robert Forbes

Source: ROM Sep 77 (1:3)
"A Payroll Program for Your Small Business"
pp. 87–95 (89–93)

program description, flowcharts
ROM OCT 77 (1:4)
"Small-Business Payroll Program
Follow-Up" pp. 89–95

A good payroll system is an essential part of a modern business. Until now, the small businessperson had to either do the payroll by hand, or contract the work out to a computer service bureau. Using microcomputers, it is now possible for a small business to have a computerized payroll system of its own. This group of programs can perform a variety of payroll functions. The system has provisions for file maintenance, payroll calculations, quarter-to-date processing, and year-to-date processing. Includes flowcharts and a sample run.

Lines: 124, 191, 31, 46, 49, 27
Version: Altair Extended Disk BASIC
Hardware: random-access file device
Software: none
Non-ANSI: not translatable

599. Payroll Program

Author: Ron Harvey

Source: *Kilobaud* Nov 77 (11)
           "Payroll Program" pp. 106–108 (107–108)

This is a payroll system for a small business. This payroll program can keep track of data such as social security numbers, marital status, and rate of pay for up to 99 employees. The only data which must be entered regularly is the number of paid hours for each employee for each week. At this point the program takes over and calculates each employee's gross pay. FICA tax, federal and state income tax, and net pay. When all the employees have been run, the program provides a payroll summary telling you how much you owe the government in social security and employee withholdings. It also shows you the net payments made and your total payroll costs. Includes a sample run.

Lines: 115
Version: SWTPC 4K BASIC
Hardware: sequential file device
Software: none
Non-ANSI: extended IF, CHR()

600. Payroll Program with Cassette Storage of Data

Author: Ron Harvey

✓ *Source:* *Kilobaud* Dec 77 (12)
             "Payroll Program (Continued)" pp. 44–48 (45–48)

This is a cassette-oriented payroll program for small businesses. This program is an extension of a payroll program in the October 1977 issue of *Kilobaud*. The program is designed to use cassette data storage that is connected in series with the terminal used.

Lines: 152
Version: SWTP 4K BASIC
Hardware: sequential file device
Software: none
Non-ANSI: extended IF, CHR( )

529. Payroll System for MSI Disk Extended BASIC

Author: Dave Gardner and Randy Jackson

Source: *Interface Age* May 79 (4:5)
           "Payday" pp. 58–69, 106–107 (62–69, 106–107)

Updates: corrections
           Interface Age Jul 79 (4:7)
           "Payday Problems" p. 90 (90)

Turning out a payroll can be one of the most complex and time-consuming bookkeeping chores of a small business. Various taxes and differing methods of computing pay make the job of getting out those paychecks a difficult task. Fortunately, it is a job that your computer can handle with ease. This set of programs forms a complete payroll system that can handle up to 300 employees. There are provisions in the system for storing and listing employee histories, printing various forms and records including W-2s, and printing out the payroll checks themselves. The program is interactive, making it simple to run.

Lines: 20 programs ranging from 14 to 118 lines
Version: MSI extended disk BASIC ver. 1.2
Hardware: 132-column printer, random-access file device, addressable-cursor video display
Software: none
Non-ANSI: not translatable

745. Payroll Program for Processor Technology Extended Disk BASIC

Author: Bernay Dusek

Source: *Kilobaud Microcomputing* Nov 79 (35)
           "Pay Up" pp. 92–93 (92–93)

One of the most complicated business functions is running a payroll. With all of those strange deductions and tax formulas, turning out a payroll can prove to be a very frustrating and time-consuming task. This payroll program is designed to get you through payday with no more than a few extra grey hairs. The program keeps employee files, recording number of dependents, FICA taxes paid, and other information, so all you have to enter each week is the number of hours worked. Includes a list of program variables.

Lines: 124
Version: Processor Technology Extended Disk BASIC
Hardware: addressable-cursor video display, random-access file device
Software: none
Non-ANSI: not translatable

PERSONAL FINANCE

483. Household Finance System

Author: Francis Ascolillo

Source: *Interface Age* Dec 77 (2:13)
"Household Finance System I" pp. 40–47
(46–47)

Interface Age Dec 77 (2:13)
"Household Finance System II" pp. 48–55
(54–55)

The Household Finance System is a system designed to give the average family a quick overview of its economic tendencies and trends. HFS I stores data from checks and produces a Monthly Record. HFS II and the Annual Report Program produce further reports. Punched tape is used to store data. Sample runs are included.

Lines: 141, 58, 95
Version: 8K MITS BASIC
Hardware: terminal with papertape punch
Software: none
Non-ANSI: extended IF, strings, WAIT, INP(), VAL(), two-letter variables, STR$(), SPC(), ON . . . GOSUB

484. Personal Accounts Payable

Author: Kevin Redden

Source: *Interface Age* Dec 77 (2:13)
"Personal Accounts Payable Program" pp. 56–61 (59–61)

This program can help you keep track of your bills. It can keep track of bills received, payments made, payment dates, and minimum payments due. Reports available include the history and present status of your household accounts. The program uses some statements peculiar to TDL BASIC: however, the article details how to convert the program for use with other BASIC systems. Includes a sample run.

Lines: 457
Version: TDL 8K BASIC
Hardware: sequential file device
Software: none
Non-ANSI: not translatable

273. Personal Budget Planner

Author: John Donohue

Source: *Creative Computer* May–Jun 78 (4:3)
"BASIC Financial Behaviorism or First Steps Toward a Real Budget" pp. 108–111
(110–111)

Most people have a tough time making ends meet. Who knows where the money goes? This program allows you to map out just exactly what your budget looks like. Knowing this, you may be able to change your budget strategy so as to get more out of the money you have. The Standard Personal Expenditures Accounting System (SPEAS) allows you to record your expenses. From this, the program can rank your various types of expenses according to how much of your budget they make up. The program lists the total amount of each type of expense, and what part of your total budget each type of expense comprises. Includes a sample run.

Lines: 124
Version: North Star BASIC
Hardware: random-access file device
Software: none
Non-ANSI: OPEN, CLOSE, READ #, WRITE, PRINT #, extended IF, HP strings, NOENDMARK( ), %( ) (used to format printouts)

628. Revolving Charge Account Calculations

Author: Len Gorney

Source: *Kilobaud* Jul 78 (19)
"Revolving Charge Account Calculations" pp. 34–35 (34–35)

Updates: improvement
Kilobaud Oct 78 (22)
"Corrections" p. 100 (100)

This program calculates various values and information for charge accounts. You enter the amount of the loan or purchase, the monthly interest rate, the monthly payment, the date of the purchase, and the minimum interest charge before a service charge is applied. The computer then prints out the monthly values for the beginning and ending balance of your account, the monthly and cumulative interest charges, and a monthly and yearly indicator to show you just how long you'll be paying for the purchase. Includes a sample run and a list of program variables.

Lines: 176
Version: not given
Hardware: none
Software: none
Non-ANSI: strings, PRINT USING

35. Checkbook Balancer

Author: Rod Hallen

Source: *Byte* Nov 78 (3:11)
"Checkbook Balancer" p. 66 (66)

This program can help you balance your checkbook at the end of the month. The program takes your balance, adds in deposits not recorded, subtracts checks not cleared, and comes up with the actual balance. The program also prints out the totals for deposits not recorded and checks not cleared.

Lines: 29
Version: Processor Technology BASIC 5
Hardware: none
Software: none
Non-ANSI: extended IF

1000. Home Expense Records

Author: Roger Ulasovetz

Source: *Personal Computing* Mar 79 (3:3)
"Where Did All the Dollars Go?" pp. 14–16 (15–16)

If you're like most of us, you usually find yourself running a bit short of cash at the end of each month. Sometimes it's hard to figure out just how your paycheck managed to dribble out of your pocket. With this home expense manager, you should be able to plug up the leaks in your financial ship of state. The program records the dates and amounts of all the purchases you make. You can print out reports of your expenses at any time. At the end of the month you can print out a detailed summary of your cash flow. This program won't give you any more money to spend but at least you'll know where all those greenbacks went. Includes a sample output.

Lines: 175
Version: Extended Benton Harbor BASIC ver. 10.01.02
Hardware: none
Software: none
Non-ANSI: CLEAR, CNTRL, strings, LINE INPUT

66. Checkbook Balancer

Author: Loring White

Source: *Byte* Jun 79 (4:6)
"Checkbook Balancing Routine" pp. 208–210 (209)

Do you dread the moment when you see your bank statement in the mail because you know it means hours of head-scratching trying to balance your checkbook? Never fear. Now you can balance your checkbook quickly and easily with this checkbook balancing program even if you can't add or subtract. (With the advent of the New Math and pocket calculators, addition and subtraction are be-

coming virtually lost arts.) Data is stored in the program in DATA statements.

Lines: 85
Version: MITS 8K BASIC Revision 3.2
Hardware: none
Software: none
Non-ANSI: strings, two-letter variables

706. Personal Finance System

Author: James McClure

Source: *Kilobaud Microcomputing* Jun 79 (30)
"A Personal Finance System" pp. 74–78 (76–78)

Kilobaud Microcomputing Jul 79 (31)
"Personal Finance System" pp. 50–56 (51–56)

Kilobaud Microcomputing Aug 79 (32)
"Personal Finance System" pp. 66–75 (70–74)

This personal finance package can give your personal budget the same computer accuracy that goes into a business budget. The system is divided into three parts. The accounts payable program keeps track of all your bills and notes when they're due. No longer will you get socked with finance charges because you forgot to pay the telephone bill. The "accounts receivable" program (actually it's more of a paycheck information recording program) records the income you get. As it records your pay, it also keeps track of how much has been taken out for various taxes and deductions. The last program summarizes and graphs the information collected by the first two programs. With it you can learn how much you've paid for various expenses and what percent of your total income each expense comprises. Includes sample runs.

Lines: 300 (plus patches), 387, 422
Version: Digital Research CBASIC
Hardware: random-access file device
Software: none
Non-ANSI: not translatable

828. Checkbook Balancing Program

Author: Stephen Sunderland

Source: *onComputing* Summer 79 (1:1)
"Checkbook Balancing Program in BASIC" pp. 100–101 (100)

If you have trouble balancing your checkbook at the end of the month, then you may want to check out this checkbook balancing program. Not only does the computer do all the arithmetic involved, with faultless precision, but at last you'll no longer be confronted by a mass of indecipherable scribbles when you try to sort out which checks were written for which things.

> *Lines:* 105
> *Version:* TDL 8K Zapple BASIC
> *Hardware:* none
> *Software:* none
> *Non-ANSI:* strings, extended IF, multi-letter variables

354. Personal Financial Model

> *Author:* James Owens
>
> *Source:* *Creative Computing* Jul 79 (5:7)
> "Personal Finances: A Model for Planning" pp. 92–95 (94)

Unless you have a "crystal ball" program running on your home computer, you probably—like most of us—have trouble seeing your financial future. Knowing what to expect tomorrow can help you plan your finances today. But how can you hope to figure out where you'll be tomorrow when it's hard enough just figuring out where you are today? One way is to use this personal finance "model." You give it information about your finances plus a few assumptions about what the future will hold in the way of inflation and other factors. The program then simulates your finances for several years into the future. By changing around your assumptions, you can see what effect various money strategies might have on your future. Includes a sample output.

> *Lines:* 129
> *Version:* not given
> *Hardware:* none
> *Software:* none
> *Non-ANSI:* two-letter variables, extended IF

1044. Liquid Asset Accounting System

> *Author:* Robert Irving
>
> *Source:* *Personal Computing* Aug 79 (3:8)
> "Liquid Asset Accounting System" pp. 53–57 (55–57)

This program helps you keep track of the money that you have squirreled away in your checking and savings accounts. The program can handle several acocunts, giving you a complete picture of your liquid assets at a glance. The program maintains current balances for each account and totals for all of the accounts. The program also keeps track of the checks you write, thus doing away with those frustrating checkbook arithmetic errors. Includes sample runs.

> *Lines:* 153 (plus patch)
> *Version:* SWTPC 8K BASIC ver. 1.0
> *Hardware:* none
> *Software:* sequential file device
> *Non-ANSI:* strings, VAL(), PORT, STR$(), LINE, PRINT #

831. Personal Check Writer

> *Author:* Andrew A. Recupero
>
> *Source:* *onComputing* Winter 79 (1:3)
> "The Personal Check Writer" pp. 59–64 (61–64)

Do you get writer's cramp making out checks to pay all your bills each month? This program can make short work of the task by automatically printing the checks. The program runs through a list of your usual creditors. With each one, you either give an amount or specify OMIT if you don't need a check for that company. When you're finished, you slip blank checks into your printer, one at a time. The program fills out each check with the proper date, company, and amount. All you have to do is sign the checks and send them off. A second program prints a "ruler" to help you set up the proper printing columns for your checks. Includes sample runs.

> *Lines:* 213, 11
> *Version:* not given
> *Hardware:* none
> *Software:* none
> *Non-ANSI:* CLEAR, strings, multi-letter variables, extended IF, SPC(), WAIT, VAL()

REAL ESTATE

490. Real Estate Analysis

> *Author:* Richard Michels
>
> *Source:* *Interface Age* Jan 78 (3:1)
> "How to Buy an Apartment Building" pp. 94–99 (99)
>
> *Updates:* corrections
> *Interface Age* Apr 78 (3:4)
> untitled p. 8

This is a program to appraise the investment potential of a piece of income property. The program computes the components of profit related to the purchase of a piece of income property. The components produced are Scheduled Gross Income, Gross Operating Income, Net Operating Income, Equity Income, Cash Flow, and Taxable Income. In addition, other information is computed including the capitalization rate of the property and the price per square foot. This information is useful not only for determining whether to buy a particular piece of property, but also for determining the effect that any of the input parameters has on profit. Included are a flow-chart and sample run.

Lines: 225
Version: SWTPC 8K BASIC
Hardware: none
Software: none
Non-ANSI: DIGITS, LINE, strings, STR$()

515. Real Estate Development Analysis

Author: W. Chellberg

Source: *Interface Age* Nov 78 (3:11)
"Building and Land Development Program"
pp. 86–89 (88)

Real estate is the "hot" investment these days. Perhaps you've thought of investing in some. If so, here is a program that should interest you. This program analyzes proposed real estate developments. The program accepts data on such things as cost of the land to be used, the number of rental units, and the projected annual expenses. From this, the program generates a "feasibility study" for the project. The report lists the net operating income you can expect, the annual cash flow, and other information. With this program you should be able to determine whether or not a given development will be profitable for you. Includes a sample run.

Lines: 108
Version: MITS 4.0 BASIC
Hardware: none
Software: none
Non-ANSI: strings, CLEAR, two-letter variables, PRINT USING, extended IF

978. Apartment House Discounted Cash Flows

Author: William Lappen

Source: *Personal Computing* Nov 78 (2:11)
"Investment Analysis" pp. 42–46 (46)

One of the most important aspects of real estate investment is analysis of cash flow. This program can analyze a given piece of property to show you how much money you can expect to receive from it each year (or how much you'll have to pay in). Note that this is different from the profit you can expect. Cash flow is the actual amount of out-of-pocket costs and income that are involved each year. It doesn't include the capital appreciation you can anticipate from the rising value of the property. The program takes into account interest, taxes, and other factors. Includes a sample run and a list of program variables.

Lines: 170
Version: TRS-80 Level I BASIC
Hardware: none
Software: none
Non-ANSI: CLS, extended IF, PRINT AT

661. Real Estate Property Locator

Author: Richard Nitto

Source: *Kilobaud Microcomputing* Jan 79 (25)
"Open House" pp. 72–77 (76–77)

If you're a real estate broker, then you know that part of your job is helping people find the houses they want. This program can help you carry out that job by showing your clients which available houses might fit their desires. The client enters information about the type, size, and features of the house desired. The program then scans data that you have previously entered about houses that are on the market. From this data, the program prints out lists of properties that fit your client's specifications. On demand, further information about selected houses can be printed out. The HEX function is used to clear the screen. The SELECT statement is used to switch output to a printer (if available). Includes a sample run, list of program variables, and flowchart.

Lines: 209
Version: Wang BASIC
Hardware: none
Software: none
Non-ANSI: HEX(), SELECT, HP strings, PRINT USING, % (used to specify format for PRINT USING)

986. Income Property Evaluation

Author: Kimball Beasley

Source: *Personal Computing* Jan 79 (3:1)
"Income Property Evaluation"
pp. 45–46 (46)

Updates: correction
Personal Computing May 79 (3:5)
"Income Property Correction" p. 4 (4)

correction
Personal Computing Dec 79 (3:12)
"Improving Income Property" p. 10 (10)

In this age of runaway inflation, real estate seems to be the only investment which is holding its value. But you can still lose your shirt even in real estate if you make a bad investment. This program evaluates properties to show you what kind of "cash flow" they have and what the long-term returns are likely to be. The program takes into account such factors as the cost of a property, what its expenses are, what your tax bracket is, and what the going rate of interest is on mortgages. Includes a sample run.

Lines: 88
Version: PET BASIC
Hardware: none
Software: none
Non-ANSI: none

1053. Real Estate Investment Analysis

Author: Larry L. Seversen

Source: *Personal Computing* Oct 79 (3:10)
"Viewing Real Estate Investments" pp. 22–25 (24–25)

Updates: commentary and corrections
Personal Computing Feb 80 (4:2)
"Real Estate Market: Bulls and Bears" pp. 6–7 (7)

More people are making more money in real estate these days than in any other time in history. Real estate, though, is like any other form of investment—there are good investments and ones that can lose you your shirt. To make money, you have to know exactly what you're buying. This program can help you select the right piece of property. It takes into account the various forms of income and expenses that a particular building or house has. It then uses this data to print out an investment report showing what the cash flow and investment potential of the property is. Includes a sample run.

Lines: 135
Version: North Star BASIC
Hardware: none
Software: none
Non-ANSI: HP strings, %() (used to format printouts), ! (used in place of PRINT)

747. Real Estate Profit Analyzer

Author: Frank Derfler

Source: *Kilobaud Microcomputing* Nov 79 (35)
"Boy, Did I Make a Killing!" pp. 112–114 (112–113)

Updates: corrections
Kilobaud Microcomputing Jan 80 (37)
"Corrections" pp. 170–171

Unlike analyzing stocks or bonds, determining how much profit a particular piece of real estate can give you is a difficult task, because many factors are involved. This program is set up to show you how much profit you can expect from a real estate investment. The program takes into account the buying and selling prices, taxes, and property maintenance costs. This information is used to give you a profitability analysis for the property. Includes a sample run and a list of program variables.

Lines: 173
Version: North Star BASIC
Hardware: none
Software: none
Non-ANSI: %( ) (used to format printouts), strings, extended IF

1062. Rental Payment Records

Author: Fred E. Guth

Source: *Personal Computing* Nov 79 (3:11)
"RENT" pp. 35–36 (36)

If you own rental property and have slow-paying tenants, one way to encourage them to pay up is to charge interest on late payments. But that can involve elaborate calculations and record keeping. This program is designed to help out by maintaining rental payment records including automatic calculations of any late charges. With it you can see exactly who owes you what. Includes a sample run.

Lines: 39
Version: TRS-80 Level II BASIC
Hardware: none
Software: none
Non-ANSI: CLEAR, CLS, two-letter variables, strings, LPRINT, LPRINT USING, STRING$(), LINE INPUT

REPORT WRITING

653. Travel Expense Report Generator

Author: not given

Source: *Kilobaud* Dec 78 (24)
"The Art of Generating Expense Reports" pp. 32–35 (33–35)

If you have to travel in your line of work, then you know what a drag it is to keep track of all those expenses for your company travel-expense reports. This program makes things easier by generating the reports for you.

The program has special provisions for creating "fake" amounts for meal expenses so that you don't have to record each and every meal (this assumes your company does not require receipts for meals.) Besides meals, the program can keep track of such expenses as taxis, hotel rooms, and rental cars. When all your expenses are recorded, the program grinds out an expense report, showing your expenses day by day. Totals are given by day and by type of expense. Includes a sample run.

Lines: 184
Version: Altair 8K BASIC
Hardware: none
Software: none
Non-ANSI: CLEAR, strings, two-letter variables, extended IF, STR$(), SPC()

520. Financial Statement Report Writer

Author: Fred LaPlante

Source: *Interface Age* Feb 79 (4:2)
"A Simple Financial Report Writer" pp. 64–69 (67–69)

Writing a new program for each task you wish to accomplish is both time-consuming and expensive. If you're just printing out reports of data you have already collected, you have another option. Rather than write a separate program for each report you wish to generate, you can print out the documents with a generalized report writer. This is one such report writer. You supply the program with data and a general description of the output. The program then takes over and "fills in" the data sections of the report. This report writer is set up to produce financial statements. Includes a sample run.

Lines: 240
Version: CBASIC ver. 1.0
Hardware: sequential file device
Software: none
Non-ANSI: not translatable

SALES

579. Sales Analysis Program

Author: Lee Wilkinson

Source: *Kilobaud* May 77 (5)
"Cure Those End-of-Month Blues" pp. 34–35 (35)

Updates: improvements
Kilobaud Sep 77 (9)
"Right on Target" p. 14 (14)

This sales analysis program gives you an instant answer to the question, "How were my sales this month?" This program takes sales data for a month and prints out a report showing what your sales were in various categories. The categories can be tailored to fit your own particular business. The report produced shows your total gross, average sale per customer, and total number of sales by category. The program does not use external files; all data is stored in memory in DATA statements. Includes a sample run.

Lines: 51
Version: MITS 8K BASIC
Hardware: none
Software: none
Non-ANSI: strings, extended IF, ON . . . GOSUB

594. Sales Receipts Tally Program

Author: Ron Harvey

Source: *Kilobaud* Oct 77 (10)
"Learn and Earn" pp. 28–30 (29)

This is a program to do a simple sales receipts tally program. This program accumulates daily cash receipts for a small business. It prints out both a daily summary and a monthly summary. It does not use external files, so some information from the previous day must be reentered at the start of each run. The program has provisions for recording sales that are exempt from sales tax. Includes a sample run.

Lines: 48
Version: SWTPC 4K BASIC
Hardware: none
Software: none
Non-ANSI: CHR()

677. Sales Forecasting

Author: Stan Tishler

Source: *Kilobaud Microcomputing* Mar 79 (27)
"The One Percent Forecasting Method" pp. 100–102 (101–102)

What does the future hold for your company? You can find out with this sales forecasting system. The system is composed of two programs. The first program allows you to enter data about past years' sales. The second program uses this information to make predictions about what sales are likely to be like in the future. Includes a list of program variables.

Lines: 96, 66
Version: TRS-80 Level II BASIC
Hardware: sequential file device
Software: none
Non-ANSI: DEFINT, CLS, PRINT #, extended IF, INPUT #, strings

532. Sales Record Keeping

Author: David Witt

Source: *Interface Age* May 79 (4:5)
"Sales Record Keeping" pp. 86–89 (87–89)

If you're a salesperson, you know that the key to higher sales is maintaining close and constant contact with your customers. To do this you'll need to keep good records about each customer and his or her needs. This system can help you handle the records you need. Using this system you can record and update information about each of your clients, including their names, addresses, phone numbers, and what products they're interested in. Space is provided for recording general comments about any particular client.

Lines: 101, 66, 79, 59
Version: MITS BASIC
Hardware: random-access file device
Software: none
Non-ANSI: not translatable

1035. Sales/Accounts Receivable System

Author: Sam Newhouse

Source: *Personal Computing* Jul 79 (3:7)
"A Program to Register More Than Cash" pp. 56–70 (62–67)

This sales/accounts receivable system keeps track of both cash and credit sales. For each transaction, the program records the items purchased, quantities, prices, taxes, and actual amounts paid. The program prints out an invoice for the customer, as well as two for your records. At the end of the every month the program outputs detailed statements for each account on your books. The program can also print out descriptions of all of your credit accounts. Includes a sample run and a flowchart.

Lines: 436
Version: Mits Disk Extended BASIC ver. 3.4
Hardware: random-access file device
Software: none
Non-ANSI: not translatable

564. Volume Prediction Program

Author: Leo P. Biese

Source: *Interface Age* Dec 79 (4:12)
"FORECAST: Volume Projection for the Small Business" pp. 60–70 (64–66)

The prediction of future sales volume is an important part of any business. Knowing how large your sales volume will be in the near future can help you intelligently plan your materials purchases. This program takes data about past volume and uses it to predict future sales volume. The program uses exponential smoothing to eliminate random fluctuations in the data. The data can be printed out in both tabular and graph form. Includes a sample run. (Though the article uses an example from a scientific setting, this program is listed in the Business section because programs of this type are used most commonly in business. The program is generalized and can be used for both business and science.)

Lines: 181
Version: Microsoft BASIC 4.1
Hardware: sequential file device
Software: none
Non-ANSI: strings, CLEAR, multi-letter variables, LINEINPUT, extended IF, OPEN, CLOSE, INPUT #, PRINT #, PRINT USING, LPRINT, LPRINT USING, SPC(), STRING$(), ' (used in place of REM)

STOCKS

464. Stock Options Program

Author: Edward Christianson

Source: *Interface Age* Feb 77 (2:3)
"Microcomputer Stock Options" pp. 29–38 (37–38)

Updates: correction
Interface Age May 77 (2:6)
untitled p. 140 (140)

Program to analyze stock market options. The article describes the options market including buy and sell strategies. Included are flowcharts and sample runs.

Lines: 183
Version: Processor Technology 5K BASIC
Hardware: none
Software: none
Non-ANSI: extended IF

603. Stock Holdings Analysis

Author: Dr. George Haller

Source: *Kilobaud* Dec 77 (12
"Who Needs a Broker?" pp. 90–92 (91)

This is a program to analyze your stock holdings. The program stores information about the stocks you own and prints out the information on demand. No external files are used; all the data is held in memory in DATA statements. Two basic reports can be generated: a dividend report and a value report. The dividend report calculates your dividends and dividend rates. The value report shows how much you have gained or lost on each stock. The program uses PRINT USING statements, but substitute code is provided for systems that do not have PRINT USING. Includes sample runs.

Lines: 68
Version: Altair Disk Extended BASIC
Hardware: none
Software: none
Non-ANSI: strings, extended IF, PRINT USING

949. Stock Market Analysis

Author: Herbert Schildt

Source: *Personal Computing* May 78 (2:5)
"Wall Street Wallop" pp. 49–57 (50–57)

Updates: correction
Personal Computing Oct 78 (2:1)
"The Case of the Missing Lines" p. 12 (12)

For a number of years, large firms and corporations have been doing market investment research by using computers. Now, with personal computers, it's possible for you to do the same sort of market analysis that the big boys do. This stock market system is composed of two programs. The first program generates statistical information about stocks. The program does regression analysis and other statistical analyses. The second program in the package prints out the information in the system. It is quite flexible about the ways it can be used to retrieve information. The program can, for example, print out information on all corporations whose price/earnings ratio is less than 10 and whose price per share is more than $30. Includes sample runs and a list of program variables.

Lines: 348, 135
Version: North Star BASIC
Hardware: random-access file device
Software: none
Non-ANSI: LINE, ! (used in place of REM), SQRT( ), OPEN, CLOSE, READ #, WRITE, extended IF, %( ) (used to format printouts), HP strings

291. Stock Options Analysis

Author: Allen Hagelberg

Source: *Creative Computing* Sep–Oct 78 (4:5)
"Evaulating Stock Options" pp. 121–122 (122)

People in the investment world frequently use computers to find the best possible investments. With this program, you can do the same thing. This program allows you to analyze stock options to find the best values. It can show you what returns to expect on a stock, given various strike prices. Includes sample runs.

Lines: 61
Version: HP 9830 BASIC
Hardware: none
Software: none
Non-ANSI: HP strings, FORMAT, WRITE, FIXED, multiple-assignment

744. Stock Market Analysis System

Author: Leslie R. Schmeltz

Source: *Kilobaud Microcomputing* Nov 79 (35)
"The Apple Goes to Market" pp. 70–76 (70–75)

Updates: correction
Kilobaud Microcomputing Jan 80 (37)
"Corrections" pp. 170–171 (170)

The key to making money in the stock market is knowing when to buy and when to sell. This system can help you make buy/sell/hold decisions. The first two programs in the system allow data about stock prices to be stored and updated. The third program computes moving averages and totals, and recommends a course of action based on advance/decline line theory. Includes a sample run.

Lines: 15, 31, 95
Version: Applesoft II
Hardware: sequential file device
Software: none
Non-ANSI: strings, STORE, RECALL, extended IF, VAL( ), FLASH

TAXES

492. Tax Calculation Program

Author: Gary Young

Source: *Interface Age* Jan 78 (3:1)
"Tax Calculation Program" pp. 158–162 (158–162)

This is a program to determine what effect earning more income or making a deductible investment would have on your taxes. The program includes data for the Federal and California State tax tables, but these can be changed to reflect your own situation. Using your adjusted gross income, the program then accepts data on additional income or tax deductible investments. Finally, the program prints the changes in your tax status and how much you stand to lose or gain. Includes a sample run.

Lines: 418
Version: North Star DOS BASIC
Hardware: sequential file device
Software: none
Non-ANSI: HP strings, OPEN, CLOSE, READ #,
           WRITE, extended IF, %() (used to format
           printouts)

942. Income Tax Form Preparer

Author: Joe Roehrig

Source: *Personal Computing* Mar 78 (2:3)
          "Deep in the Heart of Taxes" pp. 56–65
          (61–65)

Updates: correction
          Personal Computing Jun 78 (2:6)
          "Tax Amendment" p. 4

          correction
          Personal Computing Jul 78 (2:7)
          "Taxes—Author Reply" p. 5

This is a collection of three programs to help you fill out 1977 income tax forms. Though you have probably already filled out your '77 tax forms by now, you can still use this system as a model for building a system for the current year. The first program creates a blank data file. The second program supplies the tax rate data. The third, and main, program prepares the 1040 Form and Schedule A. When the program ends, you can determine if you want the input of that particular run to be saved. Includes sample runs.

Lines: 5, 23, 245
Version: not given
Hardware: sequential file device
Software: none
Non-ANSI: HP strings, OPEN, CLOSE, READ #,
           WRITE, extended IF, ! (used in place of
           PRINT), LINE, FREE(), %() (used to format
           printouts)

306. Depreciation and Taxes

Author: Gary Young

Source: *Creative Computing* Jan 79 (5:1)
          "Help For The Weary Taxpayer" pp. 41–44
          (42–44)

The Internal Revenue Service allows you to calculate depreciation on your business equipment in any one of

several ways. The way that you select can have a drastic effect on how much you will owe in taxes and on when you will have to pay them. This program can show you the best type of depreciation for your particular situation. You type in information about the asset. The output is a set of tables showing the effects each one of several methods and depreciation lifes would have on your taxes. The tax tables built into the program are set up for an unmarried Californian, but can be changed to suit your situation. Includes a sample run.

Lines: 164
Version: North Star BASIC (release 3)
Hardware: none
Software: none
Non-ANSI: %() (used to format printouts), extended IF,
           EXIT

524. Income Averaging for Income Tax Computation

Author: J. Dunn and M. Farris

Source: *Interface Age* Mar 79 (4:3)
          "Income Averaging Program" pp. 72–77
          (74–77)

One of the most aggravating things about income taxes is all the complicated forms that you have to fill out. Some people end up giving up legitimate deductions just because they can't figure out how to fill out their returns. Your computer can help you complete your income tax returns and get everything that's coming to you. This program helps you "average" your income. If your income varies considerably from year to year, income averaging can save you money. This program helps you fill out the income averaging schedules. Includes a sample run.

Lines: 247
Version: North Star BASIC
Hardware: sequential file device
Software: none
Non-ANSI: HP strings, extended IF, OPEN, READ #,
           CLOSE, EXIT, ! (used in place of PRINT), !
           # (used in place of PRINT USING), %()
           (used to format printouts)

1011. Income Tax Database

Author: Paul Holliday

Source: *Personal Computing* Apr 79 (3:4)
          "Tax Base" pp. 22–33 (28–33)

          Personal Computing May 79 (3:5)
          "Tax Base" pp. 30–37 (32–36)

You can improve your relations with the IRS by keeping accurate and complete records of your deductions. This income tax database system can help you do this. Deductions can be recorded in any of a variety of categories which you set up. At any time you can print out a detailed listing of your deductions in any category along with a running total of the amount of the deductions. The system is menu-driven to make it easy to run. Includes sample runs and lists of the program variables.

Lines: 874, 836
Version: BASIC-E
Hardware: random-access file device
Software: none
Non-ANSI: not translatable

WORD PROCESSING

583. Simulated Typesetting On a Regular Terminal

Author: Lee Wilkinson

Source: *Kilobaud* Jun 77 (6)
"Computerized Typesetting" pp. 106–108 (107–108)

This is a program to simulate the action of a typesetting composer on a regular terminal. Composers are used to print type for offset printing. Composers can "right-justify" lines; that is, they can insert space between letters to make the right-hand margin come out exactly even. On an ordinary typewriter or computer terminal you can simulate this ability by inserting spaces into the lines as you type them. This program assists you in producing "right-justified" documents. All you have to do is type in the regular unjustified copy. The computer will automatically insert the needed spaces to type out a justified document. The program does not use external files, so only one page can be handled at a time. Includes a sample run.

Lines: 62
Version: MITS 8K BASIC
Hardware: none
Software: none
Non-ANSI: CLEAR, WAIT, extended IF, two-letter variables, strings

488. Word Processor for MITS BASIC

Author: Ken Knecht

Source: *Interface Age* Jan 78 (3:1)
"The Word Processor" pp. 60–79 (75–79)

This is a word processing system for MITS BASIC. This program allows you to enter and edit documents. Fea-

tures include double spacing, justification, and page numbering. Includes a sample run. A machine-readable copy of the program on a Tarbell format phonograph record is bound into the magazine.

Lines: 315
Version: MITS Disk Extended BASIC
Hardware: random-access file device, MITS SIOA I/O board
Software: none
Non-ANSI: not translatable

631. Word Processing System for MITS Disk BASIC

Author: Donald Fitchhorn

Source: *Kilobaud* Aug 78 (20)
"DOCUFORM: A Word-Processing System for Everyone!" pp. 22–35 (25–35)

Updates: commentary and corrections
Kilobaud Microcomputing Jan 79 (25)
"What's Up, DOC?" pp. 19–20 (20)

If you do a lot of typing, here is a system that you will really appreciate. This is the DOCUFORM word processing system. DOCUFORM allows you to enter, revise, and print a wide variety of documents. With a word processing system such as this one, you only have to enter the text once. After that, the system allows you to make corrections to the text with ease. Once your work is in final form, you can have the computer print out a flawless copy. In addition, DOCUFORM has such features as line justification (three modes), hyphenation, and automatic margin control. Includes sample runs.

Lines: 892, 85
Version: MITS 4.1 Disk BASIC
Hardware: random-access file device
Software: none
Non-ANSI: not translatable

636. Page-Oriented Text Editor

Author: R. Law and D. Mitchell

Source: *Kilobaud* Sep 78 (21)
"(Con)text Editor" pp. 22–31 (25–28)

Updates: correction
Kilobaud Nov 78 (23)
"Corrections" p. 128 (128)

commentary
Kilobaud Microcomputing Jan 79 (25)
"Notice of Copyright" p. 93

commentary
Kilobaud Microcomputing Jun 79 (30)
"Computer Clinic" p. 22

Almost everyone uses some kind of editor to create and debug software. The type of editor used in most BASIC systems is so "natural" that most people don't even think that they're using an editor. Unfortunately, the BASIC type of editor is only useful for editing programs in BASIC. This editor can be used to create a variety of kinds of text. With this editor, you edit one "page" of material at a time. The editor is quite flexible, and has a variety of commands. With this editor you can Insert, Delete, Find, Print, and do a number of other operations on a given document. The program also has provisions for storing the text for later use. Includes a list of program variables, flowcharts, and a sample run.

Lines: 200
Version: MITS 8K BASIC ver. 4.0
Hardware: sequential file device
Software: none
Non-ANSI: CLEAR, strings, two-letter variables, POKE, OUT, WAIT, CSAVE, CLOAD, STR$(), VAL(), extended IF

439. Stencil Cutting Programs

Author: Richard French

Source: *Dr. Dobb's Journal of Computer Calisthenics & Orthodontia* Oct 78 (3:9) "Cutting Stencils with a Diablo Printer" p. 17 (17)

For schools and offices with small budgets, mimeographing is an inexpensive way of doing printing. Making stencils, though, can be a problem, because it's difficult to correct mistakes in them. One way to solve this problem is to use your computer to edit the text and then cut the stencil on your printer. A difficulty with this approach is that most small systems' printers don't strike the paper hard enough to cut a stencil properly. These stencil cutting programs solve this problem by printing each character several times. One program does this by simply typing each line four times. The other program does the job by printing one character at a time, striking each character several times.

Lines: 22, 51
Version: Sheppardson BASIC
Hardware: Diablo Hy-Term printer, sequential file device
Software: none
Non-ANSI: not translatable

534. Word Processing for the TRS-80

Author: C. L. Cooper

Source: *Interface Age* May 79 (4:5) "Word Processing in BASIC" pp. 96–99 (98–99)

You don't need to spend $10,000 for a word-processing system—this one runs on the inexpensive TRS-80. You type in the text that you want, along with some control information. If you make a mistake you can go back and correct it easily. When you finished with the text, you can print a flawless copy. The program has provisions for line justification, page titles, page numbers, and cassette storage of the documents. Includes a sample run.

Lines: 84
Version: TRS-80 disk BASIC
Hardware: sequential file device
Software: none
Non-ANSI: not translatable

691. Text Editor/Formatter

Author: R. M. Law and D. C. Mitchell

Source: *Kilobaud Microcomputing* May 79 (29) "A Text Formatter in BASIC" pp. 26–33 (30–32)

Updates: improvements *Kilobaud Microcomputing* Jul 79 (31) "More Formatting" p. 25 (25)

This is a combined text editor and text formatter. The editor allows you to enter (and possibly make changes in) a document. The text formatter part of the program does automatic adjustment of the material. The text formatter can perform such functions as margin justification (to get an "even" right-hand margin), centering, and automatic page numbering. You can use this system to create form letters, prepare speeches, and do many other tasks. Includes a sample run and a list of program variables.

Lines: 278
Version: not given
Hardware: sequential file device
Software: none
Non-ANSI: CLEAR, strings, two-letter variables, VAL(), STR$ (), extended IF, CLOAD, CSAVE, WAIT, INP(), OUT

64. North Star BASIC Text Editor

Author: Fred Ruckdeschel

Source: *Byte* Jun 79 (4:6) "BASIC Text Editor" pp. 156–164 (158–162)

This program frees you from typing and retyping a manuscript. Throw away your bottles of Liquid Paper. With a computer-based text editor you make changes in the copy quickly and easily. This text editor uses North Star BASIC. It has provisions for saving text on disk, justifying margins, and numbering lines. Includes a sample run.

Lines: 231
Version: North Star BASIC, ver. 6, Release 3
Hardware: random-access file device
Software: none
Non-ANSI: HP strings, %() (used to format printouts), extended IF, OPEN, CLOSE, READ #, WRITE, EXAM, FILL, ASC(), VAL()

540. Corporate Minutes Keeper

Author: Jon R. Lindsay

Source: *Interface Age* Jul 79 (4:7)
"Saving Time While Keeping Minutes" pp. 76–79 (78–79)

Virtually all corporations, large and small, keep minutes of corporate board meetings. These minutes form an important record of the actions the corporation has taken. This program aids in the preparation and printing of the minutes. The minutes automatically include routine information such as date, time, location, and persons attending the meeting. The text portion of the program allows you to enter and edit the minutes. When the minutes are complete, the program types out the final copy. Includes a list of program variables.

Lines: 266
Version: Microsoft Extended Disk BASIC (MBASIC)
Hardware: sequential file device
Software: none
Non-ANSI: CLEAR, WIDTH, LINE INPUT, strings, extended IF, LPRINT, OPEN, CLOSE, PRINT #, LINE INPUT #, EOF(), KILL, WAIT, two-letter variables

1094. Form Letter Writer

Author: Jon Lindsay

Source: *Recreational Computing* Jul–Aug 79 (8:1)
"The Dedicated Word Processor" pp. 12–13 (13)

Suppose you want to send copies of the same letter to a long list of people. One way to do the job is to let your computer do the typing. This program allows you to enter a form letter and then type out as many copies as you want. You can add that "personal touch" by including within the body of the letter phrases directed at specific individuals. The program also automatically addresses the envelopes. Includes a sample output.

Lines: 71
Version: Microsoft Disk Extended BASIC
Hardware: none
Software: none
Non-ANSI: LPRINT, strings, extended IF, WIDTH, WAIT

1140. Form-Letter Writer for Computerware BASIC

Author: Gene Embry

Source: '68' Micro Journal Aug 79 (1:6)
"Data Files" pp. 7–10 (8–10)

Updates: another version
'68' Micro Journal Sep 79 (1:7)
"Mail List" pp. 32–36 (32–36)

These two programs comprise a form-letter-writing system for Computerware BASIC. The system takes a form letter and merges it with a list of addresses to crank out as many "personalized" form letters as you want.

Lines: 222
Version: Computerware BASIC ver. 7.0
Hardware: random-access file device
Software: none
Non-ANSI: not translatable

743. Simple Text Editor for the TRS-80

Author: Roland Abe

Source: *Kilobaud Microcomputing* Nov 79 (35)
"Text Editing for the TRS-80" p. 66 (66)

This simple text editor runs on a TRS-80. It comes in two parts: a text writer and a text reader. You use the TRS-80's built-in text editor to create a message of up to 13 lines. The text writer writes this out onto the cassette. You then use the text reader to read in the lines and display them on the screen.

Lines: 21, 10
Version: TRS-80 Level II BASIC
Hardware: TRS-80
Software: none
Non-ANSI: not translatable

1066. Quickie Text Editor

Author: R. E. Langston

Source: *Personal Computing* Dec 79 (3:12)
"Two-Step Program" p. 6 (6)

Text editors have been written that use thousands of statements. Here's one that shows that a (simple-minded) editor can be written in only 9 lines. You enter a line at a time. As each line is typed, the program saves the text on cassette. When you're done, the program can play back the text from the cassette.

Lines: 9
Version: TRS-80 BASIC
Hardware: sequential file device
Software: none
Non-ANSI: CLEAR, strings, PRINT #, INPUT #, LPRINT

MISCELLANEOUS

104. Timesharing Cost Calculation

Author: LeRoy Finkel

Source: *Calculators/Computers Magazine* May 77 (1:1)
"BASIC Test Units" pp. 76–81 (79)

This program computes the amount that users on a time-sharing computer should be billed for their use of the computer. The program assumes that the users are charged varying rates for their time on the machine. Includes a sample run.

Lines: 28
Version: not given
Hardware: none
Software: none
Non-ANSI: none

955. Newspaper Advertisement Accounting System

Author: Sam Newhouse

Source: *Personal Computing* Jun 78 (2:6)
"Contract Fulfillment" pp. 28–38 (30:33)

Newspapers commonly charge companies for advertisements according to performance contracts; that is, the more lines of advertising the company buys, the less the company pays per line. Keeping track of how many lines a company has purchased is a major headache. This program takes care of that problem by taking over the accounting for newspaper advertisements. The program has a variety of features. You can type in and edit the accounting data for each day's advertising. The accounting data can be updated. The status of all accounts can be listed. The program can also accept accounting data relating to each account such as the lineage contracted for and the expiration date of the contract. Includes a sample run and a listing of program variables.

Lines: 469
Version: Altair Extended Disk BASIC ver. 3.4
Hardware: random-access file device
Software: none
Non-ANSI: not translatable

630. Retail Pricing System

Author: Phil Hughes

Source: *Kilobaud* Jul 78 (19)
"Retail Pricing System" pp. 108–110 (109–110)

This is a package of three programs designed to generate resale price reports for any small business whose retail prices can be established as a function of wholesale prices. The system facilitates price updating and generation of retail price lists. The system consists of three programs: the build program inputs the products and prices; the report program prints the reports; and the update program allows the data to be changed. Includes a sample run.

Lines: 35, 23, 32
Version: SWTP 8K BASIC
Hardware: sequential file device
Software: none
Non-ANSI: LINE, DIGITS, extended IF, PRINT #, strings

295. Critical Path Analysis

Author: Ruth Sabean, Margot Critchfield, and Thomas Dwyer

Source: *Creative Computing* Nov–Dec 78 (4:6)
"Critical Path Analysis" pp. 86–93 (91)

Scheduling a major activity can be a major headache. If the task to be accomplished has a great many steps, you'll probably find that many of the steps are dependent on prior completion of other steps. To get the right people and supplies together at the right time you will have to spend many hours adjusting and readjusting your timetable. Heaven help you if some part of the project falls behind schedule, because it will mean that other parts of the project will, no doubt, have to be juggled around. This program simplifies project planning by using a process called Critical Path Analysis. Critical path analysis can show you when things have to be done and how much "slack time" each part of the project can have without affecting other parts. Includes a sample run.

Lines: 41
Version: not given
Hardware: none
Software: none
Non-ANSI: extended IF

988. Printer's Paper-Cutting Program

Author: Stan Purinton

Source: *Personal Computing* Feb 79 (3:2)
"Stan's Paper-Cutting Program" pp. 14–15
(15)

Printers have a difficult job estimating how much paper they are going to need for any particular printing job. Paper comes in large sheets. These sheets have to be cut down to customer specifications. The number of printed pages that can be cut from one sheet depends on how the sheet is cut. This program estimates paper requirements. It uses the initial sheet size, the finished page size, the number of copies wanted, and whether grain direction is important, to compute the number of sheets needed. Includes a sample run.

Lines: 54
Version: not given
Hardware: none
Software: none
Non-ANSI: strings, extended IF, MOD(), two-letter variables

530. Check Writing Program for SSG General Ledger

Author: Eric Savage

Source: *Interface Age* May 79 (4:5)
"Interfacing with Commercial Software"
pp. 70–75 (72–75)

The Structured Systems Group (SSG) General Ledger system is a complete general ledger system for a small business. This check writing program is designed to enhance the SSG general ledger system. The problem with SSG's general ledger is that entering data for checks can be somewhat cumbersome. This program solves that problem, while at the same time retaining the overall integrity of the general ledger system. The check writer is quite flexible and can, for example, handle checks being used to pay more than one invoice or being charged to more than one ledger account.

Lines: 226
Version: CBASIC II
Hardware: random-access file device
Software: none
Non/ANSI: not translatable

1070. Service Technician Work Report

Author: Clint Hentz

Source: *Personal Computing* Dec 79 (3:12)
"Keeping Tabs on Service Technicians" pp.
63–68 (66–68)

If you are to run a profitable service-oriented business such as a TV repair shop, you must keep track of what your service technicians are doing. This program provides a system for recording just exactly who is doing what. As your crew makes house calls, they record their mileage, time spent on the job, and other data. At the end of the day, these records are turned in and entered into the computer. The computer uses this information to crank out work reports for each technician and for the repair group as a whole. You can use these reports to see whether anyone is taking too long on calls or to determine whether a new procedure is having any effect on operations. Includes a sample run.

Lines: 149, 54
Version: TRS-80 Level II BASIC
Hardware: sequential file device
Software: none
Non-ANSI: strings, LPRINT, POKE, LPRINT USING, PRINT #, INPUT #

2

GAMES

ADVENTURE GAMES

633. Swords and Sorcery

Author: Bruce Turrie

Source: *Kilobaud* Aug 78 (20)
"SWORDS AND SORCERY!" pp. 54–58
(55–58)

Updates: corrections
Kilobaud Microcomputing Feb 79 (26)
"Corrections" p. 155 (155)

You are a gallant, but broke, hero attempting to rescue an
elfin princess from the Necromancer's dungeon located
within a dark forest. In order to accomplish the rescue,
you must pass safely through the forest to the dungeon,
remove the princess, and escort her to safety. You must
also pick up enough gold along the way to pay your
creditors. Along the way you will meet a variety of good
and bad creatures including Rats, Snakes, Trolls, Goblins,
Nymphs, and Satyrs.

Lines: 372
Version: SWTP 8K BASIC ver. 2.0
Hardware: none
Software: none
Non-ANSI: DIGITS, extended IF

319. ATOM20

Author: Ray Brander

Source: *Creative Computing* Feb 79 (5:2)
"ATOM20" pp. 136–141 (137–140)

You are among the few survivors of a worldwide nuclear
war. With limited supplies, you must explore the world
around you, trying to survive. You may meet up with such
dangers as radiation poisoning and dangerous animals.
Includes a sample run.

Lines: 798
Version: CDC CYBER 70/73–26 BASIC 3.1
Hardware: none
Software: none
Non-ANSI: strings, SUBSTR()

1135. EXPLOR

Author: Tom Harmon

Source: *'68' Micro Journal* May 79 (1:3)
"Some BASIC Games" pp. 26–32 (27–32)

Updates: correction
'68' Micro Journal Jul 79 (1:5)
untitled p. 33 (33)

EXPLOR is an Adventure-type exploring game. You get
randomly dumped into a 10-by-10 matrix of rooms. From
there you must battle your way to the exit (wherever that
is). You must fight off gargoyles, dragons, warlocks,
trolls, and tax collectors. And, of course, you must try to
pick up some gold on the way.

Lines: 87, 250
Version: Computerware BASIC
Hardware: random-access file device
Software: none
Non-ANSI: OPEN, CLOSE, READ, WRITE, ON . . .
GOSUB, strings, STR$( ), FDEL, LINE,
BASE, extended IF

72. QUEST: Explore a Cave

Author: Roger Chaffee

Source: *Byte* Jul 79 (4:7)
"QUEST" pp. 176–186 (179–186)

Updates: correction
Byte Nov 79 (4:11)
"Broken Text" p. 221 (221)

commentary
Byte Dec 79 (4:12)
"QUEST Comments" p. 79

The latest rage in computer games is the "electronic adventure story." In these games you play the part of an explorer. The computer acts as your hands and eyes as you wander about the landscape. In your travels you run across a variety of strange situations to which you must respond. ADVENTURE is the granddaddy of these games. QUEST is a scaled-down version of ADVENTURE designed to run on your home computer. In this version you can only move around and explore; there are no commands for collecting objects or performing other tasks. There *is* a treasure that you can try to make off with. Includes a sample run and a list of program variables.

Lines: 528
Version: not given
Hardware: none
Software: none
Non-ANSI: extended IF, strings, MID(), LST(), NDX()

814. SPELUNKER Cave Exploration Game

Author: Thomas R. Mimlitch

Source: *Micro* Oct 79 (17)
         "SPELUNKER" pp. 15–24 (19–24)

SPELUNKER is a version of the now-famous ADVENTURE game. In this game you play the part of an explorer wandering around inside a magic cave. You run into demons which you must fight off and treasure which you can greedily haul away. This version of the game is designed for small computer systems. Descriptions of the rooms are not built into the program (you refer to descriptions printed in the article), thus saving a considerable amount of memory. By eliminating some PEEKs and POKEs, this program could probably be run on non-Apple systems.

Lines: 364
Version: Apple BASIC
Hardware: none
Software: none
Non-ANSI: not translatable

401. ADVENTURE Cave Exploration Game

Author: Ben Moser

Source: *Creative Computing* Nov 79 (5:11)
         "ADVENTURE" pp. 108–39 (126–138)

ADVENTURE is a game program originally developed at M.I.T. by Don Woods and Willie Crowther. You play the part of an explorer wandering around in a mysterious cave. Using one or two word commands, you manipulate

objects in the cave. If your wits are about you, you can fend off danger and collect all sorts of goodies. This version of the program makes extensive use of disk files for storing such things as room descriptions. Includes a sample run and a list of program variables.

Lines: 1,003
Version: HP3000 BASIC
Hardware: random-access file device
Software: none
Non-ANSI: not translatable

BACKGAMMON

281. Backgammon

Author: Paul von Autenried

Source: *Creative Computing* Jul–Aug 78 (4:4)
         "GAMMON" pp. 135–141 (138–141)

Backgammon is a game based partly on luck and partly on skill. This version of the game pits you against the computer. The computer moves are determined by sections of priority move searches. The computer tries to (in order): move two men together to form a blocked point, hit the other player (you), move safely to a previously blocked point, or move the farthest man. The program has betting capabilities. It can accept or refuse a double, or suggest a double to you. The CHAIN statement chains to a Backgammon instruction program (not supplied). This CHAIN statement may be omitted in most systems. Includes a list of variables and a sample run.

Lines: 764
Version: HP 2000 BASIC
Hardware: sequential file device
Software: none
Non-ANSI: COM, MAT ZER(), multiple-assignment,
          CHAIN, READ #, PRINT #, FILES, PRINT
          USING, IMAGE, LIN(), MAX(), HP strings,
          extended IF

BOARD GAMES

874. DODGEM

Author: Mac Oglesby

Source: *People's Computer Company* Mar–Apr 76 (4:5)
         "DODGEM" pp. 8–9 (8–9)

DODGEM is a game that can be played by two players playing against each other, or by one player playing against the computer. The game is played on a square board (you choose the size of the board). The players go in turn, moving their pieces across the board. One player moves "verticially" across the board and the other player moves "horizontally" across the board. Since the two sets of pieces are moving at right angles, they must maneuver to avoid collisions. The object of the game is to get all your pieces across the board. Includes a sample run.

Lines: 344
Version: Dartmouth BASIC
Hardware: none
Software: none
Non-ANSI: strings, SEG$(), LINPUT, POS(), CHANGE, ' (used in place of REM)

223. DODGEM

Author: Mac Oglesby

Source: Creative Computing Mar–Apr 77 (3:2) "DODGEM" pp. 117–119 (117–119)

DODGEM is a game played on a square board. You get to choose the size of the board. You can play against either the computer or another player. On the board are two sets of pieces, numbers, and letters. The letters belong to one player and the numbers to the other. The object of the game is to move your set of pieces across the board. The pieces can move horizontally or vertically at the rate of one move per turn. There are no diagonal moves, no jumps, and no captures; you must move across the board while avoiding your opponent's pieces. You forfeit the game if your move leaves your opponent with no legal move. Includes a sample run.

Lines: 344
Version: Dartmouth BASIC
Hardware: none
Software: none
Non-ANSI: LINPUT, SEG$(), multiple-assignment, POS(), CHANGE, strings, '(used in place of REM)

891. EXAGON

Author: Mac Oglesby

Source: People's Computers May–Jun 77 (5:6) "EXAGON" pp. 48–50 (49–50)

EXAGON is a game for two players. The computer can take the part of one of the players. The game is played on a hexagonal board. No rules are provided; you figure out the rules for yourself. Includes a sample run.

Lines: 248
Version: Dartmouth BASIC
Hardware: none
Software: none
Non-ANSI: strings, CHANGE, LINPUT, '(used in place of REM)

125. DROIDS

Author: Mac Oglesby

Source: Calculators/Computers Magazine Apr 78 (2:4) "DROIDS" pp. 5–10 (9–10)

DROIDS is a game played on a grid. There are two "droids" on the grid. Each droid can move one square at a time. The computer and you each "own" a droid, but each of you can control the other's droid if you so desire. The computer and you take turns moving a droid. The object of the game is to claim the most squares by moving your droid across as many squares as you can. You cannot move across a square which has already been occupied. The game continues until neither droid can move. The player with the most squares at that point wins. Includes sample runs.

Lines: 358
Version: Dartmouth BASIC
Hardware: none
Software: none
Non-ANSI: strings, LINPUT, MAT operations, SEG$( ), CHANGE, multiple-assignment, '(used in place of REM)

293. HEX

Author: James Murphy

Source: Creative Computing Sep–Oct 78 (4:5) "HEX" pp. 140–143 (141–143)

HEX is a game played on a board composed of hexagons. You and the computer alternate placing markers on the board. The object of the game is to complete a connected line of cells from one side of the board to the other. At the same time, you must stop the computer from completing its line. Includes a sample run.

Lines: 220
Version: DEC BASIC-Plus
Hardware: none
Software: none
Non-ANSI: not translatable

373. French Military Game

Author: Gerald H. Herd

Source: Creative Computing Sep 79 (5:9) "The French Military Game" pp. 116–119 (117–118)

The French Military Game (FMG) is played on a board with 11 spots. In this version of the game, you play White, who starts out with men placed on three spots at the bottom of the board. The computer plays Black, who starts out with only one man placed in the center of the board. The players are "slid" around the board until either you "pin" the computer's man (you win), or the computer's man reaches the bottom of the board (the computer wins). The program uses stored data to allow the computer to learn to play better as it gains experience. Includes a sample run.

Lines: 140
Version: not given
Hardware: sequential file device
Software: none
Non-ANSI: extended IF, STORE, LOAD

CARD GAMES

197. CONCENTRATION

Author: James Vanderbeek

Source: Creative Computing Jan–Feb 76 (2:1)
            "CONCENTRATION" p. 72 (72)

This program simulates the card game, Concentration. The computer deals out 52 cards. You pick two cards at a time. If the values of the cards match, the cards are removed and your score is increased. If not, the cards are placed back with the other concealed cards. The game thus becomes a matter of remembering where specific cards are placed. Includes a sample run.

Lines: 73
Version: not given
Hardware: none
Software: none
Non-ANSI: strings, '(used in place of REM), SEG$()

460. BLUFF: Try to Outbluff the Computer

Author: Phil Feldman and Tom Rugg

Source: Interface Age Sep 76 (1:10)
            "Games & Things" pp. 61–66 (65–66)

BLUFF is based on a card game of the same name. You and the computer are each dealt five cards per round from an 11-card deck. The remaining cards are the players' secret cards. You try to guess what the computer's secret card is, while at the same time you bluff it into incorrectly guessing yours. Includes sample runs.

Lines: 105
Version: MITS 8K BASIC
Hardware: none
Software: none
Non-ANSI: extended IF

213. TWO-TO-TEN

Author: not given

Source: Creative Computing Nov–Dec 76 (2:6)
            "Two-to-Ten" p. 88 (88)

TWO-TO-TEN is a game of chance played with a deck of cards having only the cards 2 to 10. The game is similar to blackjack. The object is to draw cards and try to come as close as possible to a goal number without going over it. The catch to the game is that you are not given the exact value of the goal number, but just a clue that is only within 15% of the goal. Includes a sample run.

Lines: 58
Version: not given
Hardware: none
Software: none
Non-ANSI: extended IF, LEFT(), strings

232. EUCHRE

Author: Victor Raybaud

Source: Creative Computing May–Jun 77 (3:3)
            "EUCHRE" pp. 120–124 (120–122)

This is the game of Euchre played against the computer. Euchre is a card game that uses a deck containing just 24 cards. Each person is dealt 12 cards in the following manner: four cards face down, four cards face up, and four cards in the person's hand. The game play is vaguely similar to bridge, with the players making bids and trying to collect tricks. The object of the game is to collect 10 points, with the number of points you get being dependent on how many tricks you collect. The program is written in two parts: the first part prints out the instructions, and the second part is the actual game. The first program CHAIN's to the second, but if you have enough RAM you can eliminate the CHAIN statement and just place both programs in memory at the same time. Includes a sample run.

Lines: 101, 574
Version: Univac 1106 BASIC
Hardware: none
Software: none
Non-ANSI: strings, CHAIN, MAT ZER(),
            multiple-assignment, INP( ), CAT$( ),
            TRM$( ), MOD( ), extended IF

916. CONCENTRATION

Author: Milan Chepko

Source: *People's Computers* Jul–Aug 78 (7:1)
"CONCENTRATION" pp. 54–55 (55)

Here is a computer version of another old standby, the card game of Concentration. In its original form, the game is played with a deck of 52 cards which are shuffled and dealt face down on a table. In turn, each player turns over two cards. If the cards match, he may take the cards and play again. If the cards do not match, they are turned face down again and the next player selects two cards. At the end of the game, the player with the most cards wins. As you can see, the player who can remember where the "non-matching" cards are has a decided advantage. This program simulates the same play (the computer does not participate in the game). At the end of the game, the computer displays the point totals for each player. Includes a flowchart and a list of program variables.

Lines: 39
Version: TRS-80 BASIC
Hardware: none
Software: none
Non-ANSI: CLS, extended IF

CHASE GAMES

200. CHASE: Avoid Killer Robots

Author: unknown; modified by Bill Cotter

Source: *Creative Computing* Jan–Feb 76 (2:1)
"CHASE" pp. 75–76 (76)

CHASE puts you in a field of high-voltage fences and posts. On the field are five killer robots, all of them out to get you. If any one of them touches you, you die. Your only hope is to make the robots run into the electrified posts. Includes a sample run.

Lines: 113
Version: Honeywell 600/6000 BASIC
Hardware: none
Software: none
Non-ANSI: ASC(), strings, CHANGE

878. SINNERS

Author: Mac Oglesby

Source: *People's Computer Company* Jul 76 (5:1)
"SINNERS" pp. 20–21 (21)

In this game, three of Satan's fiends (moved by the computer) play against a group of condemned sinners (moved by you). If the sinners win, the surviving sinners are set free. Otherwise . . . into the Black Pit! The game is played on a 5-by-5 square board. The players move around one square at a time. The sinners win if the three fiends are all in a line. The sinners lose if the fiends cannot capture a sinner at their turn. Includes a sample run.

Lines: 250
Version: Dartmouth BASIC
Hardware: none
Software: none
Non-ANSI: strings, LINPUT, CHANGE, '(used in place of REM)

569. CHASE

Author: Herman DeMonstoy

Source: *Kilobaud* Feb 77 (2)
"CHASE!" pp. 48–49 (49)

This is the game of CHASE. In the game of CHASE there are a high-voltage fence, 15 high-voltage posts, and five robots all out to get you. The object of the game is to elude the robots, and to destroy them by getting them to run into each other or into one of the posts. The program prints out a map on your terminal so that you know where you are at any given time. Includes a sample run.

Lines: 98
Version: SWTP 4K BASIC
Hardware: none
Software: none
Non-ANSI: extended IF

230. TWONKY

Author: Mark Capella

Source: *Creative Computing* May –Jun 77 (3:3)
"TWONKY" pp. 110–112 (110–111)

This game is played on a 15-by-15 playing field in which you are randomly located. The object of the game is to move to the objective square. The task is made difficult by the existence of a variety of obstacles: Relocation Squares, which when moved upon, cause you to be randomly transported to another position in the field; Walls, which you can't move onto; Super-Maze-Squares that generate a completely new maze; and The Twonky, a creature that wants to absorb you. The Twonky constantly moves toward you. He is impervious to all traps, even Walls. The game is also made more difficult by the fact that no board is printed out—you play blind. Includes a sample run.

Lines: 265
Version: not given
Hardware: none
Software: none
Non-ANSI: MAT ZER( ), non-standard strings

639. FOX AND HOUNDS

Author: Jack Inman

Source: *Kilobaud* Sep 78 (21)
"Tally Ho!" pp. 62–64 (62–64)

FOX AND HOUNDS is a variation of checkers played on a standard checkerboard. The game is played with only five pieces on the board. There are one fox and four hounds; the computer moves the fox, and you move the hounds. The object of the game is for the fox to reach the safety of "line one." If the hounds trap the fox in a location from which it cannot escape, the hounds win. Includes a sample run.

Lines: 167
Version: SWTPC 8K ver. 2.0 BASIC
Hardware: none
Software: none
Non-ANSI: strings, extended IF

146. SINNERS for the PET

Author: Mac Oglesby

Source: *Calculators/Computers Magazine*
Nov–Dec 78 (2:7) "SINNERS" pp. 36–38 (37–38)

SINNERS is a board game. Three of Satan's fiends (moved by the computer) move against a group of condemned sinners (controlled by you). The sinners and fiends move around the board with the fiends trying to capture the sinners. The sinners win if all the fiends are in a line vertically or horizontally. The sinners lose if the fiends, at their turn, cannot capture a sinner. Includes a sample run.

Lines: 166
Version: PET BASIC
Hardware: PET
Software: none
Non-ANSI: not translatable

1027. Killer Robots

Author: William Lappen

Source: *Personal Computing* Jun 79 (3:6)
"ROBOTS" pp. 60–66 (62–64)

Updates: modifications for TRS-80 Level II BASIC
Personal Computing Sep 79 (3:9)
"Level II ROBOTS" p. 7 (7)

Not all robots are loveable R2-D2 types. These robots are out to get you. You are in a large field. The robots are programmed to move toward you with every turn. To escape, you must position yourself so that all of the evil robots are destroyed by the electronic force beams which are situated around the field. Includes a sample run.

Lines: 216
Version: Radio Shack Level I BASIC
Hardware: TRS-80
Software: none
Non-ANSI: not translatable

368. HVOLT

Author: Greg Rappa

Source: *Creative Computing* Aug 79 (5:8)
"HVOLT" pp. 118–119 (118–119)

HVOLT is played on a 10-by-20 board. On the board are interceptors, high voltage posts, and offensive attackers. You move across the board one square at a time. The interceptors move in a pattern identical to yours. You try to cause all the interceptors to collide with the high voltage posts, while at the same time trying to keep out of reach of the attackers. Includes a sample run.

Lines: 180
Version: HP 2000F BASIC
Hardware: none
Software: none
Non-ANSI: HP strings, multiple-assignment, MAT operations, LIN(), extended IF, RESTORE [line number], PRINT USING, IMAGE

CHESS

655. Chess Opening Moves Instructor

Author: Tom Orr

Source: *Kilobaud* Dec 78 (24)
"Attention, Chess Buffs!" pp. 74–76 (75)

One of the keys to winning at chess is a good opening strategy. This program can be your 24-hour-a-day chess instructor to help you improve your openings. You supply the opening strategies that you desire. The program then drills you in these strategies, telling you when you make right or wrong moves. You can set up the games so that you are either white or black. With this program you should get your openings down pat in no time. Includes a sample run.

Lines: 68
Version: TRS-80 Level I BASIC
Hardware: none
Software: none
Non-ANSI: CLS

757. Chess

Author: Lou Haehn

Source: Kilobaud Microcomputing Dec 79 (36)
"Chess I for the Apple II" pp. 46–52 (47–51)

Chess is one of those games that have received a great deal of attention from programmers. At first it would seem that programming a computer to play a good game of chess should be easy—but it certainly isn't. It turns out that chess programs require so much computing that they're usually written in assembly language. However, this chess playing program is written entirely in BASIC. It has both castling and en passant. You can play either black or white, using standard algebraic notation. Includes a list of program variables.

Lines: 215
Version: Apple Integer BASIC
Hardware: Apple II
Software: none
Non-ANSI: not translatable

1068. Chess

Author: Michael J. McCann

Source: Personal Computing Dec 79 (3:12)
"BASIC Chess" pp. 48–52 (51–52)

Updates: commentary
Personal Computing May 80 (4:5)
"BASIC Chess please!" p. 81

You don't have to resort to assembly language to program a game of chess. This program (completely in BASIC) plays the game, yet it is small enough to fit into an 8K PET. It's doubtful if this program will ever make it up to grandmaster status, but it does play chess. It has a few limitations (no castling or en passant), but other than this, it plays a normal game. Patches are provided to change the program over to TRS-80 Level II BASIC. Includes a flowchart, list of program variables, and a sample run.

Lines: 219 (plus patch)
Version: PET 8K BASIC
Hardware: none
Software: none
Non-ANSI: OPEN, INPUT #, extended IF, strings,
two-letter variables, PEEK(), POKE, ASC(),
VAL(), TI(), GET, ON . . . GOSUB

CRIBBAGE

340. Cribbage

Author: Sheppard Yarrow

Source: Creative Computing May 79 (5:5)
"Cribbage" pp. 104–112 (106–112)

Updates: correction
Creative Computing Aug 79 (5:8)
"Cribbage Correction" p. 12 (12)

commentary
Creative Computing Oct 79 (5:10)
"Better Late Than Never?" p. 10

corrections
Creative Computing Oct 79 (5:10)
"CRIBBAGE Debugged" p. 16 (16)

modification
Creative Computing Nov 79 (5:11)
untitled p. 10 (10)

commentary
Creative Computing Feb 80 (6:2)
"CRIBBAGE for my PET?" p. 12

If you're an avid cribbage fan then you know the frustration of wanting to play and not being able to find an opponent. You need never lack an adversary again. CRIBBAGE plays the game of cribbage. The computer will shuffle, deal, generate cards, keep track of the running sum, and record all the points earned during play. Includes a sample run.

Lines: 648
Version: IBM BASIC
Hardware: none
Software: none
Non-ANSI: strings, PRINT USING, : (used to specify
format for PRINT USING), MIN(), MAX(),
STR(), multiple-assignment, MAT READ

DICE GAMES

164. NOTONE

Author: Robert Puopolo

Source: Creative Computing Nov–Dec 74 (1:1)
"NOTONE—A Challenge!" p. 26

Creative Computing Mar–Apr 75 (1:3)
"Not One" p. 8 (8)

NOTONE is a computerized dice game. You and the computer take turns rolling "dice." At your turn you may roll the dice as many times as you want. But watch out! If you get the same number that you rolled on your first roll, you lose all points for that turn. The player with the most points at the end of ten rounds wins. Includes a sample run.

Lines: 59
Version: not given
Hardware: none
Software: none
Non-ANSI: strings, extended IF

203. BOBSTONES

Author: Dohn Addleman

Source: Creative Computing Mar–Apr 76 (2:2)
            "BOBSTONES" pp. 72–73 (72–73)

Bobstones is a game described in the book, Watership Down. BOBSTONES lets you play the game against the computer. The game is based on each of two players rolling dice and making predictions about the outcome. As you roll, you can try to guess whether the sum of the dice will be odd or even, what the sum will be, and what the number will be on each of the two dice. Since the latter predictions are harder to make, they are awarded more points. The winner is the first player to score 11 points. Includes a sample run.

Lines: 205
Version: not given
Hardware: none
Software: none
Non-ANSI: strings

217. STRIKE 9

Author: Bruce Grembowski

Source: Creative Computing Jan–Feb 77 (3:1)
            "STRIKE 9" p. 88 (88)

This is a simple game based on the numbers 1 to 9, and a pair of computer "dice." First, the computer rolls a random number for your dice. Then you must take that number from the total of your board numbers remaining on the board. The object of the game is to remove all the numbers from the board. With each roll of the dice you must remove the total number of that roll from the board or you lose. Includes a sample run.

Lines: 115
Version: not given
Hardware: none
Software: none
Non-ANSI: strings

345. GREED

Author: Ronald Ragsdale

Source: Creative Computing Jun 79 (5:6)
            "GREED: A Game Playing Program With Adjustable Skill Level" pp. 92–93 (93)

How greedy are you? Your greed may be your undoing in this simulated dice game. You and the computer take turns rolling the "dice." Each of you gets the total that you roll added to your respective scores. You can roll as many times as you want with each turn. The rub is, if you roll your first-rolled number a second time, you lose everything for that turn. The computer's play can be adjusted to make it a good player or a poor one.

Lines: 91
Version: DEC system-10 BASIC
Hardware: none
Software: none
Non-ANSI: strings, multiple-assignment

DOTS

199. Connect-the-Dots Game

Author: Chuck Lund

Source: Creative Computing Jan–Feb 76 (2:1)
            "CONDOT" pp. 75, 77 (77)

CONDOT is a program that lets you play a game of Connect-the-Dots. The game is played on a 4-by-4 grid of dots. You connect two of the dots with each turn. The computer does likewise. When you complete a square, you get to claim the square and, in addition, take another turn. The player who has the most claimed squares at the end of the game wins. Includes a sample run.

Lines: 141
Version: not given
Hardware: none
Software: none
Non-ANSI: none

959. DOTS for the Apple Computer

Author: Fred Helliwell

Source: Personal Computing Jun 78 (2:6)
            "Dot by Dot" pp. 69–74 (72–74)

Remember the game of Dots? This is a computer version of the game. DOTS is played on a grid of "dots." You take turns with the computer. With each turn you draw a line between two of the dots. When you have completely enclosed a square, you get to claim that square and draw another line. The player who has the most squares at the end of the game wins. This version is designed to use the capabilities of an Apple computer. The author claims that the computer can never be beaten unless a special "patch" is added to reduce the computer's playing ability. Includes a sample run and a list of program variables.

Lines: 245
Version: Apple BASIC
Hardware: Apple
Software: none
Non-ANSI: not translatable

ESTIMATING GAMES

877. POUNCE: Try to Catch the Mouse

Author: Mac Oglesby

Source: People's Computer Company May 76 (4:6)
"POUNCE" p. 17 (17)

This is the game of POUNCE. You play the part of a cat trying to pounce on a mouse. You must estimate correctly how far you have to pounce in order to catch the mouse. A listing of the program is the only thing provided.

Lines: 175
Version: Dartmouth BASIC
Hardware: none
Software: none
Non-ANSI: strings, SEG$(), LINPUT, CALL, CHANGE, '(used in place of REM)

904. POUNCE

Author: Mac Oglesby

Source: People's Computers Jan–Feb 78 (6:4)
"POUNCE" pp. 20–22 (22)

POUNCE offers you the opportunity to test your ability to estimate distances. You are the cat. You are trying to pounce on a mouse. When the computer tells you to pounce, you give the distance to the mouse. If you miss the mouse, it will run away. If the mouse runs into its hole, you lose. The LIBRARY and CALL statements are not absolutely necessary. Includes a sample run.

Lines: 175
Version: Dartmouth BASIC
Hardware: none
Software: none
Non-ANSI: LIBRARY, CALL, strings, LINPUT, CHANGE, SEG$(), '(used in place of REM)

265. Paper Game

Author: Philip Tubb

Source: Creative Computing Mar–Apr 78 (4:2)
"The Computer Game 'PAPER' " p. 77 (77)

Any number of people may play Paper. This game must surely be one of the shortest game programs in existence. It is reproduced below in its entirety:

```
10 PRINT
20 GOTO 10
30 END
```

Play begins with the first person. Each player in turn types RUN. He then estimates when a full page (11 inches) of paper has gone by. He types Control/C or Break or whatever to stop the printout. Points are scored based on how close he comes to exactly one page of paper. The game continues until a player gets exactly 217 points, or until a player has 6.237 times as many points as any other player. (Look, I didn't write the rules.)

Lines: 3
Version: not given
Hardware: Gee, an IBM 370 at least . . .
Software: none
Non-ANSI: none

128. Random Rectangle Game for the TRS-80

Author: Don Inman

Source: Calculators/Computers Magazine May 78 (2:5)
"TRS-80: Games & Abstract Art" pp. 5–10 (5–7)

The object of this game is to guess the center of a randomly drawn rectangle. The rectangle is displayed on the screen of a TRS-80. You are asked to input the coordinates of the center point. The program causes the point you select to blink. When you finally guess the center point, the program tells you how many guesses it took you. The program can probably be modified to work on other systems which have a video-screen display.

Lines: 96
Version: TRS-80 Level I BASIC
Hardware: TRS-80
Software: none
Non-ANSI: not translatable

693. Darts for the Sphere Microcomputer

Author: Julie Martin

Source: *Kilobaud Microcomputing* May 79 (29)
"A Game of Darts" p. 78 (78)

This is a simulated game of darts. It is designed to run on a Sphere, but it probably could be adapted to any computer with a memory-mapped video screen. The computer displays a target on the screen. You try to hit the target by guessing the target's position.

Lines: 37
Version: Tiny BASIC Extended ver. 1.3
Hardware: Sphere microcomputer
Software: none
Non-ANSI: CLEAR, POKE, extended IF

724. NERVES

Author: Mark J. Borgerson

Source: *Kilobaud Microcomputing* Aug 79 (32)
"NERVES" pp. 100–101 (100)

The game of NERVES is basically a test of your ability to judge short (one to eight seconds) time intervals. The computer sets a time limit. You press the return key when you think that the prescribed amount of time has elapsed. The closer you come to the actual time limit, the more points you get—but if you wait *too* long you get nothing.

Lines: 50
Version: SWTP 8K BASIC
Hardware: 6800-based microcomputer
Software: none
Non-ANSI: POKE, PEEK(), USER(), strings, extended IF

GAMBLING

458. Blackjack

Author: Richard Edelman

Source: *Interface Age* Aug 76 (1:9)
"Black Jack" pp. 75–76 (75–76)

This blackjack program enables you to play head-to-head against the computer. The program plays blackjack using the same rules as those used in gambling casinos on the Las Vegas strip. It has provisions for doubling down and splitting.

Lines: 238
Version: not given
Hardware: none
Software: none
Non-ANSI: strings

462. BLACKJACK

Author: Ed Keith

Source: *Interface Age* Nov 76 (1:12)
"Expanded BLACKJACK in BASIC"
pp. 118–124 (122–124)

Blackjack is a card game in which it is possible to use skill; the game is not merely dumb luck as in some gambling games. Your knowledge of the game can determine whether the odds will be in your favor or not. This is a rather complete computer version of the game. It allows you to both split pairs and double down. You have the option of using from one to four "card decks." With each round, you bet, and stand, draw, double down, or split. Includes a sample run and a list of program variables.

Lines: 392 (plus patch)
Version: not given
Hardware: none
Software: none
Non-ANSI: none

571. HORSE RACE

Author: Herman DeMonstoy

Source: *Kilobaud* Feb 77 (2)
"At the Races" pp. 88–89 (88)

This is a horse race game. The program permits up to 10 players to bet. There are up to 10 races per game. With each race, the computer asks each player to bet some amount on one of the horses. The computer then prints out the race and pays off the players. The object of the game is to win as much as possible. The game ends when the tenth race is reached or when there is just one player remaining with money. Includes a sample run.

Lines: 155
Version: SWTP 4K BASIC
Hardware: none
Software: none
Non-ANSI: extended IF

575. KENO

Author: Gordon Flemming

Source: *Kilobaud* Mar 77 (3)
"How to Win $25,000 of Your Own Money"
pp. 84–86 (85–86)

This game is a true simulation of the game of Keno. Keno is a betting game played with Keno cards that look something like Bingo cards. The player selects from 1 to 15 numbers to play. Twenty numbers are then drawn at random from the range of 1 to 80. The payoff varies with how many numbers the player has guessed correctly. The appeal of the game lies in the fact that it is possible for a person to win as much as $25,000 with a $1 bet. Includes a sample run.

```
     Lines:  187
   Version:  not given
  Hardware:  none
  Software:  none
  Non-ANSI:  strings, extended IF
```

105. CRAPS

Author: LeRoy Finkel

Source: *Calculators/Computers Magazine* May 77 (1:1)
"BASIC Test Units" pp. 76–81 (81)

Updates: correction
Calculators/Computers Magazine Oct 77 (1:2)
untitled p. 91 (91)

This is a very simple version of the dice game craps. The computer "rolls" dice for you. On your first roll, if you get a 2, 7, or 11 you win. Otherwise the number you have rolled is your "point." You continue to roll until you either get your point (and you win), or you roll a 7 (and you lose). This is a simple version of the game and does not keep track of bets. Includes a flowchart and sample run.

```
     Lines:  21
   Version:  not given
  Hardware:  none
  Software:  none
  Non-ANSI:  none
```

247. CRAPS

Author: Thomas Dwyer

Source: *Creative Computing* Nov–Dec 77 (3:6)
"The 8-Hour Wonder" pp. 78–85 (84)

This is a simulated game of craps. You get to choose how much money you start with, and how much you want to bet each round. The computer rolls random "dice" for you. If you roll a 2, 3, or 12, you lose. If you roll an 11, you win. If you roll a 7, you win. If you roll any other number, that is your "point." You must then continue to roll until either your point or 7 comes up. If you get your point, you win. If you get a 7, you lose. The program is included in an article on beginning BASIC. Includes a flowchart and sample run.

```
     Lines:  37
   Version:  not given
  Hardware:  none
  Software:  none
  Non-ANSI:  none
```

487. INJUN POKER

Author: Kenneth Kolbly

Source: *Interface Age* Dec 77 (2:13)
"INJUN POKER" pp. 159–162 (162)

This is a version of the game of poker. You play against the computer. In INJUN POKER you each know your opponent's cards, but not your own. You bet that your own card is bigger than your opponent's card. Includes a flowchart and sample run.

```
     Lines:  120
   Version:  IMSAI Rev. 4.0 12K Extended BASIC
  Hardware:  none
  Software:  none
  Non-ANSI:  strings, extended IF
```

1127. Slot Machine for PTC BASICS

Author: Tom Digate

Source: *ROM* Dec 77 (1:6)
"The Best Slot Machine Game Ever"
pp. 34–35 (34–35)

There's no need to blow your wad in Vegas or Atlantic City—not when you can have your own private slot machine! This program allows you to simulate the action of a slot machine on your home computer. It even has jackpots. There is no commentary; only the program listing is provided. For most BASICs the SET, CALL, and ARG statements can be eliminated.

```
     Lines:  200
   Version:  PTC BASIC5
  Hardware:  video display
  Software:  none
  Non-ANSI:  CALL(), ARG(), * (used in place of REM),
             CLEAR, extended IF, SET
```

946. Test of Brock's System for Winning at Craps

Author: Timothy Purinton

Source: *Personal Computing* Apr 78 (2:4)
"Rolling the Bones" pp. 76–78 (77)

Craps is a common form of gambling which uses dice to control the play. From time to time, a variety of new "systems" appear for "beating the house." Can a person really use one of these systems to make money? This program tests out one such system by pitting it against a simulated game of craps. The output is the system's results. Includes a sample run.

Lines: 76
Version: not given
Hardware: none
Software: none
Non-ANSI: two-letter variables, extended IF

911. BLACKJACK for Denver Tiny BASIC

Author: Milan Chepko

Source: *People's Computers* May–Jun 78 (6:6)
"Tiny BLACKJACK" pp. 45–47 (47)

Updates: improvement
People's Computers Sep–Oct 78 (7:2)
untitled p. 5 (5)

Blackjack is a well-known form of card gambling. This is a computerized version designed to run on systems that use Tiny BASIC, a BASIC specially designed for systems with very little memory. This version of BLACKJACK includes provisions for splitting pairs, doubling down, and betting, and it even has a subroutine that lets the player see how many cards of each value remain in the shoe ("casing the deck"). Includes a flowchart and a list of program variables.

Lines: 138
Version: Denver Tiny BASIC
Hardware: none
Software: none
Non-ANSI: CLRS, PR, extended IF, IN

961. Roulette for the PET Computer

Author: David Conley

Source: *Personal Computing* Jul 78 (2:7)
"Roulette on your PET with Bells and Whistles"
pp. 22–24 (24)

This is a game of continuous roulette for your PET computer. In this game, you specify a starting bankroll and a number from 1 to 38. The computer then does a continuous simulation of a set of spins of a roulette wheel. The computer continues spinning the "wheel" until you run out of money. At the end of the game, the computer lists how long it took, the maximum amount of money you had, and the total number of spins. The program uses screen characters and functions specific to the PET, but it can be modified for use on other systems. Includes a sample run.

Lines: 44
Version: PET BASIC
Hardware: none
Software: none
Non-ANSI: strings, TI(), CLR, GET, extended IF

26. JACPOT: A Slot Machine Simulation

Author: Edwin Hastings

Source: *Byte* Aug 78 (3:8)
"JACPOT" pp. 166–167 (166)

Many states are now working to legalize gambling, but why wait for the bureaucratic system, when you can start a casino on your own computer? JACPOT is a simulation of a slot machine. The traditional cherries, bells, and lemons have been replaced by 8080's, 6800's, and Z-80's. You can bet as much as you want (up to the amount of money you have). Payoffs run from 2:1 to 256:1 with special surprise payoffs possible. Includes a list of program variables and a sample run.

Lines: 167
Version: DEC MU BASIC
Hardware: none
Software: none
Non-ANSI: SYS(), strings, extended IF

502. Roulette for the Compucolor Microcomputer

Author: W. Hoffer

Source: *Interface Age* Aug 78 (3:8)
"European Roulette in Color" pp. 56–60 (57–60)

Fortunes have been made and lost at the roulette tables of the world. But with this game, after the initial investment in hardware, you can play roulette without fear of losing your fortune. The game is written to take advantage of the color graphics capabilities of the Compucolor microcomputer. The game permits a variety of bets including number bets, BLACK, RED, ODD, EVEN, and others. Payoffs vary as in the real game. The object of the game is to collect as much money as possible.

Lines: 585
Version: Compucolor BASIC
Hardware: Compucolor
Software: none
Non-ANSI: not translatable

920. Horse Race for the PET

Author: Andy Stadler

Source: *People's Computers* Sep–Oct 78 (7:2)
"HORSES" pp. 46–47 (47)

This is an action horse race simulation for Commodore's PET computer. The program uses PET's graphics facilities to simulate the race. From 1 to 9 players can bet on any of 10 horses. Whenever a horse wins, its odds go down by 1; if a horse loses, its odds increase by 1.

Lines: 117
Version: PET BASIC
Hardware: PET
Software: none
Non-ANSI: not translatable

992. Craps

Author: Marolyn Pinney

Source: *Personal Computing* Feb 79 (3:2)
"Me and My TRS-80" pp. 46–51 (47–48)

Roll dem bones! This is a simulation of the dice game of craps. You and the computer take turns. If you roll a 7 or 11 on the first roll, you win. If you roll a 2, 3, or 12, you lose. If you roll anything else, you must continue to roll until you either roll the same number again (and win) or roll a 7 (in which case you lose). The program has facilities for betting. Includes a sample run.

Lines: 106
Version: TRS-80 Level I BASIC
Hardware: none
Software: none
Non-ANSI: P., IN.

1082. TRS-80 One-Armed Bandit

Source: *Recreational Computing* Mar–Apr 79 (7:5)
"SLOT" p. 31 (31)

This program simulates a slot machine on a TRS-80. There are no coins to plink and no lights to light, but it sure is a lot cheaper than the real-life one-armed bandits.

Lines: 96
Version: TRS-80 Level II BASIC
Hardware: TRS-80
Software: none
Non-ANSI: not translatable

730. Blackjack Tutor

Author: Jerry D. Howard

Source: *Kilobaud Microcomputing* Sep 79 (33)
"Beat the Computer" pp. 108–110 (109–110)

There are lots of computerized blackjack games, but here's one that shows you how to *win*. Blackjack is not purely a game of chance; there is very definitely a strategy that you can use. Using this strategy immensely improves your chances of winning—not just with computer blackjack games, but also with the real Las Vegas tables! This program tutors you in the correct blackjack playing strategy. After a brief introductory "lecture", the program gives a simulated session of blackjack to let you practice what you have learned. As you practice, the program coaches you until you have the technique down pat. Includes a sample run.

Lines: 171
Version: SWTP 8K BASIC
Hardware: none
Software: none
Non-ANSI: strings, extended IF

GAME REFEREES

839. CHOMP Referee

Author: not given

Source: *People's Computer Company* Feb 73 (1:3)
"CHOMP" p. 9 (9)

Updates: program listing reprint
People's Computer Company Nov 74 (3:2)
"Listings" p. 25 (25)

reprint
People's Computer Company Sep 75 (4:2)
"CHOMP for BASIC" p. 10 (10)

Not all computer games are played against the computer. In this game of CHOMP, the computer just acts as the game "referee." The board in this game is a big "cookie."

You specify the size of the cookie. In the upper left-hand corner of the cookie is a poison square. You alternate with another person in taking "bites" out of the cookie. The person who is forced to bite the poison square loses. It's sort of a two-dimensional NIM. Includes a sample run.

Lines: 97
Version: HP 2000 BASIC
Hardware: none
Software: none
Non-ANSI: none

875. SQUARE: Try to Form a Square Before Your Opponent

Author: Mac Oglesby

Source: People's Computer Company Mar–Apr 76 (4:5)
"SQUARE" pp. 14–15 (14)

SQUARE is a game for two players (the computer acts only as a referee). The game is played on a grid of dots. The object of the game is to select four points which form a square. At the same time, you must block your opponent from doing the same. It's sort of a square tic-tac-toe game. Includes a sample run.

Lines: 189
Version: Dartmouth BASIC
Hardware: none
Software: none
Non-ANSI: strings, LINPUT, CHANGE, SEG$(),
STR$(),VAL(), ' (used in place of REM)

259. YAHTZEE Scorekeeper

Author: Steve Elias

Source: Creative Computing Jan–Feb 78 (4:1)
"YAHTZEE" pp. 132–137 (134)

The game of Yahtzee can be played by one to four people. The computer controls the game, but does not participate as a player. Yahtzee is played with a set of "dice" and a set of "scorecards." In this version of Yahtzee, the computer replaces the dice and the scorecards. An in-depth discussion of the probabilities and computations involved in the game is provided. Includes a sample run.

Lines: 204
Version: PDP-8 Edusystem 50 BASIC
Hardware: none
Software: none
Non-ANSI: ' (used in place of REM), RANDOM, strings,
SLEEP

907. FROG RACE

Author: B. Erickson

Source: People's Computers Mar–Apr 78 (6:5)
"FROG RACE" p. 59 (59)

This is a simulation of a frog-jumping contest. One to eight players can play. Each player has a frog in the "ring." All the frogs start out at the center of the ring. The player whose frog jumps out of the ring first wins. The program allows you to bet on your frog.

Lines: 82
Version: SWTPC 8K BASIC ver. 2.0
Hardware: none
Software: none
Non-ANSI: LINE, DIGITS, strings, extended IF

133. 100: An Addition Game for Two People

Author: Paul Sowders

Source: Calculators/Computers Magazine May 78 (2:5)
"Student Programs" pp. 37–41 (40–41)

100 is an addition game for two people. The players alternately choose a number from 1 to 10. With each turn, a player is asked for a number. The numbers are continuously added together. As the player gives the number, he must also give the new total. The person who gives the number that makes the total 100 wins. This game is a good one to help students learn addition. Includes a sample run.

Lines: 58
Version: DEC BASIC-Plus
Hardware: none
Software: none
Non-ANSI: strings, extended IF, LEFT()

674. CHESS PAWN Refereee

Author: Edward Ewald, Jr.

Source: Kilobaud Microcomputing Mar 79 (27)
"CHESS PAWN" pp. 76–78 (77–78)

CHESS PAWN is a game for two people based on the standard moves of chess pawns. The game play is similar to chess except that just pawns are on the board. The object is for each player to try to move all of his or her pieces across the board. The game ends when one player cannot move. At that time, the player with the most captured pieces wins. The computer program just acts as a referee; it does not participate in the play. Includes a sample run.

Lines: 85
Version: Benton Harbor extended BASIC
Hardware: none
Software: none
Non-ANSI: strings, extended IF, LINE INPUT

736. ARENA Game Referee

Author: Richard Price

Source: Kilobaud Microcomputing Oct 79 (34)
"ARENA" pp. 110–114 (111–114)

ARENA acts as a game referee for people playing the game of Arena. Arena is a game in which two to five players fight it out in a gladiator tournament to the death. The players move around on a playing field. As the players battle, the computer keeps track of how much power each player has left. The last person alive is the winner. Includes a flowchart, sample output, and list of program variables.

Lines: 432
Version: Southwest 8K BASIC
Hardware: memory-mapped video display
Software: none
Non-ANSI: strings, LINE, extended IF, POKE, STR$(), ON . . . GOSUB

GAME SUBROUTINES

465. CHECKERS Display

Author: Marvin Mallon

Source: Interface Age Mar 77 (2:4)
"Graphics—The Easy Way" pp. 132–136 (136)

The code listed in this article is the user interface portion of a checkers playing program. It uses a Poly Morphic Systems Video Terminal Interface to display the checker board on a display screen. The program does not have the routines needed to have the computer determine what moves to make. Includes sample output.

Lines: 154
Version: MITS 8K BASIC
Hardware: Poly Morphic Systems Video Display Interface, video display
Software: none
Non-ANSI: CLEAR, PEEK(), POKE, two-letter variables, INP(), extended IF

951. Card Shuffle Routine

Author: Andrew Russakoff

Source: Personal Computing May 78 (2:5)
"Doing the 52 Card Shuffle" p. 70 (70)

Updates: modification
Personal Computing Sep 78 (2:9)
"Crooked Shuffle" p. 8 (8)

Many computer games require a computer simulation of a card shuffle. This is a quick and easy card shuffle routine which can be inserted into your program. The output is an array with 52 numbers in random order.

Lines: 11
Version: not given
Hardware: none
Software: none
Non-ANSI: none

768. Star Battle Sound Effects for the Apple II

Author: Andrew H. Eliason

Source: Micro Aug–Sep 78 (6)
"Apple II Starwars Theme" p. 13 (13)

This program creates "space battle" sounds on an Apple II.

Lines: 8
Version: Apple BASIC
Hardware: Apple II
Software: 6502 assembly language routine
Non-ANSI: POKE, CALL

772. Star Battle Sound Effects for the Apple II

Author: William Shryock, Jr.

Source: Micro Oct–Nov 78 (7)
"Improved Star Battle Sound Effects" p. 12 (12)

This program produces "star battle" sound effects on an Apple II.

Lines: 8
Version: Apple BASIC
Hardware: Apple II
Software: none
Non-ANSI: not translatable

657. Dice Rolling Routine

Author: Rod Hallen

Source: *Kilobaud Microcomputing* Jan 79 (25)
"Rolling Dice" p. 32 (32)

This is a routine for rolling computerized dice. It can be used in any program that uses such dice. The program randomly "rolls" the dice and then prints out the results. The printout is a picture of the dice with appropriate "spots" displayed. Includes a sample run.

Lines: 38 (plus patch)
Version: Processor Technology BASIC 5
Hardware: none
Software: none
Non-ANSI: CLEAR, extended IF

1015. Simple Game Playing Field

Author: L. D. Stander

Source: *Personal Computing* Apr 79 (3:4)
"A Simple Game Playing Field" pp. 50–51
(51)

Many games require a large playing field. Using an array to represent the field can be very inefficient. This subroutine does the job without costing you an arm and a leg in memory. It provides a 100-by-100 playing field without using a DIM statement. Includes a sample run.

Lines: 38
Version: Extended Benton Harbor BASIC, ver. 10.01.01
Hardware: none
Software: none
Non-ANSI: strings, STR$(), extended IF

1092. "Warp Drive" Display for the TRS-80

Author: Milan Chepko

Source: *Recreational Computing* May–Jun 79 (7:6)
"The Programmer's Toolbox" p. 62 (62)

One way to add new life to an old game is to give the game realistic graphics. Here is a subroutine that puts a little excitement into an outer space game. When called, the subroutine creates a display of "stars" that appear before you and then seem to rush past, as though you were hurling through space.

Lines: 35
Version: TRS-80 BASIC
Hardware: TRS-80
Software: none
Non-ANSI: not translatable

1093. Applesoft II Radar Scan Simulation

Author: Jim Day

Source: *Recreational Computing* May–Jun 79 (7:6)
"The Programmer's Toolbox" p. 62 (62)

This subroutine creates a radar-type display with an "arm" sweeping around a circular "screen."

Lines: 13
Version: Applesoft II BASIC
Hardware: Apple II
Software: none
Non-ANSI: not translatable

1028. Move Evaluation for Game Programs

Author: Herbert Dershem

Source: *Personal Computing* Jun 79 (3:6)
"A General Game Playing Program" pp. 70–75 (73–75)

When programming a computer to play a game such as chess, the hardest part is setting up the section of the program which determines which move the computer should select at its turn. This subroutine is a general game playing algorithm for selecting moves in any arbitrary game. The algorithm uses a "look-ahead" based technqiue; that is, it searches down the pathways of possible moves and counter-moves to figure out which move is likely to result in the best advantage. Move evaluators based on this routine are given for tic-tac-toe and kalah. Includes a list of program variables.

Lines: 80, 84, 114
Version: Radio Shack Level I BASIC
Hardware: none
Software: none
Non-ANSI: extended IF

1112. Card Shuffle Routine

Author: Eryk Vershen

Source: *Recreational Computing* Sep–Oct 79 (8:2)
"Card Shuffle" p. 63 (63)

If you're writing a card-playing program, then you'll need a routine to shuffle the cards. This routine should do the job nicely. (Reprinted from the book, *Little Book of BASIC Style*.)

Lines:	9
Version:	not given
Hardware:	none
Software:	none
Non-ANSI:	none

384. Fast Card-Shuffling Routine

Author:	Al Weiss
Source:	*Creative Computing* Oct 79 (5:10) "Better Late Than Never?" p. 10
	Creative Computing Nov 79 (5:11) untitled p. 10 (10)

Some "card-shuffling" algorithms are better than others. This one is fast and efficient. A short demonstration program shows how efficient the routine is.

Lines:	32, 20
Version:	not given
Hardware:	none
Software:	none
Non-ANSI:	none

GOMOKU

1058. Gomoku: Try to Get Five Stones in a Row

Author:	Jerry Crouch
Source:	*Personal Computing* Oct 79 (3:10) "The GOMOKU Tournament" pp. 81–85 (84–85)

Gomoku is a game that is more than 2,000 years old. It's played on a grid with black and white "stones." The object is to get five in a row of your stones. This program lets you play gomoku against the computer. Includes a list of program variables.

Lines:	91
Version:	not given
Hardware:	none
Software:	none
Non-ANSI:	none

88. GOBANG (Gomoku)

Author:	John Allwork
Source:	*Byte* Nov 79 (4:11) "BASIC Game: GOBANG" pp. 56–62 (56–58)
Updates:	commentary *Byte* May 80 (5:5) "Gomoku" p. 8

GOBANG is a program that plays a game more commonly known as gomoku. The game is played on a large checkerboard-like board. You and the computer take turns setting down pieces. The object of the game is to get five markers in a row horizontally, vertically, or diagonally. Includes a sample run.

Lines:	176
Version:	SWTPC MicroBASIC
Hardware:	none
Software:	none
Non-ANSI:	extended IF

GUESS MY NUMBER

832. NUMBER: A Number-Guessing Game

Author:	not given
Source:	*People's Computer Company* Oct 72 (1:1) "Games" pp. 8–9 (8)
Updates:	program listing reprint *People's Computer Company* Sep 74 (3:1) "Listings" pp. 24–25 (24)

This is a simple number-guessing game. The computer generates a random whole number between 1 and 100. You try to guess the number. After each guess, the computer will tell you if your guess was too high or too low. The object of the game is to guess the number in as few tries as possible. If you know the correct strategy to use, you should never need more than seven guesses. Includes a flowchart and sample run.

Lines:	27
Version:	DEC Edusystem 20 BASIC
Hardware:	none
Software:	none
Non-ANSI:	RANDOM

834. STARS: A Number-Guessing Game

Author: not given

Source: *People's Computer Company* Dec 72 (1:2) "STARS" p. 3 (3)

Updates: more compact version *People's Computer Company* May 73 (1:5) "Edusystem" pp. 18–19 (19)

program listing reprint *People's Computer Company* Sep 74 (3:1) "Listings" pp. 24–25 (24)

Most number-guessing games have the computer think up a number, and then have you guess it. The computer tells you whether your guess is too high or too low. In this version, the computer tells you about how close you are. It does this by printing out a line of stars. The farther off base you are, the fewer stars get printed out. The range of the guessing numbers and the number of tries you are allowed can be easily changed in the program. Includes a sample run.

Lines: 57
Version: DEC Edusystem 20 BASIC
Hardware: none
Software: none
Non-ANSI: RANDOM

838. TRAP Number-Guessing Game

Author: not given

Source: *People's Computer Company* Feb 73 (1:3) untitled p. 8

program listing *People's Computer Company* Sep 74 (3:1) "Listings" pp. 24–25 (24)

This is a guess-the-number type game. The computer thinks up a number, and then you try to guess what the number is. In this version, you close in on the number by specifying a range. The computer then tells you if the number is between your two numbers or not. Gradually, you can close in on what the computer's number is. Includes a sample run.

Lines: 41
Version: not given
Hardware: none
Software: none
Non-ANSI: HP strings

183. Guess My Number

Author: Danny Cohen

Source: *Creative Computing* May–Jun 75 (1:4) "Recent Trends in Mathematics Curriculum Research" pp. 64–67 (67)

In this game you try to guess what number the computer is thinking of. The number can be anywhere in the range of 0 to 25. You get only one chance per number, and the computer doesn't give hints. Includes a sample run.

Lines: 17
Version: not given
Hardware: none
Software: none
Non-ANSI: strings, extended IF, LEFT ( )

187. Guess-My-Number Game

Author: Alexander Cannara

Source: *Creative Computing* Sep–Oct 75 (1:5) "Toward A Human Computer Language" pp. 38–40 (40)

In this program you try to guess what number the computer is thinking of (between 1 and 100). The computer tells you if your guesses are too high or too low.

Lines: 16
Version: not given
Hardware: none
Software: none
Non-ANSI: HP strings

188. Guess-My-Number Game

Author: not given

Source: *Creative Computing* Sep–Oct 75 (1:5) "GUESS" p. 50 (50)

In this game, you try to guess what number the computer is thinking of (between 1 and a number you select). The computer tells you whether your guesses are too high or too low. Includes a flowchart and a sample run.

Lines: 37
Version: not given
Hardware: none
Software: none
Non-ANSI: PRI, GOT, INP

419. GUESS THE NUMBER (Tiny BASIC version)

Author: Fred Greeb

Source: *Dr. Dobb's Journal of Computer Calisthenics & Orthodontia* Mar 76 (1:3)
"Denver Tiny BASIC for 8080s" pp. 20–30 (21)

This is a guess-the-number game. The computer selects a number. You must then guess what the number is. The computer tells you when your guesses are too high or too low. This version is written for Tiny BASIC, an integer subset of BASIC.

Lines: 36
Version: Denver Tiny BASIC
Hardware: none
Software: none
Non-ANSI: IN, PR, extended IF

886. Base-Jump Number Guessing Game

Author: Mike Firth

Source: *People's Computer Company* Nov–Dec 76 (5:3)
"Another Number-Guessing Game" p. 37 (37)

In this number-guessing game, the computer has two numbers in mind: a Base and a Jump. Your goal is to catch the Base number. The trick is, the Base number is changed by the Jump each time you guess. Thus, you're aiming at a moving target. Includes a sample run.

Lines: 22
Version: not given
Hardware: none
Software: none
Non-ANSI: none

888. Yes-No Number-Guessing Game

Author: Carl Main

Source: *People's Computer Company* Mar–Apr 77 (5:5)
"The Yes-No Game" p. 35 (35)

This is a simple number-guessing game. The computer thinks up a number. You try to guess it. Each guess consists of a number, and a guess of whether the computer's number is greater than, equal to, or less than your number. With each guess, the computer tells you whether you are correct or not. Using these answers, you zero in on the mystery number. Includes a sample run.

Lines: 59
Version: PRIME 300 BASIC
Hardware: none
Software: none
Non-ANSI: strings, SUB(), extended IF

577. HI-LO

Author: Jim Huffman

Source: *Kilobaud* Apr 77 (4)
"HI-LO" p. 88 (88)

This is an elementary guessing game called HI-LO. The computer selects a random number. The object of the game is to guess what number the computer has selected. If you guess incorrectly, the computer tells you whether you have guessed too high or too low. Includes a sample run and flowchart.

Lines: 22
Version: MicroBASIC
Hardware: none
Software: none
Non-ANSI: extended IF

99. GUESS MY FRACTION

Author: Linda Schreiber

Source: *Calculators/Computers Magazine* May 77 (1:1)
"'Games Computers Play" pp. 49–52

program listing
Calculators/Computers Magazine Oct 77 (1:2)
"Guess My Fraction!" pp. 94–95 (94)

This is a structured number-guessing game. The computer thinks of a random fraction between 0 and 1. You then try to guess the fraction. The computer will give you hints as you go along. The program uses "rational" fractions (one number divided by another), and not decimal fractions. Includes a sample run.

Lines: 40
Version: Altair Extended BASIC
Hardware: none
Software: none
Non-ANSI: strings, VAL(), PRINT statements without the keyword PRINT, '(used in place of REM)

902. STARS Guessing Game for the PET

Author: Phyllis Cole

Source: *People's Computers* Jan–Feb 78 (6:4)
"STARS" p. 17 (17)

This is the game of STARS adapted for Commodore's PET computer. The computer thinks up a number. You try to guess the number. With each guess, the computer prints out a line of stars to show how close you are to the correct number. The more stars it prints out, the closer you are.

Lines: 36
Version: PET 8K BASIC
Hardware: PET
Software: none
Non-ANSI: not translatable

614. HI-LO

Author: Irwin Doliner

Source: *Kilobaud* Mar 78 (15)
"A Different Approach to HI-LO" pp. 120–122 (121–122)

This is the game of HI-LO. The object of the game is for one person to guess the number that the other player has thought up. In this version of HI-LO, you and the computer take turns guessing the number that the other has selected. You have the option of selecting what range of numbers will be used. Includes a sample run.

Lines: 113
Version: not given
Hardware: none
Software: none
Non-ANSI: strings, extended IF

285. GUESS THE NUMBER in Bally BASIC

Author: Karl Zinn

Source: *Creative Computing* Sep–Oct 78 (4:5)
"Bally Professional Arcade" pp. 56–59 (57)

This is GUESS THE NUMBER using the facilities of the Bally Arcade computer system. You try to guess the computer's number. The display is in color. The system even plays "Charge" through the speaker when you guess the number.

Lines: 17
Version: Bally BASIC
Hardware: Bally Arcade
Software: none
Non-ANSI: not translatable

144. HILO

Author: Scott Costello

Source: *Calculators/Computers Magazine* Nov–Dec 78 (2:7)
"HILO—A number-Guessing Program That Illustrates Several Math Concepts" pp. 6–8 (7)

HILO is the old number-guessing game. In this version you think up the number and the computer tries to guess it. Patches are provided to allow the program to run on a PET or TRS-80 Level I computer. Includes a sample run.

Lines: 48 (plus patches)
Version: HP 2000F BASIC
Hardware: none
Software: none
Non-ANSI: HP strings

993. Guess A Number

Author: Marolyn Pinney

Source: *Personal Computing* Feb 79 (3:2)
"Me and My TRS-80" pp. 46–51 (49)

Try to guess the computer's number. As you guess, the computer tells you when your guesses are too high or too low. Includes a sample run.

Lines: 28
Version: TRS-80 Level I BASIC
Hardware: none
Software: none
Non-ANSI: P., IN., CLS, extended IF

53. BINARY SEARCH GAME

Author: William and Alice Englander

Source: *Byte* Apr 79 (4:4)
"BASIC Cross-Reference Table Generator" pp. 190–192 (191)

This is a simple number-guessing game. You try to guess the computer's number. With each try that you make, the computer tells you whether you are guessing too high or too low.

Lines: 33
Version: CBASIC
Hardware: none
Software: none
Non-ANSI: not translatable

1100. "Guess the Number" for the TRS-80

Author: Bob Albrecht

Source: *Recreational Computing* Jul–Aug 79 (8:1)
"The Programmer's Toolbox" pp. 30–31 (30)

This program uses TRS-80 graphics to run the familiar "Guess the Number" game (you try to guess what number the computer's thinking of).

Lines: 10
Version: TRS-80 Level II BASIC
Hardware: TRS-80
Software: none
Non-ANSI: not translatable

1109. Guess My Number for the TRS-80

Author: Bob Albrecht

Source: *Recreational Computing* Sep–Oct 79 (8:2)
"Rewarding a Successful Guess" p. 62 (62)

You try to guess what number your TRS-80 is thinking of. If you guess incorrectly, the computer tells you whether your guess was too high or too low. When you guess the mystery number, the computer randomly fills its screen with stars.

Lines: 20 (plus patch)
Version: TRS-80 Level II BASIC
Hardware: TRS-80
Software: none
Non-ANSI: not translatable

GUESSING GAMES

833. LETTER: A Letter-Guessing Game

Author: not given

Source: *People's Computer Company* Oct 72 (1:1)
"Letter Guessing Game" p. 11 (11)

Updates: program listing reprint
People's Computer Company Sep 74 (3:1)
"Listings" pp. 24–25 (24)

This is a simple guessing game based on the letters of the alphabet. The computer thinks up a letter. You must then guess what the mystery letter is. After each guess, the computer will tell you if your letter occurs in the alphabet before or after the mystery letter. With the correct guessing strategy, it should take you at most five guesses to guess what the mystery letter is. Includes a sample run.

Lines: 30
Version: not given
Hardware: none
Software: none
Non-ANSI: HP strings

841. MUGWUMP: Find the Mugwump

Author: not given

Source: *People's Computer Company* Apr 73 (1:4)
"MUGWUMP" p. 3 (3)

A Mugwump is hiding in a grid. Your job is to guess where he's hiding. After each guess, the computer will tell you how far (in a direct line) your guess is from the Mugwump.

Lines: 55
Version: not given
Hardware: none
Software: none
Non-ANSI: RANDOM

844. HURKLE: Guess Where the Hurkle Is

Author: not given

Source: *People's Computer Company* Apr 73 (1:4)
"The Hurkle is a Happy Beast" p. 22 (22)

The Hurkle is hiding on a grid. You must try to find him by guessing his location. With each guess, the computer will tell you the approximate direction to go for your next guess. I don't know how the Hurkle manages to remain happy with everybody chasing him. Maybe he eats Funny Cookies. Includes a sample run.

Lines: 80
Version: not given
Hardware: none
Software: none
Non-ANSI: RANDOM

851. Capture the Snark

Author: not given

Source: *People's Computer Company* May 74 (2:5)
"SNARK" p. 3

program listing
People's Computer Company Sep 74 (3:1)
"Listings" p. 24–25 (25)

A Snark is hiding in a 10-by-10 grid. You must try to capture him. You can capture him by specifying a circular area on the grid. If the snark is in the area you have specified, the computer will tell you so. Gradually, you can reduce the size of your circle until you can pinpoint the exact spot where the snark is. Includes a sample run.

Lines: 69
Version: not given
Hardware: none
Software: none
Non-ANSI: HP strings

853. Button, Button, Who's Got the Button?

Author: Dave Kaufman

Source: *People's Computer Company* May 74 (2:5)
"Button, Button, Who's Got the Button?"
p. 10 (10)

BUTTON is a game of logic with a little twist. The object of the game is to guess which one of a "circle of friends" has the button. The catch is, when you get very close to the button holder, the button "slips away from you"! The person who has the button can (if he wants to) pass the button to someone he is sitting next to. As you make guesses, the program gives you clues as to where the button has gone. Includes a sample run.

Lines: 84
Version: not given
Hardware: none
Software: none
Non-ANSI: none

857. Capture the Hurkle

Author: not given

Source: program only
People's Computer Company Sep 74 (3:1)
"Listings" pp. 24–25 (25)

The Hurkle is hiding in a 10-by-10 grid. You can capture the Hurkle by locating where he is in the grid. You can locate the Hurkle by guessing what point on the grid he occupies. With each guess, the computer will tell you the approximate direction to go for your next guess. Includes a sample run.

Lines: 69
Version: not given
Hardware: none
Software: none
Non-ANSI: HP strings

858. Capture the Mugwump

Author: not given

Source: program only
People's Computer Company Sep 74 (3:1)
"Listings" pp. 24–25 (25)

In this game you are trying to find the Mugwump. The Mugwump is hiding in a grid. You must guess where he is. With each guess, the computer will tell you how far (in a straight line) the Mugwump is from the point you have guessed.

Lines: 54
Version: not given
Hardware: none
Software: none
Non-ANSI: HP strings

172. CHASE: Rabbit-Chasing Game

Author: Ted Park

Source: *Creative Computing* Mar–Apr 75 (1:3)
"Rabbit Chase" p. 23 (23)

This rabbit is an elusive little devil. He hops around in all directions. You must catch him by jumping on his position. Includes a sample run.

Lines: 97
Version: not given
Hardware: none
Software: none
Non-ANSI: extended IF, MIN(), HP strings

867. Witchy, The Name Witch

Author: Walter Wallis

Source: *People's Computer Company* Sep 75 (4:2)
"WITCHY" p. 11 (11)

Witchy, the Name Witch, has captured four of your friends and is holding them for ransom. If you want her to release them, you must tell her their names. The names are hidden behind fences. If a board on a fence falls down, you can see the letter behind it. Your task is to guess what name is behind each fence based on what you can see.

Lines: 93
Version: DEC EDU20-C BASIC
Hardware: none
Software: none
Non-ANSI: RANDOM, strings, PRI, ON . . . GOSUB

868. JOTTO

Author: Kent Cross

Source: People's Computer Company Sep 75 (4:2)
"JOTTO for the Altair" p. 20 (20)

JOTTO is a letter-guessing game. The computer thinks of a word. You then try to guess the word by typing words of your own. With each guess, the computer tells you how many of the letters in your word match letters in the computer's word. You have up to 15 guesses.

Lines: 27
Version: Altair BASIC
Hardware: none
Software: none
Non-ANSI: strings, extended IF

884. SNAKE

Author: Albert Bradley

Source: People's Computer Company Nov–Dec 76 (5:3)
"STORY, SNAKE, and PACK1" pp. 8–9 (9)

SNAKE is a version of Hangman without the gruesome images. The computer thinks up a word. You try to guess the letters in the word. As you guess, the computer fills in the letters that you guess correctly. As you make incorrect guesses, the "snake" vanishes. You have 12 guesses to find the correct word. Includes a sample run.

Lines: 40
Version: DEC BASIC-Plus
Hardware: none
Software: none
Non-ANSI: strings, INSTR(), & (used in place of PRINT), extended IF, LEFT (), RIGHT()

578. HANGMATH

Author: Phil Feldman and Tom Rugg

Source: Kilobaud Apr 77 (4)
"HANGMATH!" pp. 112–115 (113)

HANGMATH is a variation on the game of Hangman. In HANGMATH the object of the game is to guess the digits in a multiplication problem. The computer selects a random three-digit number and a random two-digit number. Your challenge is to guess what all the digits are. With each guess, you may guess one digit for one position. When the puzzle is completely solved (all the digits guessed) your score is the number of incorrect guesses you have made. (You try for the lowest score possible.) Includes a sample run and a list of program variables.

Lines: 48
Version: MITS 8K BASIC
Hardware: none
Software: none
Non-ANSI: strings, extended IF, STR$()

124. JOTTO in BASIC-Plus

Author: Joanne Verplank

Source: Calculators/Computers Magazine Mar 78 (2:3)
"BAGELS and JOTTO" pp. 5–16 (15–16)

JOTTO is a letter-guessing game. The computer thinks up a three-letter word. You then try to guess the word that the computer has selected. With each of your guesses, the computer gives you a clue as to how close you are to the actual word. The computer's clues consist of "jots." You get one jot for each letter in your guess that matches a letter in the mystery word. When you guess all the letters correctly you have "jotto!" Includes a sample run.

Lines: 108
Version: DEC BASIC-Plus
Hardware: none
Software: none
Non-ANSI: not translatable

147. PHANTNUM for Edusystem 20 BASIC

Author: Arlene Cram

Source: Calculators/Computers Magazine Nov–Dec 78 (2:7)
"The Phantnum Returns" pp. 48–49 (48–49)

PHANTNUM is a number-guessing game. The computer assigns "masks" to the digits 0 to 9 using the letters A through J. Your challenge is to guess what letters represent what digits. To help you guess, the computer gives you answers to basic arithmetic operations using the masked numbers. This program is a version of a game by the same name which appeared in the April 1978 issue of *Calculators/Computers Magazine*. Includes a sample run.

Lines: 103
Version: Edusystem 20 BASIC
Hardware: none
Software: none
Non-ANSI: PRI, FIX(), strings, INP, MID(), MOD(), GOT, NEX

152. CAGE

Author: Curt Torgerson

Source: *Calculators/Computers Magazine* Jan–Feb 79 (3:1)
          "Be a Computer" pp. 30–31 (30–31)

This is a word-guessing game. The computer prints out an animal name that is part of a larger word. It types dashes for the other letters of the larger word. Your challenge is to guess the mystery word. Includes a sample run and a list of program variables.

Lines: 88
Version: CDC Cyber 73 BASIC
Hardware: none
Software: none
Non-ANSI: strings, multiple-assignment, '(used in place of REM), NODATA, PRINT USING

997. Mode-Seeking Game

Author: Alan Filipski

Source: *Personal Computing* Feb 79 (3:2)
          "A Mode-Seeking Game" pp. 56–58 (58)

This is a two-dimensional guessing game. A mathematical function creates a "valley" across a square grid. You must find the lowest point of the valley. With each of your guesses, the program tells you what the slope of the function is at the point you have guessed. As written, you make your guesses using input from a Summagraphics Bit Pad. (You must supply the routines to get data from the data tablet.) With a one-line patch, however, you can enter your guesses with a simple INPUT statement.

Lines: 36 (plus patch)
Version: not given
Hardware: none
Software: none
Non-ANSI: strings

703. Name-Guessing Game

Author: Allan Joffe

Source: *Kilobaud Microcomputing* Jun 79 (30)
          "A Handle on Programming pp. 58–59 (58)

This is a name-guessing game. You try to guess what names are on a list.

Lines: 22
Version: TRS-80 Level II BASIC
Hardware: TRS-80
Software: none
Non-ANSI: not translatable

356. ZONEX

Author: Jim Madeheim

Source: *Creative Computing* Jul 79 (5:7)
          "ZONEX" pp. 106–07 (107)

ZONEX is a position-guessing game. The computer selects a target position on a board. It then "draws" two lines through the target point, dividing the board into four "zones." The zones are assigned colors. As you guess the location of the target, the computer tells you what color region your guesses have fallen into. The object is to guess the target's position with the minimum number of guesses. Includes a sample run.

Lines: 119
Version: not given
Hardware: none
Software: none
Non-ANSI: HP strings, POS( ), SEG$( ), ASC( ), STR$( ), VAL( )

KINGDOM

866. KINGDOM

Author: Lee Schneider and Todd Voros

Source: *People's Computer Company* Sep 75 (4:2)
          "KINGDOM" pp. 6–9 (8–9)

Updates: reprint and commentary
          People's Computers Sep–Oct 78 (7:2)
          "The Invasion of KINGDOM" pp. 8–15 (15)

          corrections
          Recreational Computing Jan–Feb 79 (7:4)
          "New Reader's Review" p. 6

KINGDOM is based on the premise that there are a lot of things that the average person would like to do, but, for some reason, cannot. One fantasy which seems to appeal to a great many people is being the ruler of the world. KINGDOM is a computer simulation of a medieval kingdom in game form. You are the king and make the decisions which spell prosperity or starvation for your subjects. You must deal with grain harvests, population explosions, varying land and grain prices, attacks by Huns, and other factors. It is up to you to run your kingdom so that it will prosper.

Lines: 192
Version: DEC TSS/8 BASIC
Hardware: none
Software: none
Non-ANSI: none

927. HAMURABI

Author: Joanne Verplank

Source: Personal Computing Jan–Feb 77 (1:1)
"Games & Exercises" pp. 78–82 (82)

Updates: modifications and commentary
Personal Computing Jan 79 (3:1)
"HAMURABI Solver: The Penultimate in Computer Madness" pp. 43–44 (44)

In the game of HAMURABI, you are invited to try your hand at ruling the ancient kingdom of Sumeria. You can buy land, sell land, feed your people, and plant grain. You must manage your kingdom so that it prospers. There are a variety of mistakes you can make that may bring tragedy upon your subjects. If you don't plant enough grain, your subjects may starve. Rats may eat you out of house and home. You may have to sell off your land to get grain to plant. The output of the program is a running commentary on your performance, including how many of your subjects have starved to death. Whatever happens, remember—it's all your fault! Includes a sample run.

Lines: 121
Version: DEC EDUSYSTEM 70 BASIC
Hardware: none
Software: none
Non-ANSI: CHR$()

1076. REINO: KINGDOM in Spanish

Author: Rodrigo Murillo and Jacobo Neuman

Source: Recreational Computing Jan–Feb 79 (7:4)
" 'REINO' Spanish Kingdom" pp. 46–47 (46–47)

KINGDOM is one of those computer games that have been around for quite a long time. In KINGDOM, you rule over a kingdom. You make decisions which affect how well your reign goes. This version of the program uses Spanish language output. (Note that the program still uses English BASIC keywords.)

Lines: 200
Version: TSS/8 BASIC
Hardware: none
Software: none
Non-ANSI: none

LIFE

418. LIFE Using Tiny BASIC

Author: David Piper

Source: Dr. Dobb's Journal of Computer Calisthenics & Orthodontia Jan 76 (1:1)
untitled p. 13 (13)

The game of LIFE is a game based on pattern generation. It starts with a board divided into "cells." With each passing "generation" the cells live or die depending on how many neighbors they each have. The life and death of the cells shows up as a changing pattern printed out on your terminal. By starting out with particular patterns, you can start off interesting sequences of other patterns. This version of LIFE uses an integer subset of BASIC known as Tiny BASIC Extended. Includes a sample run.

Lines: 93
Version: Tiny BASIC Extended
Hardware: none
Software: none
Non-ANSI: not translatable

429. LIFE Using the PolyMorphics Video Interface

Author: R. Broucke

Source: Dr. Dobb's Journal of Computer Calisthenics & Orthodontia Jun –Jul 77 (2:6)
"A Story of Traffic Lights, or: A BASIC Program to Play the Game of Life" pp. 12, 19 (19)

LIFE is a game that was invented in 1970 by Cambridge mathematician John Conway. It consists of a board covered with "cells" which live and die from generation to generation based on a simple set of rules: (1) cells with two or three neighbors survive, (2) cells with less than two or more than three neighbors die, and (3) new cells are "born" in empty spaces having exactly three neighbors. The birth and death of cells forms changing patterns. This program uses the PolyMorphics Video Interface to display the cell patterns on a video display. The program listing was somehow included on page 19 as the last program in another article.

Lines: 35
Version: MITS BASIC
Hardware: PolyMorphic's Video Interface, video display
Software: none
Non-ANSI: two-letter variables, POKE, extended IF

900. LIFE for Two Players

Author: Mac Oglesby

Source: *People's Computers* Nov–Dec 77 (6:3)
"SURVIVOR" pp. 48–51 (50–51)

LIFE was created by John Conway in 1970 as a board game. The game as originally designed is played by setting up a starting pattern of "cells." From there on, the cells "live" or "die" with each generation, based on specific rules. A cell survives if it has two or three neighbors. A cell dies if it has more than three or less than two neighbors. A cell is born in an empty cell if it has exactly three neighbors. Using these rules, the cells live and die, and in doing so, form a sequence of patterns. Some patterns die out. Others grow. Some evolve into stable patterns. This version of LIFE is for two people. Each person starts out with three live pieces. The object is to select a pattern that will outlive the pattern selected by your opponent. Includes a sample run.

Lines: 205
Version: Dartmouth BASIC
Hardware: none
Software: none
Non-ANSI: strings, LINPUT, CHANGE, STR$(), LIBRARY, CALL, ' (used in place of REM)

38. LIFE for BASIC-E

Author: William Englander

Source: *Byte* Dec 78 (3:12)
"Life" pp. 76–82 (76)

LIFE is based on a game that was developed in 1970 by John Conway. The game is played on a grid of squares. Each of the squares either contains a "cell" or is empty. Cells live or die from "generation" to "generation" based on the number of neighboring cells each has. The life and death of the cells forms changing patterns depending on which initial pattern you select. This version of the game

is written in BASIC-E, a version of BASIC which does not use normal BASIC line numbering. Includes a sample run.

Lines: 57
Version: BASIC-E
Hardware: none
Software: none
Non-ANSI: not translatable

776. LIFE in Color for the Apple II

Author: Richard Suitor

Source: *Micro* Dec 78–Jan 79 (8)
"LIFE for Your Apple" pp. 11–14 (11–14)

LIFE is a game of patterns. The patterns are formed by generations of "cells" which live or die by generations. This version of LIFE uses the Apple II's color graphics to display the patterns. Healthy cells show up as pink. Dying cells are brown. Cells being born are violet. You may specify which cells are to be living in the first generation by specifying individual cells or blocs of cells.

Lines: 57
Version: Apple II BASIC
Hardware: Apple II
Software: 6502 assembly language routine
Non-ANSI: not translatable

789. LIFE Aid for the PET

Author: James Stelly

Source: *Micro* Apr 79 (11)
"LIFESAVER" pp. 9–11 (10–11)

This program is an aid for the LIFE program by Dr. Covitz that appears in *The Best of Micro* (p. 65). This program allows you to enter LIFE patterns easily. You also can use this program to load and save patterns. Includes a sample run.

Lines: 65
Version: PET BASIC
Hardware: PET
Software: none
Non-ANSI: not translatable

807. LIFE for the Apple II

Author: L. William Bradford

Source: *Micro* Aug 79 (15)
"A Better LIFE for Your APPLE" pp. 22–24 (23–24)

LIFE is a game in which the life and death of "cells" forms a constantly changing pattern. The evolution of the pattern is dependent on the initial configuration of cells that you select. This version of LIFE runs in color on an Apple II. In this version of LIFE, you can move a cursor around the board to set up the initial pattern of cells.

> *Lines:* 135 (plus patch)
> *Version:* Apple BASIC
> *Hardware:* Apple II
> *Software:* none
> *Non-ANSI:* not translatable

1105. LIFE for the TRS-80

> *Author:* George E. Fleming

> *Source:* *Recreational Computing* Sep–Oct 79 (8:2)
> "TRS-80: Game of Life" p. 31 (31)

Life is a game based on changing patterns of "cells" on a board. The cells live and die from generation to generation based on how many neighbors each one has. The life and death of the cells forms patterns which vary according to the initial pattern of cells that was selected. This version of Life uses the graphics of the TRS-80.

> *Lines:* 32
> *Version:* TRS-80 Level II BASIC
> *Hardware:* TRS-80
> *Software:* none
> *Non-ANSI:* not translatable

824. 60 x 80 Life for the PET

> *Author:* Werner Kolbe

> *Source:* *Micro* Dec 79 (19)
> "A 60 x 80 Life for the PET" pp. 45–47
> (46–47)

Life is a game based on the life and death of a field of "cells." These cells live and die from generation to generation based on how many neighbors each cell has. As the cells live and die, they form constantly changing patterns. This program uses an assembly language subroutine to provide a rapidly varying display. To provide a larger working field, the program uses "windowing," displaying only part of the field at any one time.

> *Lines:* 23
> *Version:* PET BASIC
> *Hardware:* PET
> *Software:* 6502 assembly language routine
> *Non-ANSI:* not translatable

LUNAR LANDER

179. LUNAR

> *Author:* David Ahl

> *Source:* *Creative Computing* May–Jun 75 (1:4)
> "LUNAR" pp. 26—27 (27)

In this game your mission is to achieve a soft landing on the surface of the moon. You pilot a lunar excursion module (LEM), specifying how much fuel you want to burn at any given time. As you fall toward the lunar surface, you control your descent with your thrusters until you either land or run out of fuel. As you descend, the program prints out your altitude, velocity, and remaining fuel. Includes a sample run.

> *Lines:* 82
> *Version:* not given
> *Hardware:* none
> *Software:* none
> *Non-ANSI:* none

212. Lunar Lander Simulation

> *Author:* unknown; modified by Bill Cotter

> *Source:* *Creative Computing* Nov–Dec 76 (2:6)
> "LEM" pp. 86–87 (86–87)

Who needs NASA? With all these versions of LUNAR LANDER floating around, we computerniks seem to have the world's largest space fleet. Once again the object is to pilot a lunar lander safely down to the surface of the moon. In this version of LUNAR LANDER you have control of both the vertical and horizontal movement of the lander. Input is from the keyboard and output is to a regular terminal; no graphics capability is required. If you move too fast over the terrain, your LEM will flip over on touch down. Your engines will blow up if used to the limit. If you land harder than 3 meters/sec, your spacecraft disintegrates. Better take out an insurance policy before you leave. Includes a sample run.

> *Lines:* 220
> *Version:* Honeywell 600/6000 BASIC
> *Hardware:* none
> *Software:* none
> *Non-ANSI:* strings

580. Lunar Lander

> *Author:* Jim Huffman

> *Source:* *Kilobaud* May 77 (5)
> "LUNAR LANDER" pp. 100–101 (101)

Updates: correction
Kilobaud Jul 77 (7)
"Learning by Modifying" pp. 14–15 (14)

correction, new listing, flowchart
Kilobaud Aug 78 (20)
"Update: Lunar Lander" p. 69 (69)

improvements
Kilobaud Microcomputing Mar 79 (27)
"Update: 'Update: LUNAR LANDER' "
p. 22 (22)

This is a lunar lander simulation game. You play the part of a lunar lander pilot. You control the rockets which slow the lander in its descent to the moon's surface. The object of the game is to make a "soft" landing; that is, touch the surface of the moon at zero speed. This is a rather simple version of the game. Includes a sample run and flow-chart.

Lines: 38
Version: MicroBASIC
Hardware: none
Software: none
Non-ANSI: extended IF

11. Lunar Lander Simulation

Author: Stephen Smith

Source: *Byte* Nov 77 (2:11)
"Simulation of Motion (Part I): An Improved Lunar Lander Algorithm" pp. 18–22, 216–217 (216)

This program is a simulation of a lunar lander. The object is to pilot the lunar lander safely down to the surface of the moon. The pilot has control of both vertical and horizontal movement. Output is on a regular terminal; no special graphics capability is needed. As written, the program requires a joystick, but the program can be modified to accept input from the keyboard instead.

Lines: 55
Version: Tektronix 4051 BASIC
Hardware: joystick
Software: none
Non-ANSI: USR()

604. LUNAR LANDER with Joystick Control

Author: Mark Borgerson

Source: *Kilobaud* Dec 77 (12)
"Crash Landing!" pp. 100–102 (101)

Updates: improvements
Kilobaud Mar 78 (15)
"Autopilot for Lunar Lander?" pp. 13–14 (14)

This is a simulation of a lunar landing. The object is to pilot a lunar landing module safely to the surface of the moon. In this version of the game, the rate of fuel flow is taken from an A/D converter instead of from the keyboard. While the landing is in progress, the program continuously prints out the lander's altitude, speed, fuel, and burn rate. When the lander "touches down," the impact velocity and fuel remaining are printed out. Includes a sample run.

Lines: 73
Version: SWTPC 8K BASIC
Hardware: A/D converter, 6800-based microcomputer
Software: none
Non-ANSI: strings, POKE, PEEK(), extended IF, USER()

605. ROCKET PILOT

Author: Robert Bishop

Source: *Kilobaud* Jan 78 (13)
"ROCKET PILOT" pp. 90–93 (90–93)

Updates: correction
Kilobaud Mar 78 (15)
"Corrections" p. 34 (34)

This is a variation on the game of LUNAR LANDER. This version is written specifically for the Apple-II computer. It relies on a machine language subroutine which is supplied. In this version of LUNAR LANDER, the object is to fly a rocket over a mountain range. The output is displayed on a video monitor. The rocket is controlled by input from control paddles (or a joystick). Throughout the flight, your vertical and horizontal velocities, remaining fuel, and time elapsed are displayed at the bottom of the screen. Includes a sample run.

Lines: 98
Version: Apple-II BASIC
Hardware: Apple II
Software: 6502 assembly language routine
Non-ANSI: not translatable

792. LUNAR LANDER for the OSI Challenger

Author: David Morganstein

Source: *Micro* May 79 (12)
"Real-Time Games on OSI" pp. 31–33 (32–33)

This version of LUNAR LANDER uses the OSI Challenger to create a "real-time" simulation of a moon landing. You pilot the ship with keys pressed at the keyboard. The program does not pause to accept input, so if you don't press anything your landing module will crash. Program output is displayed continuously on your display screen.

Lines: 80
Version: OSI Challenger BASIC
Hardware: addressable-cursor video display
Software: none
Non-ANSI: not translatable

MASTERMIND

837. BAGELS

Author: D. Resek and P. Rowe

Source: *People's Computer Company* Dec 72 (1:2)
"BAGELS" p. 18 (18)

Updates: program listing reprint
People's Computer Company Sep 74 (3:1)
"Listings" pp. 24–25 (24)

In this game, the computer thinks up a three-digit number. You make guesses about what you think the number is. After each guess, the computer gives you clues as to how close your guess is to the actual number. The clues are given in the following manner: (Pico) one digit is in the wrong place, (Fermil) one digit is in the correct place, or (Bagels) no digit is correct.

Lines: 76
Version: HP 2000B BASIC
Hardware: none
Software: none
Non-ANSI: HP strings, ENTER

860. BULLS & CLEOTS

Author: Austin Stephens

Source: *People's Computer Company* Nov 74 (3:2)
"BULLS & CLEOTS" pp. 12–13 (13)

BULLS & CLEOTS is a word-guessing game. It is a more complicated version of BAGELS. In this game you play against the computer. Each side thinks up a random *n*-character word (you pick the *n*). Then you and the computer alternate turns guessing what the other's word is. With each guess, the opponent must respond with a certain number of "bulls" and cleots." A bull is a correct character in the correct place; a cleot is a correct character

in the wrong place. The first player to guess his opponent's mystery word wins. Includes a sample run.

Lines: 226
Version: HP 2000 BASIC
Hardware: none
Software: none
Non-ANSI: HP strings, multiple-assignment, extended IF

861. BEYOND BAGELS

Author: not given

Source: program listing only
People's Computer Company Nov 74 (3:2)
"Listings" p. 25 (25)

People's Computer Company May 75 (3:5)
"BAGELS" pp. 14–15

BEYOND BAGELS is a variation of BAGELS. In this game, the object is to guess the computer's number. With each guess you make, the computer will respond with a score. You get one point for each correct digit in the wrong place and two points for each correct digit in the correct place. Includes a sample run.

Lines: 86
Version: not given
Hardware: none
Software: none
Non-ANSI: none

201. Mastermind

Author: David Struble

Source: *Creative Computing* Mar–Apr 76 (2:2)
"Mastermind" pp. 68–69 (69)

Mastermind is a commercial adaptation of the game Bulls and Cows. In it, one player sets up a row of colored pegs. The other player tries to guess what colored pegs are in which positions. With each guess, the person who set up the pegs must give a reply, specifying how many pegs the guessing player has gotten correct. In addition, the player must say how many pegs the guessing player guessed correctly as to color, but not as to position. In this computer version of the game, the computer sets up the pegs; you take the part of the guessing player. Includes a sample run.

Lines: 90
Version: not given
Hardware: none
Software: none
Non-ANSI: strings, CHANGE, PRINT USING, : (used to specify format for PRINT USING)

215. MASTERBAGELS

Author: H. Hamilton

Source: *Creative Computing* Jan–Feb 77 (3:1)
       "MASTERBAGELS" pp. 84–85 (85)

This is the game of MASTERBAGELS, a combination of related logic games (BAGELS, MASTERMIND, BULLS AND COWS, etc.). MASTERBAGELS is designed to test your deductive ability. The computer picks a random number. Your job is to isolate the number. When prompted, you enter a valid number. The computer then responds with the number of digits that are right and in the right position, and the number of digits that are right but in the wrong position. Includes a sample run.

Lines: 92
Version: not given
Hardware: none
Software: none
Non-ANSI: none

887. MASTERMIND: A Game of Logic

Author: Jesse Heines and Gay Rosser

Source: *People's Computer Company* Jan–Feb 77 (5:4)
       "MASTERMIND—A Game of Logic" pp. 26–27 (27)

MASTERMIND is a game that challenges you to develop a logical approach to problem solving. The computer generates a secret code of four colored pegs in a specific order, using any one of six colors in each of four positions. Each time you guess a code, the computer tells you how many of your guessed pegs match the computer's in both color and position, and how many are correct in color only. If you use the correct guessing strategy it should take you no more than five guesses to break the computer's code. Includes a list of program variables and a sample run.

Lines: 233
Version: DEC TOPS-10 BASIC
Hardware: none
Software: none
Non-ANSI: strings

584. Random Number Game

Author: Harman DeMonstoy

Source: *Kilobaud* Jul 77 (7)
       "The Random Number Game" pp. 44–46 (46)

This is a number-guessing game similar to Bagels. In this game, you specify some number of digits. The computer then sets up as many random digits as you have specified. The object of the game is to guess what digits the computer has selected. You make a guess by entering a series of digits. The computer tells you how many correct digits you had in the correct places, and how many correct digits were in the wrong places. You continue guessing until you find the correct series of digits. Includes a sample run.

Lines: 83
Version: SWTP 8K BASIC
Hardware: none
Software: none
Non-ANSI: extended IF

10. MASTERMIND

Author: W. Lloyd Milligan

Source: *Byte* Oct 77 (2:10)
       "Mastermind" pp. 168–171 (168–170)

Updates: commentary, program reprint
       Byte Aug 78 (3:8)
       "Pascal versus BASIC: An Exercise" pp. 168–176 (173)

This is a set of two programs which play the game of Mastermind. Mastermind is a game in which players take turns as "codemaker" and "codebreaker." In this version, the computer is your opponent. The object of the game is to break the code of your opponent. The computer can play the part of either the codemaker or the codebreaker depending on which of the two programs is used. There are provisions for either elementary or advanced play. Includes a sample run.

Lines: 63, 112
Version: RT-11 BASIC
Hardware: none
Software: none
Non-ANSI: strings

254. MASTERMIND

Author: Steve North

Source: *Creative Computing* Nov–Dec 77 (3:6)
       "MASTERMIND II" pp. 136–139 (136–138)

Mastermind is a game normally played by two people. The two people take turns, alternating between being the "codemaker" and the "codebreaker." In this version, the computer is your opponent. The game starts out with the codemaker forming a code, or combination of "colored pegs." The codebreaker then attempts to deduce the code by placing guesses, one at a time, on the "board." After the codebreaker makes each guess, the codemaker responds by giving the codebreaker clues to indicate how close the guess was to the code. For every peg that is correct in color and position, the codebreaker gets a black peg. For every peg that is correct in color, but not position, the codebreaker gets a white peg. The object of the game is to completely guess your opponent's code. Includes a sample run.

Lines:	230
Version:	MITS 8K BASIC
Hardware:	none
Software:	none
Non-ANSI:	strings, extended IF

123. BAGELS in BASIC-Plus

Author:	Joanne Verplank
Source:	*Calculators/Computers Magazine* Mar 78 (2:3) "BAGELS and JOTTO" pp. 5–16 (14)

BAGELS is a game using secret numbers and codes. In this version of BAGELS, the secret numbers have two digits (this can be changed). Your job is to guess the secret number by making guesses. As you guess, the computer will give you clues indicating how close your guess corresponds to the secret number. "Bagels" means no digit is correct. "Fermi" means a digit is correct and in the correct position. "Pico" means a digit is correct, but in the wrong position. Includes a sample run.

Lines:	120
Version:	DEC BASIC-Plus
Hardware:	none
Software:	none
Non-ANSI:	not translatable

264. COMP IV Using Structured Programming

Author:	Alan Salisbury
Source:	*Creative Computing* Mar–Apr 78 (4:2) "Structured Software for Personal Computing" pp. 58–64 (63)

There is much talk these days of "structured programming" and "modular design." These techniques can be applied even to personal computing. This program is used to demonstrate modern programming techniques. The program is COMP IV. In COMP IV, the computer selects a random number. Then, using repeated guesses, you try to guess what the number is. With each guess, the computer tells you how many digits you guessed that were

correct regardless of sequence, and the number that were both correct and in the right position.

Lines:	124
Version:	not given
Hardware:	none
Software:	none
Non-ANSI:	multi-letter variables, strings, VAL(), extended IF

954. Guess the Hidden Number

Author:	Bruce Scott
Source:	*Personal Computing* May 78 (2:5) "No Strings Attached" p. 80 (80)
Updates:	corrections *Personal Computing* Sep 78 (2:9) "Fair Game" pp. 6–8 (6)

This game is a variation of Mastermind. The computer selects a random number. The object of the game is for you to guess the secret number. The computer gives you "hints" as you make guesses. The computer's hints consist of X's and I's. The X's represent a correct digit in the correct position; the I's represent a correct digit in an incorrect position. The game has been designed so that it can be played even under the limited form of BASIC available on the TRS-80 (Level I). Includes a sample run.

Lines:	21
Version:	TRS-80 Level I BASIC
Hardware:	none
Software:	none
Non-ANSI:	extended IF, ! (used in place of REM)

518. PICO-FUMI

Author:	Kenneth Slonneger
Source:	*Interface Age* Dec 78 (3:12) "PICO-FUMI" pp. 138–141 (141)

PICO-FUMI is a game of logical deduction. You play against the computer. You and the computer take turns thinking up two-digit numbers. Each of you tries to guess the other's number. With each guess, the other player must respond with the number of pico (digits which are correct but in the wrong place) and the number of fumi (correct digits in the correct place). The player who guesses the other's number first wins. The article contains a discussion of the computer's guessing strategy. Includes a sample run and a list of program variables.

Lines: 134
Version: not given
Hardware: none
Software: none
Non-ANSI: strings

668. SUPER MASTERMIND

Author: Tom Cardoso

Source: *Kilobaud Microcomputing* Feb 79 (26)
"SUPER MASTERMIND" pp. 100–102
(100–101)

Mastermind is a game of deduction and logic. In this version of the game, the computer generates a code formed with up to nine colors (represented by numbers). You must try to break the code by guessing the elements of the code. With each guess, the computer gives you clues as to how good your guess was. Includes a sample run.

Lines: 187
Version: SOL BASIC5
Hardware: none
Software: none
Non-ANSI: extended IF

994. BAGELS

Author: Marolyn Pinney

Source: *Personal Computing* Feb 79 (3:2)
"Me and My TRS-80" pp. 46–51 (50)

BAGELS is a number-guessing game. The computer gives you a three-digit number. You must guess the digits of the number based on clues that the computer gives you. Includes a sample run. (Reprinted from *101 Basic Computer Games*.)

Lines: 60
Version: TRS-80 Level I BASIC
Hardware: none
Software: none
Non-ANSI: not translatable

1086. MASTERMIND

Author: S. Ravn-Jensen and David Mundie

Source: *Recreational Computing* May–Jun 79 (7:6)
"Round 2: BASIC vs. PASCAL vs. BASIC"
pp. 14–15 (15)

Updates: correction
Recreational Computing Sep–Oct 79 (8:2)
"BASIC Dialects Bewilder" p. 5 (5)

commentary
Recreational Computing Sep–Oct 79 (8:2)
"Round 3: PASCAL Coolly Counters" pp. 28–30

MASTERMIND is a code-breaking game program. The computer generates a code; you try to break it. With each guess that you make about the computer's code, the computer gives you clues as to how close you are to the solution. This article compares two versions of BASIC (an unspecified "extended" BASIC, and standard BASIC) with Pascal. The program comes written in Pascal and in both versions of BASIC.

Lines: 101, 61
Version: not given
Hardware: none
Software: none
Non-ANSI: [standard BASIC version] none,
["extended" BASIC version] not translatable

MAZES

33. MAZE for the Apple I

Author: Robert Bishop

Source: *Byte* Oct 78 (3:10)
"MAZE" pp. 136–138 (138)

This program automatically generates and displays different mazes on an Apple I computer. The mazes generated are each 11-by-19 squares. The program can generate about one new maze per minute. Includes a sample output.

Lines: 54
Version: Apple I BASIC
Hardware: Apple
Software: none
Non-ANSI: not translatable

1056. MAZE: Dynamically Changing Maze for the TRS-80

Author: David Lappen

Source: *Personal Computing* Oct 79 (3:10)
"The Minotaur's Malevolent Maze" pp. 40–43 (42–43)

Updates: modification
Personal Computing Dec 79 (3:12)
"Maze Modifications" p. 6 (6)

Most maze games lack excitement; as soon as you find the way through, there's no more challenge left. Not so with this maze game for the TRS-80. With this program, your job is to work your way through a maze of walls that change constantly. The program also keeps track of how well you do. If you get through the maze, the program increases the number of walls when you try to go through again. Includes a sample output and a list of program variables.

Lines: 137
Version: TRS-80 Level II BASIC
Hardware: TRS-80
Software: none
Non-ANSI: not translatable

750. Maze Drawing Program (Two Versions)

Author: Paul Wennberg

Source: Kilobaud Microcomputing Nov 79 (35)
"A-Mazing" pp. 122–123 (123)

This program draws mazes on a regular terminal (no graphics needed). The program uses a maze-generating scheme which is both efficient and elegant. A program starts at a random point on one of the walls. It randomly walks until it becomes trapped. At this point it "backs up" until it can find an opening, and then it proceeds with its random walk. It proceeds this way until the maze is completed. Two versions of the program are provided: one which is efficient in its use of memory; and another which uses more memory but operates faster. Includes sample runs.

Lines: 52, 80 (plus patches)
Version: TDL 8K BASIC
Hardware: none
Software: none
Non-ANSI: extended IF, LPRINT, WIDTH

NIM

13. NIMBLE: The Ultimate NIM?

Author: Irwin Doliner

Source: Byte Nov 77 (2:11)
"NIMBLE: The Ultimate NIM?" pp. 172–178 (173–174)

This is a game similar to NIM, called NIMBLE. NIMBLE is a game for two players. The computer takes the role of one of the players. In this version of NIMBLE there are three piles of stones. Players alternately take stones away

from the piles. The player who removes the last stone wins. Includes sample runs.

Lines: 199
Version: not given
Hardware: none
Software: none
Non-ANSI: PRINT USING, strings, MAT operations, : (used in place of REM)

260. Van Wythoff's Game

Author: Alan Brown

Source: Creative Computing Jan–Feb 78 (4:1)
"VAN GAM" pp. 138–139 (139)

Van Wythoff's Game is similar to NIM. The computer is your opponent. In VWG there are two piles of "matches." Each pile has up to 100 matches, with you specifying the number in each pile. You and the computer alternate taking matches away from the piles. You may remove any number of matches from one pile, or an equal number of matches from each pile. The one who takes away the last match is the winner. The average user will not be able to beat the computer in nontrivial games, unless the user has been taught the winning sequences. Includes a sample run.

Lines: 94
Version: not given
Hardware: none
Software: none
Non-ANSI: SYS(), strings, STR$(), extended IF

650. 23 BYTES: NIM Via Telephone Link

Author: Stephen Gibson

Source: Kilobaud Nov 78 (23)
"Hey, Kids! It's 'Mickey Modem'!" pp. 52–57 (57)

Most computer games are played on just one computer. Here is a game that is played on two computers connected by a telephone link. The article describes how to build the modems necessary to link two computers together over the phone. The game itself is 23 BYTES, a variation of NIM. You hook up your computer over the phone lines with someone else's computer. Each of you removes "bytes" from a stack. The person who is forced to take the last byte loses.

Lines: 92
Version: TRS-80 Level II BASIC
Hardware: modem
Software: none
Non-ANSI: CLS, strings, INPUT #, PRINT #, extended IF

1065. TAC-TIX

Author: Reginald D. Gates

Source: *Personal Computing* Nov 79 (3:11)
"Structure Your Programs in English" pp.
67–72 (71–72)

TAC-TIX is a game program that lets you play a Nim-like
game against the computer. The game is played on a
square checkerboard. Initially, all the squares are covered
with markers. You and the computer alternately remove
pieces from the board. You may remove one to eight
pieces in a single move, but all the pieces must be a single
horizontal or vertical line. The player who removes the
last counter is the winner. Includes a sample run and a list
of program variables.

Lines: 238
Version: Digital Group Maxi-BASIC ver. 1.0
Hardware: none
Software: none
Non-ANSI: extended IF, strings

NUMBER GAMES

847. TAXMAN

Author: not given

Source: *People's Computer Company* Sep 73 (2:1)
"TAXMAN" pp. 6–7 (7)

Updates: comments
People's Computer Company Nov 73 (2:2)
"The Adventures of TAXMAN" p. 7

TAXMAN is a game based on factoring. The computer
prints out a list of numbers. You then remove numbers
from the list, one at a time. Your score is the total of the
numbers you take. The Taxman gets the numbers remaining that are factors of the numbers you have taken.
The object is to get a higher score than the Taxman.
Includes a sample run.

Lines: 173
Version: not given
Hardware: none
Software: none
Non-ANSI: none

854. ABASE: Game to Help Students Learn Number Bases

Author: Peter Katz

Source: *People's Computer Company* May 74 (2:5)
"ABASE" p. 15 (15)

There was a time when math students needed only to
learn how to add, subtract, multiply, and divide. What
with the "new" math and computers, students are now
being taught all sorts of strange stuff. Numbers in bases
other than 10 can be pretty strange, indeed, and boring,
too, if taught the old way. With a home computer, the task
of learning about number bases can—as has been done
here—be made into a game. In this game, the computer
selects a number. You try to guess what the number is.
The catch is, you must keep your guesses in the correct
number base.

Lines: 118
Version: not given
Hardware: none
Software: none
Non-ANSI: HP strings

168. MAGIC SQUARE

Author: David Ahl

Source: *Creative Computing* Jan–Feb 75 (1:2)
"MAGIC SQUARE" p. 13 (13)

This program makes a game out of 3-by-3 "magic
squares." You and the computer take turns placing numbers from one to nine in the squares of a tic-tac-toe board.
The goal is to make the sum of each row, column, and
diagonal equal 15. The player who first makes the sum of
any line equal something other than 15 loses. A tie game
draws a magic square! Includes a sample run.

Lines: 66
Version: not given
Hardware: none
Software: none
Non-ANSI: extended IF, FOR (used as a modifier),
CHR$()

957. Factor Game

Author: Herbert Dershem

Source: *Personal Computing* Jun 78 (2:6)
"Factor Game" pp. 44–49 (45–49)

With this educational game you can sharpen your skills in
factoring integers and you can develop analytical problem solving abilities. The game is played as follows: The
computer prints out an array of all the integers from 2 to
some number. You pick a number from the array. You
receive the same number of points as the number you
pick. The computer then scores by claiming all the factors
of the number you have picked that are left in the array.
When it is the computer's turn, you and the computer
switch roles. The player with the most points at the end of

the game wins. A TRS-80 version of the game is provided in addition to the regular listing. Includes a sample run.

Lines: 189, 93
Version: DEC System 10 BASIC, TRS-80 Level I BASIC
Hardware: none
Software: none
Non-ANSI: [DEC System 10 BASIC version] strings, MAT ZER(), STR$()
[TRS-80 Level I Basic version] not translatable

1077. CONCEPT: Binary Logic Game

Author: Ramon Zamora

Source: *Recreational Computing* Jan–Feb 79 (7:4) "TRS-80: CONCEPT Game" pp. 52–53 (53)

Updates: correction to text
Recreational Computing Mar–Apr 79 (7:5) "Correction: The Concept Game" p. 7

improvements
Recreational Computing May–Jun 79 (7:6) " 'CONCEPT' Re-Conceived" p. 5 (5)

commentary
Recreational Computing May–Jun 79 (7:6) "CONCEPT Sans Computer" pp. 40–41

CONCEPT is a game of binary logic. The goal is to identify the valid seven-digit binary numbers which satisfy a random set of concept conditions. The possible concepts are: parity, balance, majority, closure, and skip.

Lines: 79
Version: TRS-80 Level II BASIC
Hardware: none
Software: none
Non-ANSI: CLS, DEFDBL, INKEY$(), strings, extended IF

OTHELLO

7. OTHELLO

Author: Richard Duda

Source: *Byte* Oct 77 (2:10) "Othello, A New Ancient Game" pp. 60–62 (61–62)

Updates: patch for PET BASIC
Byte Aug 78 (3:8) "PET Bug?" p. 121 (121)

This game pits you against the computer in a game of Othello. Othello is a two-person board game based on the 100-year-old game of Reversi. It is similar to the game of GO. Othello is normally played on an 8-by-8 board. The object of the game is to convert a line of your opponent's pieces to your color.

Lines: 322
Version: not given
Hardware: none
Software: none
Non-ANSI: strings

1133. Othello

Author: Daniel Brodsky

Source: *ROM* Mar–Apr 78 (1:9) "OTHELLO" pp. 76–85 (78–84)

One board game that lends itself well to computer play is Othello. Othello is normally played on a 64-square matrix with two-sided (black/white) flippable disks. In this version you play against the computer. Don't count on winning; this program plays a pretty mean game. The author claims that it can win 70% of the time. The program uses positional static (no look-aheads) evaluation of the board to determine its strategy. It assumes that if it is in possession of key locations on the board it will be able to flip over more of its opponent's pieces. The program has provisions for printing out the board and for listing all of your valid moves at any time. Includes a flowchart.

Lines: 631
Version: IBM BASIC
Hardware: none
Software: none
Non-ANSI: none

90. REVERSI: Othello By Any Other Name

Author: Peter Maggs

Source: *Byte* Nov 79 (4:11) "Programming Strategies in the Game of Reversi" pp. 66–79 (76–79)

Updates: correction
Byte Feb 80 (5:2) "Correct REVERSI Termination" p. 168 (168)

corrections
Byte Mar 80 (5:3) "REVERSI Bug Makes Computer End Game Too Quickly" p. 180 (180)

Reversi is a game played on an 8-by-8 checkerboard. The players use markers which are black on one side and red on the other. Players alternate placing pieces of their respective colors on the board. When a player can "trap" an opponent's piece between two of his own, he gets to change the opponent's marker to his own color. At the end of the game, the player with the most pieces showing his color wins. This game is marketed by Gabriel Industries under the trade name, "Othello." Includes a sample run and a list of program variables.

Lines: 295
Version: not given
Hardware: none
Software: none
Non-ANSI: none

PONG

476. CRAZY BALL

Author: Elliott Myron

Source: *Interface Age* Aug 77 (2:9)
        "CRAZY BALL—EMCB" p. 171 (171)

CRAZY BALL is a one-person game of Pong. This version uses a PolyMorphic VTI display board for output. The "paddle" is controlled from the keyboard.

Lines: 105
Version: MITS 8K BASIC Rev. 3.1
Hardware: PolyMorphic VTI display board
Software: none
Non-ANSI: PEEK(), POKE, string, INP(), multi-letter
        variables, extended IF

494. CRAZY BALL for the VDM Video Driver

Author: Sy Feierstadt

Source: *Interface Age* Jan 78 (3:1)
        "CRAZY BALL with North Star Disc BASIC"
        p. 170 (170)

This game, CRAZY BALL, is a one-person version of Pong. The paddle is controlled from the keyboard. The output is on a video screen controlled by a VDM video driver.

Lines: 148
Version: North Star Disc BASIC
Hardware: VDM video driver, video display
Software: none
Non-ANSI: strings, FILL, EXAM(), INP(), !(used in place
        of PRINT), extended IF

909. PONG for the PET

Author: Martin Cohen

Source: *People's Computers* May–June 78 (6:6)
        "PONG for the PET" p. 41 (41)

PONG is the classic video simulation of a ping-pong match. This version of PONG is set up to use the graphics capabilities of the PET. The game can be played by zero—the computer playing against itself—to two players. The speed of the ball can be varied to increase or decrease the difficulty of play. The paddles are controlled from the keyboard. Includes a sample of the output.

Lines: 153
Version: PET BASIC
Hardware: PET
Software: none
Non-ANSI: not translatable

504. PING PONG

Author: Elliott Myron

Source: *Interface Age* Aug 78 (3:8)
        "PING PONG for the 8080" pp. 64–66 (66)

PING PONG (or just plain "PONG") is a familiar video game. This is a version for your home computer. It requires a CRT interface board such as the PolyMorphic VTI, as well as two control boxes. The article explains how to construct the control boxes. The game is a two-player version displayed on a video screen. Since BASIC is used to program the computer, the game runs somewhat slower than the professional machine-language versions; but it is still a good game. And you don't have to keep feeding in quarters! Includes a flowchart.

Lines: 148
Version: MITS BASIC
Hardware: PolyMorphic VTI, homemade control boxes
Software: none
Non-ANSI: multi-letter variables, strings, STR$(), VAL(),
        extended IF, INP(), POKE, PEEK()

PUZZLE SOLVERS

921. "Jumble" Word Game Solver

Author: M. Hofheinz

Source: *People's Computers* Sep–Oct 78 (7:2)
        "Jumble" p. 48 (48)

Jumble is a scrambled-word puzzle in which you are presented with several words whose letters have been rearranged. Your challenge is to unscramble the words. This is a program to assist you in unscrambling the jumbled words. It takes a group of up to six letters and prints out every possible combination of the letters.

Lines: 43
Version: PET BASIC
Hardware: none
Software: none
Non-ANSI: strings, extended IF

32. Eight Queens Problem Solver

Author: Terry Smith

Source: *Byte* Oct 78 (3:10)
"Solving the Eight Queens Problem"
pp. 122–126 (124)

Updates: improvements and commentary
Byte Feb 79 (4:2)
"Responses to the Queens" pp. 132–148
(132–140)

commentary
Byte Aug 79 (4:8)
"Permutations Bibliography" pp. 126–127

The Eight Queens Problem is a chess-related problem. The object of the puzzle is to place eight queens on a chess board in such a way that no queen can take another. This program finds solutions for this problem.

Lines: 60
Version: IBM BASIC
Hardware: none
Software: none
Non-ANSI: strings

983. Knight's Tour Chess Problem

Author: Dan Clarke

Source: *Personal Computing* Dec 78 (2:12)
"Knight's Tour" pp. 69–70 (69–70)

The Knight's Tour problem is one of the classic chess problems. The object is to have a knight visit each of the 64 squares on a chessboard without landing on any square more than once. This program works on a solution to the problem. Though no complete 64-move solution is provided, a 60-move one is given. Includes a sample run.

Lines: 121
Version: not given
Hardware: none
Software: none
Non-ANSI: extended IF

41. Eight Queens Chess-Problem Solver (Permutation Method)

Author: Richard Greenlaw

Source: *Byte* Jan 79 (4:1)
"On the Eight Queens Problem" pp. 162–165
(164)

The Eight Queens problem is a chess-related puzzle. The object of the puzzle is to place eight chess queens on a chessboard in such a way that no queen is on the same row or column as another. A program to provide solutions for this problem appeared in the October 1978 issue of *Byte*. This program does the same job, but is over 13 times faster! Includes a sample run.

Lines: 62
Version: Micropolis BASIC
Hardware: none
Software: none
Non-ANSI: AND(), OR(), extended IF

43. Eight Queens Chess-Problem Solvers

Author: Randall Matthews, James Wilcox, James
Coan, and Scott Banks

Source: *Byte* Feb 79 (4:2)
"8 Queens Forum" pp. 132–148 (136–140)

The Eight Queens problem is a chess-related puzzle. A computer solution to the problem appeared in the October 1978 issue of *Byte*. This article is a collection of comments about the problem and alternate programs to solve the puzzle. One solution uses the Apple II's color graphics to display the program results. Another program uses a permutation-of-digits algorithm. A third program uses structured programming methods.

Lines: 19, 15, 20
Version: various
Hardware: various
Software: none
Non-ANSI: various

1089. Faster Jumble Solver

Author: Peter Stark

Source: *Recreational Computing* May–Jun 79 (7:6)
"Faster JUMBLE" p. 47 (47)

Jumble is a popular word puzzle. You are presented with a group of words whose letters have been jumbled up.

You must try to unscramble the letters. This program can help you by printing out possible rearrangements of the letters. This program is a faster version of one that appeared in the September–October 1978 issue of *People's Computers*.

Lines: 59
Version: SWTPC BASIC
Hardware: none
Software: none
Non-ANSI: strings

1139. "Jumble" Puzzle Solver

Author: E. M. Pass

Source: *'68' Micro Journal* Jul 79 (1:5)
          "JUMBLE-(Basic)" p. 34 (34)

Jumble is a word puzzle that appears in many newspapers. The puzzle gives you words whose letters have been scrambled. You must figure out what the words are. This program helps you by printing out a list of all the possible ways the scrambled letters can be rearranged. But watch out—for an eight-letter combination there are over 40,000 possible arrangements of the letters. Includes a sample run.

Lines: 36
Version: SWTPC 8K BASIC
Hardware: none
Software: none
Non-ANSI: strings

1038. "Truck" Puzzler Solver

Author: David W. Stockburger

Source: *Personal Computing* Aug 79 (3:8)
          "PUZZLER" pp. 30–33 (33)

Updates: commentary
          Personal Computing Dec 79 (3:12)
          "Trucking On" p. 12

Truck is a puzzle played on a triangular board with 15 pegs. The puzzle is played by jumping pegs and removing the pegs that have been jumped. The object is to remove as many pegs as possible. This program solves the puzzle. You specify one of the pegs. The computer then tries to find the sequence of jumps which will allow it to remove the greatest number of pegs. Includes a flowchart and a list of program variables.

Lines: 205
Version: Polymorphic 88 BASIC
Hardware: memory-mapped display
Software: none
Non-ANSI: extended IF, EXIT, POKE, PLOT, CHR$(),
            TIME()

1052. Chess Knight's Tour Program

Author: Chet Dyche

Source: *Personal Computing* Sep 79 (3:9)
          "Knight on Tour" p. 66 (66)

          modifications for TRS-80
          Personal Computing Nov 79 (3:11)
          "The Knight Watch" p. 79 (79)

The Knight's Tour is a chess puzzle that has baffled chess players for centuries. The problem is to find a series of legal moves that will allow a knight to "tour" the chessboard, touching each square exactly once. This program produces a successful tour for the knight starting from any position you specify. Includes a sample run.

Lines: 66
Version: TRS-80 Level II BASIC
Hardware: none
Software: none
Non-ANSI: extended IF

87. Soma Cube and Polyomino Puzzle Solver

Author: Douglas Macdonald and Yekta Gursel

Source: *Byte* Nov 79 (4:11)
          "Solving Soma Cube and Polyomino Puzzles
          Using a Microcomputer" pp. 26–52 (34–50)

Polyominoes are groups of squares connected to form various odd shapes. A domino (two squares joined at a side) is an example of a polyomino. In polyomino puzzles, the object is to "fit" the various odd shapes together to exactly form a larger shape, such as a square. Soma Cubes are three-dimensional versions of the same type of puzzle. This program finds all the possible solutions for a given polyomino puzzle. (The program is primarily in 6502 assembly language; only "driver" sections are in BASIC.) Includes a flowchart.

Lines: 61, 64
Version: PET 8K BASIC
Hardware: 6502-based microcomputer
Software: 6502 assembly language routine
Non-ANSI: POKE, strings, multi-letter variables,
            PEEK(), SYS(), GET, extended IF

556. Hidden-Word Finder

Author: Dave Degler

Source: *Interface Age* Nov 79 (4:11)
          "The Column" pp. 21–22 (22)

You've all seen those "hidden word" puzzles where you're presented with a block of letters. The idea is to pick out the letters that form target words. This program solves such puzzles. You type in the block of letters and the hidden words. The computer then locates the words.

Lines: 83
Version: MSI BASIC
Hardware: none
Software: none
Non-ANSI: strings, extended IF, ? (used in place of PRINT), STRING

PUZZLES

422. SHOOTING STARS

Author: Mark Borgerson

Source: *Dr. Dobb's Journal of Computer Calisthenics & Orthodontia* Aug 76 (1:7) "SHOOTING STARS for Uiterwyk's 6800 Micro-BASIC" pp. 29–30 (29–30)

SHOOTING STARS is a pattern-based game. The game is played on a nine-square grid. By shooting "stars" on the grid you change the pattern of the board, converting "stars" to "black holes" and vice-versa. The object is to get a pattern with one star surrounded by black holes. This version is written in an integer version of BASIC called Micro-BASIC.

Lines: 86
Version: Micro-BASIC
Hardware: none
Software: none
Non-ANSI: extended IF

885. FROGS

Author: Mac Oglesby

Source: *People's Computer Company* Nov–Dec 76 (5:3) "FROGS" p. 16 (16)

FROGS is a reversing game played on a board nine positions long. On the board are two sets of markers (* and %). Each set of pieces is grouped at one end of the board. The goal is to reverse the positions of the two sets of pieces. To reverse the pieces, you move them one at a time across the board. At each move you can slide a piece or jump one piece over an adjacent piece. The object of the game is to do the reversal in the fewest number of moves. Includes a sample run.

Lines: 105
Version: Dartmouth BASIC
Hardware: none
Software: none
Non-ANSI: strings, ASC(), LINPUT, CHANGE, ' (used in place of REM)

466. SHOOTING STARS

Author: Herman DeMonstoy

Source: *Interface Age* Apr 77 (2:5) "SHOOTING STARS" pp. 109–112 (110–112)

This game, SHOOTING STARS, is a one-person logic game. The game is played in a 3-by-3 position "universe." In the universe are "stars" and "black holes." With each turn, the player "shoots" at one of the stars, changing it into a black hole. Each star has its own "galaxy." Shooting a star reverses the status of each position in the galaxy. The object of the game is to change the universe into eight stars surrounding one black hole. A flowchart and sample run are included.

Lines: 108
Version: TINY BASIC 6800
Hardware: none
Software: none
Non-ANSI: extended IF, GOSUB [computed line number]

243. ROTATE

Author: David Ahl

Source: *Creative Computing* Sep–Oct 77 (3:5) "ROTATE" pp. 138–139 (138)

The game of ROTATE is played on a 4-by-4 board filled randomly with the letters A through P. The game is similar to those little plastic games with sliding pieces. The object is to move the pieces around until the letters are in correct alphabetical order. The letters are moved by rotating groups of four letters clockwise, one position at a time. There is also one special move which permits you to exchange any two adjacent letters. This move can be done only once per game. Includes a sample run.

Lines: 59
Version: not given
Hardware: none
Software: none
Non-ANSI: strings, & (used in place of PRINT), FOR (used as a modifier), PRINT USING, extended IF

115. DONUTS: Simplified TOWERS OF HANOI

Author: Ron Santore

Source: *Calculators/Computers Magazine* Nov 77 (1:3)
"DONUTS for Kids" pp. 38–39 (39)

DONUTS is a simplified version of the TOWERS OF HANOI puzzle. In this game there are three "donuts": a small one, a medium one, and a large one. There are three sticks, initially, the donuts are stacked on one stick. The object is to move the donuts one at a time onto one of the other two sticks. At no time can you place a larger donut on top of a smaller one. Includes a sample run.

Lines: 70
Version: not given
Hardware: none
Software: none
Non-ANSI: strings, ! (used in place of PRINT), extended IF

652. Lucas' Puzzle

Author: William Colsher

Source: *Kilobaud* Nov 78 (23)
"Lucas' Puzzle" p. 98 (98)

Updates: corrections
Kilobaud Microcomputing Feb 79 (26)
"Corrections" p. 155 (155)

The puzzle that is the basis for this program was invented in the late nineteenth century by a French mathematician by the name of Edouard Lucas. The puzzle is a board with nine holes in it. There are two sets of pegs, one set at each end. The object is to reverse the positions of the two sets of pegs by sliding and jumping them across the board. This computer version of the puzzle uses sets of Xs and Os instead of pegs.

Lines: 78
Version: not given
Hardware: none
Software: none
Non-ANSI: HP strings, EXIT, extended IF

922. FROGS for the TRS-80

Author: Ramon Zamora

Source: *People's Computers* Nov–Dec 78 (7:3)
"TRS-80: FROGS!" pp. 17–18 (18)

FROGS is a game played on a nine-position board. There are two sets of markers ("frogs") on the board, one set at each end. The object is to reverse the positions of the two sets of markers by sliding and jumping the markers across the board. This version of the game uses the TRS-80's graphics abilities so you can watch the "frogs" as they jump. Includes a sample run.

Lines: 68
Version: TRS-80 Level II BASIC
Hardware: TRS-80
Software: none
Non-ANSI: not translatable

689. Two-Diamonds Puzzle

Author: William Colsher

Source: *Kilobaud Microcomputing* Apr 79 (28)
"Two Diamonds" p. 115 (115)

Updates: correction and improvements
Kilobaud Microcomputing Jun 79 (30)
"Polishing 'Diamonds' " pp. 23–24 (24)

The Two-Diamonds puzzle is related to Lucas' Puzzle. In the Two-Diamonds puzzle, you have a board (diamond-shaped) with two sets of markers. One set of markers is at each end of the board. The object is to reverse the positions of the two sets of markers by sliding and jumping them across the board.

Lines: 83
Version: not given
Hardware: none
Software: none
Non-ANSI: HP strings, extended IF, EXIT

1009. Tower of Hanoi Subroutine Using Recursion

Author: Herbert Dershem

Source: *Personal Computing* Apr 79 (3:4)
"Recursive Programming in BASIC" pp. 16–18 (18)

A subroutine is recursive if it calls itself. This subroutine uses recursion to solve the Tower of Hanoi problem. (The Tower of Hanoi problem is the one in which the object is to move a set of rings from one peg to another without placing a larger ring on a smaller one.)

Lines: 14
Version: Radio Shack Level I BASIC
Hardware: none
Software: none
Non-ANSI: none

355. BRAIN TEASER

Author: Hal Knippenberg

Source: *Creative Computing* Jul 79 (5:7)
"BRAIN TEASER" pp. 104–105 (104–105)

Updates: commentary
Creative Computing Sep 79 (5:9)
"Our Face is Red" p. 16

BRAIN TEASER is played on a 3-by-3 board randomly filled with ones and zeros. The object of the game is to change the pattern of ones and zeros until the board has a zero in the center and ones in all of the other positions. To make a board change, you select a square that contains a one. Depending on which position the one is in, other positions may also "flip-flop" from one to zero or from zero to one. If you end up with all zeros, you lose. The CALL statement is just used to clear the screen. Includes a list of program variables.

Lines: 171
Version: MAXI-BASIC
Hardware: none
Software: none
Non-ANSI: HP strings, CALL, extended IF, VAL()

1117. Tower of Hanoi Puzzle for the TRS-80

Author: Herbert L. Dershem

Source: *Recreational Computing* Nov–Dec 79 (8:3)
"TRS-80: Tower of Hanoi" pp. 34–35 (35)

Updates: corrections
Recreational Computing Mar–Apr 80 (8:5)
"Tower of Hanoi Correction" p. 43 (43)

The Tower of Hanoi puzzle consists of three upright rods and several "doughnuts" of varying sizes. The rings start out stacked up on one of the rods. The object of the puzzle is to move the rings, one at a time, to a new rod. At no time may you place a larger ring on a smaller one. This program lets you solve the puzzle or watch the computer solve it. You choose the number of rings used, up to a maximum of 15.

Lines: 128
Version: TRS-80 Level II BASIC
Hardware: TRS-80
Software: none
Non-ANSI: not translatable

REVERSE

845. REVERSE

Author: Peter Sessions

Source: *People's Computer Company* May 73 (1:5)
"REVERSE" p. 5 (5)

Updates: faster version
People's Computer Company May 74 (2:5)
"REVERSE" p. 17 (17)

program listing reprint
People's Computer Company Nov 74 (3:2)
"Listings" p. 25 (25)

reprint
People's Computer Company Jan–Feb 77 (5:4)
"REVERSE" pp. 17–19 (17)

This is the game of REVERSE. To win, all you have to do is rearrange a list of numbers in numerical order from left to right. With each turn, you can rearrange some of the numbers by specifying how many numbers (counting from the left) you wish to "reverse." The set of numbers that you select will be reversed in order. With one or more reverses you should be able to arrange the numbers into correct order. Includes a sample run.

Lines: 83
Version: not given
Hardware: none
Software: none
Non-ANSI: RANDOM

191. REVERSE

Author: Peter Sessions

Source: *Creative Computing* Sep–Oct 75 (1:5)
"REVERSE" pp. 58–59 (59)

Updates: commentary
Creative Computing Nov–Dec 75 (1:6)
"Our Face is Red Department" p. 41

The object of REVERSE is to rearrange a list of numbers into numerical order. With each turn, you tell the computer how many numbers (counting from the left) you would like to move. The computer then reverses the order of those digits. This process continues until you are able to move the numbers into their correct positions. Includes a sample run.

Lines: 56
Version: not given
Hardware: none
Software: none
Non-ANSI: strings

893. REVERSE Played by the Computer

Author: Carl Main

Source: People's Computers Jul–Aug 77 (6:1)
"Inverse-REVERSE" pp. 34–35 (35)

REVERSE is a game normally played by human beings. In the normal game, the computer types out a list of numbers in random order. You then try to rearrange the numbers into correct order by "reversing" the order of sections of the numbers. The sections must start with the first number in the list. In this version of the game, the computer does the reordering of the list. The object is to find out what strategy the computer is using to do the reordering. Includes a flowchart and sample run.

    Lines: 97
    Version: not given
    Hardware: none
    Software: none
    Non-ANSI: strings, SUB(), MAT operations, extended IF

925. REVERSE for the TRS-80

Author: Ramon Zamora

Source: People's Computers Nov–Dec 78 (7:3)
"REVERSE" pp. 44–45 (45)

Updates: correction
Recreational Computing Mar–Apr 79 (7:5)
"Two Keys Reversed in REVERSE" pp. 6–7 (7)

REVERSE begins with a scrambled list of the numbers from 1 to 9 (in this version you can use fewer numbers if you like). The object is to try to put the numbers into correct sequence. You do this by reversing sections of the list. The sections reversed must always start at the left-hand side. This version of the game uses the TRS-80's graphics capabilities to display the numbers. Includes a sample run.

    Lines: 80
    Version: TRS-80 Level II BASIC
    Hardware: TRS-80
    Software: none
    Non-ANSI: not translatable

SIMON

50. Musical Tone Game

Author: Steve Ciarcia

Source: Byte Apr 79 (4:4)
"The Toy Store Begins at Home" pp. 10–18 (18)

This game is a simulation of the Simon toy marketed by Milton Bradley. The game uses a player console with a tone generator, four colored lights, and four push-buttons. The computer uses the tone generator to play a series of notes. Your task is to repeat the tones that the computer plays. This becomes increasingly difficult as the computer plays longer and longer strings of notes. Plans for the player console are included in the article. Includes a flowchart.

    Lines: 60
    Version: 8K Zapple BASIC
    Hardware: player console (homemade)
    Software: none
    Non-ANSI: OUT, INP(), extended IF

562. PLAY AFTER ME: Try-to-Repeat-the-Tune Game for the Atari 400

Author: Al Baker

Source: Interface Age Dec 79 (4:12)
"Al Baker's Game Corner" pp. 34–36 (34–36)

This game is an Atari 400 version of Milton Bradley's Simon game. The computer uses the Atari's sound and color graphics to play a note and display a color. You try to repeat the musical note. If you succeed, the computer adds another note and color. You must repeat both the old note and the new one. If you repeat both notes correctly, the computer adds a third, and so on until you make a mistake.

    Lines: 110
    Version: Atari 400 BASIC
    Hardware: Atari 400
    Software: none
    Non-ANSI: not translatable

SIMULATIONS

3. BLACK FRIDAY: A Stock Market Simulation Game

Author: Robert Baker

Source: Byte Jan 77 (2:1)
"BLACK FRIDAY" pp. 56–58 (56–58)

This game provides a realistic simulation of the stock market. One to four players can play. Each player has the option to play in from three to ten years (rounds). The object of the game is to make the most money by buying and selling stocks. The computer determines the prices of the stocks and keeps track of each player's holdings.

Lines: 326
Version: DEC PDP-10 BASIC
Hardware: none
Software: none
Non-ANSI: MAT operations, strings, SPACE$(), STR$(), PRINT USING

231. SWARMS

Author: Rand Miller

Source: *Creative Computing* May–Jun 77 (3:3) "SWARMS" pp. 113–118 (114–118)

SWARMS is a game based on the book *The Swarm* by Arthur Herzog. The program puts you in charge of the defense of the entire United States when swarms of ferocious South American bees suddenly start appearing in different sections of the country. The sizes of the swarms are shown on a map printed out on your terminal, and the estimated time of arrival (ETA) of the bees to a major city is printed out in chart form. The object of the game is to destroy all of the swarms with as few casualties as possible. You have eight commands at your disposal: (1) attack scan map (print the map), (2) ETA report (print out the ETA report), (3) battle phase options (select an attack plan), (4) evacuation (evacuate a city), (5) nuclear destruction (destroy a city), (6) casualty report, (7) print a command list, and (8) cancel game. Includes a sample run.

Lines: 875
Version: DEC PDP-10 BASIC
Hardware: none
Software: none
Non-ANSI: PRINT USING, strings, MARGIN, MAT ZER(), multiple-assignment, : (used to specify format for PRINT USING)

244. NOMAD

Author: Steve Trapp

Source: *Creative Computing* Sep–Oct 77 (3:5) "NOMAD" pp. 140–42 (140–142)

Gramma Nomad is a nice old lady who has not quite made up her mind where she wants to live. She has narrowed it down to somewhere in Garbonzo City, and on a street corner. The game starts when she finds a new house. She then sends you a telegram telling you where she is. The object is to find your way to her new house. Along the way you must watch out for crash-ups, tickets, flat tires, and dead ends. If one of the town drunks hits you, you lose. In order to get to Gramma's house, you need a map which is printed in the article. The input to the game is your speed and direction at various junctions. Includes a sample run.

Lines: 322
Version: HP 2000F BASIC
Hardware: none
Software: none
Non-ANSI: HP strings, MAT CON(), extended IF, multiple-assignment

302. CORRAL: A Horse-Roping Game

Author: Colin Keay

Source: *Creative Computing* Nov–Dec 78 (4:6) "CORRAL" pp. 150–152 (152)

If you have the wild west in your blood, then this is the game for you. You are a cowboy trying to rope a reluctant horse. As you approach, the horse moves back and forth, trying to get away. If you don't move cautiously, the horse may bolt. It may also give you a kick in the ribs. Includes a sample run.

Lines: 74
Version: Microsoft BASIC
Hardware: none
Software: none
Non-ANSI: strings, extended IF

303. JOUST: A Medieval Jousting Tournament

Author: Alan Yarbrough

Source: *Creative Computing* Nov–Dec 78 (4:6) "JOUST" pp. 152–153 (153)

In this game you are a fearless knight out to win the hand of a fair maiden. To win her hand you must defeat a series of challenging knights in a jousting tournament. To the victor go the spoils! Includes a sample run.

Lines: 102
Version: Microsoft BASIC
Hardware: none
Software: none
Non-ANSI: strings, extended IF

318. GOLD MINE

Author: Royce Jones

Source: *Creative Computing* Feb 79 (5:2) "GOLD MINE" pp. 132–134 (132–134)

Here's your chance to strike it rich! Dig for your own gold mine in this game of toil and treasure. You play the part of an eager prospector. You move up, down, and sideways through a hillside digging for gold veins. The sequential file is not absolutely necessary to run the game.

Lines: 185
Version: DEC RSTS BASIC
Hardware: sequential file device, addressable-cursor video display
Software: none
Non-ANSI: not translatable

1078. AIR RAID: Try to Defuse a Bomb

Author: Milan Chepko

Source: Recreational Computing Mar–Apr 79 (7:5) "AIR RAID!" p. 15 (15)

This program takes you back to London, 1943. You get the chance to defuse an unexploded bomb left by a recent air raid. Cut the wrong wire and . . . KA-BOOM! Includes a list of program variables.

Lines: 41
Version: TRS-80 Level II BASIC
Hardware: TRS-80
Software: none
Non-ANSI: not translatable

341. Mille Bornes

Author: Richard Kaapke

Source: Creative Computing May 79 (5:5) "Mille Bornes" pp. 114–121 (118–121)

Mille Bornes is a French game played with a special deck of cards. The game simulates a series of road trips. There are four types of cards that represent things that can happen to you in your "travels": distance cards (to move), hazard cards (to simulate road hazards), remedy cards (to cancel hazards), and safety cards (to prevent hazards). This version of the game lets you play Mille Bornes against the computer. Includes a sample run.

Lines: 183
Version: CP/M Microsoft Extended BASIC
Hardware: none
Software: none
Non-ANSI: CLEAR, strings, OR(), SPACE$(), INSTR(), PRINT USING, extended IF, LINE INPUT

369. FORT: Defend a Fort from Indian Attack

Author: D. Stanley, D. Butlien, and S. Cohen

Source: Creative Computing Aug 79 (5:8) "FORT" pp. 120–123 (122–123)

In this game your task is to defend a fort from a band of rampaging Indians. You have 120 men under your command. In addition, you have 4 cannons, 20 cannon balls, and 2,300 rounds of ammo. You must deploy your forces so as to keep the Indians at bay until reinforcements can arrive. Watch out for flying arrows. Includes a sample run.

Lines: 238
Version: DEC BASIC
Hardware: none
Software: none
Non-ANSI: extended IF, strings, LINPUT

SPACE GAMES

872. MOTIE

Author: Mac Oglesby

Source: People's Computer Company Jan 76 (4:4) "MOTIE" pp. 20–21 (20–21)

In the distant future human beings control most of the galaxy. Travel between star systems involves space warp jumps. The Moties are the only intelligent nonhuman life ever discovered. The Moties are expanding out into the galaxy. You must prevent this. You control three guardian spaceships which you can maneuver to protect the galaxy. This version of MOTIE can be played by one or two players. If two people play, one person controls the Moties. The Moties win if they remain untrapped after 15 moves or if they reach "location zero." Includes a sample run.

Lines: 297
Version: Dartmouth BASIC
Hardware: none
Software: none
Non-ANSI: strings, STR$(), LINPUT, SEG$(), ASC(), CHANGE, VAL(), MAT operations, ' (used in place of REM)

873. RESCUE

Author: Mac Oglesby

Source: People's Computer Company Jan 76 (4:4) "RESCUE" pp. 22–23 (22–23)

Lines: 270
Version: Honeywell 600/6000 BASIC
Hardware: none
Software: none
Non-ANSI: DAT$( ), strings

421. STAR TREK for Tiny BASIC

Author: Erik Mueller

Source: *Dr. Dobb's Journal of Computer Calisthenics &
Orthodontia* Jun–Jul 76 (1:6)
"Tiny TREK" pp. 36–37 (37)

Updates: correction
*Dr. Dobb's Journal of Computer Calisthenics &
Orthodontia* Aug 76 (1:7)
"MINOL: Tiny Trek—More Details & a
Correction" p. 31 (31)

STAR TREK is a game based on the television series of
the same name. The object is to wipe out the Klingons.
This version is one written for Tiny BASIC systems. It has
Klingons, stars, and starbases.

Lines: 68
Version: Tiny BASIC
Hardware: none
Software: none
Non-ANSI: not translatable

879. TINY TREK

Author: Li-Chen Wang

Source: *People's Computer Company* Jul 76 (5:1)
"TINY TREK" pp. 22–23 (23)

Another version of STAR TREK. This one is written for
Tiny BASIC (a class of BASIC designed to run on systems
with very little RAM). Tiny Trek has the usual commands, including Report, Sensors, Phasers, Torpedos,
and Warp Engines.

Lines: 130
Version: Tiny BASIC
Hardware: none
Software: none
Non-ANSI: not translatable

2. STAR TREK

Author: Gerald Herd

Source: *Byte* Sep 76 (13)
"A BASIC STAR TREK Trainer" pp. 40–42
(40–41)

Updates: correction
Byte Jan 77 (2:1)
"A Glitch Pair in Close Orbit" p. 99 (99)

This is a game of interplanetary combat. The object of the
game is to enter commands so as to guide the *Enterprise* in
combat against a Klingon (run by the computer). There
are seven commands including "fire phasers," "maneuver
to attack," and "surrender" (if you're a coward). The
output is on a regular terminal and does not require a
special graphics terminal. Includes a sample run.

Lines: 202
Version: Data General BASIC
Hardware: none
Software: none
Non-ANSI: multiple-assignment, GOSUB . . . OF

4. STAR TREK: Flights of Fancy with the Enterprise

Author: David Price

Source: *Byte* Mar 77 (2:3)
"Flights of Fancy with the Enterprise" pp.
106–113 (106–109)

Updates: correction
Byte Aug 77 (2:8)
"Bug Report on 'Flights of Fancy . . .'" pp.
10–12 (12)

This is a rather large version of STAR TREK. You command the *Enterprise*; the computer commands a fleet of
Klingon ships. The object of the game is to rid the galaxy
of the hated Klingons. The program runs on a normal
terminal and does not require a special graphics terminal.
Includes a flow chart, sample run, and a list of program
variables.

Lines: 399
Version: not given
Hardware: none
Software: none
Non-ANSI: HP strings, PRINT USING, IMAGE, MAT
operations, multiple-assignment, LIN(),
SPA(), extended IF

929. STAR TREK

Author: L. Cochran

Source: *Personal Computing* Mar–Apr 77 (1:2)
"A STARTREK Walkthrough" pp. 126–130
(128–129)

Updates: correction
Personal Computing Mar 78 (2:3)
"Starburst" p. 5 (5)

STAR TREK is a strategy game in which you, as the captain of the *Enterprise,* attempt to destroy the Klingon cruisers which threaten to obliterate the Federation. You have a limited amount of time and energy to complete your mission. The playing field is a galaxy laid out in an 8 quadrant-by-8 quadrant matrix. Each quadrant consists of 64 sectors, each also arranged in an 8-by-8 matrix. Within the galaxy are Klingons, stars, starbases, and the *Enterprise* itself. You have six commands: warp engines, short range sensors, long range sensors, phasers, photon torpedoes, and galactic records. When you move, a map of your sector is printed out. Includes a sample run.

Lines: 144
Version: not given
Hardware: none
Software: none
Non-ANSI: strings, STR$(), extended IF, ASC()

467. Apple STAR-TREK

Author: Robert Bishop

Source: *Interface Age* May 77 (2:6)
"Apple STAR-TREK" pp. 132–134 (134)

This is the game of STAR TREK for the Apple computer. You must pilot the *Enterprise* and drive the Klingons from the galaxy. The galaxy is divided into quadrants, with the quadrants being themselves divided into sectors. You must destroy the 7 Klingon spaceships within 15 stardates. You have six commands available including "short range sensor scan" and "move the *Enterprise.*"

Lines: 88
Version: Apple BASIC
Hardware: Apple computer
Software: none
Non-ANSI: not translatable

240. UFO

Author: Raymond Kernay

Source: *Creative Computing* Jul–Aug 77 (3:4)
"UFO" pp. 141–143 (141–142)

UFO is a strategy game in which you play against the computer in a life-and-death struggle for superiority in space. It takes place after a space war with another planet in which both planets were destroyed. only you and an enemy ship are left. You command a ship with heavy guns, warheads, and lazers (*sic*). The object of the game is to destroy the enemy spacecraft before it can destroy you. The enemy has capabilities similar to yours. This game is essentially a variation on STAR TREK. Includes a sample run.

Lines: 121
Version: not given
Hardware: none
Software: none
Non-ANSI: SLEEP, LINPUT, strings

644. STAR TREK for the TRS-80

Author: Ed Juge

Source: *Kilobaud* Oct 78 (22)
"Action on the *Enterprise*" pp. 76–78 (77–78)

Updates: corrections
Kilobaud Microcomputing Jan 79 (25)
" 'Action' . . . Elucidation" p. 21 (21)

This is STAR TREK written for TRS-80 Level I BASIC. This version of STAR TREK uses the TRS-80's graphics capabilities to make the game more interesting. Information is displayed continuously on the screen. Your objective, as usual, is to wipe out all the Klingons. You have the standard set of features including warp drive, phasers, and scanners. Includes a list of the program variables.

Lines: 127
Version: TRS-80 Level I BASIC
Hardware: TRS-80
Software: none
Non-ANSI: not translatable

TIC-TAC-TOE

475. Tic-Tac-Toe

Author: Bud Shamburger

Source: *Interface Age* Aug 77 (2:9)
"TIC TAC" p. 170 (170)

This is the game of Tic-Tac-Toe played against the computer. In this version, the computer deliberately makes mistakes once in a while just to make the game a little more interesting. Program listing only.

Lines: 187
Version: MITS BASIC ver. 4.0
Hardware: none
Software: none
Non-ANSI: DEFINT, strings, ' (used in place of REM)

117. SQUARE: A "Square" Version of Tic-Tac-Toe

Author: Mac Oglesby

Source: *Calculators/Computers Magazine* Nov 77 (1:3)
"SQUARE" pp. 84–90 (86–89)

SQUARE is a game you can play against the computer or against another player in a "square" version of Tic-Tac-Toe. You work on a 5-by-5 board. You and the other player take turns choosing positions on the board. The object of the game is to choose four points that form a square, while at the same time blocking your opponent from doing the same. Includes a sample run.

Lines: 328
Version: Dartmouth BASIC
Hardware: none
Software: none
Non-ANSI: strings, LINPUT, CHANGE, SEG$(), VAL(), MAT operations, multiple-assignment, STR$(), ' (used in place of REM)

617. 3-D Tic-Tac-Toe

Author: Joseph Roehrig

Source: *Kilobaud* Apr 78 (16)
"3-D Tic-Tac-Toe" pp. 66–69 (67–69)

Updates: correction
Kilobaud Jun 78 (18)
"Demystifying the April Tic-Tac-Toe Program" pp. 20, 110 (20, 110)

improvements
Kilobaud Sep 78 (21)
"Another Dimension of 3-D Tic-Tac-Toe" p. 19 (19)

This is a high-powered type of Tic-Tac-Toe played against the computer. In this version of Tic-Tac-Toe there are 4 separate boards, each 4-by-4. The boards may be thought of as being "stacked" on top of each other so as to form a "cube." As in Tic-Tac-Toe, the object is to get a straight line filled with your markers. In 3-D Tic-Tac-Toe, not only can you get a line on any one of the boards, but you can get a line through the cube as well. There are three versions of the game provided. The first version is a simple 4-by-4 board (not 3-D). The second version is the 3-D version. This version can be beaten. The third version is an almost unbeatable 3-D game. The version listed is the third one. The other two versions are created by adding patches. Includes a flowchart, list of variables, and a sample run.

Lines: 61 (plus patches)
Version: Altair 3.2 BASIC
Hardware: none
Software: none
Non-ANSI: strings, extended IF

39. Beatable Tic-Tac-Toe

Author: Mike Stoddard

Source: *Byte* Dec 78 (3:12)
"Tic-Tac-Toe in BASIC" pp. 174–176 (175–176)

Updates: correction
Byte Feb 79 (4:2)
"Tic-Tac?" p. 43 (43)

commentary
Byte Apr 79 (4:4)
"Successful Transformation" p. 8

The problem with Tic-Tac-Toe is that between two good players every game ends in a draw. Here is a Tic-Tac-Toe player that livens up the game a little by making mistakes from time to time. If you're clever, you should be able to find out the patterns of moves that fool the computer, and thus be able to beat the machine every time. (By making a one-line change in the program, you can also make it unbeatable.) Includes a sample run.

Lines: 159
Version: not given
Hardware: none
Software: none
Non-ANSI: HP strings

60. Unbeatable Tic-Tac-Toe

Author: Delmer Hinrichs

Source: *Byte* May 79 (4:5)
"Tic-Tac-Toe" pp. 196–203 (198–202)

Updates: corrections
Byte Aug 79 (4:8)
"Tic Tac Bug" p. 194 (194)

commentary
Byte Oct 79 (4:10)
"Tic-Tac-Tactics" p. 175

commentary
Byte Jan 80 (5:1)
"Tic Tac Rebuttal" p. 14

This program plays an unbeatable game of Tic-Tac-Toe. The computer never loses; the best you can hope for is a draw.

Lines: 200
Version: TDL 8K BASIC
Hardware: none
Software: none
Non-ANSI: extended IF, strings

WAR GAMES

163. Depth Charge Game

Author: Dana Noftle

Source: *Creative Computing* Nov–Dec 74 (1:1)
"Depth Charge" pp. 18–19 (19)

In this game, you are the captain of the destroyer USS Digital. An enemy submarine lurks in the waters beneath. You must destroy the sub by accurately dropping a depth charge on it. To do this, you specify a position and depth to drop a depth charge. With each depth charge, the computer tells you about how far off you were and in what direction. Includes a sample run.

Lines: 31
Version: not given
Hardware: none
Software: none
Non-ANSI: strings, extended IF

176. GEOWAR: Missile Firing Game

Author: Gary Lorenc; modified by David Ahl

Source: *Creative Computing* May–Jun 75 (1:4)
"GEOWAR" pp. 10–11 (10)

Updates: commentary
Creative Computing Sep–Oct 75 (1:5)
" 'Feature' Letter to the Editor" p. 9

GEOWAR is a simple missile-firing game. You try to hit an enemy target by aiming a missile. As you shoot, the enemy moves around. Includes a sample run.

Lines: 240
Version: BASIC-PLUS
Hardware: none
Software: none
Non-ANSI: extended IF

177. ICBM

Author: Paul Calter

Source: *Creative Computing* May–Jun 75 (1:4)
"ICBM" p. 12 (12)

Your radar screen springs to life and picks up an enemy missile headed your way. In this missile-against-missile game you must guide your own surface-to-air missile

(SAM) against the enemy. As the game progresses, the computer prints out the positions of both missiles so that you can guide your own missile in on the foe. Includes a sample run.

Lines: 50
Version: not given
Hardware: none
Software: none
Non-ANSI: strings

181. SEAWAR

Author: David Paxton; modified by Mary Dobbs

Source: *Creative Computing* May–Jun 75 (1:4)
"SEAWAR" pp. 32–33 (33)

In this game you command a fleet of ships. An enemy force is attacking you. You must fire back with depth charges and guns, specifying the elevation to raise your guns to. Includes a sample run.

Lines: 221
Version: Hewlett-Packard 2000F BASIC
Hardware: none
Software: none
Non-ANSI: HP strings, PRINT USING, IMAGE, extended IF, multiple-assignment, ENTER

190. CIVIL: Civil War Game

Author: L. Cram, L. Goodie, and D. Hibbard

Source: *Creative Computing* Sep–Oct 75 (1:5)
"Civil War" pp. 55–57 (57)

CIVIL is a program that simulates 14 battles of the Civil War. You play the part of a Confederate Commander. For each battle, you decide how much to spend on food, salaries, and ammunition, as well as which battle strategy you wish to employ. The program controls other factors such as the number of men and the amount of money each side will have. The CIVIL simulation uses this information to determine the outcome of the battle. It compares the casualties of the simulated battle with those of the actual battle. Includes a sample run.

Lines: 237
Version: not given
Hardware: none
Software: none
Non-ANSI: none

195. Artillery Game for Several Players

Author: Brian West

Source: *Creative Computing* Jan–Feb 76 (2:1)
"WAR 3" pp. 69–70 (70)

This artillery game lets two or more players lob cannon balls at each other. (The computer doesn't participate.) You specify the distances between the players and the muzzle velocities of the various guns. The players then take turns raising their weapons to the appropriate angles and firing way. Includes a sample run.

Lines: 143
Version: H-P 2000 BASIC
Hardware: none
Software: none
Non-ANSI: HP strings, MAT ZER()

581. Artillery Practice

Author: Herman DeMonstoy

Source: *Kilobaud* Jun 77 (6)
"Artillery Practice" pp. 34–36 (36)

This program is a game that simulates practice firing of artillery. This game can be played by one to ten players. The object of the game is to hit a "target." The only information you are given is the X and Y coordinates of the target. From this you must estimate the angle to elevate the artillery and the angle to rotate it, so as to hit the target. Includes a flowchart and sample run.

Lines: 133
Version: SWTP 8K BASIC
Hardware: none
Software: none
Non-ANSI: DIGITS, strings, extended IF

496. WORLD POWER

Author: Joe Jaworski

Source: *Interface Age* Feb 78 (3:2)
"WORLD POWER" pp. 167–171 (171)

WORLD POWER is a war game played against the computer. The object of the game is to conquer all of the computer's countries by wiping out each country's forces. The game consists of 10 countries with 5 defenses and 4 shores for each country. The defenses include troops, planes, artillery, tanks, and missiles. There are five com-

mands: "show country status," "transport defenses," "show global status," "spy mission," and begin attack." The article describes some strategy for the game. Includes a sample run.

Lines: 144
Version: SWTPC 8K BASIC ver. 2.0
Hardware: none
Software: none
Non-ANSI: strings, extended IF, LINE

629. BATTLESHIP

Author: Harley Dyk

Source: *Kilobaud* Jul 78 (19)
"BATTLESHIP!" pp. 84–87 (85–86)

The game of BATTLESHIP pits you against your computer in sea combat. Both you and the computer have 10-by-10 grids. On these grids are "ships" (rows of markers) placed vertically or horizontally. Each player's board is hidden from the other. You and the computer alternate taking "shots." If either you or the computer scores a hit, the other must give the name of the ship hit. The object of the game is to sink all of the computer's ships. Includes a sample run.

Lines: 122
Version: MITS Extended BASIC
Hardware: none
Software: none
Non-ANSI: CLEAR, RUN (used as a program statement), extended IF, strings, two-letter variables, ON . . . GOSUB

964. Artillery Game

Author: Laurence Dishman

Source: *Personal Computing* Jul 78 (2:7)
"Gunner Game" pp. 64–66 (64–65)

This game is a simulation of an artillery battle. The object is to knock out the computer's guns before they can destroy you. You are given the range in meters to each enemy gun. You then enter an elevation for your gun. If you hit the enemy gun, you destroy it. At the same time, the computer will be firing back at you, trying to destroy your position. At the end of your "mission" you will be assigned a rating based on your gunnery efficiency. Includes a sample run.

Lines: 108
Version: North Star BASIC V6 R3
Hardware: none
Software: none
Non-ANSI: HP strings, DEF . . . FNEND, extended IF, SQRT(), %() (used to format printouts)

394. USWAR: United States War Game

Author: Garth Dollahite

Source: *Creative Computing* Oct 79 (5:10)
           "USWAR" pp. 140–144 (141–144)

USWAR is a modern-day civil war game which uses a map of the United States as a playing board. The battle is between the East and the West; you take one side, the computer takes the other. You control bases, missiles, armies, and mines. The object is to try to defeat the opposing side by strategically deploying your forces. Includes a sample run.

Lines: 584
Version: Microsoft BASIC
Hardware: none
Software: none
Non-ANSI: strings, RESTORE [line number], extended IF, LINE INPUT, PRINT USING

WARI

896. Mini-KALAH

Author: Jon Stedman

Source: *People's Computers* Sep–Oct 77 (6:2)
           "The Bead Game" pp. 35–39 (38–39)

Mancala is a class of ancient games found in many parts of the world. In Africa it goes by the names Wari and Awari. In Syria the game is known as Kalah. Mini-KALAH is a computer version of this game. You can play against either the computer or another player. The game is played in a ring of 10 cups. The cups have beads in them. With each turn, you take the beads from one cup and distribute them counterclockwise to other cups in the circle. You score points when beads fall into your "scoring" cup. Includes sample runs.

Lines: 220
Version: UNIX BASIC-Plus
Hardware: none
Software: none
Non-ANSI: strings, LEFT(), extended IF, ! (used in place of REM)

749. Wari

Author: L. D. and P. H. Stander

Source: *Kilobaud Microcomputing* Nov 79 (35)
           "Wari" pp. 118–120 (118–120)

Just because a game is simple to play, it doesn't necessarily mean that the game can't have high strategy. An example of this is the game of wari (sometimes known as mancala). In this game, two players face off over a set of 12 cups. The cups contain stones. Each player in his turn picks up a cup and distributes the stones in the cup into succeeding cups, one stone per cup. Play continues until one player has no stones to move, and thus loses. This computer version of the game gives you the option of playing against the computer or another human. Includes a flowchart and sample runs.

Lines: 153
Version: Extended Benton Harbor BASIC
Hardware: none
Software: none
Non-ANSI: strings, LINE INPUT, SPC(), ASC(), extended IF, PAUSE, CLEAR

WORD SEARCH PUZZLES

121. WORDFIND

Author: Mac Oglesby

Source: *Calculators/Computers Magazine* Feb 78 (2:2)
           "WORDFIND" pp. 64–68 (66–68)

WORDFIND generates a 20-by-24 grid of letters in which are hidden words from one of several categories. You may choose one of four categories (computers, flowers, animals, unusual words), or you may make up your own category. The computer then arranges the words in horizontal, vertical, or diagonal order. The letters in the word may be printed out in either forward or reverse order. The computer "hides" the words by picking random letters to surround the words. The object of the game is to find the words in the matrix and circle them. A list of the words is printed out on the worksheet along with the puzzle. Includes a sample run.

Lines: 238
Version: Dartmouth BASIC
Hardware: sequential file device
Software: none
Non-ANSI: strings, LINPUT, SEG$(), MAT operations, CHANGE, FILE, TYP(), INPUT #, ' (used in place of REM)

304. Word Search Puzzle Generator

Author: Leor Zolman

Source: *Creative Computing* Nov–Dec 78 (4:6)
           "Puzzle" pp. 154–155 (154–155)

Updates: modification
            Creative Computing May 79 (5:5)
            "Word Search Program" p. 10 (10)

This program creates word search puzzles. Word search puzzles are the type of puzzle that consists of a large block of scrambled letters. Somewhere in the letter block are hidden words. The words can run horizontally, diagonally, or vertically. This program generates such puzzles from words that you supply. Includes a sample run.

Lines: 129
Version: Microsoft BASIC
Hardware: none
Software: none
Non-ANSI: CLEAR, strings, extended IF, ASC(), multi-letter variables, POS()

WUMPUS

863. Hunt the Wumpus

Author: not given

Source: program listing only
People's Computer Company Jan 75 (3:3)
"Listings" p. 24 (24)

The Wumpus lives in a cave of 23 rooms. Each room has three tunnels leading to other rooms. Your job is to hunt down the Wumpus. While wandering around in the caves, you must beware of hazards. There are bottomless pits and superbats (the Wumpus is not bothered by the hazards because he has sucker feet and is too big for a bat to lift). On each turn you may move or shoot a crooked arrow. You have five arrows, each of which can go into one to five rooms. If you run out of arrows, you lose.

Lines: 225
Version: not given
Hardware: none
Software: none
Non-ANSI: strings, extended IF

189. Hunt the Wumpus

Author: Gregory Yob

Source: *Creative Computing* Sep–Oct 75 (1:5)
"Hunt the Wumpus" pp. 51–54 (54)

The Wumpus lives in a cave with 20 rooms. Each room has three tunnels leading to other rooms. You must try to shoot the Wumpus with one of your "crooked" arrows (they can zigzag around). While stalking the Wumpus you must beware of Superbats and Bottomless Pits. You must also beware of the Wumpus itself, since it will be trying to eat *you!* Includes a sample run.

Lines: 228
Version: not given
Hardware: none
Software: none
Non-ANSI: strings, extended IF

194. WUMPUS II

Author: Gregory Yob

Source: *Creative Computing* Jan–Feb 76 (2:1)
"Wumpus 2" pp. 66–68 (67–68)

The Wumpus lurks around in caves. In this version of the Wumpus-hunting game, you can scramble around in a variety of cave setups. As always, the object is to hit the Wumpus with one of your "crooked" arrows (they're called crooked arrows because they can turn corners). At the same time you must avoid Bottomless Pits, Superbats, and you also must avoid getting eaten by the Wumpus itself. Includes a sample run.

Lines: 317
Version: not given
Hardware: none
Software: none
Non-ANSI: HP strings, extended IF, GOSUB . . . OF

568. HUNT THE WUMPUS

Author: Joe Kasser

Source: *Kilobaud* Feb 77 (2)
"Beware the Wumpus" pp. 40–42 (41–42)

Updates: correction
Kilobaud Jun 77 (6)
"Corrections" p. 141 (141)

This is the game of HUNT THE WUMPS. The Wumpus is a strange animal. It lives in a burrow of 20 caves that it shares with its mate, friends, and superbats. The object of this game is to find the Wumpus, kill it, and bring it back to the surface. This task is made difficult by "earthquakes," "Freddy, the fearless bat," "bottomless pits," and the fact that you are given only five arrows to shoot. Includes a sample run.

Lines: 146
Version: MITS BASIC
Hardware: none
Software: none
Non-ANSI: strings, extended IF, ON . . . GOSUB

912. WUMPUS for TRS Level I BASIC

Author: Clyde Farrell

Source: *People's Computers* May–Jun 78 (6:6)
"TRS-80 Talk" pp. 54–57 (55)

The object of WUMPUS is to descend into a labyrinth of caves to hunt a Wumpus and then return to the surface with your catch. On your way, you must cope with a variety of hazards. You have a limited supply of arrows with which to shoot the Wumpus. This version of WUMPUS uses TRS Level I BASIC abbreviations for the BASIC commands. Includes a sample run.

Lines: 90
Version: TRS Level I BASIC
Hardware: none
Software: none
Non-ANSI: not translatable

MISCELLANEOUS

192. SPLAT2: Sling Mud at a "Schmoo"

Author: Frederick Bell

Source: *Creative Computing* Sep–Oct 75 (1:5) "Schmoo" pp. 59–60 (60)

Schmoos love to have mud thrown at them (talk about masochists!). You type in a direction and elevation to lob the mud balls. With a little practice you should be able to give the schmoos exactly what they want. Includes a sample run.

Lines: 90
Version: not given
Hardware: none
Software: none
Non-ANSI: strings

207. WATCHMAN

Author: Mac Oglesby

Source: *Creative Computing* Sep–Oct 76 (2:5) "WATCHMAN" pp. 74–75 (74–75)

This is a version of the "draw a figure without retracing or lifting your pencil" puzzle. You act as a watchman hired to patrol a small village. You must do this as efficiently as possible. This means that you must find a path that does not cause you to retrace your steps at any point. Includes a sample run.

Lines: 283
Version: Standard BASIC
Hardware: none
Software: none
Non-ANSI: strings, multiple-assignment, CHANGE, MAT operations, SST(), VAL(), ASC(), STR$()

882. Secret Code Game

Author: Franz Armbruster

Source: *People's Computer Company* Sep–Oct 76 (5:2) "HATS" p. 31 (31)

Updates: more readable listing *People's Computer Company* Nov–Dec 76 (5:3) "The Readable Listings Page!" p. 43 (43)

The computer is acting as a "spy". It has a code system which it is using to communicate with other spies. Your task is to try to break the code. You do this by giving the computer numbers. It then responds with another number. You continue with this until you can figure out what system the computer is using to generate its responses. When you guess one code system, the computer moves on to a harder one. We're not sure how the hats got into all of this.

Lines: 165
Version: not given
Hardware: none
Software: none
Non-ANSI: nonstandard strings, CHAR()

426. ZAPP

Author: Dan Elliott

Source: *Dr. Dobb's Journal of Computer Calisthenics & Orthodontia* Feb 77 (2:2) "ZAPP . . . Converted to 12K BASIC" p. 24 (24)

ZAPP is a game for the VDM video display board. Originally written in CASUAL, this program has been converted to BASIC. The object is to hit a "moon man" with lightning bolts. The moon man is at the top of the screen. You launch bolts from the bottom of the screen.

Lines: 34
Version: MITS 12K BASIC
Hardware: VDM video interface
Software: none
Non-ANSI: OUT, POKE, INP(), extended IF

226. FLIP

Author: John James

Source: *Creative Computing* Mar–Apr 77 (3:2) "FLIP" p. 126 (126)

There are many situations in life where the name of the game is, "Guess what the other person is thinking." Competitive bargaining is such a situation. In such "games," the other person will be trying to vary the strategy so as to anticipate your anticipation. Here is a computer game that models those situations. In this game, the computer guesses "yes" or "no." Your job is to anticipate what the computer will print. The rub is, the computer watches your behavior and tries to make its decisions so as to increase the chances that you will be wrong. To make things even more difficult, the computer does not strictly maximize its chances—it throws a little randomness into its decisions. The game ends after 50 turns; a score of 24 or more correct answers is good. Includes a sample run.

> *Lines:* 84
> *Version:* not given
> *Hardware:* none
> *Software:* none
> *Non-ANSI:* strings

889. ZOT

> *Author:* Marc LeBrun

> *Source:* *People's Computer Company* Mar–Apr 77 (5:5)
> "ZOT" pp. 38–39 (38–39)

In the game of ZOT, two (human) players compete to get the last bite of a rectangular "cookie." A move, called a "ZOT," consists of taking all the stars in a line between a given side of the board and a particular star (pretend you're an anteater). You get to choose how many rows and columns the board has.

> *Lines:* 216
> *Version:* HP BASIC
> *Hardware:* none
> *Software:* none
> *Non-ANSI:* HP strings

892. CAPTURE

> *Author:* Mac Oglesby

> *Source:* *People's Computers* Jul–Aug 77 (6:1)
> "CAPTURE" pp. 24–27 (26–27)

In CAPTURE, the computer generates a board randomly filled with letters. You can play against the computer or against another player. With each turn, you select a letter on the board. You capture all the characters within 1 centimeter of the one you have selected. The object is to capture the most characters. Includes a sample run.

> *Lines:* 235
> *Version:* not given
> *Hardware:* none
> *Software:* none
> *Non-ANSI:* strings, LINPUT, CHANGE, MAT operations, SEG$( ), multiple-assignment, ' (used in place of REM)

588. TIME BOMB

> *Author:* Dave Culbertson

> *Source:* *Kilobaud* Aug 77 (8)
> "Time Bomb Game" pp. 82–83 (83)

This is a Time Bomb game. The object of the game is to deactivate a bomb within a given time limit. The bomb has a red wire, a green wire, a blue wire, and a set of purple wires. The purple wires all detonate the bomb. Of the red, green, and blue wires, one detonates the bomb, one does nothing, and one defuses the bomb. The program comments on your progress and keeps track of the time. When the time runs out, the bomb explodes. Boom.

> *Lines:* 57
> *Version:* MITS 8K BASIC
> *Hardware:* none
> *Software:* none
> *Non-ANSI:* extended IF, OUT, INP()

932. Petals Around the Rose

> *Author:* Ken Jackman

> *Source:* *Personal Computing* Sep–Oct 77 (1:5)
> "We're A-Leavin' Big D" pp. 120–123
>
> *Personal Computing* Jul 78 (2:7)
> "Petals Around the Rose Revisited" pp. 30–31 (31)

> *Updates:* commentary
> *Personal Computing* Dec 78 (2:12)
> "Petals Around the Rose Revisited" p. 6 (6)

In this game, the object is to guess the secret algorithm. The computer rolls a set of "dice." You then guess a number based on the numbers rolled. If you guess correctly, the computer says so. If you fail to guess the right number, the computer tells you the correct answer. This continues until you can guess what algorithm the computer is using to generate numbers. Includes a sample run.

> *Lines:* 108
> *Version:* not given
> *Hardware:* none
> *Software:* none
> *Non-ANSI:* none

8. BUG: Race to Build a Bug

> *Author:* David Higgins

> *Source:* *Byte* Oct 77 (2:10)
> "Structured Program Design" pp. 146–151 (148–151)

This game is included in an article on structured programming. The game of BUG pits you against the computer in a race to build a "bug." Play is controlled by the roll of computer "dice."

Lines: 130
Version: not given
Hardware: none
Software: none
Non-ANSI: multi-letter variables, extended IF, multiple-assignment, ; (used in place of PRINT), FIX@(), strings

493. TAX MAN

Author: Gary Young

Source: *Interface Age* Jan 78 (3:1)
"The Tax Man" pp. 164–169

listing
Interface Age Feb 78 (3:2)
"The Tax Man—Part 2" pp. 140–141
(140–141)

This is the game of Tax Man. The idea of the game is to fill out a 1040 form. If you get a refund, you win. If you end up owing Uncle Sam money, you lose. To make the game more complete, California State income tax and FICA are also calculated. The game has three modes: "new," "old update," and "old list." In "new" mode, the initial tax data are entered. "Old update" mode is then used to modify the data. "Old list" is used to print out the tax forms and calculate the tax. Includes a sample run.

Lines: 518
Version: North Star DOS BASIC
Hardware: sequential file device
Software: none
Non-ANSI: HP strings, OPEN, CLOSE, READ #, WRITE, extended IF, %() (used to format printouts)

277. BLACK BOX

Author: Jeff Kenton

Source: *Creative Computing* May–Jun 78 (4:3)
"BLACK BOX" pp. 142–143 (142)

Updates: adaptations for TRS-80 Level I BASIC
Creative Computing Nov–Dec 78 (4:6)
"Investment Analysis . . . Coming Up!"
p. 12 (12)

version for PET
Creative Computing Feb 80 (6:2)
"BLACKBOX for the PET" pp. 112–117
(116–117)

BLACK BOX is an 8-by-8 square in which several "atoms" are hidden. The object of the game is to discover the positions of the atoms by projecting "rays" at them from the sides of the box and noticing how these rays are deflected, reflected, or absorbed. Rays enter the box across one of the four edges and travel horizontally or vertically. To play the game, you first specify how many atoms are in the box. Then you send a ray into the box. The computer tells you whether the ray has been absorbed or reflected. If the ray is reflected, the program prints out what the deflection is. Includes a sample run.

Lines: 37
Version: MITS 8K BASIC
Hardware: none
Software: none
Non-ANSI: extended IF

503. MISFIT

Author: Bruce Scott

Source: *Interface Age* Aug 78 (3:8)
"*MISFIT*" p. 63 (63)

Misfit is a computer game for one to five players. The players compete against each other. To score, a player must recognize a relationship between four items which the computer presents. The first person to spot the misfit in the set gains a point or "letter." The object of the game is to build up enough letters to form the word "*Misfit*." Players can also gain points by challenging other players to state similarities in the sets presented. As written, the program has six sets of terms. You can add more as needed.

Lines: 47
Version: DEC BASIC-PLUS
Hardware: none
Software: none
Non-ANSI: strings, ! (used in place of REM), VAL(), NUM$(), RIGHT(), LEFT()

897. SANDPILE: Level a Sandpile With a Bulldozer

Author: Mac Oglesby

Source: *People's Computers* Sep–Oct 78 (6:2)
"SANDPILE" pp. 44–47 (46–47)

In this game you are at the controls of a giant bulldozer. Your job is to level a pile of sand without losing any. The sandpile is on a 7-by-7 board. As you move the bulldozer around, you push the sand across the board. Any sand that falls off the sides of the board is lost. Includes sample runs.

Lines: 189
Version: Dartmouth BASIC
Hardware: none
Software: none
Non-ANSI: strings, SEG$(), LINPUT, CHANGE, ' (used in place of REM)

778. WALL BREAK for the PET

Author: Alan Christensen

Source: *Micro* Dec 78–Jan 79 (8)
"Continuous Motion Graphics or How to Fake a Joystick with the PET" pp. 23–26 (24–26)

This is the game of WALL BREAK for the PET computer. Two "walls" and a "bat" are displayed on the screen. A ball bounces back and forth across the screen. Each time it hits a wall, the ball takes out part of the wall. The object is to direct the ball with the bat so that the ball breaks through the left wall before it can penetrate the right wall.

Lines: 63
Version: PET BASIC
Hardware: PET
Software: none
Non-ANSI: not translatable

658. Billiards

Author: Phil Feldman and Tom Rugg

Source: *Kilobaud Microcomputing* Jan 79 (25)
"Pseudo Graphics: An Inexpensive Approach" pp. 34–39 (37–38)

Billiards is supposed to be a game for aristocrats. Now you can be an aristocrat too with this billiards program. The program can run (with slight modifications) on any video terminal with an addressable cursor. The screen displays the cue ball and the two object balls. You specify the angle of your shot. The computer then makes the shot for you, bouncing the cue ball off the cushions and displaying the target ball strikes (if any). A patch is provided to allow the program to run on a Commodore PET. Includes a sample run.

Lines: 150 (plus patches)
Version: Altair 8K BASIC, ver. 3.2
Hardware: addressable-cursor video display
Software: none
Non-ANSI: extended IF, two-letter variables, strings, WAIT, OUT

1072. TRS-80 Memory Game

Author: Ramon Zamora

Source: *Recreational Computing* Jan–Feb 79 (7:4)
"TRS-80: The Memory Game" p. 15 (15)

How good is your memory? Test it with this memory tester for the TRS-80. The computer will flash a series of digits on the screen for about one second. You must then repeat the digits. As you get better, the string of digits gets longer.

Lines: 52
Version: TRS-80 Level II BASIC
Hardware: TRS-80
Software: none
Non-ANSI: not translatable

348. INSPECTOR CLEW-SO
Detective Game

Author: Ronald Carlson

Source: *Creative Computing* Jun 79 (5:6)
"INSPECTOR CLEW-SO" pp. 104–106 (106)

simultaneous printing of article
Recreational Computing May–Jun 79 (7:6)
"INSPECTOR CLEW-SO" pp. 42–43 (43)

Updates: commentary
Recreational Computing Sep–Oct 79 (8:2)
"The Perils of Publishing" p. 7 (7)

INSPECTOR CLEW-SO is a computerized detective game loosely patterned after the board game of Clue. A murder has occurred in a guest house. Your job is to track down the culprit. You use skillful questioning of the suspects to deduce the murderer's identity and bring the murderer to justice. Includes a list of program variables and a sample run.

Lines: 161
Version: Digital Group Maxi BASIC
Hardware: none
Software: none
Non-ANSI: HP strings, extended IF, EXIT, DEF . . . FNEND

1031. COMPUTE FOUR

Author: Mark Sawusch

Source: *Personal Computing* Jul 79 (3:7)
"Compute 4" pp. 42–45 (44–45)

COMPUTE FOUR is a computerized version of Milton Bradley's "Connect Four" game. The game is played on a 6-by-8 board which you can imagine as being placed on one end. You and the computer take turns "dropping" pieces down the columns of the board. The object is to get four pieces in a row while keeping the computer from doing likewise. Includes a flowchart.

Lines: 183
Version: Radio Shack Level II BASIC
Hardware: TRS-80
Software: none
Non-ANSI: not translatable

393. PRESS UPS

Author: Ron Behrns

Source: Creative Computing Oct 79 (5:10)
         "PRESS UPS" pp. 136–139 (138)

PRESS UPS is a program that simulates a game of the same name manufactured by Invicta. The game is played on a board filled with red, blue, and yellow pegs. The red and the blue pegs belong to each of two players; the yellow pegs are neutral. You alternate pressing down pegs; either your own, your opponent's, or neutral pegs. The peg you choose must be adjacent to a previously pressed peg. The game ends when there are no legal moves remaining. The player with the most pegs pressed down at that point wins. In this computer simulation, you can either play against the computer or let the computer act as a referee in a game between two humans. Includes a sample run.

Lines: 210
Version: SWTPC 8K BASIC ver. 2.0
Hardware: none
Software: none
Non-ANSI: strings, extended IF

740. Touch: The Game of Personal Contact

Author: Adrian R. Thornton

Source: Kilobaud Microcomputing Oct 79 (34)
         "Touch" pp. 166–167 (167)

"Touching" is one of the great social taboos of our culture. Except under very limited conditions, personal contact is out. This program deliberately uses touching to make a great party game. You gather together a group of people. The computer then randomly tells members of the group to touch various parts of their anatomies to other peoples'. The result is an uproarious mass of people trying to satisfy the computer's dictates. Includes a sample run.

Lines: 90
Version: Extended Benton Harbor BASIC
Hardware: none
Software: none
Non-ANSI: strings, CNTRL, extended IF, LINE
          INPUT, STR$(), PAUSE, MAX()

1119. Bingo for the TRS-80

Author: Karen D. Chepko

Source: Recreational Computing Nov–Dec 79 (8:3)
         "TRS-80 Bingo" p. 46 (46)

This game referee runs a bingo game for you. The program "calls out" random number-letter combinations, none of which are repeats of previously called combinations. The program maintains a continuous display of the combinations that have been called. Just the thing for church socials.

Lines: 47
Version: TRS-80 Level II BASIC
Hardware: TRS-80
Software: none
Non-ANSI: not translatable

3
MATH

ALGEBRA

612. Solve Polynomial Equations

Author: Mel Baker

Source: *Kilobaud* Mar 78 (15)
"Number-Crunching Time" pp. 42–46 (46)

Updates: *Kilobaud* Aug 78 (20)
"What's Your Sine?" p. 17

This program uses a brute force technique for solving polynomial equations. Many kinds of polynomial equations can be solved by fairly straightforward techniques. Others require a great deal of head-scratching even for a mathematician. If you don't require a general solution to a particular polynomial equation, answers to some difficult problems can be solved by brute force. The technique involves selecting an interval where the equation is known to cross the X-axis, and then gradually reducing the size of the interval until an approximate answer is found. This program uses this approach. Includes a flowchart, sample runs, and a list of program variables.

Lines: 43
Version: not given
Hardware: none
Software: none
Non-ANSI: none

563. Brute Force Equation Solvers

Author: Alfred Adler

Source: *Interface Age* Dec 79 (4:12)
"The Micro Mathematician" pp. 37–40 (39–40)

Sometimes, the easiest way to solve an equation is use a "brute force" method, as do these two programs. The first program uses the following method: Juggle the equation

so that one side equals zero. Iteratively step toward a likely root (a place where the equation equals zero). Compute trial values at intervals as you approach the approximate location of the root. When you pass the root and the sign of your results change, reverse your direction and reduce your interval. By sweeping back and forth over the area of the root, and constantly reducing your step size, you can come arbitrarily close to the root, thus solving your equation. The second program uses a refinement of the first technique known as the Newton-Raphson method. Includes sample runs.

Lines: 30, 26
Version: North Star BASIC (release 5)
Hardware: none
Software: none
Non-ANSI: EXIT, %() (used to format printouts), ! (used in place of PRINT)

ARITHMETIC

572. Multiplication Drill

Author: Jack Inman

Source: *Kilobaud* Feb 77 (2)
"7×9=56 . . . Right?" pp. 111–112 (111)

Updates: reprint
People's Computer Company Mar–Apr 77 (5:5)
"7×9=56 . . . Right?" pp. 28–29 (29)

This is a program to drill a child in multiplication tables. The child is given a series of sample problems and is asked to answer them. If the child types in an incorrect answer, he or she is asked to try again. If the correct answer is typed, the child is rewarded with randomly generated praise. The computer prints out the number of correct and incorrect answers at intervals. Includes a sample run.

Lines: 62
Version: Tiny BASIC
Hardware: none
Software: none
Non-ANSI: PR

229. Mathematics Drill and Practice

Author: David Ahl

Source: *Creative Computing* May–Jun 77 (3:3)
"CAI: Mathematics Drill and Practice"
pp. 82–85 (83–85)

Computer Assisted Instruction (CAI) was one of the earliest uses of computers in education. This is a group of four CAI programs to drill a student in mathematics. The first program presents vertical addition problems. The computer provides an addition problem, and the student is asked to answer it. The computer does not keep score. By adding 10 statements to the first program, you get the second program which can drill a student in both addition and subtraction. The third program generates multiplication problems. The student's name is used liberally in comments throughout the exercise. The fourth program presents nine different types of horizontal and vertical addition and subtraction problems. Includes sample runs.

Lines: 23, 33, 34, 122
Version: not given
Hardware: none
Software: none
Non-ANSI: strings

234. Addition Drill

Author: David Ahl

Source: *Creative Computing* Jul–Aug 77 (3:4)
"CAI: Structuring the Lesson to the Student"
pp. 62–64 (63)

The problem with most arithmetic drill programs is that they do not allow the student to "progress." Ideally, in Computer Assisted Instruction, as the student becomes proficient in one set of problems, the computer should begin to present the student with harder and harder problems. This program does just that with addition problems. As the student begins to master the exercises, the computer uses the student's current performance to decide when to move on to harder material. If the student begins to "backslide," the computer can also throw in easier problems until the student has caught up again. In this way, the computer can custom tailor an exercise drill to each individual student. Includes a sample run.

Lines: 35
Version: not given
Hardware: none
Software: none
Non-ANSI: none

109. Multiplication Drill

Author: Barbara Zanzig

Source: *Calculators/Computers Magazine* Oct 77 (1:2)
"Teaching Using Computers" pp. 69–73
(71–72)

This is a CAI multiplication drill. The program gives the student one-digit-times-one-digit multiplication problems. The problems can be in either vertical or horizontal format. Includes a list of program variables and a sample run. (Appeared originally in *Calculators, Computers, and Elementary Education.*)

Lines: 146
Version: none
Hardware: none
Software: none
Non-ANSI: strings

596. WORDMATH

Author: Mac Oglesby

Source: *Kilobaud* Oct 77 (10)
"Try WORDMATH!" pp. 90–92 (91–92)

WORDMATH generates worksheets of simple arithmetic problems written in words. These worksheets are designed to provide arithmetic practice for students. The worksheets require a student to read and write the word names for the numbers from 0 to 99, and to read the words for the four basic operations: addition, subtraction, multiplication, and division. The program prints both the problems and a separate list of answers for use as a correction key. Includes a sample run.

Lines: 104
Version: Dartmouth BASIC
Hardware: none
Software: none
Non-ANSI: strings, STR$(), ' (used in place of REM)

12. Program to Drill Students in Multiplication and Addition

Author: Robert Lloyd

Source: *Byte* Nov 77 (2:11)
"Simple Math Lessons" p. 60 (60)

This is a simple program to drill a student in multiplication and addition. The computer prints out sample multiplication and addition problems, and asks the student to answer them.

Lines: 65
Version: Tiny BASIC
Hardware: none
Software: none
Non-ANSI: PR

116. Division to Any Number of Decimal Places

Author: Douglas Scott

Source: *Calculators/Computers Magazine* Nov 77 (1:3)
"How Many Digits Do You Want?" pp. 75–80 (78)

One of the facts of life for users of both computers and calculators is the inherent limitation on the number of digits that can be handled in doing computations. Even computers with very long word lengths or double-precision arithmetic can handle only a relatively small number of digits. There are a variety of ways to get around these limitations. This program demonstrates one technique for doing computations to extreme accuracies. This program does division by placing each digit of the numbers involved in an array. Includes a sample run and a list of program variables.

Lines: 38
Version: not given
Hardware: none
Software: none
Non-ANSI: strings

246. Addition, Subtraction, Multiplication Drill

Author: Laura McLaughlin

Source: *Creative Computing* Nov–Dec 77 (3:6)
"CAI: Further Considerations for Presenting Multiple-Problem Types" pp. 74–77 (76–77)

This program presents students with practice problems in addition, multiplication, and subtraction. It is part of a series on Computer Assisted Instruction. The previous article in this series discussed a method of calculating a sliding grade level based on the range of the numbers presented in a particular problem. This program expands on the earlier program by recording each student's performance in a data file. The program constantly adjusts the student's grade level (and thus the level of difficulty of the problem presented) for each type of problem. This data, along with the student's name, is recorded for future sessions. Includes a sample run.

Lines: 140
Version: BASIC-E ver. K1.4
Hardware: sequential file device
Software: none
Non-ANSI: not translatable

601. Math Tutor

Author: Sanford Schumacher

Source: *Kilobaud* Dec 77 (12)
"The 'Learning Machine' " pp. 62–64 (64)

This is a program to help a student learn multiplication and division. The student is given a series of problems to solve, with the computer keeping track of right and wrong answers. The features of this program include: The student's name is used throughout the session. The student can select the type of problems to work on (multiplication or division). The same problem is immediately repeated when the student makes a mistake. The range of digits can be selected. The student can ask for his or her score at any time. Missed problems are remembered and repeated a little later. Includes a sample run.

Lines: 83
Version: MITS BASIC
Hardware: none
Software: none
Non-ANSI: strings, two-letter variables, VAL(), INSTR(), extended IF, ASC()

118. Math Homework Checker

Author: Karen Schreiber

Source: *Calculators/Computers Magazine* Jan 78 (2:1)
"Letter from Karen Schreiber" pp. 5–6 (6)

This program allows a student to check arithmetic homework. The student can specify addition, subtraction, multiplication, or division problems. The program accepts two numbers and asks the student for the correct answer. If he or she cannot answer correctly, the program will, after three tries, give the solution. Includes a sample run.

Lines: 65
Version: Altair Extended BASIC
Hardware: none
Software: none
Non-ANSI: strings, extended IF, ' (used in place of REM)

263. Multiplication Practice Using a Video Screen

Author: Laura McLaughlin

Source: *Creative Computing* Mar–Apr 78 (4:2)
"CAI: Interaction Between Student and Computer" pp. 44–49 (48–49)

This is the fourth in a series of articles on Computer Assisted Instruction. In this part of the series, the author investigates some of the more subtle areas of student-computer interaction. The program presented is a three-part system to drill students in multiplication. The first part of the program asks the student to multiply a number up to three digits long by a one-digit number. The program keeps track of how long it takes the student to answer. The next part of the program is a set of "flash-card" type problems. The third part is a set of "long" multiplications. The student must show all the intermediate steps in the multiplication. The program uses a nonstandard line-numbering system. It should be possible to change it over to regular numbering. Includes a sample output.

Lines: 300
Version: CBASIC ver. 1.0
Hardware: addressable-cursor video display
Software: none
Non-ANSI: not translatable

19. Multiplication Trainer

Author: Dennis Barbour

Source: Byte Apr 78 (3:4)
"User's Report: The SOL-20" pp. 126–130 (128)

This is a program to help a student learn multiplication by drilling in sample problems. The student specifies the numbers to be multiplied. The computer then asks what the answer is. The accompanying article describes the SOL-20 system. The SOL-20 system is not required to run the program. Included is a sample run.

Lines: 36
Version: SOL BASIC-5
Hardware: none
Software: none
Non-ANSI: none

132. Arithmetic Drill (Multiple Choice)

Author: Steve Robbins

Source: Calculators/Computers Magazine May 78 (2:5)
"Student Programs" pp. 37–41 (39)

This program drills a student in the four basic arithmetic operations: addition, subtraction, multiplication, and division. The program presents a series of problems to the student. For each problem, three answers are listed. The student must pick the correct answer. If he or she picks the correct answer, the student gets a point. If the student guesses incorrectly, he or she loses a point. At the end of the exercises, the program reports the student's score.

Lines: 100
Version: IBM BASIC
Hardware: none
Software: none
Non-ANSI: strings, : (used in place of REM)

953. Math Drill

Author: Mike Donahue

Source: Personal Computing May 78 (2:5)
"Math for Minors" pp. 75–76 (75)

This is a math drill to help students learn mathematical functions. The drill provides exercises in addition, subtraction, multiplication, and division. You can select the level of difficulty of the problems presented. You can also select what types of problems are presented: addition, subtraction, multiplication, division, or a combination of problems. The program provides the student with immediate feedback on how he or she is doing. The student's score is printed after every 10 problems; at the end of 50 problems the program ends. Includes a sample run.

Lines: 105
Version: SWTPC 4K BASIC
Hardware: none
Software: none
Non-ANSI: extended IF

511. Addition Practice with Stars to Count

Author: Karen Wolfe

Source: Interface Age Sep 78 (3:9)
"Child's Play Number Game for Beginning Micro-Bugs" pp. 128–129 (129)

This is an addition drill program for students just starting out. The program prints out practice addition problems in both horizontal and vertical formats. In addition, the program prints out groups of stars so the student can see and count the stars to get the answer. Includes a sample run.

Lines: 45
Version: North Star BASIC
Hardware: none
Software: none
Non-ANSI: HP strings, %() (used to format printouts)

512. Bilingual Math Tutor

Author: Marvin Mallon; modified by Alan Samov

Source: Interface Age Sep 78 (3:9)
"On a Bi-Lingual Math Tutoring Program" pp. 130–133 (131–133)

Teachers run into special problems where minority students are concerned. Often these students do not have an easy time learning English. This language problem makes it difficult for non-English-speaking students to learn math. This is a CAI math tutor that gets around this problem by doing its instruction in Spanish. The student can be drilled in addition, subtraction, multiplication, and division. Problems can be chosen so as to make the session easy or more difficult. Two versions of the program are supplied, one version in English and one version in Spanish. Only the program conversation is in Spanish; the Spanish language program uses the standard English language BASIC keywords. Includes a sample run.

Lines: 168, 180
Version: not given
Hardware: none
Software: none
Non-ANSI: strings, POKE, extended IF

919. Math Drill Using the Apple-II

Author: John Gaines

Source: *People's Computers* Sep–Oct 78 (7:2)
"Apple Math" pp. 41–43 (42–43)

Updates: correction
Recreational Computing May–Jun 79 (7:6)
"No End to Apple Math" p. 7 (7)

This is a Computer Assisted Instruction program that uses the Apple-II computer. The program drills a student in addition, multiplication, division, or subtraction. Includes a sample run.

Lines: 258
Version: Apple-II BASIC
Hardware: Apple-II
Software: none
Non-ANSI: not translatable

44. Unlimited Precision Division

Author: Jef Raskin

Source: *Byte* Feb 79 (4:2)
"Unlimited Precision Division" pp. 154–156 (154–156)

Updates: commentary
Byte May 79 (4:5)
"Periodic Answers" p. 210

How many digits of precision does your computer have? Seven? Fourteen? No matter how much precision your computer has, sooner or later you're going to need more.

Here is a demonstration program that shows you how to do division to any number of digits. The division of some numbers results in answers that are seemingly endless. For example, with this program you could divide 99,991 by 99,989 and get over 2,500 decimal digits with no repetition. Includes a sample run.

Lines: 15 (plus patches)
Version: Apple II Integer BASIC
Hardware: none
Software: none
Non-ANSI: extended IF

1102. Arithmetic/Negative Numbers Drill

Author: Tony Pola

Source: *Recreational Computing* Jul–Aug 79 (8:1)
"MATH" pp. 51–53 (52–53)

This is a drill to help students learn addition, multiplication, subtraction, and negative numbers. The student selects the category, and the computer presents problems in groups of ten. The problems get progressively harder, but the student must get at least seven out of ten right before being allowed to move from one level of difficulty to the next. Includes a sample run.

Lines: 221
Version: Wang BASIC
Hardware: none
Software: none
Non-ANSI: HEX(), KEYIN, SELECT, strings

1116. Elementary Math Trainer

Author: Karen D. Chepko

Source: *Recreational Computing* Nov–Dec 79 (8:3)
"TRS-80: Elementary Math" p. 27 (27)

This program drills children in elementary math operations. The program presents a child with problems in addition, subtraction, multiplication, and division. The program adjusts the difficulty of the problems based on what grade the child is in.

Lines: 64
Version: TRS-80 BASIC
Hardware: none
Software: none
Non-ANSI: CLS, DEFINT, strings, extended IF, PRINT USING

BAR CHARTS

684. Bar-Graph Generator for the PET

Author: Frederick Luffman

Source: *Kilobaud Microcomputing* Apr 79 (28)
"Bar-Graph Generator" pp. 90–92 (91–92)

Bar graphs are used commonly in business and science to display information. Sometimes called histograms, these graphs make it possible to quickly convey a general point about some data. Such a graph might, for example, show that the price of a stock has risen consistently for the last several years. This program uses the PET's graphics capabilities to generate bar graphs. The program is a general-purpose one, so the graphs can be easily changed around to accommodate many different types of data. Includes a sample output.

Lines: 108
Version: PET BASIC
Hardware: PET
Software: none
Non-ANSI: not translatable

1024. Bar Charts

Author: Robert Nicholson

Source: *Personal Computing* Jun 79 (3:6)
"The Thoughts Behind the Structure" pp. 29–36 (30–34)

Updates: correction
Personal Computing Aug 79 (3:8)
"Cut That Out!" p. 11 (11)

This program produces general bar charts. These charts can be used to represent a wide variety of data. You type in the data, along with information about labeling and scaling, for the chart. The computer then grinds out the bar chart. Includes a flowchart, list of program variables, and a sample run.

Lines: 175
Version: not given
Hardware: none
Software: none
Non-ANSI: strings, extended IF

1039. Quickie Bar Graph Printer

Author: James W. Cerny

Source: *Personal Computing* Aug 79 (3:8)
"Visual Aids for Business, Home and School" pp. 38–42 (40–42)

Updatse: correction
Personal Computing Jan 80 (4:1)
"Aiding Visual Aids" p. 7

Bar graphs (or histograms) are charts which use bars to represent quantities of things in different categories. This is a program for making up quickie bar graphs. You give the title of the chart and the number of items in each category. (The program does *not* do the counting and sorting by category for you.) The program then prints out a bar graph of the data. Includes sample runs.

Lines: 189
Version: not given
Hardware: none
Software: none
Non-ANSI: strings

CURVE FITTING

598. Curve Fitting Routines

Author: Russell Adams

Source: *Kilobaud* Nov 77 (11)
"Reliable Conversion Techniques" pp. 58–60 (58–60)

These are two programs to fit curves to sets of data points. The first program finds the straight line which best describes ("fits") a set of data points. The second program does the same thing, except it can fit not just a straight line, but also polynomials up to the sixteenth degree. The program can, for example, fit a parabola to a set of points. This second program is based on Chebyshev polynomials. Curve fitting programs such as these are often used to filter out random noise from analog data readings. Includes a list of program variables.

Lines: 15, 103
Version: not given
Hardware: none
Software: none
Non-ANSI: extended IF, two-letter variables, ' (used in place of REM)

289. Linear Model of Data (Regression Analysis)

Author: Kenneth Travers

Source: *Creative Computing* Sep–Oct 78 (4:5)
"A Computer Activity for Building a Linear Model of Data" pp. 104–105 (105)

Suppose you wish to draw the "best" line through a group of data points on a graph. How do you go about it? This process is known as linear modeling. You are trying to find a mathematical equation that models the data. This program allows you to model a group of data points by trying out various lines (models) to see which line produces the best "fit" (produces the smallest root mean square error). Includes a sample run. (Reprinted from *School Science and Mathematics*.)

Lines: 44
Version: not given
Hardware: none
Software: none
Non-ANSI: multiple-assignment

513. Approximating Data With Functions

Author: Endre Simonyl

Source: *Interface Age* Oct 78 (3:10)
"A Special Function Approximation Method and Its Application" pp. 74–77 (77)

Updates: corrected listing of program
Interface Age Feb 79 (4:2)
"Alan Miller Solves a Problem" pp. 6–10 (9–10)

commentary and corrections
Interface Age Dec 79 (4:12)
"More on a Function Approximation Program" pp. 13–14 (14)

Often in science or engineering you must do calculations using data that are in tabular form. This can be difficult and time-consuming. A better way to handle the problem than using the data directly is to find a function which approximates the data closely. This program accepts sets of data. It then tests up to 1,296 different functions, looking for the one which best describes the data. Approximation functions considered include linear, parabolic, exponential, hyperbolic, and elliptical functions. Includes a flowchart.

Lines: 105
Version: not given
Hardware: none
Software: none
Non-ANSI: ACOS(), ASIN(), strings, extended IF, ON . . . GOSUB

317. Multiple Regression Analysis

Author: David Chereb

Source: *Creative Computing* Feb 79 (5:2)
"Multiple Regression Analysis—Simplified" pp. 126–129 (127–129)

Multiple regression is a statistical technique for finding a relationship among a set of variables. The article uses the example of U.S. imports. The amount of imports in any given year is dependent on the Gross National Product, the size of the labor force, and other factors. But what is the exact relationship? Multiple regression can give you the answer. Given information about the factors, the program can generate an equation that gives the best estimate possible for the relationship of each of the factors to the dependent variable—in this case, U.S. imports. Includes a flowchart.

Lines: 235
Version: TRS-80 Level I BASIC
Hardware: none
Software: none
Non-ANSI: CLS, PRINT @, strings, extended IF

85. Parabolic Curve Fitting

Author: Fred R. Ruckdeschel

Source: *Byte* Oct 79 (4:10)
"Curve Fitting with Your Computer" pp. 150–160 (150–152)

Updates: commentary and correction
Byte Mar 80 (5:3)
"Correspondence Regarding 'Curve Fitting with Your Microcomputer' " p. 16

Very often in scientific and mathematical applications, you want to know what line best "describes" a set of data points. You can use linear regression to find out which straight line best fits the data. But sometimes a parabola or other curve might give you a better approximation of the data. This program is a least squares curve fitting routine that calculates which second-degree curve best fits the data points you specify. Includes sample runs.

Lines: 83
Version: North Star BASIC, Release 2, ver. 3
Hardware: none
Software: none
Non-ANSI: %() (used to format printouts), extended IF, SQRT()

DIFFERENTIAL EQUATIONS

315. Differential Equations

Author: Bruce Barnett

Source: *Creative Computing* Feb 79 (5:2)
"An Analysis of Change: Differential Equations" pp. 110–112 (112)

We live in a changing world. Many of the changes in our world can be expressed mathematically by what are known as differential equations. These equations express a rate of change in terms of the variables upon which the change is based. Examples of processes which can be described by differential equations include radioactive decay and compound interest. This program solves differential equations numerically. You type in the differential equation and the starting conditions. The program computes the results for varying intervals of the independent variable. Includes a sample run.

Lines: 41
Version: not given
Hardware: none
Software: none
Non-ANSI: none

546. Discrete Model Simulation Program

Author: Dennis E. Bahr

Source: *Interface Age* Aug–Sep 79 (4:8)
"Discrete Model Simulation Program" pp. 94–101 (99–101)

This simulation program can be used to simulate causal systems described by coupled first-order differential equations. It can be used to solve linear and nonlinear differential equations. Output is in the form of printed plots. Includes sample runs.

Lines: 282
Version: not given
Hardware: none
Software: none
Non-ANSI: strings, LPRINT, extended IF, DEF . . . FNEND, FNRETURN, LPRINT USING, SPC()

FACTORIALS

171. Computing Very Large Factorials

Author: Walter Koetke

Source: *Creative Computing* Mar–Apr 75 (1:3)
"Computing Factorials—Accurately" pp. 9–11 (9–11)

These programs show how to compute and print the factorials of very large numbers. The first program shows the normal way of computing factorials. The second program demonstrates an algorithm that allows for the com-

puting and printing of factorials with arbitrarily large numbers of digits. The third program is an improved version of the second. Includes sample runs.

Lines: 7, 19 (plus patches), 30
Version: not given
Hardware: none
Software: none
Non-ANSI: none

457. Extended Precision Factorials and Powers

Author: Tom Rugg and Phil Feldman

Source: *Interface Age* Aug 76 (1:9)
"Games & Things" pp. 54–55, 66 (54–55)

Most BASIC interpreters can't work with numbers that have more than a few significant digits. One method to get around this is to store the numbers in arrays, using one number in an array to represent one digit in the final number. This program uses this method to generate factorials and powers of numbers to arbitrarily large values. Includes a sample run.

Lines: 42
Version: Mits 8K BASIC
Hardware: none
Software: none
Non-ANSI: CLEAR, strings, STR$(), extended IF,

432. Factorial Using Iterative and Recursive Techniques

Author: Jef Raskin

Source: *Dr. Dobb's Journal of Computer Calisthenics & Orthodontia* Aug 77 (2:7)
"Friend Finds Factorial Flaw" p. 31 (31)

The factorial of a number n (denoted $n!$) is $1 \times 2 \times 3 \ldots \times n$. This program demonstrates two different ways of computing factorials. One way uses the standard iteration technique, simply going through a loop $n-1$ times. The other way a factorial can be computed is using a recursive function; that is, a function that actually calls itself. This program demonstrates both these techniques. Includes a sample run.

Lines: 39
Version: PolyMorphic System 5 BASIC
Hardware: none
Software: none
Non-ANSI: DEF . . . FNEND, extended IF

1080. Recursive Factorial Program

Author: Dennis Allison

Source: *Recreational Computing* Mar–Apr 79 (7:5)
"Two Recursive Functions in BASIC" p. 27
(27)

A procedure is recursive if it is defined in terms of itself. This program uses a recursive subroutine to compute the factorial function.

Lines: 12
Version: TRS-80 BASIC
Hardware: none
Software: none
Non-ANSI: extended IF

1007. Factorial Recursively and Iteratively

Author: Herbert Dershem

Source: *Personal Computing* Apr 79 (3:4)
"Recursive Programming in BASIC" pp. 16–18 (17)

A recursive subroutine is one that calls itself. An iterative subroutine is one that repeats the same process several times. These two subroutines compute the factorial function using, respectively, recursion and iteration.

Lines: 12, 9
Version: Radio Shack Level I BASIC
Hardware: none
Software: none
Non-ANSI: extended IF

65. Factorial Using Stirling's Approximation Technique

Author: Alan Miller

Source: *Byte* Jun 79 (4:6)
"BASIC Factorial" p. 206 (206)

This program calculates the factorials of numbers using the Stirling Approximation technique. Includes a sample run.

Lines: 8
Version: not given
Hardware: none
Software: none
Non-ANSI: none

550. Factorials of Large Numbers

Author: Walter L. Pragnell

Source: *Interface Age* Oct 79 (4:10)
"The Micro-Mathematician" pp. 39–46
(42–46)

The product of all the numbers from 1 to some number n is called "factorial n" and is denoted $n!$. Factorials are commonly used in statistics and in probability. These two programs compute the factorials of large numbers (i.e., n greater than 50). The first program computes $n!$ exactly, digit for digit, up to very large numbers. The second program generates factorials by adding the logarithms of their factors. Includes sample runs.

Lines: 25, 50
Version: not given
Hardware: none
Software: none
Non-ANSI: ! (used in place of PRINT), extended IF, %() (used to format printouts), CHR$()

FACTORING

870. Number Factoring

Author: Dick Whipple and John Arnold

Source: *People's Computer Company* Nov 75 (4:3)
"Tiny BASIC Runs" p. 11 (11)

This is a program to reduce a number to prime factors. Includes a sample run.

Lines: 34
Version: Tiny BASIC
Hardware: none
Software: none
Non-ANSI: none

876. Factors of a Range of Numbers

Author: Mac Oglesby

Source: *People's Computer Company* May 76 (4:6)
"Concision Has Its Place & So Do People" p. 16 (16)

This program prints out the factors of a list of numbers. You specify the range of numbers. The program then lists the numbers, giving the factors of each number. Two versions of the program are given: a regular version, and a compressed version with the remarks and excess spaces taken out. Includes a sample run.

Lines: 80, 51
Version: Dartmouth BASIC
Hardware: none
Software: none
Non-ANSI: strings, STR$(), ' (used in place of REM)

283. Prime Factors

Author: Jay Jeffery

Source: *Creative Computing* Jul–Aug 78 (4:4)
"Prime Factoring with Quasi-Primes" p. 143 (143)

A program that yields the prime factors of integers comes in handy at various levels of mathematics. It can be used to reduce fractions to lowest terms, to find greatest common factors, to find least common multiples, and to test if numbers are prime. This program uses a fast method to generate prime factors. The program is based on the generation of "quasi-primes." These quasi-primes greatly reduce the number of divisions required to screen possible prime factors. The program output is a list of the prime factors of the numbers entered. Includes a sample run.

Lines: 30
Version: not given
Hardware: none
Software: none
Non-ANSI: none

403. Prime Factors Program

Author: J. Jeffery

Source: *Creative Computing* Nov 79 (5:11)
"Prime Factors" p. 140 (140)

This program prints out the prime factors of numbers that you type in. Includes a sample run.

Lines: 30
Version: not given
Hardware: none
Software: none
Non-ANSI: not translatable

FIBONACCI NUMBERS

952. Fibonacci Numbers

Author: Donald Spencer

Source: *Personal Computing* May 78 (2:5)
"Playing the Game" pp. 73–74 (74)

The Fibonacci numbers are a series of numbers such that every number in the series equals the sum of the two previous numbers. This program prints out the first 22 Fibonacci numbers. Includes a flowchart. (This program appeared originally in the book *Game Playing with BASIC*.)

Lines: 14
Version: not given
Hardware: none
Software: none
Non-ANSI: none

1008. Fibonacci Numbers Recursively and Iteratively

Author: Herbert Dershem

Source: *Personal Computing* Apr 79 (3:4)
"Recursive Programming in BASIC" pp. 16–18 (17)

A recursive subroutine is one that calls itself. An iterative subroutine is one that repeats the same process several times. These two subroutines compute the nth number in the Fibonacci series using, respectively, recursion and iteration.

Lines: 14, 10
Version: Radio Shack Level I BASIC
Hardware: none
Software: none
Non-ANSI: extended IF

GEOMETRY

120. Geometric Figure Exercises

Author: Mac Oglesby

Source: *Calculators/Computers Magazine* Jan 78 (2:1)
"GEOPAGES" pp. 50–60 (57–60)

This program generates exercises in analytic geometry. The program prints out the vertices of various geometric figures. These figures can be rectangles, parallelograms, trapezoids, triangles, or quadrilaterals. If desired, the program can also print out the area and length of the perimeter of the figure presented. The figures that this program prints out can be used to teach students how to calculate the areas and perimeters of various geometric figures. Includes sample runs.

Lines: 284
Version: Dartmouth BASIC
Hardware: none
Software: none
Non-ANSI: ' (used in place of REM), strings, LINPUT, PRINT USING, ON . . . GOSUB

58. Cartesian/Spherical Coordinate Translators

Author: David Beard

Source: *Byte* May 79 (4:5)
"Spacewar in Tiny BASIC" pp. 110–115
(115)

When writing games that involve three-dimensional space, it is usually convenient to have the programs use rectangular (X − Y) coordinates. At the same time, data entry is often best done using spherical coordinates involving angles. These two routines convert back and forth between rectangular and spherical coordinates. Required ARCTAN and SINE routines are supplied in the same article.

Lines: 36, 15
Version: Tiny BASIC
Hardware: none
Software: none
Non-ANSI: extended IF

1098. Area-of-a-Circle-Section Problem

Author: Newett Awl

Source: *Recreational Computing* Jul–Aug 79 (8:1)
"Newett Awl and the Goat" p. 27

Recreational Computing Sep–Oct 79 (8:2)
"Newett Awl and the Goat" pp. 38–39 (39)

Updates: new program
Recreational Computing Sep–Oct 79 (8:2)
"Responses to the Newett Awl Challenge" p. 71 (71)

new program
Recreational Computing Nov–Dec 79 (8:3)
"Newett Awl's Goat Once Again" p. 54 (54)

Suppose you had a circular lawn 20 feet in diameter and you wanted to stake a goat at the edge of the circle so that the goat would eat exactly half the grass. How long would the rope have to be? You can put your computer to work on the problem using this program. Includes a sample run. (Reprinted from the *Homebrew Computer Club Newsletter* Jan–Feb 1979.)

Lines: 37
Version: not given
Hardware: none
Software: none
Non-ANSI: extended IF, SQRT()

366. Double Precision Rectangular/Polar Coordinate Conversion

Author: Delmar D. Hinrichs

Source: *Creative Computing* Aug 79 (5:8)
"Double Precision: Does Your BASIC Have It? Now It Can . . ." pp. 110–114 (112–113)

One of the shortcomings of TRS-80 Level II BASIC is that although it has double precision variables, it does not have double precision functions. You can get around this problem by doing the function calculations in these programs. These two programs convert rectangular coordinates to polar coordinates and vice-versa. They use double precision subroutines to get double precision results.

Lines: 17, 28
Version: TRS-80 Level II BASIC
Hardware: none
Software: none
Non-ANSI: CLS, DEFDBL, DEFINT, ' (used in place of REM), two-letter variables, extended IF

1108. Pythagorean Triples for the Apple II

Author: Jim Day

Source: *Recreational Computing* Sep–Oct 79 (8:2)
"Graphic Triples for Apple II" p. 56 (56)

Pythagorean triples are a special type of triangle. This program draws pictures of such triangles on an Apple II.

Lines: 18
Version: Applesoft BASIC
Hardware: Apple II
Software: none
Non-ANSI: not translatable

GRAPHING

425. Function Plotter for Video Displays

Author: not given

Source: *Dr. Dobb's Journal of Computer Calisthenics & Orthodontia* Jan 77 (2:1)
"Lawrence Livermore Lab's 8080 BASIC" pp. 8–62 (12)

This program plots a function on a video display. The user changes a few lines in the program to select the function desired. The program then plots the function on a display. The program plots a set of axes and labels the plot. The program requires a set of assembly language routines to do the plotting. Includes a sample run.

Lines: 62
Version: MCS80 BASIC
Hardware: video display, 8080-based microcomputer
Software: 8080 assembly language routines
Non-ANSI: CALL

431. Plotting With the PolyMorphic Systems Video Terminal Interface

Author: R. Broucke

Source: *Dr. Dobb's Journal of Computer Calisthenics & Orthodontia* Jun–Jul 77 (2:6)
"Curve Plotting on a T.V. Screen With the PolyMorphics Video Interface and MITS BASIC" pp. 17–19 (18–19)

This is a group of three programs to demonstrate the abilities of the PolyMorphic Systems Video Terminal Interface. The VTI allows you to plot graphics on a video terminal or TV. The data to be displayed is accessed directly from memory. The first program plots a sine function. The second program allows a table of points to be displayed. Such a program might be useful where you have obtained the results of an experiment and wish the data plotted. The program automatically determines the lower and upper limits of the data so that it can be properly scaled. The third program belongs with a LIFE article on page 12.

Lines: 17, 27, 35
Version: MITS BASIC
Hardware: PolyMorphic Systems Video Terminal Interface
Software: none
Non-ANSI: POKE, PEEK(), OR(), two-letter variables, extended IF

122. Graph Reading Drill

Author: Robert Schenk

Source: *Calculators/Computers Magazine* Feb 78 (2:2)
"A Graphing Drill for CAI" pp. 77–79 (79)

This program drills a student in interpretation of graphs. The student is presented with a graph and then is asked to get information from it. The type of graph used is called a "scatter diagram." The program CHAIN's to another program as part of a CAI system. This CHAIN statement can be eliminated by most users. Includes a sample run.

Lines: 71
Version: not given
Hardware: none
Software: none
Non-ANSI: LIN(), CHAIN, HP strings

24. Plot 3-D Equations on a Terminal

Author: Mike Stoddard

Source: *Byte* May 78 (3:5)
"PLOT3D: A Function Plotting Program" pp. 60–61 (61)

This is a program to plot simulated 3-D plots of mathematical functions. Usually programmers have to resort to pen plotters and expensive high-power graphics software to get 3-D plots. Here is a simple program to get 3-D plots. No special graphics capability is needed; an ordinary terminal is used for output. Lines which are hidden are properly concealed. The main limitation of the program is that the Z-axis of the output must lie along the line of the terminal carriage. Includes a sample output.

Lines: 39
Version: not given
Hardware: none
Software: none
Non-ANSI: HP strings, extended IF, multiple-assignment

130. Graphs of Polar Equations

Author: Kurt Endress

Source: *Calculators/Computers Magazine* May 78 (2:5)
"Student Programs" pp. 37–41 (37)

Most students are used to working in "rectangular" coordinates. That's the kind of graphing system where you plot things on a "grid". There is another kind of graphing system known as the "polar" system. This is one in which the "lines" on the graph run out from a center point. This program draws polar graphs of equations. You can control how much of the graph is plotted (up to 360 degrees). The size of the graph can be from 1 to 7 inches. The output is on a regular terminal; no special graphics facility is needed.

Lines: 76
Version: HP-2000 BASIC
Hardware: none
Software: none
Non-ANSI: MAT ZER( )

914. Function Plotter for the PET Computer

Author: Philip Gash

Source: *People's Computers* Jul–Aug 78 (7:1) "PLOT" pp. 44–45 (45)

Updates: correction
People's Computers Sep–Oct 78 (7:2) "PET Bloopers" p. 45 (45)

This is a simple program to plot single-valued functions on a PET. The program can plot a variety of functions on the PET screen. Includes sample output.

Lines: 49
Version: PET BASIC
Hardware: PET
Software: none
Non-ANSI: not translatable

294. Contour Mapping of Three-Dimensional Functions

Author: William Games

Source: *Creative Computing* Nov–Dec 78 (4:6) "Patterns" pp. 78–81 (79)

Determining what a three-dimensional function looks like can be a difficult task. With a two-dimensional function you can just plot a section to get a feel for how the function acts. But with three-dimensional functions you run into the problem that paper is a two-dimensional medium. This program can assist you in understanding and visualizing three-dimensional functions by creating contour maps for such functions. You specify the function, the range of the function values (this can be computed automatically), and the size of the plot you want. The computer then prints out a contour map of the function using dark and light characters to represent the "height" of the function in different areas. The program uses a standard terminal; no special graphics capability is needed. Includes sample runs and a list of program variables.

Lines: 69
Version: not given
Hardware: none
Software: none
Non-ANSI: HP strings, LIN(), LINPUT, PRINT USING, extended IF

150. Function Lesson

Author: Kendell Hyde and David Tolman

Source: *Calculators/Computers Magazine* Jan–Feb 79 (3:1) "Computer Supplemented Calculus" pp. 20–23 (21–22)

Learning math can be a tedious process. The process can be made a bit less dreary by using a computer to take care of the busy work. This is a set of two programs to teach students about functions. A student types in a function. The computer responds with the value of that function at several points. This output can be used to teach students about how functions are graphed. Includes a sample run.

Lines: 75, 73
Version: PDP-10 BASIC
Hardware: none
Software: none
Non-ANSI: ' (used in place of REM), strings, CHAIN, MAT INPUT, multi-letter variables

324. Function Graphing Using Program-Entered Functions

Author: Douglas Schiffer

Source: *Creative Computing* Mar 79 (5:3) "Individual Graphing of Mathematical Functions" pp. 122–123 (123)

If you're graphing a set of functions, you have to enter the functions into the program in some way. You could have the program stop at some point, have the user type in a DEF statement, and then restart the program. But this is too complicated for someone just starting out with computers. This program demonstrates how to get around this problem by having the program actually modify itself to enter a function. Two versions of the program are given, one in DEC 11/40 BASIC and one in MITS 12K BASIC. The DEC version modifies a program on disk, and then CHAINs to it. The MITS version modifies itself in memory.

Lines: 40, 12, 38
Version: DEC 11/40 BASIC, MITS 12K BASIC
Hardware: sequential file device
Software: none
Non-ANSI: not translatable

1079. TRS-80 Three-Dimensional Plots

Author: Milan Chepko

Source: *Recreational Computing* Mar–Apr 79 (7:5) "TRS-80: 3D Plots" p. 21 (21)

Visualizing three-dimensional functions is sometimes difficult. It's possible to draw a two-dimensional picture of a three-dimensional plot, but this usually takes a lot of high-powered software. This is especially true if "hidden" lines are to be removed from the display. There is, however, a technique which can produce plots of three-dimensional functions with very little effort. This program demonstrates this technique using the TRS-80's display. Includes a sample output.

Lines: 33
Version: TRS-80 Level II BASIC
Hardware: TRS-80
Software: none
Non-ANSI: not translatable

335. Vertical and Bar Graphs

Author: Robert Barrett

Source: *Creative Computing* Apr 79 (5:4)
"Vertical Graphs and Bar Charts" pp. 146–151 (147–151)

Updates: improvements
Creative Computing Aug 79 (5:8)
"Vertical Printer Graphing" p. 10 (10)

Graphing is not very hard to do if you run the axis of the plot perpendicular to the paper. Producing vertically-oriented plots is somewhat harder. This is a set of programs which demonstrate how to produce such vertical graphs. One program plots a function. Another plots the function plus its derivative. There is also a program which produces bar graphs. Includes sample runs.

Lines: 46, 62, 62, 33
Version: Hewlett-Packard BASIC-X
Hardware: none
Software: none
Non-ANSI: MAT ZER()

696. Function Graphing for the TRS-80

Author: Curtis Gerald

Source: *Kilobaud Microcomputing* May 79 (29)
"Graphing with the TRS-80" pp. 100–104 (100–104)

Computers can help mathematics come alive. Examples of this are these two function graphing programs. You don't need to get bogged down in the tiresome chore of point-by-point plotting when you have a computer that can do it for you. These programs use the display of the TRS-80 to do the graphing of any function you specify. One of the programs does only straight graphing. The other can draw "scaled" graphs. Includes a sample output and a list of program variables.

Lines: 34, 53
Version: TRS-80 Level I BASIC
Hardware: TRS-80
Software: none
Non-ANSI: not translatable

388. Graphs of Sine Wave Approximations

Author: Project Solo

Source: *Creative Computing* Oct 79 (5:10)
"Trigonometric Functions and Tchebychev Approximations" pp. 116–119 (116–118)

When is a sine function not a sine function? When it's a ploynomial approximation to a sine function. Because sine values cannot be computed directly, computers compute values for the SIN function using polynomials which provide values very near to true sine values. These three programs plot graphs of sine approximations. (The printout uses a normal terminal; no special graphics capability is required.) One program uses the built-in SIN function to get the sine values. The other two programs use less sophisticated polynomials. Includes a sample output.

Lines: 13, 10, 8
Version: not given
Hardware: none
Software: none
Non-ANSI: none

MAGIC SQUARES

193. De La Loubere and Franklin Magic Squares

Author: Donald Piele

Source: *Creative Computing* Jan–Feb 76 (2:1)
"Magic Squares on the Computer" pp. 28–34 (32–33)

Magic squares are number squares in which all of the rows and all of the columns add up to the same number. These two programs use two different methods to generate up to 11-by-11 magic squares. Includes sample runs.

Lines: 130, 198
Version: not given
Hardware: none
Software: none
Non-ANSI: MAT operations

1137. Magic Square Generator

Author: Paul Pennington

Source: *'68' Micro Journal* Jun 79 (1:4)
"MAGIC SQUARES" p. 39 (39)

A magic square is an array of numbers arranged in a square so that the sum of each row and column, as well as the two diagonals, is the same. This program uses the following method to generate magic squares: Place a 1 in the middle square of the top row. Proceed numbering up and to the left diagonally ("wrapping around" as needed) until a filled square is reached. Then drop down one square and continue. Includes a sample run. (This program is reprinted from the *CSRA Computer Club Newsletter*.)

Lines: 27
Version: not given
Hardware: none
Software: none
Non-ANSI: extended IF

MATRIX ARITHMETIC

894. Matrix Arithmetic Subroutines

Author: Tim Scully

Source: *People's Computers* Jul–Aug 77 (6:1)
"8080 Matrix Subroutines" p. 41 (41)

Scientists in many fields often have a need to use matrix operations to solve various problems. More advanced versions of BASIC have matrix operations built in. Most BASICs, however, don't. To get around this problem, you can program the functions yourself. These are two BASIC subroutines to do matrix arithemetic. The first subroutine inverts square matrices. The second subroutine finds the roots (eigenvalues) of symmetric matrices. The second routine also returns the eigenvectors of the matrices.

Lines: 36, 56
Version: Altair Extended BASIC
Hardware: none
Software: none
Non-ANSI: ' (used in place of REM), extended IF, multi-letter variables

551. Matrix Arithmetic Program

Author: Walter Pragnell

Source: *Interface Age* Oct 79 (4:10)
"The Micro-Mathematician" pp. 39–46 (44–45)

Updates: commentary
Interface Age Nov 79 (4:11)
"The Micro-Mathematician" pp. 30–36

Matrix (plural: *matrices*) is just a fancy mathematical term for an array (you know, DIM A(100), etc.?). Mathematicians have developed a whole set of arithmetic operations to manipulate matrices. This program performs these *matrix arithmetic* operations. The program can do matrix addition, multiplication, transposition, and inversion of matrices up to 9 by 9. Includes a sample run.

Lines: 151
Version: not given
Hardware: none
Software: none
Non-ANSI: strings, INP(), %() (used to format printouts), extended IF, ! (used in place of PRINT)

1142. Matrix Multiplication Subroutine

Author: David Eagle

Source: *'68' Micro Journal* Oct 79 (1:8)
untitled p. 8 (8)

Matrix is another term for array. It's possible to multiply two matrices using an operation called *matrix multiplication*. This operation is frequently used in linear algebra and computer graphics. This subroutine performs matrix multiplications

Lines: 12
Version: SWTPC 8K BASIC, V2.3
Hardware: none
Software: none
Non-ANSI: none

NUMBER BASES

173. Binary

Author: Ted Park

Source: *Creative Computing* Mar–Apr 75 (1:3)
"BINARY" p. 37 (37)

This program tests your binary-to-decimal and decimal-to-binary conversion skills. The computer gives you ten binary numbers and challenges you to convert them to their decimal equivalents. It then gives you ten decimal numbers and asks for the binary equivalents. Includes a sample run.

Lines: 53
Version: not given
Hardware: none
Software: none
Non-ANSI: HP strings

590. Hexadecimal/Decimal Converter

Author: Phil Hughes

Source: *Kilobaud* Aug 77 (8)
"HEXDEC" p. 105 (105)

This is a hexadecimal/decimal number conversion program. It converts any decimal number, from 0 to 65,535, to its hexadecimal equivalent, or any hexadecimal number, from 0 to FFFF, to its decimal equivalent. Includes a sample run.

Lines: 47
Version: SWTPC 8K BASIC
Hardware: none
Software: none
Non-ANSI: strings, extended IF, VAL(), ASC()

108. Convert Fractional Numbers Between Bases

Author: Lud Braun

Source: *Calculators/Computers Magazine* Oct 77 (1:2)
"Easy Fractional Conversion From/To Base-10 To/From Any Lower Base" pp. 63–67 (67)

It is in working with computers that most people first learn that there can be uses for numbers in bases other than 10. Base 2, 8, and 16 are all commonly used in the computer world. Converting numbers from base 10 to these other bases can be a problem—especially if the number to be converted is a fraction. This program converts fractional numbers from base 10 to any other base in the range 2 to 9.

Lines: 60
Version: not given
Hardware: none
Software: none
Non-ANSI: none

250. Changing Bases

Author: Jim West

Source: *Creative Computing* Nov–Dec 77 (3:6)
"Changing Bases" p. 130 (130)

When working with computers, it is often useful to convert base 10 numbers to other bases. This program takes a positive base 10 integer and gives you the equivalent number in any new base between 2 and 16. Includes a sample run.

Lines: 35
Version: not given
Hardware: none
Software: none
Non-ANSI: strings

481. Test Your Knowledge of Number Bases

Author: Irwin Doliner

Source: *Interface Age* Nov 77 (2:12)
"CONVBASE: Getting Down to Bases" pp. 158–161 (161)

This is a program to help you lean how to convert between different number bases. The article contains a discussion of number bases. The program tests you by giving you numbers in one base and asking you to convert them to another. Includes a sample run and list of program variables.

Lines: 121
Version: not given
Hardware: none
Software: none
Non-ANSI: strings

482. Number Base Conversion Program

Author: Mark Winkler

Source: *Interface Age* Nov 77 (2:12)
"Number Base Conversion Program—MWNBCP" pp. 162–164 (164)

This program accepts decimal, binary, octal, split-octal, or hexadecimal numbers, and converts them into any of the other bases. A flowchart is included.

Lines: 148
Version: 8K 3.1 MITS BASIC
Hardware: none
Software: none
Non-ANSI: strings, two-letter variables, extended IF, ASC( )

651. Universal Number Converter

Author: Easton Beymer

Source: *Kilobaud* Nov 78 (23)
"Universal Number Converter" p. 67 (67)

Updates: corrections
Kilobaud Microcomputing Feb 79 (26)
"Conversion" p. 19 (19)

If you're still struggling along in assembly language, you may find this program useful. This program is a universal number converter. It takes numbers in any base from 2 to 16 and converts them into any other base in the same range. Includes a sample run.

Lines: 43
Version: PET BASIC
Hardware: none
Software: none
Non-ANSI: strings, multi-letter variables, ASC(), extended IF

48. Split-Octal to Decimal Conversion

Author: Paul Poduska

Source: Byte Mar 79 (4:3)
"Building the Heath H8 Computer" pp. 12–13, 124–140 (138–139)

This program converts split-octal bytes to the equivalent decimal numbers. You type in the octal value of a byte and the computer responds with the corresponding decimal value.

Lines: 12
Version: not given
Hardware: none
Software: none
Non-ANSI: none

1081. Base 10 to Base 16 Translator

Author: Dennis Allison

Source: Recreational Computing Mar–Apr 79 (7:5)
"Two Recursive Functions in BASIC" p. 27 (27)

This program takes base 10 numbers you type in and prints out the hexadecimal (base 16) equivalents.

Lines: 15
Version: TRS-80 BASIC
Hardware: none
Software: none
Non-ANSI: extended IF, CHR$(), AND()

446. Decimal to Another Base Converter

Author: Theodore Hines

Source: Dr. Dobb's Journal of Computer Calisthenics & Orthodontia May 79 (4:5)
"Changing Bases" p. 15 (15)

This program converts numbers between decimal and any other base between 2 and 16. The program can also convert numbers back to base 10.

Lines: 68
Version: Processor Technology Extended Cassette BASIC
Hardware: none
Software: none
Non-ANSI: HP strings, DEF . . . FNEND, SEARCH, VAL(), extended IF

536. Binary/Octal/Decimal/Hex Converter

Author: Alfred Adler

Source: Interface Age Jun 79 (4:L6)
"The Micro-Mathematician" pp. 35–40 (38)

Updates: modifications
Interface Age Oct 79 (4:10)
" 'FIX' Conversions" pp. 8–11

This simple number base converter converts numbers between binary, octal, decimal, and hexadecimal. A patch is provided for users who do not have the ASC() function. Includes a sample run.

Lines: 75 (plus patch)
Version: PolyMorphic BASIC, ver. A00
Hardware: none
Software: none
Non-ANSI: HP strings, extended IF, ASC(), VAL(), ! (used in place of PRINT)

708. Decimal to Octal and Hex Number Conversion

Author: Rod Hallen

Source: Kilobaud Microcomputing Jun 79 (30)
"Number Conversion" p. 96 (96)

This program takes a decimal number and prints it out in octal and hex.

Lines: 21
Version: Processor Technology Extended BASIC
Hardware: none
Software: none
Non-ANSI: HP strings

1040. Decimal/Octal/Hex Number Converter

Author: Rod Hallen

Source: Personal Computing Aug 79 (3:8)
"Let's Have a BALL" pp. 44–52 (46–47)

Updates: modifications for Applesoft II BASIC
Personal Computing Dec 79 (3:12)
"Applesoft Conversions" p. 10 (10)

Computers "think" in binary. Keeping track of all those printed 1s and 0s can get a bit tedious. So most programmers represent binary values using octal (base 8) or hex (base 16) notation. This is fine as long as you stick with one system or the other. The problems come when you need to enter an octal program into a computer using a monitor that accepts only hex or vice-versa. This program can help you out by translating numbers in decimal, octal, or hex into each of the other two notations. The program uses HP format strings, but a patch is provided for DEC format strings. Includes a sample run and a list of program variables.

Lines: 66 (plus patch)
Version: Processor Technology Extended Cassette BASIC
Hardware: none
Software: none
Non-ANSI: HP strings, RESTORE [line number], single character INPUT, extended IF, CHR()

1148. Number Base Converter

Author: Art Weller

Source: *'68' Micro Journal* Nov–Dec 79 (1:9)
untitled pp. 27–28 (28)

In computing, many numbers are not in regular base 10 notation. Base 2 (binary), base 8 (octal), and base 16 (hexadecimal) are all commonly used. This program can help you switch numbers between different bases. The program can handle numbers in any base from 2 to 16.

Lines: 38
Version: not given
Hardware: none
Software: none
Non-ANSI: strings

758. Hex to Decimal Converter

Author: Allan S. Joffe

Source: *Kilobaud Microcomputing* Dec 79 (36)
"Implementing an Algorithm" pp. 76–77 (76)

Hexadecimal (base 16) is a number system which uses 16 symbols. The first 10 symbols are 0 through 9, which carry their usual values. The letters A through F carry the values 10 through 15. This program converts hexadecimal (hex) format numbers into decimal, printing out the value of each digit as the digit is translated. A patch allows

the program to convert any base up to base 16. Includes a sample run.

Lines: 19 (plus patch)
Version: TRS-80 BASIC
Hardware: none
Software: none
Non-ANSI: CLS, strings, ASC(), extended IF, multi-letter variables, CLEAR

NUMBER SEQUENCES

137. 4-2-1 Loop Problem

Author: Jim Wilson

Source: *Calculators/Computers Magazine* Sep–Oct 78 (2:6)
"Loops" pp. 37–41 (41)

This program demonstrates the 4-2-1 loop problem. The problem is as follows: Take a whole number. Apply the following rules: (1) if the number is even, divide by two; (2) if the number is odd, multiply by three and add one. Apply the two rules to the result and all subsequent results. Eventually you will get into the pattern of four, followed by two, followed by one (a pattern which repeats itself endlessly). This program lets you test numbers to see if they always result in the 4-2-1 pattern. Includes a sample run.

Lines: 76
Version: not given
Hardware: none
Software: none
Non-ANSI: strings

138. Number Patterns

Author: Bob Albrecht

Source: *Calculators/Computers Magazine* Sep–Oct 78 (2:6)
"Number Patterns on the TRS-80" pp. 58–61 (60)

This program allows you to explore the patterns that are created by squaring each number of a sequence of numbers. You enter the sequence and the computer grinds out the patterns. Includes a sample run.

Lines: 11
Version: TRS-80 Level II BASIC
Hardware: none
Software: none
Non-ANSI: CLS

61. Puzzling Rotation

Author: Ken Barbier

Source: *Byte* May 79 (4:5)
"Puzzling Rotation" p. 216 (216)

Updates: commentary
Byte Aug 79 (4:8)
"Puzzling Rotation Explained" p. 8

This program starts with a six-digit integer formed from the first six digits of the reciprocal of the number seven. This number is repeatedly added to itself to form a column of six digit numbers with curious properties.

Lines: 8
Version: not given
Hardware: none
Software: none
Non-ANSI: none

565. Number Patterns

Author: Bob Albrecht

Source: *Interface Age* Dec 79 (4:12)
"My TRS-80 Likes Me" pp. 114–115 (114)

This program is designed to teach students about number sequences. The sequences are generated by adding a constant to the previous number. Each time you press the space bar, the computer types out the next number in the sequence.

Lines: 16
Version: TRS-80 BASIC
Hardware: none
Software: none
Non-ANSI: CLS, strings, multi-letter variables, INKEY$(), extended IF

PI

267. Computing the Value of Pi by Convergence

Author: not given

Source: *Creative Computing* Mar–Apr 78 (4:2)
"Convergence" p. 132 (132)

Certain constants such as *e* and *pi* can be calculated as the sum of a number of elements in a series. The series which converges on *pi* is $1 - 1/3 + 1/5 - 1/7 + 1/9$ . . . One of the two programs supplied uses this method to compute *pi*. Also supplied is a method of converging on *pi* by the use of polygons. Includes sample runs.

Lines: 11, 6
Version: not given
Hardware: none
Software: none
Non-ANSI: none

279. Calculate Pi by Inscribed Polygons

Author: George Ball

Source: *Creative Computing* Jul–Aug 78 (4:4)
"Convergence Revisited" p. 70 (70)

Updates: commentary
Creative Computing Jul 79 (5:7)
"North Star Criticism" p. 14

Pi is a number without end. It starts out 3.14159 . . . and continues on forever. It has many interesting properties, not the least of which is that the area of a circle is *pi* times the radius of the circle squared. This program makes a start at calculating *pi* using the Inscribed Polygon method. The value the program generates is accurate to 13 decimal places. Includes a sample run.

Lines: 20
Version: not given
Hardware: none
Software: none
Non-ANSI: PRC()

769. Pi Computation

Author: Robert Bishop

Source: *Micro* Aug–Sep 78 (6)
"Apple Pi" pp. 15–16 (15–16)

Updates: commentary and correction
Micro Oct–Nov 78 (7)
"Microbes" p. 27

Pi is a number without end. It starts out 3.14159 . . . and goes on forever! In times gone by, mathematicians have spent their entire lives trying to extend the known value of *pi* out a few more digits. This program uses an expansion series to compute *pi* to as many digits of accuracy as you want. A sample run of the program shows the value of *pi* to 1,000 digits (it took almost 40 hours to calculate the value).

Lines: 82
Version: Apple Integer BASIC
Hardware: none
Software: none
Non-ANSI: CALL, VTAB, multi-letter variables,
GOSUB [computed line number], PEEK(),
POKE, OR(), MOD(), extended IF

694. Computing Pi by Alternating Series

Author: Wallace Kendall

Source: *Kilobaud Microcomputing* May 79 (29)
"Prettyprinting with Microsoft BASIC" p. 80
(80)

This program computes the value of *pi* using the alternating series method. With each term in the series, the adjusted value of *pi* is printed. Includes a sample run.

Lines: 17
Version: OSI Microsoft BASIC
Hardware: none
Software: none
Non-ANSI: none

709. Calculating Pi Using the Leibnitz Method

Author: E. M. McCormick

Source: *Kilobaud Microcomputing* Jun 79 (30)
"Calculating Pi . . . The Leibnitz Method" p.
97 (97)

In 1694 Leibnitz discovered a simple method for computing the value of *pi*. This program uses this method to calculate the value of that strange number. The program uses double-precision numbers.

Lines: 10
Version: TRS-80 Level II BASIC
Hardware: none
Software: none
Non-ANSI: none

390. Finding Rational Approximations for Pi

Author: Robert G. Hoffman

Source: *Creative Computing* Oct 79 (5:10)
"Blunder Programming" pp. 124–125 (124)

Rational numbers are those numbers that can be represented by the division of two whole numbers. *Pi* is not a rational number because there are no two numbers that you can divide to get *Pi*. These two programs are designed to look for rational fractions which come close to *pi*. One program just prints out all the fractions resulting from all the possible numerators and denominators less than 100. The other program uses a "guided search" method to look for *pi* values.

Lines: 6 (plus patch), 9 (plus patch)
Version: TRS-80 Level II BASIC
Hardware: none
Software: none
Non-ANSI: Extended IF, DEFDBL

PRIME NUMBERS

591. Printing a List of Primes

Author: Robert Hinkley, Robert Calbridge, David
Meltzer, and John McGaw

Source: *Kilobaud* Sep 77 (9)
"Programming Problem" p. 18

Kilobaud Dec 77 (12)
"Solutions for September's Programming
Problem" pp. 18–20 (18–20)

These are four programs by four different authors to print out lists of prime numbers. The lists include all the prime numbers between one and an arbitrary limit. Includes a sample output.

Lines: 44, 11, 22, 5
Version: various
Hardware: none
Software: none
Non-ANSI: strings, extended IF, SQRT()

783. Visual Sieve of Eratosthenes for the PET

Author: Gary Bullard

Source: *Micro* Feb 78 (9)
"The Sieve of Eratosthenes" p. 8 (8)

The Greek geographer-astronomer Eratosthenes devised a method for finding prime numbers that involves making a list of numbers and then crossing off all the multiples of known primes. This program uses a visual variation of this technique using the display screen of the PET. The character positions on the PET's screen are thought of as integers. The program then sets or clears any particular position according to whether or not it corresponds to a prime number. This produces a "bathroom tile" effect on the screen. At the end, a list of the primes found is printed out.

Lines: 20
Version: PET BASIC
Hardware: PET
Software: none
Non-ANSI: not translatable

PROBABILITY

185. Coin Tossing Simulation

Author: Jeffrey Moskow

Source: *Creative Computing* Sep–Oct 75 (1:5)
"Odd or Even?" p. 24 (24)

This program simulates the tossing of a coin. You specify how many times to toss the "coin." The computer then simulates the coin tossing and prints out how many times the coin came up heads and how many times it came up tails. Includes a sample run.

Lines: 14
Version: not given
Hardware: none
Software: none
Non-ANSI: none

915. Coin Tossing Simulation

Author: Bob Kahn

Source: *People's Computers* Jul–Aug 78 (7:1)
"Gambler's Paradox" pp. 48–53 (52–53)

These two programs are designed to introduce you to some elementary concepts of statistics using the age-old game of "coin flipping." The first program, FLIPME, is a coin-tossing simulator. The computer simulates coin tosses. You try to guess what the toss will be. If you guess correctly, you win "morps." If you guess wrong, you lose morps. With a little statistics, it should be easy to see that on the average you should just break even. The second program, GESTRA, demonstrates various guessing strategies to show that no matter what guessing scheme you use, you will always, on the average, just break even. Includes sample runs.

Lines: 170, 115
Version: Data General BASIC
Hardware: none
Software: none
Non-ANSI: HP strings, extended IF, PAUSE

136. Probability Machine Simulation for the PET

Author: Mac Oglesby

Source: *Calculators/Computers Magazine* Sep–Oct 78 (2:6)
"MARBLESTAT" pp. 34–36 (36)

Have you ever seen a "probability machine" in a math lab or science museum? It's one of those machines that have a lot of balls that fall down among a pyramid of metal pins and finally land in collecting pockets at the bottom. This program simulates such a device on a PET. In normal mode, the program uses the PET's graphics to display the balls as they fall. At any time you can have the program print out a bar graph of the number of balls in each collecting pocket. Includes a sample run.

Lines: 151
Version: PET BASIC
Hardware: PET
Software: none
Non-ANSI: not translatable

286. Simulations and Probability

Author: John Camp

Source: *Creative Computing* Sep–Oct 78 (4:5)
"Computer Simulations and Problem-Solving in Probability" pp. 69–71 (70–71)

Computer simulations can be a powerful tool in understanding the laws of probability. They have a unique advantage in that it is not necessary for you to fully understand the theory in order to solve problems. With simulations you can start in immediately and learn as you go. These three programs use simulation techniques to solve sample probablity problems. The three problems are a Population Planning problem, a Bubblegum Card problem, and a System Reliability problem.

Lines: 9, 17, 17
Version: not given
Hardware: none
Software: none
Non-ANSI: HP strings, MAT operations, extended IF

290. Chance That Two People in a Group Have the Same Birthday

Author: Sanderson Smith

Source: *Creative Computing* Sep–Oct 78 (4:5)
"Common Birthdays" p. 106 (106)

If you have a group of people, what is the probability that two people in the group have the same birthday? Probably greater than you think! In a group of 10 randomly chosen people, there is only about a 12% chance that two of them share a common birthday. With 40 people, though, there is an 89% chance that two people in the group have the same birthday. This program prints out a table showing what the chances are for a given number of people. Includes a sample run.

Lines: 10
Version: not given
Hardware: none
Software: none
Non-ANSI: none

641. Coin Flipping

Author: Charles Carpenter

Source: *Kilobaud* Oct 78 (22)
"Not So Tiny" pp. 44–45 (44–45)

This program flips a computer "coin" 50 times, then prints the number of heads in each 50 flips. The program comes in two versions: a regular BASIC version and a version for Tiny BASIC. Includes a sample run.

Lines: 17, 32
Version: Tiny BASIC, standard BASIC
Hardware: none
Software: none
Non-ANSI: PR

332. Expected Value Probability Simulations

Author: Glenda Lappan and M. J. Winter

Source: *Creative Computing* Apr 79 (5:4)
"What Will Happen If . . . ?" pp. 100–104 (101–104)

How much can you expect to win on a bet? For a large class of games of chance, a study of the probabilities involved can give you the answer. This group of programs demonstrates ideas in expected value probability. In one problem, you are asked whether you would prefer to play a game in which you pay $10, roll three dice, and get an amount equal to the sum of the dice; or whether you would rather pay $12, roll two dice, and get the product of the dice. The computer then simulates the games and shows you how much you have won in each. Similar programs are presented to demonstrate other concepts in probability. Includes sample runs.

Lines: 16, 23, 31, 16, 27
Version: Tektronix 4051 BASIC
Hardware: none
Software: none
Non-ANSI: none

346. Coin Tossing Simulation

Author: N. B. Winkless, Jr.

Source: *Creative Computing* Jun 79 (5:6)
"Two Million Frantic Frenchmen: A Study in Probability" pp. 94–95 (95)

Updates: commentary
Creative Computing Oct 79 (5:10)
"Borel's Frantic Frenchmen" p. 8

commentary
Creative Computing May 80 (6:5)
"Still Flipping Frenchman" p. 8

If two million Frenchmen started flipping coins at the rate of one flip per second, and if each stopped only when he had flipped an equal number of heads and tails, how long would it be before the last man finished flipping? On the average, heads and tails will always eventually come out even. But as this simulation demonstrates, "eventually" can sometimes be an awfully long time. Includes a sample run.

Lines: 32
Version: Micropolis BASIC
Hardware: none
Software: none
Non-ANSI: extended IF, strings, CHAR$(), FMT()

377. Craps Probability Simulations

Author: Elliott A. Tanis

Source: *Creative Computing* Sep 79 (5:9)
"Simulations In The Game of Craps" pp. 140–141 (141)

Most gambling games are based on probability. These two simulation programs study the game of craps. The first program "rolls" the dice 1,000 times and prints out how many winning throws occur. The second program simulates the number of rolls needed to lose $5. For 25 trials it lists the number of rolls needed to exhaust the $5 and the maximum capital accumulated during the trial. Includes sample runs.

Lines: 31, 73
Version: Tektronix 4051 BASIC
Hardware: none
Software: none
Non-ANSI: INIT, extended IF, PAGE, PRINT @ (used in place of PRINT #), PRINT @ USING (used in place of PRINT # USING), IMAGE

RANDOM NUMBERS

642. Random Number Generator Tester

Author: Bill Rogers

Source: *Kilobaud* Oct 78 (22)
"Randomness is Wonderful" pp. 62–63 (63)

Updates: commentary
Kilobaud Dec 78 (24)
"Variety is the Spice of Microcomputing" pp. 16–17

Contrary to popular belief, random numbers are not always random. The random number generators in most BASICs use "pseudo-random" numbers. These are sequences of numbers that appear to be random, but really are not. For most practical purposes you'd never know the difference. It's nice, though, to check to see how random your random number generator really is. This program tests random number generators to see what their output looks like. The program produces a table showing the relative frequencies with which certain ranges of numbers show up. If the random numbers generated are truly random, then all the numbers should appear with approximately equal frequency. Includes a sample run.

Lines: 95
Version: not given
Hardware: none
Software: none
Non-ANSI: none

148. Normally Distributed Random Numbers

Author: Douglas Scott

Source: *Calculators/Computers Magazine* Nov–Dec 78 (2:7)
"Two Kinds of Random Numbers" pp. 60–62 (62)

Most versions of BASIC have some provisions for producing random numbers. Commonly, the function RND(x) is used to produce random numbers in the range 0.0000 to 0.9999. The numbers so produced are called a "rectangular" distribution. This means that any number has the same chance of being produced as any other. Many times in the real world, however, random events occur in "normal" distribution. That is, they tend to clump together around the middle of their range. This program generates normally distributed random numbers. The program prints out a bar graph of the frequencies of numbers produced. Includes sample runs.

Lines: 32
Version: not given
Hardware: none
Software: none
Non-ANSI: none

989. Histogram of Random Numbers

Author: John Nevison

Source: *Personal Computing* Feb 79 (3:2)
"BASIC With Style" pp. 17–22 (22)

This program prints a histogram of the distribution of *n* random numbers. Includes a sample run and a list of program variables.

Lines: 61
Version: not given
Hardware: none
Software: none
Non-ANSI: none

69. Pseudorandom Number Generators

Author: C. Brian Honess

Source: *Byte* Jun 79 (4:6)
"Three Types of Pseudorandom Sequences" pp. 234–246 (236–242)

Updates: corrections
Byte Oct 79 (4:10)
"Pseudorandom Errors" p. 209 (209)

Many computer applications use random numbers. But generating truly random numbers is a difficult task. Fortunately, few programs require truly random numbers. Most can make do with "pseudorandom" numbers. Pseudorandom numbers are number sequences which appear to be random but which actually repeat after a certain number of numbers. These programs demonstrate several ways of generating pseudorandom numbers. The center squared method, the Fibonacci series method, and the power residue method are discussed.

Lines: 11, 11, 15, 13, 6
Version: not given
Hardware: none
Software: none
Non-ANSI: none

715. Chi-Square Analysis of Randomness

Author: John Cameron and Alette Comrack

Source: *Kilobaud Microcomputing* Jul 79 (31)
"Randomness Is More Than It Seems" pp. 64–65 (64)

Random numbers are not always random. When asked to write down a list of random numbers, a typical human will write down numbers that turn out to be very unrandom, statistically speaking. This program does Chi-square tests to determine how random the RND function in your system really is. Includes sample runs.

Lines: 33
Version: Xitan SuperBASIC
Hardware: none
Software: none
Non-ANSI: PRECISION, two-letter variables, extended IF, ? (used in place of PRINT)

STATISTICS

947. Calculating Seasonal Indexes

Author: Karen Wolfe

Source: *Personal Computing* Apr 78 (2:4) "Calculating Seasonal Indices" pp. 101–102 (102)

When statistics are presented to the public, they are often "seasonally adjusted." What does this mean? It means that the data under consideration "normally" move up or down during different parts of the year. If you wish to look at changes in the data, it makes sense to take this seasonal difference into account. You would not want to say that employment among department store Santa Clauses is down just because there are fewer of them employed in July compared to last December! This program calculates seasonal indexes so that you can seasonally adjust your data. You can use this type of index to predict next year's sales, analyze your personal budget, or examine data you see printed in the newspaper. The FILL statements in the program are for a North Star printer; they may be omitted on most systems. Includes a sample run.

Lines: 50
Version: North Star BASIC
Hardware: none
Software: none
Non-ANSI: FILL, HP strings, ! (used in place of PRINT), %() (used to format printouts)

42. Computation of Means and Standard Deviations

Author: Alan Forsythe

Source: *Byte* Jan 79 (4:1) "Elements of Statisitical Computation" pp. 182–184 (183–184)

Updates: commentary
Byte May 79 (4:5)
"Improving Statistic Accuracy" p. 223

correction
Byte Jun 79 (4:6)
"Statistical Computations Recomputed" p. 193

commentary
Byte Feb 80 (5:2)
"Algebraic Identities Are Not Numerical Identities" p. 174

Two of the most basic of all statistical elements are the *mean* and the *standard deviation*. The mean of a group of figures is a number which represents the average or typical value of the group. The standard deviation is a number which tells you how the numbers are grouped around the average. A large standard deviation tells you that the data vary greatly. This article discusses mean and standard deviation and shows some of the surprising pitfalls of computer calculation of these simple numbers. The programs demonstrate good and bad ways of doing the calculations. Includes flowcharts and sample runs.

Lines: 13, 10, 17, 18
Version: not given
Hardware: none
Software: none
Non-ANSI: SQRT()

339. Correlation

Author: Price

Source: *Creative Computing* May 79 (5:5) "And Then There *Was* One" pp. 67–69 (67)

This program computes the statistical correlation between two variables. The data is stored in DATA statements in the program. Includes a sample run. (Appeared originally in *Elementary Psychological Statistics*.)

Lines: 44
Version: not given
Hardware: none
Software: none
Non-ANSI: none

531. Statistics Package

Author: John Lehman

Source: *Interface Age* May 79 (4:5) "SABR Statistical Analysis for Business Research" pp. 76–85 (81–85)

Updates: commentary
  Interface Age Oct 79 (4:10)
  "Comments on TDL BASIC" p. 14 (14)

There are many computer programs that do statistics. The problem with many of these programs is that if you wish to do more than one statistical test, you have to reenter the data again. This statistics package allows you to enter the data just once, then use it again and again for various functions. The data may be edited as it is entered. Once the data is entered, a variety of routines can be called including correlation, regression, histograms, and covariance. When you're finished, the data can be saved on cassette. Includes a sample run and a list of program variables.

  Lines: 228, 106, 158, 16
  Version: TDL 8K BASIC
  Hardware: sequential file device
  Software: none
  Non-ANSI: strings, two-letter variables, ? (used in place of PRINT), extended IF, ASC(), VAL(), STR$(), SWITCH, TRACE, LPRINT

TRIGONOMETRY

245. Triangle Angles

  Author: Geoffrey Chase

  Source: *Creative Computing* Nov–Dec 77 (3:6)
    "New Benchmark Program" pp. 50–51 (51)

Given the length of each side of a triangle, it is possible to calculate what each of the corner angles is. This program does that. Given the lengths of the sides of a triangle, it prints out the angles both in radians and in degrees. The program is designed to be a "benchmark" program—that is, one designed to serve as a reference for testing and comparing the speeds of various computers or computer system implementations. A comparison of the running times for several different languages is provided. Includes a sample run.

  Lines: 63
  Version: EDUCOMP BASIC V2.0
  Hardware: none
  Software: none
  Non-ANSI: PI( ), strings, ! (used in place of REM)

142. Trigonometric Addition Problems

  Author: Samuel Spero

  Source: *Calculators/Computers Magazine* Sep–Oct 78 (2:6)
    "Calculators and Computers: Graphical Addition" pp. 87–90 (90)

Besides using the computer directly as a training tool, you can also use it to generate noncomputer problems. This program generates trigonometric addition problems. The problems generated ask the student to graph a function of the form: Y = A sin Bx + C cos Dx. The program also generates solution sheets for the teacher. Includes a sample run.

  Lines: 41
  Version: not given
  Hardware: none
  Software: none
  Non-ANSI: strings

59. Trigonometric Calculations Using CORDIC Techniques

  Author: John Ball

  Source: *Byte* May 79 (4:5)
    "Trigonometry in Two Easy Black Boxes" pp. 184–194 (189–190)

This program performs two functions. First, it performs rotations in Cartesian coordinates. If you have a point on a circle, and then you rotate it through a specified arc, the program can give you the new location of the point. Second, the program can calculate the displacement angle necessary to rotate a vector to a given position on a circle. Using these two features, the program can perform a wide variety of calculations, as discussed in the article. It can, for example, convert between Cartesian and polar coordinates or compute arctangent. The program uses CORDIC (COordinate Rotation DIgital Computer) techniques to perform the calculations. Two versions of the program are given, one for the binary number system and one for the decimal number system. Includes sample runs.

  Lines: 92, 86
  Version: not given
  Hardware: none
  Software: none
  Non-ANSI: none

362. Sine, Cosine, and Tangent Values for a Point on a Circle

  Author: Project Solo

  Source: *Creative Computing* Aug 79 (5:8)
    "Circular Functions" pp. 100–102 (101)

When you place a point on a circle whose center is at the origin, the line from the origin to the point forms an angle with the X-axis. Given the coordinates of the point, this program computes the sine, cosine, and tangent of the angle formed. Includes a flowchart and sample run. (This is a reprint of a Project Solo module.)

Lines: 22
Version: not given
Hardware: none
Software: none
Non-ANSI: strings

MISCELLANEOUS

167. Palindrome Program

Author: Tom Karzes

Source: *Creative Computing* Jan–Feb 75 (1:2)
"Palindromes: For Those Who Like to End at
the Beginning" pp. 10–12 (12)

Updates: commentary, new programs
Creative Computing May–Jun 75 (1:4)
"Follow-up on Palindromes" p. 18 (18)

A palindrome is a work, verse, number, or what-have-you
that reads the same backward as forward. This program
tests whether a given number is a palindrome. If the
number isn't a palindrome, the program goes on to form
it into one. Includes a sample run.

Lines: 17
Version: not given
Hardware: none
Software: none
Non-ANSI: extended IF

178. Palindromic Reversal Programs

Author: Gregory Yob

Source: *Creative Computing* May–Jun 75 (1:4)
"Follow-up on Palindromes" p. 18 (18)

Updates: commentary
Creative Computing Sep–Oct 75 (1:5)
" 'Feature' Letter to the Editor" p. 9

A palindromic number is one whose digits read the same
foward as backward. 8998 is an example of a palindromic
number. These two programs generate palindromic
numbers from "seed" numbers by using a process of
successive reversals and additions. Includes sample runs.

Lines: 22, 45
Version: HP 3000 BASIC
Hardware: none
Software: none
Non-ANSI: HP string

184. Odd or Even?

Author: Jeffrey Moskow

Source: *Creative Computing* Sep–Oct 75 (1:5)
"Odd or Even?" p. 24 (24)

This program takes an integer (whole number) and tells
whether it is odd or even. Includes a sample run.

Lines: 10
Version: not given
Hardware: none
Software: none
Non-ANSI: none

266. Computing the Logarithmic Constant E

Author: not given

Source: *Creative Computing* Mar–Apr 78 (4:2)
"Convergence" p. 132 (132)

Certain constants such as *e* and *pi* can be calculated as the
sum of a number of elements in a series. The logarithmic
constant *e* can be represented by the series: $1 + 1/1 + 1/2
+ 1/6 + 1/24 + \ldots$ This short program computes the
value of *e* using this convergence series. Includes a sample
run.

Lines: 10
Version: not given
Hardware: none
Software: none
Non-ANSI: none

25. Roman Numeral Arithmetic

Author: Laurence Dishman

Source: *Byte* Jun 78 (3:6)
"Those Calculating Romans" pp. 109–111
(109–111)

Today we use a system of numbers based on the digits 0
through 9. In ancient Rome a different number system
was used. That system was based on digits that included I
(1), V (5), and X (10). Roman numbers were formed by
combining the Roman digits according to a special set of
rules. This program can help you to learn about Roman
numerals. With this program you can add, subtract, multiply, divide, or translate Roman numerals. Includes a list
of program variables and a sample run.

Lines: 193
Version: North Star BASIC
Hardware: none
Software: none
Non-ANSI: HP strings, FILL, extended IF

322. Pascal's Triangle

Author: Jordan Mechner

Source: *Creative Computing* Mar 79 (5:3)
"Pascal's Triangle: What's It All About?" pp. 112–113 (112–113)

Updates: commentary
Creative Computing Jul 79 (5:7)
"Pascal's Triangle" p. 14

Pascal's Triangle is a "triangle" of numbers. The triangle has many amazing properties! Each row is symmetrical. The sums across the ascending diagonals form the Fibonacci sequence. Each row corresponds to the digits of a power of 11. There are many more. In this article there are two different programs to print out Pascal's Triangle. Includes sample runs.

Lines: 15, 15
Version: not given
Hardware: none
Software: none
Non-ANSI: none

528. Arithmetic of Complex Numbers

Author: Alfred Adler

Source: *Interface Age* May 79 (4:5)
"The Micro-Mathematician" pp. 39–42 (42)

Complex numbers are used frequently in many branches of science, mathematics, and engineering. Doing arithmetic using complex numbers can be somewhat involved, because you must keep track of both the real and imaginary parts of the numbers. This program can do arithmetic using complex numbers. The program can perform multiplication, division, roots, and powers. Where a number has more than one root, all of the roots are given. Includes a sample run.

Lines: 63
Version: PolyMorphic BASIC, ver. A00
Hardware: none
Software: none
Non-ANSI: strings, extennded IF, ! (used in place of PRINT)

360. Extended Precision Multiplication, Exponentiation, and Factorials

Author: Bruce Barnett

Source: *Creative Computing* Aug 79 (5:8)
"Accuracy Plus: Multiprecision Multiplication" pp. 82–84 (84)

Updates: commentary
Creative Computing Dec 79 (5:12)
"Accuracy [?] Plus" p. 12

How many digits of precision can your BASIC handle? Eight? Sixteen? More? It doesn't matter how great the precision is; sooner or later you're going to run into a problem where you need more than you have. This program demonstrates how multiplication can be done to virtually any accuracy you desire using strings to hold the data. The program also does extended precision exponentiation and factorials. Includes a sample run and a list of program variables.

Lines: 157
Version: Northstar BASIC
Hardware: none
Software: none
Non-ANSI: HP strings, STR$(), VAL(), DEF . . . FNEND, PRINT #, extended IF

4
PERSONAL INTEREST

ALCOHOL

586. Sobriety Tester

Author: Al Gerbens

Source: *Kilobaud* Aug 77 (8)
"Sobriety Tester Program" pp. 40–42 (42)

This is a program to determine whether or not you have had too much to drink. The program has two parts: first it accepts data about you, and then it conducts a skill test to determine how sober you are. In the first part of the program you are asked questions to determine how much you have had to drink, what your body weight is, what your tolerance for booze is, and whether or not you have had something to eat. In the second part of the test, you are given tests to gauge your reaction time and memory. From this information the program decides how bombed you are. Includes a sample run.

Lines:	156
Version:	Digital Group Maxi-BASIC ver. One
Hardware:	none
Software:	none
Non-ANSI:	strings, extended IF, INP(), # (used in place of PRINT)

965. Computerized Bartender

Author: Sam Newhouse

Source: *Personal Computing* Aug 78 (2:8)
"Computing on the Rocks" pp. 22–34 (29–34)

Do you get befuddled when you have to tend bar? If so, this program can help. It is a computerized bartending program. The program can't dispense drinks, but can do just about everything else. It can provide you with the recipes for a wide variety of drinks. The program can tell you what garnishes go with what drinks and what type of bar glass you should serve each drink in. It can even print out pictures of each type of glass. You can name a specific spirit, and then have the program display all the recipes that use that ingredient. Finally, the program can print

out a shopping list for the quantity of ingredients necessary to prepare the number of drinks you specify. Includes a flowchart and sample run.

Lines:	528
Version:	MITS 3.4 Disk Extended BASIC
Hardware:	none
Software:	none
Non-ANSI:	CLEAR, strings, WIDTH, two-letter variables, extended IF, ON . . . GOSUB

139. Alcohol Effects Program

Author: John Cook

Source: *Calculators/Computers Magazine* Sep–Oct 78 (2:6)
"How to Get Dead Drunk and Survive" pp. 66–68 (67)

Can you handle your booze? This program shows you just how alcohol affects people. You type in your body weight, what kind of alcohol you plan to drink, how long you plan to drink, and how much you plan to drink. The computer then types out what your blood alcohol percentage will be and how it will proabably affect your behavior. Includes a sample run.

Lines:	90
Version:	Hewlett Packard 2000 BASIC
Hardware:	none
Software:	none
Non-ANSI:	none

AMATEUR RADIO

649. Morse Code Reader

Author: Robert Kurtz

Source: *Kilobaud* Nov 78 (23)
"World of the Brass Pounders: Receive Morse Code the Easy Way" pp. 34–36 (34)

Updates: modifications
      Kilobaud Microcomputing Jan 79 (25)
      "A Blow for Standardization" p. 21 (21)

Now your home computer can help you receive ham radio transmissions. This program decodes and prints out Morse code. The program has self-adaptive adjustment for changes in code speed, so it can adjust to anyone's "fist." The program can detect the ends of words and print out the spaces needed. The article describes the interface circuit needed to attach your receiver to your computer. Includes a flowchart.

Lines: 37
Version: 9K Microsoft BASIC
Hardware: interface circuit
Software: none
Non-ANSI: strings, PEEK(), AND(), two-letter variables, extended IF

795. Morse Keyboard for the OSI Challenger

Author: William Taylor

Source: *Micro* Jun 79 (13)
      "The Basic Morse Keyboard" pp. 13–15 (15)

Updates: correction
      Micro Sep 79 (16)
      untitled p. 34 (34)

Are you a ham radio operator? Is your finger getting tired from all of those dots and dashes? Let your computer do the keying! This program takes input from the keyboard of an Ohio Scientific Instruments Challenger. It then translates the ASCII characters into Morse code and outputs them to your transmitter or tone generator.

Lines: 119
Version: MicroSoft BASIC
Hardware: Ohio Scientific Instruments Challenger
Software: none
Non-ANSI: POKE, PEEK(), extended IF, USR()

ART

849. Flower-Pot Art

Author: Joel McCormack

Source: *People's Computer Company* Sep 73 (2:1)
      "Joel & Andy's Page" p. 16 (16)

This program prints out an art pattern that resembles a plant in a flower pot. Includes a sample run.

Lines: 68
Version: not given
Hardware: none
Software: none
Non-ANSI: HP strings, MAX()

850. Art Patterns Based on Your Sun Sign

Author: Jane Wood

Source: *People's Computer Company* Nov 73 (2:2)
      "SUNSIGN" p. 17 (17)

With this program you can generate a pattern based on your name and sun sign. The pattern is composed of blanks, zeros, and asterisks. The asterisks indicate "expanding stuff." The zeros show "contracting stuff." The blanks indicate "no stuff." The outer part of the design is your outward image (how you look to others). The inner part of the design is your inward being. Your situation lies in the arrangement of your expanding stuff, contracting stuff, and space. Includes a sample run.

Lines: 160
Version: not given
Hardware: none
Software: none
Non-ANSI: HP strings, ENTER

852. MANDALA: Computer Art Program

Author: Marc LeBrun

Source: *People's Computer Company* May 74 (2:5)
      "MANDALA" p. 8 (8)

The dictionary defines "mandala" as "a schematized representation of the cosmos, chiefly characterized by a concentric organization of geometric shapes, each of which contains an image or attribute of a deity." I'm not sure about the deities, but this program does seem to produce some interesting artistic patterns. The patterns are printed out on an ordinary terminal; no special graphics capability is required. You can specify the size of the pattern to be generated, as well as input constants to define the characteristics of the pattern to be created. Includes sample runs.

Lines: 64
Version: not given
Hardware: none
Software: none
Non-ANSI: none

170. "Love" Poster

Author: David Ahl

Source: *Creative Computing* Jan–Feb 75 (1:2)
"Love" p. 19 (19)

This program prints out copies of Robert Indiana's "Love" poster. The program uses the letters in the word love to form a large poster with the word love printed on it in stylized form. Includes a sample output.

Lines: 34
Version: DEC RSTS-11 BASIC-PLUS
Hardware: none
Software: none
Non-ANSI: strings, OPEN, CLOSE, PRINT #, MID(),
extended IF

864. Generating Patterns Based on Your Name

Author: Richard Mickelsen and Magdalena Muller

Source: *People's Computer Company* Mar 75 (3:4)
"Generating Patterns from People's Names"
p. 23 (23)

The technique of generating patterns from people's names is known by most handweavers. However, drawing patterns by hand to determine if they are interesting enough to actually weave is quite tedious. This program does the job automatically. In the process, it produces some very interesting artistic patterns. The patterns are all the more interesting because you can have one based on your own name. In effect, you have your own personal pattern. That pattern can be printed out on a regular terminal; no special graphics terminal is needed. Includes a sample run.

Lines: 76
Version: DEC BASIC-Plus
Hardware: none
Software: none
Non-ANSI: strings, CHANGE, ASCII(), extended IF,
LEFT()

224. Artistic Patterns Based on Pascal's Triangle

Author: Charles Lund

Source: *Creative Computing* Mar–Apr 77 (3:2)
"PASART" pp. 122–123 (122–123)

Mathematics can often be merged with art. Here is an example. This program generates artistic patterns on a regular terminal, based on Pascal's triangle. Pascal's triangle is a famous mathematical number pattern. The triangle consists of six rows. The first two rows contain only 1s. Each of the other rows contains a 1 at each end, and numbers in between such that each of the numbers in the row is the sum of the two numbers to the right and left in the row above. The program provides the user with three options: (1) print a single triangle, (2) print two triangles, and (3) print four triangles. Option 1 simply allows you to examine an artistic picture of the relative positions of the multiples of any number in the array. Option 2 allows you to create a picture based on triangles in opposite corners of a square array. Option 3 allows you to create a picture based on Pascal's triangles in the four corners of a square. Includes sample runs.

Lines: 126
Version: not given
Hardware: none
Software: none
Non-ANSI: MAT INPUT

239. Anamorphic Art

Author: Andy Zucker

Source: *Creative Computing* Jul–Aug 77 (3:4)
"Anamorphic Art" pp. 137–140 (138–139)

Anamorphic art is a certain popular kind of "distorted" art. The distorted images look normal only when reflected from a curved mirror. This program is designed to produce cylindrically distorted anamorphic art. You start by creating a normal picture on a 60-by-60 grid. You enter this into the computer using routines to draw curves, lines, and points. The computer then takes this internal image and mathematically distorts it. The final image is then printed out on a regular terminal; no special graphics capability is required. Includes sample runs.

Lines: 90
Version: DEC BASIC-Plus
Hardware: none
Software: none
Non-ANSI: strings, extended IF, PI( ), FOR (used as a
modifier)

241. Art & Mathematical Structures

Author: R. Chandhok and M. Critchfield

Source: *Creative Computing* Sep–Oct 77 (3:5)
"Art & Mathematical Structures" pp. 61–64
(64)

The Algebra of Symmetry is a mathematical system based not on numbers, but instead on the changing positions of a given polygon. The system elements include rotations, flips, mirrors, and identity. Designs based upon these symmetrics can be quite striking. The program given calculates the rotations and reflections of a regular polygon of *n* sides. The output is a set of tables which represent the transformations. Translated into graphic design elements, these patterns can form abstract works of art. Includes a sample run.

Lines: 86
Versions: not given
Hardware: none
Software: none
Non-ANSI: PRINT USING, strings, extended IF

242. Lissajous Art

Author: Larry Ruane

Source: *Creative Computing* Sep–Oct 77 (3:5)
"Lissajous" p. 132 (132)

A Lissajous pattern is a pattern based on harmonics. This program prints out Lissajous patterns. You enter the relative x and y frequencies, and the phase. The program then prints out a Lissajous pattern on your terminal; no special graphics capability is required. Two versions of the program are provided. One is in MITS Extended BASIC. The other is in IBM 370 BASIC. They produce identical results. Includes a sample output.

Lines: 39, 41
Version: IBM 370 BASIC, MITS Extended BASIC
Hardware: none
Software: none
Non-ANSI: [MITS version] FIX( )
[IBM version] ASN( ), RAD( ), multiple-assignment

271. Light-Pen Crayon for the Compucolor 8051

Author: not given

Source: *Creative Computing* May–Jun 78 (4:3)
"Color Graphics with a Light-Pen" pp. 92–95

This demonstration program shows off the color graphics abilities of the Compucolor 8051. The program creates artistic displays in color using information that you supply via a light-pen. As written, the program generates a display that is basically an ellipse with random vectors inside it. You control the colors used and the arrangement of the vectors. The program can be modified to produce other types of displays. Includes a description of the program and samples of the output (in color). (Appeared originally in *BASIC and the Personal Computer*.)

Lines: 30
Version: Compucolor BASIC
Hardware: Compucolor 8051, light-pen
Software: none
Non-ANSI: not translatable

272. Computer Art: STARGATE

Author: Joe Jacobson

Source: *Creative Computing* May–Jun 78 (4:3)
"Computer Art: STARGATE" p. 107 (107)

Some computer art programs embody generalized routines, and can draw a wide range of different pictures in response to various parameters entered through the keyboard. Other programs are designed solely to draw a particular picture thought up by the designer. This program is a computer art program of the latter type. The design it creates is a star pattern on a background of concentric circles. The author drew the pattern using a Tektronix 4051 terminal. The program could, however, be modified for use with other graphics devices. Includes a sample of the output.

Lines: 114
Version: Tektronix BASIC
Hardware: Tektronix 4051
Software: none
Non-ANSI: Not translatable

619. Snoopy on the TRS-80

Author: Tom Kasper

Source: *Kilobaud* May 78 (17)
"Best User Program of the Quarter" pp. 8–9, 20–21 (9, 20–21)

This program plots a display of Snoopy cursing the Red Baron. The program is designed to run on a TRS-80 computer. Includes a sample of the output.

Lines: 86
Version: TRS-80 Level I BASIC
Hardware: TRS-80
Software: none
Non-ANSI: not translatable

288. Drawing Gumowski-Mira Patterns on a Tektronix 4051

Author: John Lansdown

Source: *Creative Computing* Sep–Oct 78 (4:5)
"GUMOWSKI" pp. 88–89 (88)

This program generates interesting computer art patterns on the screen of a Tektronix 4051. The program can probably be adapted to draw patterns on other video displays. Includes a sample output.

Lines: 25
Version: Tektronix 4051 BASIC
Hardware: Tektronix 4051
Software: none
Non-ANSI: not translatable

301. Snowflake Patterns

Author: James Jones

Source: *Creative Computing* Nov–Dec 78 (4:6)
"Snowflake Plotting in ALGOL and BASIC"
pp. 146–149 (148–149)

Snowflakes form some of the most beautiful designs in nature. This program generates snowflake patterns. The program output is just a list of coordinates. If you wish to see the patterns drawn, you'll have to write your own driver for a graphics device. An ALGOL version of the program is included in addition to the BASIC version. Includes a list of program variables.

Lines: 168
Version: MITS BASIC
Hardware: none
Software: none
Non-ANSI: multi-letter variables, MOD(), extended IF

785. High-Resolution Lissajous and Hypocycloid Patterns

Author: John Sherburne

Source: *Micro* Mar 79 (10)
"High-Resolution Plotting for the PET" pp. 19–23 (19–23)

Updates: modifications for OSI
Micro Oct 79 (17)
"Hypocycloids" pp. 52–53 (53)

Using assembly language routines, it is possible to do "high-resolution" (80-by-50) plotting on the screen of your PET. These programs draw various figures based on mathematical equations using this high-resolution feature. Includes a sample output.

Lines: 10, 14, 12 (plus patch), 12, 19
Version: PET BASIC
Hardware: PET
Software: 6502 assembly language routine
Non-ANSI: not translatable

1084. Rose Leaf Patterns for the Apple II

Author: Jim Day

Source: *Recreational Computing* Mar–Apr 79 (7:5)
"APPLE ROSE" p. 55 (55)

This program plots "rose leaf" patterns on an Apple II using high-resolution graphics. Includes a sample output.

Lines: 16
Version: Applesoft II BASIC
Hardware: Apple II
Software: none
Non-ANSI: not translatable

331. Superose

Author: Michael Zorn

Source: *Creative Computing* Apr 79 (5:4)
"Superose" pp. 98–99 (99)

This program draws a variety of artistic line patterns based on the formula $r = a \sin n$. The program is set up to use the PET's plotting abilities, but you should be able to modify it for other systems fairly easily. Includes a sample output.

Lines: 13
Version: PET BASIC
Hardware: PET
Software: none
Non-ANSI: not translatable

1091. Cascading Display for the PET

Author: Harry Saal

Source: *Recreational Computing* May–Jun 79 (7:6)
"SPOT" pp. 52–55 (55)

This program creates a display which "cascades" down the screen of a PET.

Lines: 58
Version: PET BASIC
Hardware: PET
Software: none
Non-ANSI: not translatable

344. Lissajous Figures Using the Diablo HyTerm Printer

Author: Tom McDonough

Source: *Creative Computing* Jun 79 (5:6)
"Computer Graphics With the Diablo" pp.
32–35 (34–35)

Updates: corrections
Creative Computing Oct 79 (5:10)
"Diablo Graphics" p. 14 (14)

Lissajous figures are created by plotting two sine waves of different frequencies on a graph. One sine wave is used for the x component of the graph; the other wave is used for the y component. This program plots such figures using the graphics capabilities of the Diablo HyTerm printer. Includes a sample output.

Lines: 124 (plus patch)
Version: North Star disk BASIC
Hardware: Diablo HyTerm printer
Software: none
Non-ANSI: strings, extended IF, OUT, ASC()

395. Mondrian Designs for the TRS-80

Author: Stephen Gray

Source: *Creative Computing* Oct 79 (5:10)
"TRS-80 Strings" pp. 170–176 (170)

These programs produce designs on a TRS-80 that are reminiscent of paintings by Mondrian. Mondrian's works consist mainly of intersecting black horizontal and vertical stripes on a white canvas. Includes a sample output.

Lines: 5, 5 (plus patch), 7, 12
Version: TRS-80 BASIC
Hardware: TRS-80
Software: none
Non-ANSI: not translatable

746. United States Flag Display for the PolyMorphic Poly-88

Author: David L. Johnson

Source: *Kilobaud Microcomputing* Nov 79 (35)
"Wave the Flag" p. 110 (110)

This program draws a picture of the United States flag on the screen of a PolyMorphic Poly-88.

Lines: 43
Version: POLY ver. A00 BASIC
Hardware: Poly-88
Software: none
Non-ANSI: not translatable

416. TRS-80 Key Character Patterns

Author: not given

Source: *Creative Computing* Dec 79 (5:12)
"TRS-80 Strings" pp. 154–161 (156)

This program creates patterns on the screen of a TRS-80. The patterns are based on key characters that you type in. (This program was reprinted from the *Radio Shack Newsletter*.)

Lines: 8
Version: TRS-80 BASIC
Hardware: TRS-80
Software: none
Non-ANSI: not translatable

ASTROLOGY

665. Funny Horoscopes

Author: Adrian Thornton

Source: *Kilobaud Microcomputing* Feb 79 (26)
"Madam Dupre's House of the Zodiac" pp.
48–49 (49)

This program generates sarcastic horoscopes. There are twelve horoscopes built into the program (one for each sign of the zodiac). Includes a sample run.

Lines: 138
Version: Heath Extended Benton Harbor Cassette BASIC
Hardware: none
Software: none
Non-ANSI: strings, extended IF

527. Astrology Program

Author: Michael Erlewine

Source: *Interface Age* Apr 79 (4:4)
"Astrological Horoscope Program" pp.
146–149 (148–149)

Updates: uncorrected errors
Interface Age Aug–Sep 79 (4:8)
"Horoscope Program Problem" p. 11

commentary
Interface Age Oct 79 (4:10)
"Letters" p. 10

commentary
Interface Age Jan 80 (5:1)
"Who's Playing Games?" p. 14

If you're into astrology then this program should be of interest to you. This program computes the planetary positions of the Zodiac as well as all 12 of the House Cusps including the Rising Sign. You can use the program to check out the conditions of the Cosmos at the moment of your birth, or at any time that you select. Includes a sample run.

Lines:	198
Version:	PET 8K BASIC
Hardware:	none
Software:	none
Non-ANSI:	strings, VAL(), STR$(), two-letter variables, GET, extended IF, RUN (used as a program statement)

AUTOMOBILES

9. Program to Compute Gas Mileage

Author: John Bauernschub

Source: *Byte* Oct 77 (2:10)
"Analyze Your Car's Gas Economy with Your Computer" pp. 166–167 (167)

This program allows you to analyze your car's gas economy. To do this you need to keep track of how much fuel you buy and what your mileage is at the time of each purchase. The computer takes this information and outputs your average gas mileage as well as other information. Includes a sample run.

Lines:	67
Version:	SWTPC BASIC
Hardware:	none
Software:	none
Non-ANSI:	extended IF, strings

14. Simulation of an Automobile Suspension System

Author: Stephen Smith

Source: *Byte* Dec 77 (2:12)
"Simulation of Motion (Part II): An Automobile Suspension" pp. 112–116 (116)

This program is a simulation of an automobile suspension system. Given information concerning road conditions and the automobile suspension, the program simulates the action of an automobile suspension system. The output is on a regular terminal; no special graphics capability is needed. Includes a list of program variables.

Lines:	75
Version:	Tektronix 4051 BASIC
Hardware:	none
Software:	none
Non-ANSI:	none

280. Auto Maintenance Record

Author: Rob Lufkin

Source: *Creative Computing* Jul–Aug 78 (4:4)
"Does Your Car Need Oil?" pp. 79–80 (79)

Anyone who has ever owned an automobile or similar type of complicated equipment has probably, at one time or another, been faced with the problem of determining when maintenance is due. It's not difficult to conclude that you need new brakes if pushing the brake pedal fails to slow your car. However, most car maintenance is more mundane and more difficult to remember. This program takes over the job of maintaining records for your car. Initially, you enter the maintenance schedule for your car. Then, from time to time, you run the program, which prints out a check-list of the repairs or service which needs to be done. The check-list is based on your car's current mileage, the date, and what previous service has been done. Work that is overdue by 50% or more is flagged with double asterisks. Includes a sample run.

Lines:	38
Version:	not given
Hardware:	none
Software:	none
Non-ANSI:	strings, STR$()

918. Automobile Miles Per Gallon

Author: Milan Chepko

Source: *People's Computers* Sep–Oct 78 (7:2)
"Decimals in Tiny BASIC" pp. 34–35 (35)

The price of gas is going up all the time. This program won't help your car get any better mileage, but it can at least tell you what kind of mileage it does get. Every time you fill up, you record the number of gallons you buy and your car's odometer reading. Using this information, the program computes your car's MPG. Includes a flowchart and a list of program variables.

Lines: 37
Version: Denver Tiny BASIC
Hardware: none
Software: none
Non-ANSI: CLRS, PR, RET, IN, extended IF

1073. TRS-80 Miles Per Gallon Program

Author: Milan Chepko

Source: *Recreational Computing* Jan–Feb 79 (7:4)
"TRS-80: Miles Per Gallon Program" pp. 16–18 (17–18)

Updates: corrections and improvements
Recreational Computing May–Jun 79 (7:6)
"Author Refines 'MPG' " p. 7 (7)

One way to keep your car in tip-top shape is to keep track of what kind of mileage you're getting. If your mileage starts to gradually fall off, then you know it's time for a tune-up. In order to accurately track your car's MPG you'll want a program like this one to record the details. This program records how many gallons you get and what your mileage is at each fill-up. It then uses this information to compute how many miles you are getting out of every gallon of gas. Includes a flowchart.

Lines: 88
Version: TRS-80 Level II BASIC
Hardware: TRS-80
Software: none
Non-ANSI: not translatable

728. Mileage Calculator

Author: Phil Feldman and Tom Rugg

Source: *Kilobaud Microcomputing* Sep 79 (33)
"Happy Motoring!" pp. 48–50 (48)

As the cost of gasoline goes through the roof, you may be becoming more concerned about what kind of gasoline mileage your car is getting. This program keeps records of how much gasoline your car gets at each fill-up and how far it has traveled. From these records, the program can compute your car's mileage. Includes a sample run and a list of program variables.

Lines: 65 (plus patch)
Version: PET BASIC
Hardware: sequential file device
Software: none
Non-ANSI: two-letter variables, strings, extended IF, OPEN, CLOSE, PRINT #, INPUT #, GET, SPC(), POKE, STR$(), ON . . . GOSUB

BANNERS

211. Print Out Posters on a Regular Terminal

Author: Bradford Huntress

Source: *Creative Computing* Nov–Dec 76 (2:6)
"POSTER" pp. 84–85 (85)

This program prints out banners on ordinary hard-copy terminals. The letters are made up of groups of regular-size terminal characters. The lettering on the banners produced runs "sideways" down the length of the paper. All the letters have rounded corners where appropriate. The computer asks you for the height, width, and left-hand margin in inches. It next asks for your message. Using this information, the computer then prints out your banner. Includes sample runs.

Lines: 179
Version: DEC EDU250 BASIC
Hardware: none
Software: none
Non-ANSI: ! (used in place of REM), LINPUT, CAT(), strings, extended IF, FIX(), MID()

233. Papertape Message Printer

Author: Bill Gardner and Jim Larus

Source: *Creative Computing* May–Jun 77 (3:3)
"TICKERTAPE" p. 126 (126)

This program inputs a line of characters from a Teletype, and then punches the shape of each letter on papertape. The program can handle the letters from A to Z, as well as numbers from 0 to 9. The program cannot print out special symbols. The letters are formed by an 8-by-5 dot matrix on the tape. The program uses PDP-8 BASIC internal representation of the numbers and letters, so it will not work with other systems. Includes a sample output.

Lines: 27
Version: PDP-8 BASIC
Hardware: PDP-8, terminal with papertape punch
Software: none
Non-ANSI: not translatable

936. BANNER

Author: Ed Bernstein

Source: *Personal Computing* Jan 78 (2:1)
"Banner Fun" pp. 85–87 (86)

This program can print out banners of different sizes on your terminal. The characters are formed by a 5-by-7 "dot" matrix. There are 79 characters including lower-case characters (you can print lower-case banners even if your terminal does not have lower-case characters). The characters on the banner can be any size. The program has many special capabilities. You can print "reverse" (white-on-black) characters. You can align the characters in several different ways. The program uses Data General strings, which are similar to Hewlett-Packard strings. Includes a sample output.

Lines: 393
Version: Data General Nova 1200 BASIC
Hardware: none
Software: none
Non-ANSI: HP strings, RESTOR

635. Sign Printer

Author: Joseph Roehrig

Source: *Kilobaud* Aug 78 (20)
"Computer-Generated Signs: Put Your TTY to Work!" pp. 90–93 (90–91)

Updates: commentary
Kilobaud Microcomputing Feb 79 (26)
"Looking Before Leaping" p. 19

This program generates signs. The characters on the sign are formed by groups of regular terminal characters. Each letter on the sign is ten characters wide and seven characters high. Each letter is formed from groups of the corresponding normal-letter. Includes a sample run.

Lines: 47
Version: not given
Hardware: none
Software: none
Non-ANSI: HP strings, ! (used in place of PRINT), ASC(), extended IF

676. Dot Matrix Banner Program

Author: Jonathan Rotenberg

Source: *Kilobaud Microcomputing* Mar 79 (27)
"ULTRA BANNER" pp. 90–93 (91)

Updates: corrections
Kilobaud Microcomputing Sep 79 (33)
" 'Banner' Headline" p. 21 (21)

ULTRA BANNER is a banner printing program. The program combines the letters printed out by your terminal into groups to form the larger letters of the banner.

This program uses the "dot matrix" technique for forming letters. The letters in the banner can run either horizontally or vertically across the printout. If you have a Practical Automation DMTP-6 uP printer, the program can make use of the printer's double-width character capabilities. The program also has provisions for user-defined characters. Includes a sample run.

Lines: 53 (plus patch)
Version: TDL 8K BASIC, ver. 1.1
Hardware: none
Software: none
Non-ANSI: LPRINT, ASC(), strings, LWIDTH, extended IF

555. Poster Program

Author: Alan Miller

Source: *Interface Age* Oct 79 (4:10)
"Announce Your Next Meeting With Posters" pp. 139–142 (140–142)

Updates: corrections
Interface Age Mar 80 (5:3)
"On Alan Miller and Software" p. 8 (8)

This program prints out posters using a regular printing terminal or printer. This poster program prints out signs with 1-by-3/4-inch block letters. The letters are composed of As overprinted with Ws. The program draws a border around the sign. At the bottom of the sign you can have a line in small letters. Includes a sample output.

Lines: 244
Version: Microsoft BASIC
Hardware: none
Software: none
Non-ANSI: ' (used in place of REM), CLEAR, DEFINT, two-letter variables, strings, STR$( ), LINE INPUT, extended IF, LPRINT, SPACE$( ), MOD( ), ASC( ), SPC( )

BIORHYTHMS

859. Biorhythm Plotter

Author: not given

Source: *People's Computer Company* Nov 74 (3:2)
"BIOSIN" pp. 6–7 (7)

Updates: more readable listing
People's Computer Company Mar 75 (3:4)
"BIOSIN" p. 24 (24)

The biorhythm theory postulates that there are certain metabolic rhythms that have a constant cycle in the human body. The theory says that there are three of these cycles (known as inner clocks): the physical cycle, the sensitivity cycle, and the cognitive cycle. These cycles vary at regular intervals. The midpoints in the cycles are known as critical days and have a special significance. At these points a person is supposedly more prone to accidents. This program can plot your biorhythms. The output is on a regular terminal; no special graphics capability is needed. Includes a sample run.

Lines: 155
Version: not given
Hardware: none
Software: none
Non-ANSI: HP strings, MAT READ, extended IF

865. BIOSIN for a Tiny Edusystem

Author: not given

Source: *People's Comupter Company* Jul 75 (4:1)
"BIOSIN for a Tiny Edusystem" pp. 10–11 (10)

According to the biorhythm theory, there are metabolic cycles which govern our lives. There are many biorhythm plotting programs available. This one is designed for use on systems that don't have much memory. Includes a sample run.

Lines: 85
Version: DEC EDU20-C BASIC
Hardware: none
Software: none
Non-ANSI: strings, LINPUT, PRI, extended IF

1. Compute and Plot Your Biorhythms

Author: Joy and Richard Fox

Source: *Byte* Apr 76 (8)
"Biorhythm for Computers" pp. 20–23 (22)

Updates: correction
Byte Jul 76 (11)
"Patching the Biorhythm Program" p. 100 (100)

correction
Byte Nov 76 (15)
"Patch of a Patch" p. 90 (90)

According to the biorhythm hypothesis, humans have life rhythms which govern their actions. These rhythms are divided into three classes: emotional, physical, and men-

tal. When your cycles are up, you feel physically strong, emotionally high, and mentally alert. When your cycles are down, you feel correspondingly low. At the critical midpoints, you are in transition, and are especially prone to accidents and illness. This program plots these rhythms on a terminal. Included are a flowchart and a sample run.

Lines: 127
Version: not given
Hardware: none
Software: none
Non-ANSI: HP strings

454. Biorhythm Plotter

Author: Paul Greene

Source: *Interface Age* Aug 76 (1:9)
"Biorhythm" pp. 6, 64 (64)

According to the Biorhythm hypothesis, the human body is governed by three cycles. These cycles—the emotional, mental, and physical cycles—supposedly control how you act and feel on any given day. The cycles start at birth and vary over periods ranging from 23 to 33 days. This program plots these cycles on a terminal. (No special graphics display is needed.)

Lines: 72
Version: Altair 8K BASIC (ver. 3.0)
Hardware: none
Software: none
Non-ANSI: strings, extended IF

455. Biorhythm Plotter

Author: William Donham

Source: *Interface Age* Aug 76 (1:9)
"Biorhythms in Practice" pp. 48–51 (50–51)

Biological rhythms (biorhythms) are based on the theory that the energy of the brain and nervous system varies in cycles of fixed durations. These variations affect your physical, emotional, and intellectual powers. This program plots biorhythm cycles. Includes sample runs.

Lines: 88
Version: IMSAI 8K BASIC
Hardware: none
Software: none
Non-ANSI: multi-letter variables, strings, SPC(), POS(), STR$(), extended IF

480. Plot Your Biorhythms

Author: William Mitchell

Source: *Interface Age* Oct 77 (2:11)
"BIORHYTHM" pp. 138–144 (142–144)

Updates: complete rework of program
Interface Age Dec 77 (2:13)
"Biorhythm" pp. 140–146 (144–146)

correction
Interface Age Feb 78 (3:2)
"More Biorhythm Corrections" p. 8 (8)

This is a program to plot your biorhythms. According to
the biorhythm theory, there are three metabolic cycles in
the human body. The three main cycles are the 23-day
physical cycle, the 28-day emotional cycle, and the 33-day
intellectual cycle. When a cycle is low, you feel low in that
particular respect. When a cycle is high, you are at your
best in that area. At the midpoints in the cycles are critical
days when your performance is unstable. This program
produces a graph of these cycles. Includes sample runs.

Lines: 106
Version: not given
Hardware: none
Software: none
Non-ANSI: strings, PRINT #, extended IF

934. Biorhythms

Author: Phil Hughes

Source: *Personal Computing* Nov–Dec 77 (1:6)
"Biorhythm & Readout" pp. 94–97 (96–97)

Biorhythms, and the theory of their charting, rest on the
premise that three cycles, beginning on the day of birth,
affect you throughout your life. Each of the three cycles
has its own period; the Physical lasts 23 days, the Sensitivity or Emotional cycle lasts 28 days, and the Cognitive or
Intellectual cycle lasts 33 days. Critical days occur when
you cross the midpoint of each cycle. During this time,
you are more likely to feel unsure and indecisive about
the things that the particular cycle deals with (i.e., clumsy
when the physical cycle crosses the midpoint, indecisive
during cognitive crossings, emotionally upset while sensitivity crosses). This program plots your biorhythms on
your terminal. Includes a sample run.

Lines: 140
Version: SWTPC 8K BASIC
Hardware: none
Software: none
Non-ANSI: strings, PORT, extended IF

256. Biorhythms with Bio-Index

Author: J. Robertson

Source: *Creative Computing* Jan–Feb 78 (4:1)
"How Was I Yesterday?" pp. 74–78 (75–77)

The theory of biorhythms, which has been around since
the late 1800s, speculates that each person is guided by
three cycles that begin at birth. The intellectual, physical,
and emotional cycles are each sine curves with amplitude
one and periods of 33, 23, and 28 days, respectively. This
program plots your set of biorhythms on your terminal;
no special graphics capability is required. This version of
BIORHYTHM includes a Bio-Index, a quantity that
summarizes your biorhythm state. Includes a sample run.

Lines: 166
Version: not given
Hardware: none
Software: none
Non-ANSI: strings

CLOCKS

663. VDM Clock Program

Author: James Brennan

Source: *Kilobaud Microcomputing* Jan 79 (25)
"VDM Clock Program" p. 95 (95)

With this program you can use your computer as a (very
expensive) digital clock. The clock can be adjusted to run
slower or faster.

Lines: 75
Version: Altair BASIC, 12K ver. 3.2
Hardware: Video Display Module (VDM)
Software: none
Non-ANSI: two-letter variables, OUT, VAL(), POKE,
extended IF, strings

75. Telling Time with a Digital Clock Chip

Author: Steven Ciarcia

Source: *Byte* Aug 79 (4:8)
"Anyone Know the Real Time?" pp. 50–59
(58)

One way to let your computer know the time of day is to
add a digital clock circuit to your system. This article

describes how to use a digital clock integrated circuit (the kind used in digital watches) to give your computer a time-of-day clock. You can use such a clock, for example, to turn your house lights on and off at different times to scare away burglars when you are not at home. The demonstration program reads the clock and prints the time. Includes a flowchart.

Lines: 16
Version: Micro Com 8K Zapple BASIC
Hardware: digital clock circuit (homemade)
Software: none
Non-ANSI: OUT, INP(), AND(), extended IF

387. TRS-80 Digital Clock

Author: Delmer Hinrichs

Source: *Creative Computing* Oct 79 (5:10)
"Graphics Digital Clock" pp. 110–113
(112–113)

Updates: modifications
Creative Computing Mar 80 (6:3)
"Tick Tock for the TRS-80 Clock" p. 14 (14)

correction
Creative Computing Apr 80 (6:4)
" 'Turning Over' The Clock" p. 10 (10)

This program uses the TRS-80's graphics to display a 12- or 24-hour digital clock. It provides a continuous display of the time in hours, minutes, and seconds. The characters used are four centimeters high, so you can read the time all the way across the room. The program needs no real-time clock because the operation of the TRS-80's microprocessor is stable enough to give the correct time, accurate to within a fraction of a second per day. Includes a sample output.

Lines: 104
Version: TRS-80 Level II BASIC
Hardware: TRS-80
Software: none
Non-ANSI: not translatable

762. Heathkit H8 Alarm Clock Program

Author: Adrian Thornton

Source: *Kilobaud Microcomputing* Dec 79 (36)
"H8 Alarm Clock Program" pp. 160–161
(161)

With its nine-digit LED display and internal speaker, the Heathkit H8 computer is a natural as an alarm clock. This program keeps time by referencing the H8's internal clock tick counter. You can set the "alarm" for any time you want. The current time is displayed on the LED display. You also have the option of an audible "tick tock." Includes a sample run.

Lines: 56
Version: Heathkit Extended Cassette BASIC
Hardware: Heahtkit H8
Software: none
Non-ANSI: strings, LINE INPUT, PEEK(), POKE, SEG(), AND(), VAL(), extended IF, PAUSE

CODES

428. Playfaire Coder-Decoder

Author: Marvin Winzenread

Source: *Dr. Dobb's Journal of Computer Calisthenics & Orthodontia* May 77 (2:5)
"Jack Armstrong's Super Decoder Ring— Revisited" p. 9 (9)

Want to play James Bond? Here is a computer-driven message coder-decoder system for you. The system is based on the Playfaire-Digraphic Cryptographic Cypher, a cypher system used during World War II. The code is generated using a "key word" and a 5-by-5 letter matrix. Simple letter substitution cyphers are easily broken using statistical analysis of the frequencies with which characters occur in the code text. This system avoids this problem by applying the cypher to letter pairs, thus destroying normal letter frequencies. A description of the coding system is given in *DDJ* Vol. 1, No. 9. Includes a sample run.

Lines: 40
Version: ALTAIR 8K BASIC
Hardware: none
Software: none
Non-ANSI: CLEAR, strings, extended IF

249. Cryptarithmetic

Author: Donald Piele and Larry Wood

Source: *Creative Computing* Nov–Dec 77 (3:6)
"Thinking Strategies with the Computer: Contradiction" pp. 86–89 (89)

Computers are very good at using predetermined algorithmic methods for solving specific problems. Humans, on the other hand, excel at the use of heuristic methods. In the heuristic approach, the nature of the solution to a general problem is guessed, and then proved to be correct. This program simulates a heuristic problem-solving method for a specific problem. The problem solved is one of cryptarithmetic. Cryptarithmetic is a type of problem in which letters have been substituted for the digits in an arithmetic problem. This program solves a cryptarithmetic problem. Includes a sample run.

Lines: 49
Version: not given
Hardware: none
Software: none
Non-ANSI: LIN(), extended IF

969. Coder/Decoder

Author: Stephen Smith

Source: Personal Computing Aug 78 (2:8)
"Secrecy and Your Personal Computer" pp.
75–78 (76)

Security is a hot topic in the data processing world these days. Almost every company is aware of the dangers of allowing its databases to remain unprotected. One way to protect data is to encode it. That way, even if someone does manage to gain access to the data, they would not be able to use it unless they had the decoding scheme. The problem of encoding and decoding has been around for a long time because of the need to send secret messages. Due to this, a wide variety of coding methods are available. This program uses a character substitution method to code and decode messages that you give it. Includes a sample run.

Lines: 72
Version: Microsoft 6502 BASIC
Hardware: none
Software: none
Non-ANSI: strings, ASC(), extended IF

381. Simple Cipher Program

Author: Gregory Yob

Source: Creative Computing Sep 79 (5:9)
"Personal Electronic Transactions" pp.
178–182 (180–181)

Are you a closet James Bond? Want to send some secret messages? Here is a simple message encrypting program. The program encodes text by adding a value you specify to the ASCII values of the characters in the text to come up with new encoded characters. To decode the messages, the process is reversed. Includes a sample run.

Lines: 16 (plus patch)
Version: PET BASIC
Hardware: none
Software: none
Non-ANSI: extended IF, strings, ASC()

382. Cipher Program

Author: Gregory Yob

Source: Creative Computing Sep 79 (5:9)
"Personal Electronic Transactions" pp.
178–182

Creative Computing Nov 79 (5:11)
untitled p. 10 (10)

This cipher program uses the "keyword" method to encode and decode messages. You enter the keyword and your message. The computer displays the encoded message in 5-letter blocks. To decode the message, you enter the keyword and the encoded text. The computer quickly translates the text into the original uncoded message.

Lines: 80
Version: PET BASIC
Hardware: none
Software: none
Non-ANSI: strings, extended IF, GET, ASC()

396. Random Number Generator-Based Cypher

Author: Gregory Yob

Source: Creative Computing Oct 79 (5:10)
"Personal Electronic Transactions" pp.
180–183 (183)

This program uses a nifty trick to encode and decode messages. On the PET and on some other computers, the random number generator (RND) can be "seeded" with a number you select. This seed will cause the RND function to output the same sequence of "random" numbers every time. This program uses this idea to encode messages using the random numbers to scramble the message text. Because the same seed produces the same random numbers every time, the messages can be unscrambled if the seed number is known. Note that not all BASICs allow the RND function to be seeded this way.

Lines: 44
Version: PET BASIC
Hardware: none
Software: none
Non-ANSI: strings, extended IF, GET

DRAWING

899. Drawing Pictures on the PET

Author: Phyllis Cole

Source: *People's Computers* Nov–Dec 77 (6:3)
"Our PET's First Steps" pp. 8–10 (10)

The Commodore PET computer has a good graphics capability. This program demonstrates this capability. It is a sketchpad drawing program. When the program starts up, a "drawing symbol" is displayed in the middle of the PET video screen. By using PET's keypad, you can move the drawing point around, drawing a line as you move. The symbol used to do the drawing can be changed at any time. The program has provisions for erasing sections of the screen.

Lines: 48
Version: PET 8K BASIC
Hardware: PET
Software: none
Non-ANSI: not translatable

903. DRAW 8K: Sketchpad with Picture-Save for the PET

Author: Larry Tesler and Dave Offen

Source: *People's Computers* Jan–Feb 78 (6:4)
"DRAW" pp. 18–19 (19)

Updates: more readable listing
People's Computers Mar–Apr 78 (6:5)
"DRAW Revisited" pp. 56–57 (57)

correction
People's Computers May–Jun 78 (6:6)
"DRAW Update" p. 43 (43)

The Commodore PET computer system can be used as a sketchpad. Using the PET and this program, you can draw whatever doodles your heart desires. The computer displays a "target cell" on the screen of the PET. Using the keypad, you can move the target around. As you move, the computer leaves a trail of whatever character you have designated as the drawing character. You can erase sections of the display if you wish. When you are finished, you can save your picture for later display. Includes list of program variables.

Lines: 126
Version: PET BASIC
Hardware: PET
Software: none
Non-ANSI: not translatable

17. Color Sketchpad for the Apple II

Author: Carl Helmers

Source: *Byte* Mar 78 (3:3)
"An Apple to Byte" pp. 18–24, 30–46 (42)

This is a sketchpad program for the Apple II Computer. The article describes the Apple II Computer and its capabilities. The program allows you to draw patterns on the color monitor. A sample of the output is included.

Lines: 91
Version: Apple II 5K BASIC
Hardware: Apple II, joystick
Software: none
Non-ANSI: not translatable

278. Sketchpad for the Apple-II

Author: David Ramsey and Dennis Freeze

Source: *Creative Computing* Jul–Aug 78 (4:4)
"High-Resolution Graphics for the Apple-II"
pp. 30–31 (30)

Updates: correction to credits
Creative Computing Nov–Dec 78 (4:6)
"(Our Face is Red Dept.)" p. 6

This program allows you to draw a shape in the high-resolution graphics mode from the keyboard of an Apple II system. The program simultaneously assembles a vector table for the shape in memory. This vector table is a map of the shape, which allows it to be stored and recalled later. The program recognizes seven cursor-control commands: move up, move down, move left, move right, invert point status, start over, and shape finished. The shape you create may be stored on a cassette player and may subsequently be restored. The program requires the use of the Apple high-resolution subroutines which must be stored in RAM. Includes a sample output.

Lines: 67
Version: Apple II BASIC
Hardware: Apple II
Software: 6502 machine language routines (not supplied)
Non-ANSI: not translatable

1074. Apple II High Resolution Drawing Program

Author: Carl Swenson

Source: *Recreational Computing* Jan–Feb 79 (7:4)
"Building a HI-RES Shape Table for the Apple II" pp. 26–28 (28)

The Apple II system has the ability to store and recall high-resolution pictures. These pictures can subsequently be used to augment programs. This program allows you to draw and store such images. You use a cursor to draw the figure you wish. The picture can then be stored on tape for later use. Includes a sample output and a list of program variables.

Lines: 75
Version: Apple Integer BASIC
Hardware: Apple II
Software: none
Non-ANSI: not translatable

825. "Etch-a-Sketch" Drawing Program for the OSI Challenger C1P

Author: William Taylor

Source: *Micro* Dec 79 (19)
"Graphics and the Challenger 1P" pp. 61–65 (62)

This "etch-a-sketch"-type drawing program uses the graphics capabilities of the Ohio Scientific Challenger C1P. As you press various keys on the keyboard, the program draws a line on the video screen. Different keys cause the line to be drawn in different directions so that you can draw a picture.

Lines: 63
Version: Microsoft OSI BASIC
Hardware: OSI Challenger C1P
Software: none
Non-ANSI: POKE, PEEK()

ELECTRONICS

459. Reactance

Author: Bruce Scott

Source: *Interface Age* Sep 76 (1:10)
"BASIC—An Easy Programming Language" pp. 34–36 (34)

Given frequency (hertz) and capacitance (farads), this program computes reactance (ohms). Includes a sample run.

Lines: 9
Version: not given
Hardware: none
Software: none
Non-ANSI: none

587. Electronic Design Package

Author: Jim Huffman

Source: *Kilobaud* Aug 77 (8)
"Electronic Design by Computer" pp. 60–70 (62–66)

This is a package of programs to do various electronic design calculations. The package is divided up into four separate programs, each doing different calculations. Here are some of the calculations that the package can handle: Peak-to-Peak to RMS, RMS to peak-to-peak, Voltage divider problems, Reactance of L and C circuits, Inductor problems, Capacitance of parallel plates, Copper wire problems, Pi-network impedance matching, DBM conversions. There are also Pi and Tee attenuator programs. The article describes how several of the calculations are derived. Includes a sample run.

Lines: 162, 40, 75, 110
Version: SWTPC 6800 8K BASIC
Hardware: none
Software: none
Non-ANSI: extended IF, DIGITS, LINE, ASC(), strings

261. Electrical Networks

Author: Alan Brown

Source: *Creative Computing* Jan–Feb 78 (4:1)
"KIRKOF and NETWRK" pp. 140–143 (141–142)

This is a package of two programs designed to describe simple electrical networks. An electrical network is a set of resistors and DC potential difference sources. The first program, KIRKOF, inputs data describing the network and calculates the current in each line using Kirchhoff's Laws. The program allows up to 10 junctions and 22 possible current-bearing lines. The second program, NETWRK, prints a diagram of the network. Includes a sample run.

Lines: 84, 61
Version: PDP-11 MU BASIC
Hardware: none
Software: none
Non-ANSI: COMMON, SYS(), CHAIN, extended IF, TRM$(), STR$(), SEG$(), strings

499. Resistor Value Computing Program

Author: Lucille Moody

Source: *Interface Age* Apr 78 (3:4)
"Use Your Computer to Sort Resistors" pp. 167–168 (167–168)

This program determines the resistance value of a resistor when given its color bands. When the program starts, it prints a table of resistor band colors with their associated values. The program asks you to enter the band numbers. Using this, the program determines the resistance and tolerance of the resistor. Includes a sample run.

>
    Lines: 48
    Version: SWTPC 4K BASIC, ver. 2.0
    Hardware: none
    Software: none
    Non-ANSI: none

506. TV Test Pattern Generator for the Apple II

>
    Author: Robert Harr, Jr. and Gary Poss

>
    Source: *Interface Age* Aug 78 (3:8)
    "T.V. Pattern Generator" pp. 80–82, 160 (160)

One annoying feature of color television sets is that the color on such sets frequently goes out of whack, turning Walter Cronkite a weird shade of green. This program generates a series of test patterns to help you return dear Walter to his normal rosy hue. The program generates six different patterns: a solid color to test for purity, a rainbow of colors to adjust the color controls, a dot matrix to converge the color guns, vertical and horizontal patterns to test gain and linearity, and a crosshatch to check for barrel or pincushion distortion. Includes samples of the output (in color) and a flowchart.

>
    Lines: 45
    Version: Apple II BASIC
    Hardware: Apple II
    Software: none
    Non-ANSI: not translatable

509. Circuit Analysis

>
    Author: Tim Gates

>
    Source: *Interface Age* Aug 78 (3:8)
    "Circuit Analysis" pp. 116–119 (118–119)

LOGIC.BAS is a simple logic-circuit analysis program. Logic circuits may be entered and tested under changing input conditions. All of the nodes in the cirucit are monitored on an iterative basis, and their states are printed after each cycle. The program can use any of eight different logic gates: AND, NAND, OR, NOR, NOT, BUFT, XOR, and XNOR. The program consists or four functions: CIRCUIT, SEQUENCE, ANALYSIS, and END. The first stage in the circuit analysis is done by CIRCUIT. CIRCUIT inputs a list of the logic gates to be used, and

their interconnections. The circuit generated is stored away in a file. SEQUENCE generates a testing sequence for the circuit. ANALYSIS performs the actual cicuit testing by doing a cycle-by-cycle simulation of the circuit. With each cycle, the states of the various nodes in the circuit are printed out (high, low, or unknown). Includes a sample run.

>
    Lines: 327
    Version: not given
    Hardware: sequential file device
    Software: none
    Non-ANSI: OPTION, WIDTH, strings, OPEN, CLOSE, PRINT #, INPUT #, AND(), NOT(), OR(), VAL(), LINE INPUT, extended IF, EOF(), MAX(), ' (used in place of REM), two-letter variables

1087. TV Test Pattern Generator

>
    Author: Milan Chepko

>
    Source: *Recreational Computing* May–Jun 79 (7:6)
    "T.V. Test Pattern" p. 44 (44)

Adjusting the picture on a TV set requires a constant, stable pattern so that you can see the effects of what you are doing. This program can generate two such patterns for black and white television sets: a "cross-hatch" pattern and a dot pattern. The program uses output from a TRS-80. An RF generator is required to convert the TRS-80's video signal to a normal television signal.

>
    Lines: 22
    Version: TRS-80 BASIC
    Hardware: RF generator, TRS-80
    Software: none
    Non-ANSI: not translatable

541. Integrated Circuit Tester for Pragmatic Designs' ICTM-1

>
    Author: Tim Barry and Ed Ingber

>
    Source: *Interface Age* Jul 79 (4:7)
    "Integrated Circuit Testing for Hobbyists" pp. 82–86 (86)

>
    Updates: commentary
    Interface Age Nov 79 (4:11)
    "Circuit Testing" p. 17

Pragmatic Designs' ICTM-1 is an integrated circuit tester which operates off of a microcomputer. The demonstration program shows how integrated circuits can be tested using TBASIC, a version of BASIC designed for use with the ICTM-1.

Lines: 45
Version: Tester Extended BASIC (TBASIC)
Hardware: Pragmatic Designs' ICTM-1 integrated
circuit tester
Software: none
Non-ANSI: not translatable

Lines: 109
Version: PET BASIC
Hardware: none
Software: none
Non-ANSI: POKE, ASC(), strings, extended IF

712. Integrated Circuit Logic Tester

Author: F. R. Ruckdeschel

Source: *Kilobaud Microcomputing* Jul 79 (31)
"IC Logic Tester and Parallel I/O Expander"
pp. 26–39 (28–35)

In the old days of vacuum-tube companies it was easy to find burned-out circuits. All you had to do was turn out the lights and look for the tube that wasn't glowing. With integrated circuits the job is a bit more difficutl, because a defective chip looks no different than a good one. This IC logic tester is a combined hardware/software system for checking the operation of integrated circuits. You plug in the suspect chip and the computer checks whether the circuit's operation is as it should be. If you have an integrated circuit with an obliterated ID number, the program can automatically search for a match to the mystery chip's outputs. Includes sample runs. The listing given is only a partial one; the complete listing is available from the author.

Lines: 420
Version: North Star BASIC, ver. 6, Release 3
Hardware: logic tester (homemade)
Software: none
Non-ANSI: HP strings, OUT, INP(), extended IF

800. Boolean Equation Reducer

Author: Alan Christensen

Source: *Micro* Jul 79 (14)
"Boolean Equations Reduced on the PET"
pp. 23–26 (23–26)

It never fails. Just when you're on the verge of completing some digital circuit, you realize that you need a part you don't have. So what do you do? Wait six weeks for the part to come by mail? It may be possible for you to build up the needed circuit from basic logic gates. This program can help you by showing you what circuit would be the best one for the outputs you want. You specify what the outputs should be for a given set of inputs. The program then figures out what the best arrangement of gates would be. Includes a sample run.

ENERGY

103. Electric Bill Calculation

Author: LeRoy Finkel

Source: *Calculators/Computers Magazine* May 77 (1:1)
"BASIC Test Units" pp. 76–81 (78)

This program computes your bill for electric power. It assumes that you are billed according to a rate scale that varies with the amount of electricity that you use. Includes a sample run.

Lines: 25
Version: not given
Hardware: none
Software: none
Non-ANSI: none

257. Power Generation Simulation

Author: David Ahl

Source: *Creative Computing* Jan–Feb 78 (4:1)
"How to Write a Computer Simulation" pp. 88–93 (90–91)

In this simulation, you are the director of the U.S. Federal Power Commission. It is up to you to direct the national energy program. You approve the building of new power generating facilities to keep up with the nation's need for energy. An important part of your job is knowing how much additional power will be required in the future. You have at your disposal a computer simulation of the U.S. power generation system. The model will ask for your decisions on new generating capacity every five "years," and then will give you the results of your decision. You may run the model for 25 to 100 years. The output of the simulation is five-year charts of energy capacity and usage for a variety of fuels including coal, oil, gas, nuclear, and hydroelectric potential. The program makes a great many assumptions about the national power system; these assumptions can be modified to study their effects. Includes a sample run and flowchart.

Lines: 162
Version: not given
Hardware: none
Software: none
Non-ANSI: strings, FOR (used as a modifier), PRINT USING, extended IF, ! (used in place of REM)

443. Home Heating Improvement Cost/Benefit Analysis

Author: Michael Trombetta

Source: *Dr. Dobb's Journal of Computer Calisthenics & Orthodontia* Jan 79 (4:1)
"Performing A Cost-Benefit Analysis of an Improvement Designed to Reduce Home Fuel Costs" pp. 36–37 (36–37)

Can you actually save money by making your home energy efficient? This program might give you the answer. When considering whether or not to pay for home improvements such as insulation or solar waterheaters, you must take into account a great number of factors. You must consider not only the cost of the improvement and the fuel savings you will get, but also the effect of the investment on your taxes and the way in which inflation is likely to affect your fuel bills. This program takes all these and more factors into account in determining whether it will be to your benefit financially to invest in a particular improvement. Includes a sample run.

Lines: 88
Version: IBM CALL-OS BASIC
Hardware: none
Software: none
Non-ANSI: PRINT USING, : (used to specify format for PRINT USING), multiple-assignment

1046. Electricity Usage Analysis

Author: Howard Berenbon

Source: *Personal Computing* Sep 79 (3:9)
"Electric Usage Analysis Program" pp. 18–20 (19–20)

In these days of skyrocketing energy costs, it pays to do everything you can to keep down your use of power. This program can help you monitor (and possibly reduce) your use of electricity. The program prints out a table that compares your current use of electricity with that of a base year. From this you see whether you are using more or less electricity in any given month. Includes a sample run.

Lines: 80
Version: not given
Hardware: none
Software: none
Non-ANSI: none

82. Electric Power Usage

Author: Karen S. Wolfe

Source: *Byte* Oct 79 (4:10)
"POWER Helps Analyze Electric Bills" pp. 48–54 (50)

Updates: commentary
Byte Jan 80 (5:1)
"A Stitch in Time?" p. 16

Has your electric bill gone through the roof? If it has, then this program called POWER may help you to reduce your use of electricity. The program first uses data from your electric bill to determine your cost per kilowatt-hour of power used. It then uses this information to generate the cost per hour and per month to run the various appliances in your house based on their electrical specifications. Includes a sample run.

Lines: 52
Version: North Star BASIC
Hardware: none
Software: none
Non-ANSI: HP strings

756. Electric Bill Report

Author: Edward and Sandra Back

Source: *Kilobaud Microcomputing* Dec 79 (36)
"Electric Bill Watchdog" pp. 32–33 (33)

Does your electric bill look like the national debt? Perhaps it's time you cut back on the amount of power you use. This program can help you keep track of your electricity usage. You enter data about the cost of electricity in your area and what your electric meter readings have been. The program then types out an "energy report" showing how much power you've used, how much it has cost you per day and to date, and how much it will cost you in the future. Includes a sample run.

Lines: 105
Version: TRS-80 Level I 4K BASIC
Hardware: TRS-80
Software: none
Non-ANSI: not translatable

FOOD

143. Recipe Servings Adjustment

Author: Linda Schreiber

Source: *Calculators/Computers Magazine* Nov–Dec 78 (2:7)
"Made to Order" pp. 4–5 (5)

Your new recipe is so great that everyone loves it. It's so good, in fact, that they've asked you to serve it at the next bridge club meeting. Unfortunately, your recipe makes four servings and there are 25 people in your club. How do you expand your recipe? You could haul out a pencil and paper to figure out how much of everything you need. Or you could let your computer do the work. This program adjusts the amounts of the ingredients in recipes to make the recipes larger or smaller. The program can handle measures in cups, teaspoons, or tablespoons. You type in your recipe ingredients, how many servings the recipe makes, and how many servings you want. The program types out the new adjusted recipe. Includes a sample run.

Lines: 98
Version: Altair Extended BASIC
Hardware: none
Software: none
Non-ANSI: CLEAR, strings, multi-letter variables, LINEINPUT, extended IF, INSTR( ), VAL( ), ' (used in place of REM)

157. Menu Planner

Author: Linda Schreiber

Source: *Calculators/Computers Magazine* Jan–Feb 79 (3:1)
"Meals in Minutes" pp. 56–58 (57–58)

Do you have trouble trying to decide what to have for dinner? Do you come back from the market with a bag full of impulse purchases because you didn't shop with a shopping list? If so, this program can simplify your life and possibly save you some money on your grocery bills. The program creates a daily menu for up to one month based on a list of foods you select. After the monthly menu is printed out, the program generates a shopping list for you. Includes a sample run.

Lines: 283
Version: Altair Extended BASIC
Hardware: none
Software: none
Non-ANSI: ' (used in place of REM), strings, multi-letter variables, extended IF, ON . . . GOSUB

990. Menu Planner

Author: Carolyn Busch and Sam Newhouse

Source: *Personal Computing* Feb 79 (3:2)
"Menu Planning" pp. 26–34 (30–34)

Updates: correction
Personal Computing May 79 (3:5)
"Some Missing Bytes in the Menu Plan" p. 4 (4)

commentary
Personal Computing Sep 79 (3:9)
"Menu Planning Notes" p. 9

This program is designed to help you plan and monitor your diet. Called MENUPLAN, this program generates nutritionally balanced menus based on your specifications. You enter the number of menus you want, the number of people who will be eating with you, and the average number of calories for each dinner menu. The program then composes a set of menus that are varied and nutritionally balanced. After the basic meals are selected, you have the option of making changes. Once you are satisfied with the bill of fare, the program prints out a complete list of the menus, along with a detailed shopping list. Includes a sample run.

Lines: 608
Version: MITS Disk Extended BASIC ver. 3.4
Hardware: none
Software: none
Non-ANSI: strings, extended IF, STR$(), two-letter variables, ON . . . GOSUB

1019. Supermarket Prices

Author: Sam Newhouse

Source: *Personal Computing* May 79 (3:5)
"Tracking Prices at the Store" pp. 38–41 (40–41)

Prices are going up all the time. You need all the help you can get to keep your grocery bills in line. This program can help you by showing the average prices of groceries. You enter the prices of various products during the recent past. The program then prints out a list showing what the average price has been for each product. You can use this information to spot bargains and avoid overpriced goods. Includes a sample run and flowchart.

Lines: 75
Version: Altair BASIC ver. 3.4
Hardware: none
Software: none
Non-ANSI: strings, NULL, CLEAR, WIDTH, extended IF, multi-letter variables

1032. Recipe Cost

Author: Lon Poole and Mary Borchers

Source: *Personal Computing* Jul 79 (3:7)
"Three Practical Programs" pp. 46–50 (46)

Don't let a tight budget keep you from throwing that dinner party you've been wanting. The key to keeping the cost down to less than an arm and a leg is good planning. This program can take a recipe and compute how much it will cost to produce; both in total and per serving. Includes a sample run. (This program is reprinted from *Some Common BASIC Programs*.)

Lines: 31
Version: not given
Hardware: none
Software: none
Non-ANSI: none

FORM LETTERS

613. Consumer Form Letter

Author: Joseph Roehrig

Source: *Kilobaud* Mar 78 (15)
"Consumer Computer, Inc." pp. 64–65 (64)

Have you ever had a problem with a credit-card billing company? No matter what you sent them, they still kept sending you form letters. This program can help you fight back by sending out your own anti-form-letter-letter. You are asked to type in answers to eight questions. The computer then takes over and generates a form letter for you to send out. Includes a sample run.

Lines: 48
Version: not given
Hardware: none
Software: none
Non-ANSI: HP strings, ! (used in place of PRINT), %() (used to format printouts)

305. Christmas Form Letter

Author: Gordon Flemming

Source: *Creative Computing* Nov–Dec 78 (4:6)
"Season's Greetings!" pp. 156–158 (157–158)

Save on Christmas cards this year. Instead of sending out cards, send out your own Christmas form letters. This program generates pseudo-personalized Christmas letters. The letters not only include your own Christmas sentiments, but also contain a yuletide design and a calendar for the new year. Includes a sample run.

Lines: 180
Version: not given
Hardware: none
Software: none
Non-ANSI: CLEAR, strings, extended IF, two-letter variables

54. Equipment Order Form Letter

Author: Andrew Carpenter

Source: *Byte* Apr 79 (4:4)
"Label and File Program" pp. 222–223 (222–223)

Do you order computer parts by mail? If so, then this equipment order form letter program can help you keep track of your orders. You type in the parts you need and the address that the order is to be sent to. The program then prints out two copies (one for your files) of a standard parts order letter and two mailing labels. The program uses LIST statements to print out data stored with the program.

Lines: 91
Version: SWTPC 6800 BASIC
Hardware: none
Software: none
Non-ANSI: not translatable

GARDENING

945. Vegetable Garden Planner

Author: Gary Dozier

Source: *Personal Computing* Apr 78 (2:4)
"A Plentiful Harvest" pp. 57–70 (61–70)

Would you like to keep yourself in vegetables by planting your own vegetable garden? This program can help you. It is entitled HARVEST. The purpose of HARVEST helps you decide on what vegetables to grow, based on your preferences and the soil conditions in your garden. If it should prove desirable to change the soil conditions, HARVEST can help you plan the changes. Using this program, you can set up your garden so that it produces the greatest yield for your labors.

Lines: 330
Version: not given
Hardware: none
Software: none
Non-ANSI: strings, multi-letter variables

998. Houseplant Care Program

Author: Pat Tanner

Source: *Personal Computing* Feb 79 (3:2)
"PLANTMAN" pp. 60–62 (61–62)

PLANTMAN is a program that can help you keep your house green. House plants can make any room in your home look better. The trouble with greenery is that it can be difficult to maintain. This program can help you select the best plants for your house. It can also show you what the needs are of plants you already own. Includes a sample run.

Lines: 147
Version: PolyMorphic Poly BASIC
Hardware: none
Software: none
Non-ANSI: HP strings, EXIT, extended IF, ! (used in place of PRINT)

GENEALOGY

1050. Genealogy (Family Tree) System for the TRS-80

Author: John J. Armstrong

Source: *Personal Computing* Sep 79 (3:9)
"Roots and Branches" pp. 41–53 (48–53)

Updates: corrections
Personal Computing Dec 79 (3:12)
"Family Tree Update" pp. 6–8 (7–8)

modifications and corrections
Personal Computing Feb 80 (4:2)
"Genealogy Program Translated for Altair"
p. 7 (7)

This genealogy system should be an invaluable aid to anyone trying to trace his or her family tree. Broken into two programs (a "name adder" program and an editor/printer program), this system can organize, record, and print out data that you collect about your ancestors. Once you've collected and stored the information, the system can do selective searches and printouts of data you might be interested in. It can, for example, print out all the people on file with a particular last name or who were living in a particular year. The system can do "tree" printouts showing either the ancestors or the descendants of someone in the database. Just don't blame the computer if your family tree is full of fruits and nuts. Includes sample runs, flowcharts, and listings of program variables.

Lines: 65, 340
Version: Radio Shack Disk BASIC ver. 1.1
Hardware: TRS-80, random-access file device, 132-column printer
Software: none
Non-ANSI: not translatable

81. Genealogical Program

Author: Stan W. Merrill

Source: *Byte* Oct 79 (4:10)
"Tracing Your Own Roots" pp. 22–46 (30–46)

Do you have that craving to find out about your family heritage? This program can help you discover your family tree by recording and organizing genealogical data. You enter the information that you know about your ancestors. The program records this information and allows you to review the data you've collected in a systematic manner. Besides the usual information about births, deaths, and marriages, the program also records data about the existence of "vital records," those documents needed to verify the genealogical data. On command, the program can print out a pedigree chart for any person you have on file. Includes sample runs.

Lines: 491
Version: DEC BASIC Plus 2
Hardware: random-access file device
Software: none
Non-ANSI: not translatable

HUMOR

646. Chinese Fortune Cookie Program

Author: Peter Stark

Source: *Kilobaud* Oct 78 (22)
"Ready for the Nuthouse?" p. 108 (108)

This program simulates a Chinese fortune cookie. No, you can't eat it. What it does is print out a randomly selected one-line message each time you run it. The messages can be profound—or just silly. Includes a sample run.

Lines: 24
Version: not given
Hardware: none
Software: none
Non-ANSI: strings, extended IF

386. HORRIBLE HARRY:
Wisecracking Ghost for the TRS-80

Author: Joe Weisbecker

Source: *Creative Computing* Oct 79 (5:10)
"HORRIBLE HARRY" pp. 108–109 (109)

Let Horrible Harry add a new, insulting twist to your Halloween this year! Horrible Harry is a wisecracking ghost that you can conjure up on the screen of your TRS-80. He moves his eyes back and forth, and comes up with any one of fourteen snappy sayings. Includes a sample output.

Lines: 87
Version: TRS-80 Level II BASIC
Hardware: TRS-80
Software: none
Non-ANSI: not translatable

LOGIC

228. Five Sailors and a Monkey Problem

Authors: Donald Piele and Larry Wood

Source: *Creative Computing* May–Jun 77 (3:3)
"Thinking Strategies with the Computer: Working Backward" pp. 76–78 (78)

Five sailors and a monkey are on an island. One evening the sailors gather up a pile of coconuts. They decide to divide up the coconuts the next day. During the night, a sailor wakes up, takes one fifth of the coconuts, and gives one to the monkey. He goes back to his hammock. He is followed by each of the other sailors who do the same thing. The next morning the remaining nuts are divided up, with one remaining nut going to the monkey. What is the least number of coconuts the sailors could have begun with? This program solves this problem. It uses a problem-solving technique based on "working backward" from the goal to the given information. That monkey is a real operator, don't you think? Includes a flowchart and sample run.

Lines: 21
Version: not given
Hardware: none
Software: none
Non-ANSI: none

248. Whodunit?

Author: Donald Piele and Larry Wood

Source: *Creative Computing* Nov–Dec 77 (3:6)
"Thinking Strategies with the Computer: Contradiction" pp. 86–89 (88)

Four men, one of whom is known to have committed a certain crime, confront an inspector from Scotland Yard. They each give (conflicting) statements about the crime. This program solves the crime by using a problem-solving method known as "proof by contradiction." The program accepts the suspects' statements (the statements can be changed), and deduces who actually committed the crime. Includes a sample run.

Lines: 37
Version: not given
Hardware: none
Software: none
Non-ANSI: LIN(), MAT ZER(), HP strings

905. Bucket-Filling Problem

Author: Mac Oglesby

Source: *People's Computers* Mar–Apr 78 (6:5)
"BUCKETS" pp. 26–27 (27)

A standard problem in mathematical logic is the Bucket-Filling problem. In this problem, you are given two "buckets." By filling the buckets with water and pouring the water between the buckets, you are to measure out a certain amount of water. You must measure out the water precisely (no fair "estimating" how much you have poured into a bucket). BUCKETS solves this problem by printing out the possible outcomes for the bucket sizes you specify. Includes a sample run.

Lines: 127
Version: Dartmouth BASIC
Hardware: none
Software: none
Non-ANSI: strings, LINPUT, SEG$(), PRINT USING, multiple-assignment, ' (used in place of REM)

334. Syllogism Solver

Author: Michael Orlove

Source: *Creative Computing* Apr 79 (5:4)
"Lewis Carroll" pp. 138–141 (141)

Updates: modifications
Creative Computing Oct 79 (5:10)
"Lewis Carroll Revisited" p. 8 (8)

A syllogism is a group of sentences called "premises" which imply a sentence called a "conclusion." For example: It is raining. When it rains, the sun does not shine. Therefore the sun is not shining. This program reads in and analyzes such syllogisms. The program can find the conclusion when none is supplied. You can also type in a conclusion and ask the computer if your conclusion is valid. Includes a sample run.

Lines: 254
Version: not given
Hardware: none
Software: none
Non-ANSI: CLEAR, strings

MAGIC TRICKS

967. Computer Card Trick

Author: Timothy Purinton

Source: Personal Computing Aug 78 (2:8)
"The Marvelous Micro Mentalist" pp. 48–51 (50–51)

Updates: correction
Personal Computing Nov 78 (2:11)
"Marvelous Mistake" p. 6 (6)

Card tricks are always popular at parties. With this program, your computer can get into the act with a card trick of its own. This program allows your computer to become a "mind reader." Includes a sample run.

Lines: 115
Version: not given
Hardware: none
Software: none
Non-ANSI: two-letter variables, strings, extended IF, PEEK(), POKE

829. Computer Card Trick

Author: Chris Morgan

Source: onComputing Fall 79 (1:2)
"Magic for Your Micro" pp. 18–22 (21–22)

Updates: modifications for the PET
onComputing Winter 79 (1:3)
"Magic for Your Micro" p. 81 (81)

modifications for the TRS-80
onComputing Winter 79 (1:3)
"Mysterious Magic" p. 82 (82)

Amaze your friends! Let your computer turn into a magician with this simple, but effective card trick. You pick a card. The computer then makes a series of guesses as to the suit, color, and number of the card—making a *correct* guess each time.

Lines: 155 (plus patch)
Version: Apple Integer BASIC
Hardware: none
Software: none
Non-ANSI: HP strings, ASC(), GOTO [computed line number]

MUSIC AND SOUND

835. Musical Overtone and Harmonics Analysis

Author: Peter Sessions

Source: People's Computer Company Dec 72 (1:2)
"BASIC Music" pp. 14–17 (15–16)

Updates: article reprint
People's Computer Company Jul 76 (5:1)
"BASIC Music: Overtone Series" pp. 6–8 (6–7)

This is a group of three programs to do musical harmonics analysis. The first program is an overtone series generator. Given a fundamental frequency, this program generates a table of the overtones of that frequency. The second program is a scale frequency generator. This program asks you for a base frequency and the number of tones per octave. The program then grinds out the frequencies of the tones. The third program is a harmonic beat-frequency analyzer. First, the program asks for the base frequency you wish to use and the lower and upper limits of your critical range. Next, the program asks for the two chromatic scale tones you wish to examine. The program then computes the difference tone produced by these frequencies and the difference tones of their overtones, as well as other information. Includes sample runs.

Lines: 17, 16, 29
Version: not given
Hardware: none
Software: none
Non-ANSI: none

836. Random Melody Generator

Author: Peter Sessions

Source: People's Computer Company Dec 72 (1:2)
untitled p. 17 (17)

Updates: article reprint
People's Computer Company Jul 76 (5:1)
untitled p. 8 (8)

Who says computers can't be artistic? Here is a (slightly mad) computer music composer. You give it a key to work in and the number of notes you want (up to 100), and the program outputs a melody. The melody is printed out as a series of letter representations of notes. You might try to hitch this program up with an audio music generator. That way, the computer could play the music it composes! Includes a sample run.

Lines: 51
Version: HP 2000C BASIC
Hardware: none
Software: none
Non-ANSI: HP strings, MAT ZER()

840. Pythagorean Scale

Author: Peter Sessions

Source: *People's Computer Company* Feb 73 (1:3)
"BASIC Music" p. 15 (15)

Updates: reprint
People's Computer Company Sep–Oct 76 (5:2)
"BASIC Music" p. 40 (40)

Pythagoras' gifts to music and musicians are many. One of them is a scale based on mathematical concepts. Here is a program that computes and prints out the frequencies of the Pythagorean scale. Includes a sample run.

Lines: 30
Version: DEC PDP-8 BASIC
Hardware: none
Software: none
Non-ANSI: none

842. Musical Scales (Tempered and Seven-Note)

Author: Peter Sessions

Source: *People's Computer Company* Apr 73 (1:4)
"BASIC Music" pp. 6–7 (6–7)

Updates: reprint
People's Computer Company Nov–Dec 76 (5:3)
"BASIC Music" pp. 28–29 (28–29)

These are two musical scale programs. One prints out the tone frequencies of tempered scales. The other produces seven-note scales. Includes a sample run.

Lines: 10, 19
Version: not given
Hardware: none
Software: none
Non-ANSI: RANDOM

218. Musical Superparticular Ratios

Author: Donald Piele and Larry Wood

Source: *Creative Computing* Mar–Apr 77 (3:2)
"Thinking Strategies with the Computer: Inference" pp. 96–99 (98)

The Greek mathematician, Pythagoras, first discovered a basic relationship between musical harmony and numbers. The relationship is this: pluck a stretched string; it will sound a certain pitch. Allow only half of the string to vibrate and the pitch will rise an octave. Other changes in the length of string allowed to vibrate will produce other predictable changes in pitch. These changes are governed by "superparticular ratios." This program is used to find superparticular ratios and to discover properties about them. In music, these ratios are studied with the aid of a medieval bowed instrument with a single string. The instrument came to be known as the "Nun's Fiddle." Thus this program has been named the NUN'S FIDDLE. Includes a sample run and flowchart.

Lines: 40
Version: not given
Hardware: none
Software: none
Non-ANSI: MAT operations, LIN()

219. Musical Note Tester

Author: J. Quentin Kuyper

Source: *Creative Computing* Mar–Apr 77 (3:2)
"Music More Music" p. 109 (109)

This program prints a five-line musical staff with either a treble or a bass clef sign. A note is randomly chosen and the student is asked to type its letter name. If he gives the correct answer, the note is erased and a new note is printed. No ledger lines are used. A note is never used twice in a row. The computer keeps track of the number of correct and incorrect answers. The student may skip to the end of the program at any time by typing the word "stop." This program uses cursor addressing and reverse video. The character sequences are designed for the SUPERBEE terminal, but can be changed for other terminals.

Lines: 120
Version: HP 2000/Access BASIC
Hardware: addressable-cursor video display
Software: none
Non-ANSI: HP strings, LIN(), ENTER, IMAGE, UPS$(), PRINT USING, SPA(), multiple-assignment, extended IF

220. Musical Scale Practice

Author: Marvin Thostenson

Source: *Creative Computing* Mar–Apr 77 (3:2)
"Scales" p. 112 (112)

You can use this program to practice and observe the differences among the scales. Eleven different types of scales can be generated. These include major, natural minor, harmonic minor, Hungarian minor, dorian, phrygian, lydian, mixolydian, locrian, and whole tone. When you run this program, you will be asked, "Which type of scale is wanted?" You then respond by typing in the first two letters of the name of the desired scale, followed immediately by the desired key. The lower case "b" is used to denote flats; the "#" is used to denote sharps. Sample inputs would be *phe* for phrygian starting on E, *maf#* for major on F-sharp, and *whg* for whole tone on G. Includes a sample run.

Lines: 117
Version: HP 2000/Access BASIC
Hardware: none
Software: none
Non-ANSI: HP strings, multiple-assignment, LIN(),
UPS$(), extended IF

221. Music Key Signature Drill

Author: J. Quentin Kuyper

Source: *Creative Computing* Mar–Apr 77 (3:2)
"Sharps & Flats" p. 114 (114)

This program will help you practice naming key signatures. The computer names a key (such as F# minor) and asks you to respond with the correct key signature. Since a knowledge of key signatures, to be useful, must be almost immediate, the program keeps track of how much time you require to complete 20 questions. This information, along with the number of correctly answered questions, is printed out at the end of each run.

Lines: 132
Version: HP 2000/Access BASIC
Hardware: none
Software: none
Non-ANSI: LIN(), TIM(), multiple-assignment, ENTER,
HP strings

222. Musical Magic Squares

Author: Fred Hofstetter

Source: *Creative Computing* Mar–Apr 77 (3:2)
"Musical Magic Squares" p. 116 (116)

In music, the term "magic square" refers to the compositional matrix used by composers of 12-tone music. This school of music was started by Arnold Schoenberg, who discovered that if music was composed such that one of the 12 tones is repeated until every other tone is used, an atonal texture results (atonal means that there is no tonic, or that there is no "do-re-mi"). To use the program, you enter a set of numbers from 1 to 12 typed in any order with no repetitions (the numbers correspond to a 12-tone row). The computer then generates a "magic square." The magic square is the transpositions, inversions, retrograde inversions, and retrogrades of the row printed in a matrix. Includes a sample run.

Lines: 42
Version: not given
Hardware: none
Software: none
Non-ANSI: MAT operations, extended IF

1125. Computer Music Synthesizer

Author: Dorothy Siegel

Source: *ROM* Oct 77 (1:4)
"Scott Joplin on Your Sci-Fi Hi-Fi"
pp. 61–65 (64–65)

Updates: corrections
ROM Dec 77 (1:6)
untitled p. 6

Now, you too can get a computer to play music. This program uses a very simple home-built music interface to generate computer music. The program is called SCORE. It takes notes that you specify, and converts them into pitch and duration constants for the 8080 assembly language routine PLAY. PLAY, in turn, outputs the music to the music interface for playing. The program's abilities are limited to controlling the frequency and duration of each note played; there are no provisions for controlling the envelope or timbre of the music. The tempo of the music can be adjusted by changing a constant in SCORE. As written, the program SCORE generates the score for the song "The Entertainer" by Scott Joplin; however, you can write your own music. The November 1977 issue of *ROM* contains more music for this system. A-one-ana-two . . .

Lines: 98
Version: North Star BASIC
Hardware: music interface board (homemade),
8080-based microcomputer
Software: 8080 assembly language routine
Non-ANSI: HP strings, extended IF, FILL, CALL

1126. More Computer-Generated Music

Author: Dorothy Siegel

Source: *ROM* Nov 77 (1:5)
"Make Me More Music, Maestro Micro" pp. 58–63 (58–62)

Updates: comments
ROM Jan 78 (1:7)
untitled p. 6

The October 1977 issue of *ROM* contains a computer music generator. The system is based on a simple music interface, an assembly language routine called PLAY, and a program in BASIC called SCORE. In this issue, three more pieces of music are given. The first is "Bourree Anglaise" from Bach's A Minor Unaccompanied Flute Sonata. The second is Chopin's Waltz in D Flat, Op. 64, No. 1. For this second piece, the program SCORE has been rewritten to give it more capabilities. The third piece is Bach's Invention No. 4 in D Minor. It uses the modified version SCORE. This piece is designed to be a duet for you and the computer to play together.

Lines: 70, 220, 55
Version: North Star BASIC
Hardware: music interface board (homemade), 8080-based microcomputer
Software: 8080 assembly language routine
Non-ANSI: HP strings, extended IF, FILL, CALL

602. "The Twelve Days of Christmas" Lyrics

Author: Jill Zimmerman

Source: *Kilobaud* Dec 77 (12)
"The Twelve Days of Christmas" pp. 84–85 (84)

This program generates the lyrics to the song, "The Twelve Days of Christmas." Includes a sample run.

Lines: 31
Version: not given
Hardware: none
Software: none
Non-ANSI: strings

763. Apple II Bugle Call

Author: Marc Schwartz

Source: *Micro* Dec 77–Jan 78 (2)
"Ludwig von Apple II" p. 19 (19)

Updates: commentary, assembly language listing
Micro Feb–Mar 78 (3)
"Machine Language Used in 'Ludwig von Apple II' " p. 8 (8)

Did you know that your Apple II can make music? It can. This program demonstrates the Apple II's musical abilities by playing a "horse racing" bugle call.

Lines: 35
Version: Apple II BASIC
Hardware: Apple II
Software: none
Non-ANSI: not translatable

262. Newtech Music Generator Software

Author: Steve North

Source: *Creative Computing* Mar–Apr 78 (4:2)
"Computer Music" pp. 28–37 (34–37)

Many computer music-generating systems require tons of complicated (and expensive) electronics gear. Here is a system which uses a very simple and inexpensive music interface board designed by Newtech. The software consists of a BASIC music "compiler" and a machine language music player. The music compiler translates your musical scores into an internal form. On your command, it then loads a machine language music-playing routine. The music-playing routine outputs the music to the Newtech music board.

Lines: 380 (plus patch)
Version: MITS Extended BASIC
Hardware: Newtech Model 6 Music Board, 8080-based microcomputer, sequential file device
Software: none
Non-ANSI: strings, CLEAR, extended IF, HEX$(), VAL(), POKE, DEFUSR, STR$(), OUT, ASC()

950. Music Key Transposer

Author: Linda Schreiber

Source: *Personal Computing* May 78 (2:5)
"Music from A to G pp. 68–69 (69)

Music directors and those of you who enjoy a good sing-along with friends or family often have a problem with songs written out of the vocal range of the group. The solution to this problem is to change the key of the music. But this is an annoying and time-consuming task. This program takes over that burden by transposing the notes of a particular piece of music from one key to another. The musical notes are stored in the program in DATA statements. You type in the original key and the key desired. The program then outputs the notes transposed into the new key. Once the notes have been entered, they can be transposed as many times as desired. Includes sample runs.

Lines: 54
Version: Altair Extended BASIC
Hardware: none
Software: none
Non-ANSI: strings, ' (used in place of REM)

314. Music Composition

Author: Steven Roberts

Source: *Creative Computing* Feb 79 (5:2)
"Music Composition: A New Technique" pp. 42–43 (42–43)

There are many microprocessor-driven music generator boards available on the market today. However, most of the music programs around require you to compose your own music or to use music written by some other human. This article discusses several methods for creating computer-composed music. Each of the programs demonstrates one of the techniques that you might use. The first program simply generates random notes. The second program uses a slight variation on the random note technique. The third, and most musically pleasing, program uses a method based on "1/f" noise. No discussion of how to output to a music board is given.

Lines: 9, 17, 44
Version: not given
Hardware: music generating board, interface
Software: none
Non-ANSI: OUT, BINAND(), BINXOR(), extended IF

1134. Music for Tiny BASIC

Author: Noel and Sharon Thompson

Source: *'68' Micro Journal* Feb 79 (1:1)
"Tiny Music" pp. 20–27 (21–26)

Fancy music synthesizers and high-powered music software aren't needed to get a computer to whistle a tune. This article describes a simple digital-to-analog converter that can be used to output music. Several programs show how it can be used. The programs range from one that just plays a little run up a scale to one that plays a complete computer-generated melody.

Lines: 6, 5, 34, 95
Version: Pitman's Tiny BASIC
Hardware: D/A converter (homemade), 6800-based microcomputer
Software: 6800 machine-language routine
Non-ANSI: not translatable

47. Beep Demo for the Heath H8

Author: Paul Poduska

Source: *Byte* Mar 79 (4:3)
"Building the Heath H8 Computer" pp. 12–13, 124–140 (138)

The Heath H8 computer can produce a beep tone. This short demonstration program generates a tone sequence with timing that follows a sine curve.

Lines: 4
Version: not given
Hardware: Heath H8
Software: none
Non-ANSI: POKE

320. PET Music Programs

Author: Gregory Yob

Source: *Creative Computing* Mar 79 (5:3)
"Personal Electronic Transactions" pp. 33–37 (34–37)

Updates: corrections
Creative Computing Sep 79 (5:9)
"More March Mix-ups" p. 16 (16)

You can use the CB2 line in the User Port of a PET to generate tones. Strung together, these tones can be made into music. This is a collection of programs to demonstrate PET music. One program figures out which of the PET's 255 possible tones come closest to being musical notes. Other programs generate white music (random notes) and brown music (randomly fluctuating music). Also included is a music player that plays Scott Joplin music. Some of the programs are created by adding lines to other programs; the number of lines given are for the individual program fragments.

Lines: 18, 20, 6, 6, 11, 16, 93, 80
Version: PET BASIC
Hardware: PET, music hardware (homemade)
Software: none
Non-ANSI: not translatable

329. Random Music Composition in Four-Part Harmony

Author: Nancy Altmayer

Source: *Creative Computing* Apr 79 (5:4)
"Music Composition: A Different Approach"
pp. 74–85 (76–83)

For those of you interested in computerized music composition who are not satisfied with simple melodies, here is a program that composes computer music in four-part harmony. You can select major or minor keys and any one of four tempos. Because the program is large, it has been broken into two parts which CHAIN to each other. Includes a sample run and a list of program variables.

Lines: 220, 300
Version: Honeywell BASIC
Hardware: sequential file device
Software: none
Non-ANSI: FILES, READ #, WRITE, CHAIN, TIM(), CALL

71. Musical Pitch Structures in Normal Form

Author: Hubert S. Howe, Jr.

Source: *Byte* Jul 79 (4:7)
"Creativity in Computer Music" pp. 158–173
(162)

Pitch structures are sets of musical notes related by transposition. (Transposition is the addition or subtraction of a constant interval to each tone in a collection, moving the set up or down by a uniform amount.) This program computes pitch structures in normal form.

Lines: 28
Version: TRS-80 Level I BASIC
Hardware: none
Software: none
Non-ANSI: extended IF

1103. Texas Instruments TI-99/4 Music Demos

Author: Don Inman

Source: *Recreational Computing* Sep–Oct 79 (8:2)
"The Sounds from Texas Instruments" pp. 9–15 (11–15)

The Texas Instruments TI-99/4 has the ability to produce musical tones. These tones can be used to create a variety of interesting programs. This set of programs shows off the TI-99/4's sound capabilities. Among the demos are a musical scale player, a random-note player, and a tone guessing game. (These programs have been reprinted from the book, *Introduction to TI BASIC*.)

Lines: 6, 20 (plus patch), 11 (plus patch), 10, 26 (plus patch), 37, 39 (plus patch)
Version: TI BASIC
Hardware: TI-99/4
Software: TI BASIC
Non-ANSI: not translatable

1113. Atari Music Demos

Author: Herb Moore

Source: *Recreational Computing* Nov–Dec 79 (8:3)
"See What You Hear & Hear What You See"
pp. 8–10 (9–10)

Updates: corrections
Recreational Computing Jan–Feb 80 (8:4)
"See What You Hear & Hear What You See"
pp. 42–44 (42–44)

The Atari computer system has provisions for making a wide variety of sounds. These short demos show off the Atari's musical abilities.

Lines: various
Version: Atari BASIC
Hardware: Atari computer
Software: none
Non-ANSI: not translatable

1121. Soundware Music Amplifier Demos for the PET

Author: Alfred J. Bruey

Source: *Recreational Computing* Nov–Dec 79 (8:3)
"Making Music on the PET" pp. 49–51
(50–51)

There are many ways to use a computer to make sounds or music. These programs show how you can make music on a PET using a Soundware amplifier. The first program plays one note. The second program plays scales. The third program plays "Happy Birthday."

Lines: 7, 20, 22
Version: PET BASIC
Hardware: Soundware music amplifier
Software: none
Non-ANSI: POKE, TI()

**414. Micro Technology Unlimited
Music Demo for the Pet**

Author: Gregory Yob

Source: *Creative Computing* Dec 79 (5:12)
"Personal Electronic Transactions" pp.
146–149 (147)

Your PET can make music using Micro Technology
Unlimited's K-1002-2 digital-to-analog converter board.
This program uses the MTU board to produce various
tones. The program loads data, which is then executed by
MTU software.

Lines: 61
Version: PET BASIC
Hardware: PET, Micro Technology Unlimited K-1002-2
D/A board
Software: MTU music software
Non-ANSI: POKE, PEEK( ), extended IF, ON . . .
GOSUB

MYSTERY PROGRAMS

616. Mystery Program

Author: Tom Rugg and Phil Feldman

Source: *Kilobaud* Apr 78 (16)
"Kilobaud's Mystery Program" pp. 22–23
(23)

Updates: author's address
Kilobaud Jun 78 (18)
"Corrections" p. 112

solution
Kilobaud Jul 78 (19)
"Let's Hear It for the Mystery Program" p. 20

Most people try to make their programs as easy to understand as possible. In this program, the authors have deliberately disguised the function of the program. Your job is
to figure out what the program actually does. You have
two ways to find out: you can read the listing and try to
deduce what the program does, or you can try out the
program on a computer. It's elementary, my dear Wat-
son.

Lines: 65
Version: Altair 8K BASIC
Hardware: none
Software: none
Non-ANSI: CHR$()

155. Mystery Programs

Author: not given

Source: *Calculators/Computers Magazine* Jan–Feb 79
(3:1)
"The Microchallenge" p. 49 (49)

This is a group of three short mystery programs. Your
challenge is to figure out what the programs do. You are
asked to answer (without running the programs first)
such things as how many numbers the programs will print
out and what the largest number printed will be.

Lines: 9, 10, 11
Version: TRS-80 BASIC
Hardware: none
Software: none
Non-ANSI: CLS, strings

999. Mystery Word Programming
Puzzle

Author: Colin Wells

Source: *Personal Computing* Mar 79 (3:3)
"Ugly BASIC" p. 12 (12)

Updates: corrected copy of program
Personal Computing Jun 79 (3:6)
"Ugly BASIC Bugs" p. 8, 101 (8)

With this puzzle, the object is to figure out what the
computer is going to print. On the surface, this would
seem a simple task because the program is mostly PRINT,
GOTO, FOR, and NEXT statements. In practice, it takes
careful bookkeeping. Of course, you can always cheat and
just run the program. (This program appeared originally
in the Australian computer journal *COM-3*).

Lines: 23
Version: not given
Hardware: none
Software: none
Non-ANSI: none

1022. Hidden Word Puzzle

Author: Jonathon Cook

Source: *Personal Computing* Jun 79 (3:6)
"Ugly BASIC Bugs" pp. 8, 101 (8)

This program prints a "mystery" word. See if you can
figure out what word will be printed, without running the
program.

Lines: 30
Version: TRS-80 BASIC
Hardware: none
Software: none
Non-ANSI: extended IF

1023. Programming Puzzles

Author: James Boettler and Ed Dolney

Source: *Personal Computing* Jun 79 (3:6)
"BASIC Without Style" pp. 10, 104, (10)

Think you're a skilled programmer? Test your ability to decipher strange problems with these puzzling little oddities. Includes sample runs.

Lines: 9, 8, 8, 10
Version: Educomp BASIC
Hardware: none
Software: none
Non-ANSI: ! (used in place of REM), extended IF

PETS

485. Aquarium Maintenance Program

Author: Timothy O'Shaughnessy

Source: *Interface Age* Dec 77 (2:13)
"Aquarium Maintenance" pp. 64–69 (66)

This is a program to monitor and maintain the conditions in an aquarium. The program monitors three aquarium parameters: temperature, salinity, and pH. Special sensor probes and an A/D converter are required.

Lines: 135
Version: not given
Hardware: sensor probes, A/D converter
Software: none
Non-ANSI: HP strings, PEEK(), POKE, MOD()

PHOTOGRAPHY

710. Photography Lab Program

Author: Michael Avery

Source: *Kilobaud Microcomputing* Jun 79 (30)
"Personal Computing, Meet Photography"
pp. 114–118 (115–118)

Updates: address of author
Kilobaud Microcomputing Jul 79 (31)
"Corrections" p. 172

Getting your photos to come out right is no easy task. Even after you've taken that perfect picture, you can still blow it in the lab. You have to worry about setting the correct f-stop and exposure time for a variety of film formats. Now your home computer can do all the photo lab calculations, so you can spend your time in the field instead of in the darkroom. This program can help you set things up so that you get perfect prints every time. The program takes into account such factors as print size, paper grade, highlight density, and shadow density. Includes a sample run.

Lines: 311
Version: SWTP 8K BASIC
Hardware: none
Software: none
Non-ANSI: extended IF, CHR(), On . . . GOSUB, CHR$()

POETRY

855. Haiku Writer

Author: John Morris, modified by G. Yob

Source: *People's Computer Company* Jul 74 (2:6)
"How to Write Poems with a Computer" p. 8
(8)

You don't need rhyme, meter, or even grammar to write a poem. What you need is a fresh way of seeing things and a new way of saying them. Some people say that computers are uncreative because they are "mindless." But it is just this mindlessness that can make a computer very creative indeed. Because a computer never worries about being conventional or rational, it can turn out works that no human being would think of writing. This program can turn out examples of this. Haikus are a form of poetry that has been around for thousands of years; yet no one has ever thought of turning out the kind of haikus that the computer does! Includes a sample run.

Lines: 45
Version: Datapoint 2200 BASIC
Hardware: none
Software: none
Non-ANSI: HP strings, extended IF, CLICK, multiple-assignment, PRINT #, PRINT statements without the keyword PRINT

204. Haiku Writer

Author: Paul Emmerich

Source: *Creative Computing* Sep–Oct 76 (2:5)
"Haiku Generator" pp. 34–35 (35)

The *Haiku* is a Japanese form of poetry. One form of haikus consists of three lines containing, respectively, five, seven, and five syllables. The objective of the haiku writer is to form a striking image. This program generates random haikus. You supply the basic words and the computer grinds out as many haikus as you want. The haikus usually don't mean anything, but they do have their own odd sort of beauty. Includes a sample run.

Lines: 111
Version: Data General NOVA BASIC
Hardware: none
Software: none
Non-ANSI: HP strings, ON . . . GOSUB, multiple-assignment

205. Computer Poetry Programs

Author: David Ahl

Source: *Creative Computing* Sep–Oct 76 (2:5)
"Roses are red, Computers are blue" pp. 36–38 (37)

What is poetry but words strung together to convey some emotional or other feeling of the author? These two programs string together words to form computer poetry. The first program prints out dark and sinister poems based on phrases from Edgar Allan Poe. The second program uses phrases that you type in. You can change the type of poems created from sentimental to just plain weird. Includes a sample output.

Lines: 34, 24
Version: not given
Hardware: none
Software: none
Non-ANSI: strings, OPEN, CLOSE, PRINT #, extended IF

722. Haiku Composer

Author: John Krutch

Source: *Kilobaud Microcomputing* Aug 79 (32)
"Haiku Composer" pp. 80–82 (81)

Updates: commentary
Kilobaud Microcomputing Nov 79 (35)
"Getting Haiku" p. 20

new author address
Kilobaud Microcomputing Nov 79 (35)
"Corrections" p. 198

Haikus are a form of poetry which originated in Japan over four centuries ago. The haiku is a short passage which creates a single mental image. This program allows your computer to compose haikus. Not bound by logic or reason, the program is capable of generating some rather fanciful imagery. Includes a sample output.

Lines: 169
Version: TRS-80 Level II BASIC
Hardware: TRS-80
Software: none
Non-ANSI: not translatable

RANDOM PATTERNS

848. Patterns of Plus Signs

Author: Andy Fire

Source: *People's Computer Company* Sep 73 (2:1)
"Joel & Andy's Page" p. 16 (16)

This program prints out computer art composed of more-or-less random patterns of plus signs. Includes a sample run.

Lines: 23
Version: HP 2000 BASIC
Hardware: none
Software: none
Non-ANSI: none

856. Impressionistic Paintbrush

Author: Gregory Yob

Source: *People's Computer Company* Jul 74 (2:6)
untitled p. 27 (27

You don't need a fancy graphics display to produce works of art with your computer. Here are two programs which turn out works of "impressionistic art" on an ordinary terminal. The works produced are more-or-less random patterns of certain characters. Includes sample runs.

Lines: 22, 12
Version: Datapoint 2200 BASIC
Hardware: none
Software: none
Non-ANSI: HP strings, PRINT #, extended IF, PRINT
statements without the keyword PRINT

129. Abstract Art for the TRS-80

Author: Don Inman

Source: *Calculators/Computers Magazine* May 78 (2:5)
"TRS-80: Games & Abstract Art" pp. 5–10
(8–9)

Computers can be thought to have a limited amount of artistic talent, especially if your tastes run to abstract art. This program generates abstract images on the screen of a TRS-80 system. The pictures are composed of randomly drawn rectangles. You get to choose the number and sizes of the rectangles. The computer then randomly draws the shapes on the screen. This program can probably be modified for use on other systems that have a video screen. Includes a sample output.

Lines: 34
Version: TRS-80 Level I BASIC
Hardware: TRS-80
Software: none
Non-ANSI: not translatable

910. KALEIDOSCOPE for the PET

Author: Dave Offen

Source: *People's Computers* May–Jun 78 (6:6)
"KALEIDOSCOPE" p. 42 (42)

KALEIDOSCOPE is a program that continuously draws patterns on the screen of the Commodore PET. The patterns drawn vary continuously. Includes a sample of the output.

Lines: 27 (plus patch)
Version: PET BASIC
Hardware: PET
Software: none
Non-ANSI: not translatable

514. Graphics Demo for the Apple II

Author: Mike Tautkus

Source: *Interface Age* Nov 78 (3:11)
untitled p. 14 (14)

This is a short program to produce a random display on an Apple II. No explanation is given of what the program produces.

Lines: 17
Version: Apple II BASIC
Hardware: Apple II
Software: none
Non-ANSI: not translatable

923. Random Patterns on a TRS-80

Author: Ramon Zamora

Source: *People's Computers* Nov–Dec 78 (7:3)
"Random Patterns" p. 23 (23)

If your idea of a hot way to spend an evening is to sit up watching TV test patterns, then this is the program for you. This program draws random patterns on a TRS-80. The patterns are composed of a single character which you select.

Lines: 6
Version: TRS-80 Level II BASIC
Hardware: TRS-80
Software: none
Non-ANSI: not translatable

154. APPLE ART

Author: Jim Day

Source: *Calculators/Computers Magazine* Jan–Feb 79
(3:1)
"High-Resolution Apple Art" pp. 46–48 (47)

The Apple computer system has a truly remarkable color graphics capability. In its high-precision mode, the system can make detailed plots in a variety of colors. This program demonstrates the Apple's abilities by producing random art using circles, rectangles, and triangles. Includes a sample output.

Lines: 43
Version: Applesoft II BASIC
Hardware: Apple II
Software: none
Non-ANSI: not translatable

1016. Apple II Pop Art Program

Author: Raymond Vizzone and Del Cornali

Source: *Personal Computing* Apr 79 (3:4)
"Apple II, Artist Extraordinaire" pp. 58–60
(59–60)

ARTPAC.3 is a pop art program for the Apple II. This program draws (semi-randomly) color patterns on the Apple II's screen. The patterns are composed of dots, lines, rectangles, and squares. Though the patterns are essentially random, you can rate the various elements to give the computer an idea of the type of display you wish. Includes sample output (in color).

Lines: 167
Version: Apple II BASIC
Hardware: Apple II
Software: none
Non-ANSI: not translatable

1020. Random "City" Patterns on the PET

Author: Eric Olson

Source: *Personal Computing* May 79 (3:5)
"CITY" pp. 42–44 (44)

Updates: TRS-80 version, modifications
Personal Computing Aug 79 (3:8)
"CITY for the TRS-80" p. 9 (9)

new program
Personal Computing Dec 79 (3:12)
"TRS-80 CITY" p. 10 (10)

This program produces random patterns on the screen of a PET. The output can be compared to a city in that the computer prints new characters over old, like a city; building and then rebuilding a minute later. Includes a sample output.

Lines: 25
Version: PET BASIC
Hardware: PET
Software: none
Non-ANSI: not translatable

68. Random Graphics for the TRS-80

Author: M. Parris

Source: *Byte* Jun 79 (4:6)
"A Peek at Poke" pp. 212–213 (212)

This program fills the screen of a TRS-80 with random characters. A patch allows the program to call a machine language routine to do the same thing.

Lines: 3 (plus patch)
Version: TRS-80 Level II BASIC
Hardware: TRS-80
Software: none
Non-ANSI: not translatable

370. Random and "Wallpaper" Patterns on a TRS-80

Author: Stephen B. Gray

Source: *Creative Computing* Aug 79 (5:8)
"TRS-80 Strings" pp. 126–130 (126–127)

Updates: corrections
Creative Computing Dec 79 (5:12)
"TRS-80 Strings" pp. 154–161 (154)

This set of programs produces random patterns on a TRS-80. The first two programs produce a single random pattern. The second two programs repeat the individual patterns to create a "wallpaper" effect. Includes a sample output.

Lines: 5, 5 (plus patches), 10 (plus patch), 17 (plus patches)
Version: TRS-80 Level II BASIC
Hardware: TRS-80
Software: none
Non-ANSI: not translatable

371. "Op Art" for the TRS-80

Author: Mark Richard Cusumano

Source: *Creative Computing* Aug 79 (5:8)
"TRS-80 Strings" pp. 126–130 (130)

This program produces "op art" patterns on a TRS-80 by drawing random horizontal and vertical lines.

Lines: 16
Version: TRS-80 Level II BASIC
Hardware: TRS-80
Software: none
Non-ANSI: not translatable

1036. Random "City Patterns" on the TRS-80

Author: Robert McDaniel

Source: *Personal Computing* Aug 79 (3:8)
"CITY for the TRS-80" p. 9 (9)

This program produces random patterns on the screen of a TRS-80. The output can be compared to a city in that the computer prints new characters over old, like a city; building and then rebuilding a minute later.

Lines: 34
Version: TRS-80 Level II BASIC
Hardware: TRS-80
Software: none
Non-ANSI: not translatable

383. Kaleidoscope
Programs for the TRS-80

Author: Stephen B. Gray

Source: *Creative Computing* Sep 79 (5:9)
"TRS-80 Strings" pp. 186–190 (186–188)

These two programs draw "kaleidoscope" patterns on the screen of a TRS-80. The first program draws random patterns. Patches build it up into a kaleidoscope program. The second kaleidoscope program provides for user-defined pattern sizes. Includes a sample output.

Lines: 6 (plus patches), 14 (plus patches)
Version: not given
Hardware: TRS-80
Software: none
Non-ANSI: not translatable

830. Random Color Points and Lines
on the Apple II

Author: Robert Jellinghaus

Source: *onComputing* Winter 79 (1:3)
"The Talcott Mountain Science Center" pp. 34–46 (44)

Updates: commentary
onComputing Spring 80 (1:4)
"Talcott Mountain" p. 6

This program creates random abstract drawings on an Apple II. The drawings consist of points and lines in various colors. The display changes constantly until you stop it. Includes a list of program variables.

Lines: 34
Version: not given
Hardware: Apple II
Software: none
Non-ANSI: not translatable

1059. Random Patterns on a TRS-80

Author: Franklyn Miller

Source: *Personal Computing* Nov 79 (3:11)
"Random Patterns" p. 8 (8)

This program draws random patterns on the screen of a TRS-80.

Lines: 9
Version: TRS-80 Level II BASIC
Hardware: TRS-80
Software: none
Non-ANSI: not translatable

RECORD KEEPING

430. Personal Daily Reminder
Calendar

Author: Bob Moody and Steve Williams

Source: *Dr. Dobb's Journal of Computer Calisthenics & Orthodontia* Jun–Jul 77 (2:6)
"SCHDL: A BASIC-Coded 'Daily Reminder' for Home and Office Use" pp. 15–16 (15–16)

Do you think it's time to get your life more organized? This program can help. It is a personal daily calendar and schedule. To use the program, you first input the schedule of your activities. Later, you can print out a complete display of your activities for the month. You can use this program to make sure you don't forget your spouse's birthday, the next Rams-Vikings game, and other important dates. Includes a sample run.

Lines: 117
Version: North Star Extended Disk BASIC
Hardware: sequential file device
Software: none
Non-ANSI: OPEN, CLOSE, READ #, WRITE, HP strings, ! (used in place of PRINT), extended IF, %() (used to format printouts)

589. Record Keeping Program

Author: Randy Miller

Source: *Kilobaud* Aug 77 (8)
"Try a Do-All Program!" pp. 84–89 (86–89)

Updates: improvements
Kilobaud May 78 (17)
"5 Minutes or 5 Hours?" pp. 100–102 (101–102)

This is a do-all record keeping program. It can maintain a great variety of record lists. Some of the kinds of lists it might be used for are a list of your record collection, grouped by subject matter, or a list of names, addresses, and phone numbers. The program can be used to keep and balance your checkbook. It has commands to load records, dump records, add or remove records, sort, and print all or some of the records. Includes a sample run.

Lines: 198
Version: not given
Hardware: sequential file device
Software: none
Non-ANSI: CLEAR, multi-letter variables, strings, extended IF

940. Note Storing Program

Author: Sam Newhouse

Source: *Personal Computing* Mar 78 (2:3)
"The Bob-Up Program" pp. 24–25 (24–25)

How many times have you forgotten an appointment? What about locker combinations, your mother's birthday, or your wedding anniversary? This program can help you keep track of all of the above and more. This program allows you to store notes to yourself for later recall. You store each note with a "keyword." Then, when you want to recall the information, you type in the keyword. The computer will output all the notes associated with that keyword. The program also has provisions for removing notes (for things you'd rather forget).

Lines: 250
Version: Altair Disk Extended BASIC ver. 3.4
Hardware: random-access file device
Software: none
Non-ANSI: not translatable

962. Record Album Data Management System

Author: Rodger Pogue

Source: *Personal Computing* Jul 78 (2:7)
"Music in Your Memory" pp. 43–52 (48–50)

Updates: modification
Personal Computing Feb 79 (3:2)
"Index Statement" p. 4 (4)

This is a system for maintaining information about your music collection. The program can perform a variety of tasks. The program can list and sort record albums (or tapes) according to a variety of categories. The program keeps track of information such as record title and artist. It has provisions for adding, deleting, and correcting information in the database. Because the system is disk based, it includes commands to assist you in organizing the disk. These include disk initialization and disk record movement. As written, the system requires a disk (or

other random-access medium) and 48K of RAM. The author claims that the program can be changed to use tape files and as little as 14K of RAM. The program can also be modified to manage information for other things such as books or coins. Includes a sample run and a list of program variables.

Lines: 460
Version: Micropolis Extended Disk BASIC
Hardware: random-access file device
Software: none
Non-ANSI: not translatable

296. Computer-Generated Subject Index

Author: Timothy Craven

Source: *Creative Computing* Nov–Dec 78 (4:6)
"Need a Subject Index? Use NEPHIS" pp. 94–95 (95)

NEPHIS (NEsted PHrase Indexing System) is a computer-assisted subject indexing system. The NEPHIS program takes input records that you type in and creates a whole series of records from each one. After NEPHIS generates the entries, you can use a sorting program and then a formatting program (these are not supplied) to automatically print out a complete, cross-referenced subject index. Using this system you can create subject indexes for a collection of books, magazine articles, or just about anything. Includes a sample output.

Lines: 115
Version: PDP-10 BASIC
Hardware: two sequential file devices
Software: none
Non-ANSI: FILES, SCRATCH, MARGIN, INPUT #, PRINT #, strings, END()

298. Simple Data Retrieval System

Author: Tom McCalmont

Source: *Creative Computing* Nov–Dec 78 (4:6)
"Microurologistically, Of Course" pp. 130–131 (131)

Suppose you have a short list of data—a list of magazine articles, for example, How do you quickly find the single entry you want? This is a quick and easy program to do just that task. You store information in data statements in the program. Then, to find something, you run the program. The program searches for a target character string that you specify. All the entries that contain the target string are printed out. In our example, you could type in a word and have the program type out all the magazine titles that have that word in them.

Lines: 15
Version: Cromemco Control BASIC
Hardware: none
Software: none
Non-ANSI: HP strings, POS(), extended IF

1075. Electronic Desk Calendar for the TRS-80

Author: Clyde Farrell

Source: *Recreational Computing* Jan–Feb 79 (7:4)
"An Electronic Desk Calendar" pp. 29–31
(30–31)

This electronic desk calendar allows you to make notes to yourself and be reminded automatically on the requested date. As a side benefit, the calendar can tell you the day of the week for any date you specify. Includes a sample run.

Lines: 84
Version: TRS-80 Level II BASIC
Hardware: TRS-80
Software: none
Non-ANSI: not translatable

521. Notary Public Records

Author: Jim Schreier

Source: *Interface Age* Feb 79 (4:2)
"Notary" pp. 81–83 (82–83)

Notary Publics are people who record and notarize documents. Notaries must keep complete and precise records of all the documents they have stamped. This program helps notaries by keeping notary records on computer where they can be indexed and accessed with ease. The program has provisions for storing, updating, and displaying notary records.

Lines: 211
Version: SWTPC disk BASIC ver. 3.0
Hardware: two sequential file devices
Software: none
Non-ANSI: OPEN, CLOSE, PRINT #, READ #, EOF(),
WRITE, SCRATCH, KILL, RESTORE #,
LINE, RENAME, strings, extended IF, KILL

333. Intelligent Calendar

Author: Gary Young

Source: *Creative Computing* Apr 79 (5:4)
"An Intelligent Calendar" pp. 128–131
(129–131)

Updates: revised program
Creative Computing Jan 80 (6:1)
"Intelligent Calendar Revisited" pp. 120–121
(120–121)

This program can help you keep track of loan payment dates, birthdays, and other important dates. It's an intelligent calendar. Most calendars just record information. This one does that job, but it also can automatically record events that occur on a routine basis. The program can even list what your payments are on bills and how much you have left to pay off. The calendars generated have room for you to enter other information. Includes a sample run.

Lines: 323
Version: Northstar BASIC, release 4
Hardware: random-access file device
Software: none
Non-ANSI: HP strings, extended IF, %() (used to format
printouts), OPEN, CLOSE, WRITE, READ
#, TYP()

337. Book Notes

Author: Derek Kelly

Source: *Creative Computing* May 79 (5:5)
"Beyond the Text Editor" pp. 32–33 (32)

If you do a lot of reading then you'll probably want to record notes about what you've read. You could do this by recording your references on paper. By the time your desk drawer is awash in scraps of paper, you may decide to use your computer to keep abreast of things. This program records book notes and basic information about each book. The data is stored in DATA statements. As written, the program just prints out the stored data, but it can be modified to perform other jobs.

Lines: 17
Version: not given
Hardware: none
Software: none
Non-ANSI: strings, GET, two-letter variables

695. TRS-80 Cross-Index

Author: John Records and Bob Wine

Source: *Kilobaud Microcomputing* May 79 (29)
"A TRS-80 Cross-Index" pp. 94–98 (94–95)

Are you becoming lost in a sea of paper? Get better organized with this cross-indexing program. It allows you to record information about a group of documents.

Then, using this information, you can have the program list the reference numbers of those documents which match your current interest. The data about the documents is stored on tape. You type in a selection criteria. The program scans the tape and prints out the documents that fit your specifications. Two versions of the program are given: one with detailed instructions and one without. Includes a flowchart.

Lines: 99, 25
Version: TRS-80 Level II BASIC
Hardware: sequential file device
Software: none
Non-ANSI: CLS, INPUT #, PRINT #, extended IF, ON . . . GOSUB, strings

1030. Photograph Collection Records

Author: Loyd Bulmer

Source: Personal Computing Jul 79 (3:7)
"FOTO FINDER" pp. 36–41 (38–40)

Updates: commentary
Personal Computing Sep 79 (3:9)
"Research Retrieval" p. 9

commentary
Personal Computing Oct 79 (3:10)
"Copyright Questions Yield Few Answers" p. 7

Now where is that photo of Aunt May that I took out in front of her house in 1954? FOTO FINDER is a program designed to help photo bugs keep track of their collections. The program records information about each picture, such as where it was taken, when it was taken, and its description. This data is stored on cassette tape. You can then later have the program print out a list of those photos that fit your specifications. This program should be easy to adapt for other types of collections besides photographs. Includes a sample run.

Lines: 164
Version: Radio Shack Level II BASIC
Hardware: sequential file device
Software: none
Non-ANSI: strings, CLS, PRINT @ , CLEAR, extended IF, STRING$(), INPUT #, PRINT #

726. Inventory System

Author: Richard A. Blessing

Source: Kilobaud Microcomputing Sep 79 (33)
"INVENTORY" pp. 28–32 (28–32)

Updates: additional program
Kilobaud Microcomputing Nov 79 (35)
"Corrections" pp. 198–200 (200)

corrections
Kilobaud Microcomputing Jan 80 (37)
"Corrections" pp. 170–171 (171)

Everyone needs to keep inventory lists of one kind or another. Perhaps you might want to keep a list of the records in your record collection. Or maybe you might want to keep track of magazine articles. This program is a general purpose inventory program to do such tasks. It maintains lists of things that you enter. The program can search for occurrences of a given string in the file to help you locate items of interest. As written, the program requires an Otto OEM-1000 TVT terminal, but it should be fairly easy to change the input routine so that only a normal terminal is required. Also provided is a sorting program that can sort the records according to your specifications. An assembly language sorting routine is given in addition to the BASIC one, in case you want very fast sorting.

Lines: 131, 64
Version: North Star BASIC
Hardware: random-access file device, Otto OEM-1000 TVT
Software: none
Non-ANSI: not translatable

735. Calendar Program

Author: Steve Tabler

Source: Kilobaud Microcomputing Oct 79 (34)
"Calendar Program" p. 102 (102)

This program prints out calendars for a single month or a full year. Combine it with a computer art program to make your own pinup calendars. Includes a sample run.

Lines: 79
Version: Southwest Technical Products 8K BASIC, ver. 2.3
Hardware: none
Software: none
Non-ANSI: strings, LINE, PRINT #, extended IF

1055. Coin Collection Program (Hobby and Profit-Minded Versions)

Author: Charles D. Sternberg

Source: Personal Computing Oct 79 (3:10)
"Coin Collecting" pp. 30–36 (31–36)

Some people collect coins as a hobby; others are interested in coins as an inflation hedge. This coin collection program comes in two versions—one for each type of collector. Both versions record data about the coins that you have on hand. With both versions you can selectively print out lists of coins based on date, denomination, mint mark, or type of coin. The version for profit-minded collectors also keeps track of purchase dates, costs, and current coin values. Includes sample runs and lists of program variables. (Reprinted from the book, *BASIC Computer Programs for the Home.*)

Lines: 113, 143
Version: not given
Hardware: none
Software: none
Non-ANSI: strings

742. Computerized Information Cross-Referencing System

Author: Joseph Jay Sanger

Source: *Kilobaud Microcomputing* Nov 79 (35)
"The Electronic Librarian" pp. 44–62
(46–62)

This set of programs forms a system for cross-indexing journals, magazine articles, or other information. The system is flexible and can be tailored to fit a wide variety of data requirements. The system is based on the use of keyword cross-indexes. You type in data about an article. At the same time, you type in a set of keywords. When you want to find information about a particular subject, you enter one or more keywords. The computer then rummages around in the database and prints out all the articles that have the desired keywords. The system has complete provisions for creating, editing, and sorting the databases. Includes a sample run and flowchart.

Lines: 551, 162, 145
Version: BASIC-E
Hardware: random-access file device
Software: none
Non-ANSI: not translatable

1071. Periodical Guide

Author: Margaret Whack

Source: *Personal Computing* Dec 79 (3:12)
"Create Your Own Periodical Guide" pp.
69–70 (69)

Do you read stacks of magazines each month? If so, you may be having trouble remembering where you read just what. This program can help you keep track of those interesting articles, advertisements, and what-not. For each entry, you store in a DATA statement the magazine,

subject, title, date, and page, as well as a subject category. When you want to find something, you select from the computer's list of available categories. The computer will print out a list of all the entries under that category. Includes a sample run.

Lines: 46
Version: PET BASIC
Hardware: none
Software: none
Non-ANSI: strings, extended IF, GET

RELIGION

225. BIBLE QUIZ

Author: Steve Wentworth

Source: *Creative Computing* Mar–Apr 77 (3:2)
"BIBLE QUIZ" p. 124 (124)

This is a quiz which tests your knowledge of biblical events, places, and persons. The BIBLE QUIZ program administers up to 25 questions about the Bible. All the questions require one-word answers. All the answers must be spelled correctly. If an incorrect answer is given, the program gives the correct answer. After the question has been answered, the biblical reference is given. At the end, your percentage of correct answers is given. Includes a sample run.

Lines: 90
Version: not given
Hardware: none
Software: none
Non-ANSI: strings

906. Tibetan Prayer Wheel

Author: Edrid

Source: *People's Computers* Mar–Apr 78 (6:5)
"Prayer Wheel Program" p. 44 (44)

This program endlessly recites Tibetan chants. The program keeps a permanent record of the number of chants performed.

Lines: 19
Version: North Star BASIC
Hardware: sequential file device
Software: none
Non-ANSI: HP strings, OPEN, CLOSE, READ #,
WRITE, PRINT statements without the
keyword PRINT

721. Shavasan Meditation Program

Author: Ian Thurston

Source: *Kilobaud Microcomputing* Aug 79 (32)
"Shavasan Meditation Program" pp. 64–65
(64–65)

Is life getting you "up-tight"? Let your computer become your automated guru and show you the way to *nirvana*. This program coaches you in the *Shavasan* method of meditation. This method is based on controlled breathing exercises. The computer guides you in these special exercises.

Lines: 51
Version: TRS-80 Level-II BASIC
Hardware: none
Software: none
Non-ANSI: multi-letter variables, extended IF, strings, PRINT @, CLS

1049. "Who Am I?" Bible Quiz

Author: John B. Palmer

Source: *Personal Computing* Sep 79 (3:9)
"Who Am I?" pp. 38–40 (40)

Updates: modifications, new program listing
Personal Computing Mar 80 (4:3)
"Bible Translations" pp. 8–9 (8–9)

How's your knowledge of the Bible? Test it against this "Who Am I?" Bible quiz. The computer thinks of a biblical character. You try to guess the person by asking one or more of eight possible questions. The computer answers "yes" or "no" to your questions until you guess who the mystery figure is. If you misspell a person's name, the computer tries to figure out who you're referring to and then corrects you. Includes a sample run.

Lines: 138
Version: Processor Technology Extended BASIC
Hardware: none
Software: none
Non-ANSI: HP strings, extended IF, VAL( )

SELF-REPRODUCING PROGRAMS

928. Self-Reproducing Program

Author: Kenneth Jackman

Source: *Personal Computing* Mar–Apr 77 (1:2)
"The UNGAME" pp. 114–119 (114–115, 118–119)

This is a package of programs to create a self-reproducing program. The package uses recursion and bootstrapping to generate the final program. The output of the final program is copies of itself. The program is unique in that it manages to print out itself without the use of strings.

Lines: 40, 36, 105, 315
Version: not given
Hardware: none
Software: none
Non-ANSI: none

227. Self-Reproducing Program

Author: Donald Bell

Source: *Creative Computing* May–Jun 77 (3:3)
"Computer Recreations" p. 66 (66)

One of the criteria of life is "the ability to reproduce." Can a computer program be a living thing? Maybe. Here is a program that prints exact copies of itself. It doesn't *do* anything interesting, but I guess you can't have everything.

Lines: 18
Version: not given
Hardware: none
Software: none
Non-ANSI: strings

380. PET Self-LISTing Program

Author: Gregory Yob

Sources: *Creative Computing* Sep 79 (5:9)
"Personal Electronic Transactions" pp. 178–182 (179–180)

Updates: modifications
Creative Computing Feb 80 (6:2)
"Personal Electronic Transactions" pp. 156–161 (157)

This program LISTs itself by examining the internal PET BASIC interpreter code and translating it back into text form. You can use it to get a better idea of how BASIC interpreter code is stored in the PET.

Lines: 39
Version: PET BASIC
Hardware: none
Software: none
Non-ANSI: not translatable

SIMULATIONS

For more entries in this category, see specific topics.

574. Program to Simulate the Growth of Home/Hobby Computing

Author: Rich Diadday

Source: *Kilobaud Microcomputing* Mar 77 (3)
"Looking Ahead" pp. 13–15 (14)

This is a program to graphically simulate the growth of home/hobby computing. Simulation is a powerful tool for predicting the future behavior of complex systems. Simulation is divided into two categories: structural models and aggregate models. In structural models the individual units of the system are modeled. In aggregate models only measurements concerning the system are modeled. This program is used as an example of aggregate modeling. You can modify the model to see what effect various assumptions about the model have on the output. The output consists of a growth chart printed on your terminal. Includes sample runs.

> *Lines:* 110 (plus patch)
> *Version:* not given
> *Hardware:* none
> *Software:* none
> *Non-ANSI:* strings

15. Model Rocket Flight Simulator

Author: Stephen Smith

Source: *Byte* Jan 78 (3:1)
"Simulation of Motion (Part III): Model Rockets and Other Flying Objects" pp. 144–149 (148)

Updates: correction
Byte May 78 (3:5)
"A Note About Simulations, Part 3" p. 155 (155)

This is a simulation of the flight of a model rocket. The simulation takes into account such factors as drag, thrust, and rocket mass to produce a listing of the rocket's altitude, range, and speed at various times after launch. No special graphics terminal is required. This program is part of a continuing series of articles on simulation. This article in the series details the simulation of moving objects in flight.

> *Lines:* 102
> *Version:* Tektronix 4051 BASIC
> *Hardware:* none
> *Software:* none
> *Non-ANSI:* none

255. World Simulation

Author: James Murphy

Source: *Creative Computing* Jan–Feb 78 (4:1)
"WORLD2" pp. 48–53 (49–51)

In the book *World Dynamics*, Jay Forrester presents a world population model interrelating many variables including population, natural resources, food supply, pollution, capital investment, and quality of life. Forrester's model predicts that the world will become overpopulated and the quality of life will decline sharply. This program is a version of the same model. The various assumptions about the world and its resources are written into the program. The output of the program is a graph plotted on your terminal. On the graph are plotted the world's population, resources, quality of life, pollution, and capital investment. By changing the data in the program you can change the assumptions upon which the model is based. The program comes in two parts: the program itself, and a section of comments listing the program data variables. Includes a sample output.

> *Lines:* 315, 85
> *Version:* not given
> *Hardware:* none
> *Software:* none
> *Non-ANSI:* ! (used in place of REM), MAT operations, strings, CHANGE, extended IF, ' (used in place of PRINT)

16. Ship Motion Simulator

Author: Stephen Smith

Source: *Byte* Feb 78 (3:2)
"Simulation of Motion (Part IV): Extended Objects, Applications for Boating" pp. 42–51 (50–51)

This is a simulation of the motion of a boat in the water. The article is part of a continuing series on the simulation of motion. This article in the series discusses the simulation of complex forces acting on objects. The program simulates the motion of a boat by printing out the boat's vertical and angular positions at various time intervals. No special graphics capability is required. A sample run is included.

> *Lines:* 90
> *Version:* Tektronix 4051 BASIC
> *Hardware:* none
> *Software:* none
> *Non-ANSI:* none

131. Airplane Simulator

Author: Alex Siegel

Source: *Calculators/Computers Magazine* May 78 (2:5)
"Student Programs" pp. 37–41 (38)

In this game you have control of an airplane. The object of the game is to navigate safely to a landing field 2,000 miles away. The airplane can climb, dive, accelerate, slow down, and turn. It can also run out of gas, crash, and stall. As the simulation proceeds, you are given a constant read-out on your altitude, gas, speed, position, banking angle, and distance to the runway. When you land (or crash), the program gives you a pilot rating.

Lines: 104
Version: IBM BASIC
Hardware: none
Software: none
Non-ANSI: strings, PRINT USING, : (used to specify format of PRINT USING)

276. ART AUCTION

Author: C. William Engel

Source: *Creative Computing* May–Jun 78 (4:3)
"Art Auction" pp. 140–141 (141)

In this simulation, you are given the opportunity to participate in an art auction. The objective is to make as much money as possible by buying and selling paintings. In order to buy a painting, you must bid against a secret bid made by another buyer. After you buy your paintings, you are given a chance to sell them. You receive from one to five offers (you do not know in advance how many offers you will get). Sometimes it is wiser to accept a low bid, rather than risk losing out altogether on a sale. When all the paintings you have bought have been sold, you are given your total profit for all the transactions. Includes a flowchart, a list of program variables, and a sample run. (Appeared originally in the book *Stimulating Simulations.*)

Lines: 47
Version: not given
Hardware: none
Software: none
Non-ANSI: strings, two-letter variables, extended IF

979. Model Rocket Simulation

Author: Geoffrey Landis

Source: *Personal Computing* Nov 78 (2:11)
"Model Rocket Altitude Program" pp. 52–53 (53)

Up, up and away with this model rocket simulation. This program simulates the flight of a rocket by listing its altitude, velocity, and acceleration at 0.05-second intervals. You can specify the rocket's mass, body diameter, and drag coefficient. Includes a sample run and list of program variables.

Lines: 69
Version: not given
Hardware: none
Software: none
Non-ANSI: strings, extended IF

SPEECH

681. Cassette-Oriented Speech Routine for the TRS-80

Author: Jim Wright

Source: *Kilobaud Microcomputing* Apr 79 (28)
"Free Speech Lessons for the TRS-80" pp. 66–67 (67)

You don't have to spend hundreds of dollars for a speech synthesizer in order to get your TRS-80 to talk. This routine uses the TRS-80's cassette recorder to generate verbal output. You use the program provided (either alone or as part of another program) to record messages on tape. Then, when you run the program that needs speech output, the program can use PRINT # statements to stop and start the recorder.

Lines: 27
Version: TRS-80 Level I BASIC
Hardware: TRS-80
Software: none
Non-ANSI: not translatable

811. Speech Processor

Author: Charles Husbands

Source: *Micro* Sep 79 (16)
"Speech Processor for the PET" pp. 35–39 (36–39)

Updates: commentary
Micro Nov 79 (18)
"Note on Charles Husbands' Speech Processor for the PET" p. 45

One way to create speech is to record the sounds in digital form, and then later reconstruct them. The DATA-BOY Speech Processor developed by Mimic Electronics uses this technique to produce speech and other sounds. This program demonstrates the abilities of the DATA-BOY. It allows you to record and play back various sounds. The program also has a facility for saving the sound data on tape. Includes a flowchart.

Lines: 101 (plus patch)
Version: PET BASIC
Hardware: DATA-BOY Speech Processor, sequential file device, 6502-based microcomputer
Software: 6502 assembly language routine
Non-ANSI: strings, POKE, PEEK(), GET USR(), OPEN, CLOSE, PRINT #, INPUT #

SPORTS

862. Bicycle Gear Ratio

Author: Steve Rogowski

Source: People's Computer Company Jan 75 (3:3)
"Bicycle Gear Ratio" p. 18 (18)

Today's derailleur bicycles are typically 10-speed models. They have a wide range of gear ratios which make for easy pedaling under many conditions. Ideally, your feet turn the pedals of the bike at a constant rate. The only thing that changes is the rate that the wheels of the bicycle turn. Using a little physics, it is possible to prove that using the correct gear optimizes the transfer of power from your feet to the wheels of the bicycle. The purpose of this program is to compute your speed for given pedal-turning rates. It asks information about your gear ratio and what cadence range you wish, and outputs a table of bike speeds for given pedal-turning rates. Includes a sample run.

Lines: 22
Version: not given
Hardware: none
Software: none
Non-ANSI: strings, extended IF, PRINT statements without the keyword PRINT

567. Compute Golf Handicaps

Author: George Haller

Source: Kilobaud Jan 77 (1)
"Computers in Golf" pp. 96–98 (96)

This is a program to compute golf handicaps. Golf handicaps are computed by taking the average of the 10 best scores from the most recent 20 games played. From this average the United States Golf Association course rating is subtracted, and the result is multiplied by 0.96 and

rounded. This result is then the individual player's handicap. These handicaps are used to match players of varying degrees of skill. The program accepts golf scores from a group of players. It computes their handicaps and prints a summary of the results. Includes a sample run.

Lines: 57
Version: MITS Extended BASIC
Hardware: none
Software: none
Non-ANSI: strings, two-letter variables, SWAP, DEFINT, extended IF

931. Golf Handicaps

Author: O. Dial

Source: Personal Computing Jul–Aug 77 (1:4)
"GOLFCAP" pp. 46–51 (50–51)

Computing golf handicaps takes a fair amount of work. Most golf courses and clubs farm out the work to computer service bureaus. One way to use your microcomputer to earn a little cash would be to start up a business computing these handicaps. This program does this job. The program accepts the names and scores of a list of players. The program then computes the handicaps and outputs an alphabetical list of the players and their handicaps. The data in the program is stored in DATA statements and is continuously stored by resaving the program each time more data is added. Includes a sample run.

Lines: 112
Version: MITS Extended BASIC
Hardware: none
Software: none
Non-ANSI: CLEAR, strings, extended IF, ' (used in place of REM), two-letter variables, SWAP, PRINT USING, CONSOLE

937. Boxing Match

Author: Joseph Roehrig

Source: Personal Computing Jan 78 (2:1)
"Boxing by Computer" pp. 88–91 (91)

This game simulates a round of boxing matches. The program presents you with a list of fighters. You select from this two fighters who then engage in a simulated boxing match. The play is controlled by variables governing the capabilites of each boxer with regard to their various offensive and defensive abilities. The program simulates the match by giving a blow-by-blow account of the fight. At the end of the fight, a winner is declared. This is then used to "rank" each player. By winning fights against higher ranked boxers, a boxer can move up in

Is your finger worn out from dialing your telephone? Get relief from calloused fingers with this telephone dialer. You type in the phone number you want. The program then dials the number using a simple homemade relay circuit. Patches to the program add the ability to store and recall telephone numbers. As written, the program uses the cassette control jack on a TRS-80 to operate the relay circuit but any computer with a digital output interface should be able to use the program with slight changes.

Lines: 26 (plus patches)
Version: TRS-80 BASIC
Hardware: telephone dialer circuit (homemade)
Software: none
Non-ANSI: strings, multi-letter variables, extended IF, OUT, ASC()

TIME

470. Local Mean Time

Author: James Brennan

Source: Interface Age Aug 77 (2:9)
"Local Mean Time (LMT)" p. 32 (32)

This program calculates the difference between Greenwich Mean Time (GMT) and Local Mean Time (LMT). A sample run is included.

Lines: 27
Version: not given
Hardware: none
Software: none
Non-ANSI: extended IF

471. Calculate Sidereal Time

Author: James Brennan

Source: Interface Age Aug 77 (2:9)
"Local Sidereal Time & Date" pp. 33–34 (33–34)

This program calculates Greenwich Mean Time (GMT), Greenwich Sidereal Time (GST), Greenwich Sidereal Date (GSD), Julian Date (JD), corrected Local Mean Time (LMT), and Local Sidereal Time (LST). Includes a sample run.

Lines: 142
Version: not given
Hardware: none
Software: none
Non-ANSI: two-letter variables, DEFDBL, strings, extended IF

1130. Computing When Easter Occurs

Author: Lichen Wang

Source: ROM Feb 78 (1:8)
"Western Easters & When They Come" pp. 66–67 (67)

Easter is one of those weird holidays that seem to jump all over the calendar. The rule is: "Easter falls on the first Sunday after the first full moon after March 21." Simple. Well, figuring out when Easter occurs in any particular year turns out to be a major headache. This program takes care of that problem by printing out all the Easter Sundays between 1978 and the year 2001. The program can be modified to print out Easter for any particular year between 464 A.D. and 32767 A.D. (Appeared originally in the Nov–Dec 77 issue of The Homebrew Computer Club Newsletter.)

Lines: 40
Version: Palo Alto Tiny BASIC
Hardware: none
Software: none
Non-ANSI: PRINT #, extended IF

145. Day of the Week

Author: Douglas Scott

Source: Calculators/Computers Magazine Nov–Dec 78 (2:7)
"What Day of the Week . . . ?" pp. 26–29 (29)

Do you know on what day of the week you were born? With this program you can find out. It computes the day of the week of any given date. You type in a date and the computer types out what day of the week that date falls on. You can use the program to find out the day of a holiday or the day of the week of an important historical event. Includes a sample run and a list of program variables.

Lines: 82
Version: not given
Hardware: none
Software: none
Non-ANSI: strings, SEG$()

1034. Day of the Week Program

Author: Lon Poole and Mary Borchers

Source: Personal Computing Jul 79 (3:7)
"Three Practical Programs" pp. 46–50 (50)

Updates: modification for PET
Personal Computing Sep 79 (3:9)
"Pet Peculiarity" p. 9 (9)

commentary
Personal Computing Jan 80 (4:1)
"Pet Anomaly" p. 6

This program calculates the day of the week of a given date. Includes a sample run. (This program is reprinted from *Some Common BASIC Programs*.)

Lines:	43
Version:	not given
Hardware:	none
Software:	none
Non-ANSI:	none

78. Day of the Week Derived from Date

Author: W. B. Agocs

Source: *Byte* Sep 79 (4:9)
"Day of the Week and Elapsed Time Programs" pp. 126–129 (129)

Updates: modifications
Byte Jun 80 (5:6)
"Computing Time Between Dates" p. 202 (202)

This program uses *Zeller's congruence* to determine the day of the week of a given date. You type in a date; the computer tells you what day of the week that date falls on.

Lines:	23
Version:	not given
Hardware:	none
Software:	none
Non-ANSI:	strings, extended IF

79. Number of Days Between Two Dates

Author: W. B. Agocs

Source: *Byte* Sep 79 (4:9)
"Day of Week and Elapsed Time Programs" pp. 126–129 (129)

This program uses a matrix method to determine how many days there are between two given dates. The MAT statement is just used to set all the numbers in an array to ones.

Lines:	59
Version:	not given
Hardware:	none
Software:	none
Non-ANSI:	MAT CON(), DCL, mutliple-assignment

1143. Days Between Two Dates Subroutines

Author: David Eagle

Source: '68' *Micro Journal* Oct 79 (1:8)
untitled p. 8 (8)

This subroutine calculates a date "factor." The number of days between two dates is the factor of one minus the factor of the other.

Lines:	13
Version:	SWTPC 8K BASIC, ver. 2.3
Hardware:	none
Software:	none
Non-ANSI:	none

1144. Julian Date Subroutine

Author: David Eagle

Source: '68' *Micro Journal* Oct 79 (1:8)
untitled p. 8 (8)

This subroutine calculates Julian Dates when given dates in regular month, day, and year format.

Lines:	13
Version:	SWTPC 8K BASIC, V2.3
Hardware:	none
Software:	none
Non-ANSI:	extended IF

405. Years, Months, and Days Between Two Dates

Author: Joe Ligori

Source: *Creative Computing* Nov 79 (5:11)
"Date Conversion" p. 141 (141)

This program computes the years, months, and days between two dates. Such calculations are important in the business world where they are used in computing interest. The program makes calculations based on the 30-day month and 360-day year commonly used in business. Includes a sample run.

Lines: 14
Version: not given
Hardware: none
Software: none
Non-ANSI: strings, extended IF, VAL()

1115. YR.DAY Calendar Subroutines

Author: H. Frank Andersen

Source: *Recreational Computing* Nov–Dec 79 (8:3)
"CALENDAR" pp. 25–26 (26)

Because there aren't the same number of days in a month as months in a year, and because there are different numbers of days in various months, manipulating dates can be a difficult task. These subroutines simplify things by setting up a system of time which uses dates in the format YR.DAY (for example, January 3, 1975 becomes the number 75.03). Subroutines are provided for adding dates, subtracting dates, and for converting dates to and from conventional form.

Lines: 154
Version: Northstar BASIC, ver. 6
Hardware: none
Software: none
Non-ANSI: extended IF

TRAVEL

5. Program to Compute Distance and Bearing Between Two Points

Author: Rene Pittet

Source: *Byte* Jul 77 (2:7)
"How Far—Which Way?" pp. 118–119 (119)

This is a navigation program. Given the latitudes and longitudes of two points, the program prints out the distance between the two points and the bearing from one point to the other. This program may be useful to people who fly or sail, who need to navigate from point to point. Includes a sample run.

Lines: 58
Version: SWTPC 8K BASIC
Hardware: none
Software: none
Non-ANSI: LINE, DIGITS

948. Trip Planner

Author: Sam Newhouse

Source: *Personal Computing* May 78 (2:5)
"If It's Tuesday . . . This Must be Seattle" pp. 38–45 (40–45)

Without proper planning, your summer vacation across the country by car could turn into a disaster. You could end up 500 miles from home with two vacation days left and only $5 in your pocket. With this program, you'll know beforehand whether you can fit visits to particular cities into your trip. You'll know whether or not you can finance your trip. The program can also be used as a game; compete with your friends to see whose trip plan will cost the least money and take the least travel time. The planner's cost figures in the program are based on American Automobile Association (AAA) estimates. The expenses taken into account include gas, oil, lodging, food, taxes, and sightseeing costs. Includes a sample run and a list of the variables used in the program.

Lines: 328
Version: Altair BASIC ver. 3.4
Hardware: none
Software: none
Non-ANSI: CLEAR, WIDTH, NULL, strings, two-letter variables, extended IF, ON . . . GOSUB

505. Computation of Direction by Celestial Observation

Author: Gene Szymanski

Source: *Interface Age* Aug 78 (3:8)
"The Computation of Direction" pp. 72–76 (76)

Many people require a precision determination of direction in their activities. Surveyors, navigators, sailors, and astronomers all need a precise determination of direction from time to time. One very precise means of doing this is by taking "azimuth" observations of celestial bodies. The azimuth of a celestial body such as the sun or moon is simply its direction from the observer. The computation of azimuth requires the application of spherical trigonometry to account for the curvature of the earth. Such calculations can be quite tedious, making them an ideal application for a small computer. This program performs this task. The user enters latitude, longitude, the declination of the observed body, and the Greenwich hour angle of the body. The program then computes the azimuth, or true direction of the body from the observer. Includes a sample run.

Lines: 59
Version: MITS 8K BASIC
Hardware: none
Software: none
Non-ANSI: strings, two-letter variables, CLEAR, extended IF

682. Aircraft Flight Plan

Author: Jack Adams

Source: *Kilobaud Microcomputing* Apr 79 (28)
"Let's Go Flying" pp. 68–70 (68–70)

If you fly an airplane, then you know the importance of filing flight plans. If your airplane should go down, your flight plan may be the only tool search parties can use to locate you. Unfortunately, generating an accurate flight plan can be a tedious job. This computer program does this task for you. You supply it with data about where you are starting out, what your destination is, your air speed, and other information. The program uses this data to grind out a complete flight plan. The OPEN and CLOSE statements are used to switch output to a printer (if available). Includes a sample run.

Lines: 250
Version: Digital Group Business BASIC
Hardware: none
Software: none
Non-ANSI: OPEN, CLOSE, DATE(), HP strings, %()
           (used to format printouts), DEF . . .
           FNEND, SQRT(), extended IF, # (used in
           place of PRINT)

MISCELLANEOUS

235. Change for a Dollar Bill

Author: Donald Piele and Larry Wood

Source: Creative Computing Jul–Aug 77 (3:4)
          "Thinking Strategies with the Computer:
          Subgoals" pp. 87–90 (89–90)

This is a set of two programs. One program computes the number of ways that change can be made for a dollar; the other does the same thing for any amount up to $5. These programs illustrate a problem-solving method based on the location and definition of subgoals in a problem. Includes a flowchart and sample run.

Lines: 14, 26
Version: not given
Hardware: none
Software: none
Non-ANSI: multiple-assignment

933. Conference Message Center

Author: Gene Dial

Source: Personal Computing Nov–Dec 77 (1:6)
          "CONFEREE" pp. 71–81 (72–74)

One problem frequently encountered during conferences is the difficulty of maintaining and organizing a message center. CONFEREE is a program designed to take over this function. CONFEREE can perform many message center functions. The program can maintain and update a message board. The program can also generate lists of conference attendees sorted in various ways. Shorter lists of selected people can be generated. Lists of this type might be used for special meetings at the conference. Includes a sample run.

Lines: 324
Version: MITS 4.0 Disk BASIC
Hardware: 132-column printer
Software: none
Non-ANSI: CLEAR, WIDTH, CONSOLE, strings,
           ' (used in place of REM), extended IF, SWAP,
           SAVE (used as program statement)

486. Program to Produce Random Number Combinations

Author: David Mann

Source: Interface Age Dec 77 (2:13)
          "Random Number Program for Security
          Combinations" p. 148 (148)

The purpose of this program is to produce a list of randomly-generated lock combinations. Includes a sample run.

Lines: 54
Version: not given
Hardware: none
Software: none
Non-ANSI: PRINT USING, : (used to specify format for
           PRINT USING)

491. Computerese Speech Writer

Author: Ashok Nagrani

Source: Interface Age Jan 78 (3:1)
          "Computer(ese) Speech Writer" pp.
          150–152 (152)

This is a program to create computer-generated reports in that rather bizarre tongue, Computerese. Anyone who has hung around a corporate computer center long enough knows that English is on the skids. It is being replaced by a variant known as Computerese. The first axiom of Computerese is, "It doesn't matter what you say as long as you use long sentences with big words." Computerese is marked by cryptic jargon and obscure acronyms. Reports in Computerese tend to be impressive-sounding, but nearly meaningless. The purpose of this program is to generate suitably unintelligible Computerese reports to impress your boss or associates. The reports are randomly generated and may be any length. Includes a flowchart and sample run.

Lines: 143
Version: Altair's Extended BASIC ver. 3.2
Hardware: none
Software: none
Non-ANSI: CLEAR, strings, two-letter variables

939. Controlling a Homemade Robot

Author: Sam Newhouse

Source: *Personal Computing* Feb 78 (2:2)
"Building Your BASIC Robot" pp. 56–62
(59–61)

Have you ever wanted to build your own personal robot? Sam Newhouse has built his. This article describes his robot and two BASIC programs for controlling it. The first program is a control program for moving the robot under computer control. The program generates commands to drive the robot forward, backward, and to turn it. The second program allows the operator to control the robot directly using a joystick and a SWTPC GT6144 graphics display.

Lines: 188, 64
Version: SWTPC 8K BASIC ver. 2.0
Hardware: homemade robot, joystick, graphics display
Software: none
Non-ANSI: strings, PRINT #, PORT, LINE, PEEK( ),
extended IF, ON . . . GOSUB

620. Vote Tally Program

Author: Dr. Lance Leventhal

Source: *Kilobaud* May 78 (17)
"The Top-Down Approach" pp. 68–73 (73)

The purpose of this program is to count ballots and print the totals for an election. The vote counts are listed in descending order starting with the candidate who has received the most votes. The program has provisions for handling votes for write-in candidates, illegal votes (two or more candidates marked), and blank ballots. The program is included in an article on structured programming as an example of the top-down approach to program design. Includes a sample run and flowchart.

Lines: 90
Version: not given
Hardware: none
Software: none
Non-ANSI: none

958. Partner Matching Program

Author: Harriet Morrill

Source: *Personal Computing* Jun 78 (2:6)
"Partner Matching" pp. 54–59 (58–59)

People-matching services can be used for a number of applications. You can pair tennis or bridge partners according to skill for a local tournament, match roommates, or pair up people looking for rides. This is a program to do this "matching up." The program is specifically designed for "compatibility matching," but it can be used for other purposes. The program operates by accepting data from people about their likes and dislikes. It then finds the couples with the smallest differences between their answers, based on the answers and the weight each person has assigned to each question. An optional part of the program prints out "human readable" paired names on papertape. Includes a sample run and a list of program variables.

Lines: 140
Version: Applesoft (Floating Point BASIC)
Hardware: none
Software: none
Non-ANSI: strings, OPEN, CLOSE, PRINT #, MID(),
extended IF

510. Dress Pattern for the Apple II

Author: William Smith III

Source: *Interface Age* Sep 78 (3:9)
"The Automated Dress Pattern for the Apple II" pp. 76–81 (78–81)

More useful applications for microcomputers are turning up every day. This is an automated dress pattern maker for the Apple II comptuer system. The pattern is stored in a compress data format by one program. A second program uncompresses the data and produces a printout of the pattern on a line printer. The dress pattern fits sizes 9 to 13, but there are no provisions for adjusting the pattern size under program control. Machine readable copies of the programs and data are bound into the magazine in a phonograph record. Includes a sample run.

Lines: 65, 125
Version: Apple II BASIC
Hardware: Apple II, 132-column printer
Software: none
Non-ANSI: not translatable

975. Haunted House Controller

Author: Peter Henry

Source: *Personal Computing* Oct 78 (2:10)
"Techno Turkey and the Haunted House" pp. 24–36 (34–36)

Here's an unusual microcomputer application. This program, used in conjunction with power-control equipment described in the article, allows your computer to control a "haunted house." Using this system you can scare the wits out of your friends with rattling noises and flying "spooks." Everything is controlled by your computer through a set of power-switching triac circuits. Plans for these circuits are described in the article. Besides operating a haunted house, the circuits can be used anywhere in your house where you want to control a household gadget with your computer. The control program can also be adapted to other uses.

Lines: 273
Version: not given
Hardware: triac circuits (homemade)
Software: none
Non-ANSI: INP(), OUT, extended IF

36. Light Detector Programs

Author: Steve Ciarcia

Source: Byte Nov 78 (3:11)
"I've Got You in My Scanner!" pp. 76–89 (84–88)

Updates: correction
Byte Jan 79 (4:1)
"Motor Bug" p. 53

This is a set of three programs to demonstrate the use of a scanning light detector system. The light detector is a photo detector and reflector mounted on a stepping motor. The first program detects a light value read by an analog-to-digital converter. The second program tests the stepping motor system by making it sweep back and forth. The third program causes the system to sweep back and forth while searching for a light source. When the scanner finds one, it stops and points at the source.

Lines: 17, 32, 48
Version: Micro Com 8K Zapple BASIC
Hardware: scanning light detector system
Software: none
Non-ANSI: OUT, INP(), extended IF

982. Home Security System

Author: Peter Henry

Source: Personal Computing Dec 78 (2:12)
"Techno Turkey's Home Security System" pp. 54–60 (59)

Worried about things that go bump in the night? This home security system might be able to give you some peace of mind. The program allows your home computer to act as a security monitor, checking on sensors that you place around your house. The program scans the sensors, looking for possible signs of a break-in. The system does not just look for an open circuit and then turn on a siren. It is designed to check for specific patterns that indicate trouble. This is designed so that if you get up in the middle of the night for a snack, you won't wake up the neighborhood if you accidentally trip one of the sensors.

Lines: 266
Version: not given
Hardware: sensors (homemade)
Software: none
Non-ANSI: extended IF, OUT, INP(), AND()

995. Friend Program

Author: Marolyn Pinney

Source: Personal Computing Feb 79 (3:2)
"Me and My TRS-80" pp. 46–51 (51)

Longing for companionship? Why not let your computer be your friend? This program can carry on a short, chatty conversation with you. Includes a sample run.

Lines: 62
Version: TRS-80 Level I BASIC
Hardware: none
Software: none
Non-ANSI: CLS, strings, extended IF, IN.

675. Exterior Ballistics

Author: David Dixon

Source: Kilobaud Microcomputing Mar 79 (27)
"Exterior Ballistics with the Home Computer" pp. 80–81 (80)

Ballistics is important for accurate hunting or target shooting. This program calculates ballistics information. You type into the program the ballistic coefficient of your bullet, the muzzle velocity of your rifle, the range it is zeroed to, and the range at which trajectories are to be calculated. From this, the program uses McGehee Ballistic functions to calculate the remaining velocity, sight corrections, and point of impact. Includes a sample run.

Lines: 40
Version: SWTPC 8K BASIC
Hardware: none
Software: none
Non-ANSI: LINE, DIGITS

797. Color Detector for the Apple II

Author: Neil Lipson

Source: *Micro* Jun 79 (13)
"The Color Gun for the Apple II" pp. 31–32
(32)

With some rather inexpensive hardware, you can turn your Apple II Computer into a color detector. Using cadmium sulphide photo cells mounted in a "gun," the Apple II can determine what color an object is. One use for such a detector is determining the temperature of a glowing object; the brighter and whiter the object is, the higher its temperature. The program accepts input from the photo cells and calculates the color being observed. A second program computes color "correction factors."

Lines: 38, 21
Version: Applesoft 2 BASIC
Hardware: homemade color detector
Software: none
Non-ANSI: PDL(), HTAB, VTAB, extended IF, CALL

1099. TRS-80 Birthday Card

Author: Bob Albrecht

Source: *Recreational Computing* Jul–Aug 79 (8:1)
"The Programmer's Toolbox" pp. 30–31
(30)

Here is a program for all of you who are too cheap to send your own mother a birthday card. It writes "Happy Birthday Mother" and draws a box around the outside edge of your TRS-80's screen.

Lines: 14
Version: TRS-80 Level II BASIC
Hardware: TRS-80
Software: none
Non-ANSI: not translatable

367. Aphorism Generator

Author: J. D. Robertson

Source: *Creative Computing* Aug 79 (5:8)
"Blip is the Blap of Bleep" p. 116 (116)

An *aphorism* is a terse saying embodying a general truth, such as "necessity is the mother of invention." This program generates reams of pseudo-profound aphorisms by filling in random words in the phrase, "_____ is the _____ of _____." Includes a sample run.

Lines: 35
Version: not given
Hardware: none
Software: none
Non-ANSI: strings

1107. VAR/80 Input/Output Demo

Author: Don Inman

Source: *Recreational Computing* Sep–Oct 79 (8:2)
"The Outside Connection" pp. 48–50 (50)

The VAR/80, manufactured by Telesis Laboratory, is a device that allows you to control appliances and other equipment with your computer. This short program demonstrates how the VAR/80 can be used to sense whether a pair of windows are open or closed.

Lines: 11
Version: TRS-80 Level II BASIC
Hardware: Telesis Laboratory VAR/80, TRS-80
Software: none
Non-ANSI: not translatable

739. Pig Latin Translator

Author: Ken Klosson

Source: *Kilobaud Microcomputing* Oct 79 (34)
"Pig Latin" pp. 162–163 (162)

Pig Latin is a "language" used by people who don't want others to understand what's being said. It's based on the English language. The basic rule for "Pig-Latinizing" words is that any consonants at the beginning of a word must be moved to the end of the word and "ay" added. Thus, "scram" becomes "amscray" in Pig Latin. This program takes text and converts it into Pig Latin. Includes a list of program variables.

Lines: 59
Version: Microsoft 8K BASIC (OSI 6502 version)
Hardware: none
Software: none
Non-ANSI: strings, two-letter variables, extended IF

398. Appliance Controller Demo

Author: Mark Garetz

Source: *Creative Computing* Nov 79 (5:11)
"Today We Control the House, Tomorrow . . ." pp. 60–64

Creative Computing Dec. 79 (5:12)
"Today We Control the House, Tomorrow . . ." pp. 64–71 (68)

Would you like to be able to control the lights and appliances in your house with your computer? You can do it with a BSR System X10 controller and a homemade interface. The controller (also marketed by Sears as the Sears Home Control System and by Radio Shack as the Plug 'n Power) operates by transmitting digital signals over your house's power lines. You plug appliances into control modules. The control modules pick up the digital signals and use them to turn on and off whatever is plugged into the modules. The homemade interface and clock circuit described in the article allow your computer to control the controller. The demonstration program supplied turns appliances on and off at preset times.

Lines: 90
Version: North Star BASIC
Hardware: BSR System X10 controller, homemade interface and clock circuit
Software: none
Non-ANSI: OUT, strings, VAL(), ! (used in place of PRINT), extended IF, INP()

1064. "Alien" Names Creator

Author: Donald W. Fairhurst

Source: *Personal Computing* Nov 79 (3:11) "Alien Names Made Easy" pp. 56–57 (57)

Science fiction writers have a problem: How do you think up names for your alien characters that sound "alien" but can still be pronounced by humans? This program can "think up" as many out-of-this-world-sounding names as you need. Includes a sample run.

Lines: 28 (plus patch)
Version: Radio Shack Level II BASIC
Hardware: none
Software: none
Non-ANSI: RANDOM, strings

1122. Research Paper Title Creator

Author: Jack A. Taylor

Source: *Recreational Computing* Nov–Dec 79 (8:3) "CHOOSE-A-TITLE" pp. 52–53 (53)

Updates: modifications
Recreational Computing Mar–Apr 80 (8:5) "An Improvement on CHOOSE-A-TITLE" p. 43 (43)

Whether you're a student looking for a topic for a term paper or a professional in need of a research paper, this program can pick up the subject for you. It takes phrases in your field of study and combines them in random ways

to come up with proposed titles. As written, the program produces music education titles, but it can easily be adapted to other fields. Includes a sample run.

Lines: 83
Version: CDC Cyber 70 BASIC ver. 2.1
Hardware: none
Software: none
Non-ANSI: HP strings

1123. Ticket Printing Program

Author: David J. Beard

Source: *Recreational Computing* Nov–Dec 79 (8:3) "Compute-a-Ticket" p. 55 (55)

This program prints out sequentially numbered tickets for your next club party, school dance, or whatever. The program prints out 16 tickets per sheet.

Lines: 38
Version: Programma 2.0 BASIC
Hardware: none
Software: none
Non-ANSI: HP strings, CLEAR, PRINT #

1146. Winning Football Pool Tickets Finder

Author: Weldy Moffatt

Source: *'68' Micro Journal* Nov–Dec 79 (1:9) untitled p. 26 (26)

This program assumes you have a football pool with winning numbers spread across many booklets of tickets. The program prints out the numbers of the booklets with winning score combinations. Includes a sample run.

Lines: 59
Version: SWTPC BASIC 3.0
Hardware: none
Software: none
Non-ANSI: LINE, strings, PORT, extended IF

411. I.Q. Tester

Author: Howard Berenbon

Source: *Creative Computing* Dec 79 (5:12) "What's Your Math IQ?" pp. 116–117 (116–117)

Updates: commentary
         Creative Computing Mar 80 (6:3)
         "More on Math I-Q" p. 12

Think you're smart, don't you? Find out with this math I.Q. tester. You have 15 minutes to solve 20 number-series questions. From the number of questions that you get right, you can determine your I.Q.

Lines:	157
Version:	not given
Hardware:	none
Software:	none
Non-ANSI:	none

Lines: 18, 8, 52, 76
Version: HP-2000 BASIC
Hardware: sequential file device
Software: none
Non-ANSI: HP strings, PRINT #, READ #, END#(), LIN(), FILES

186. Alphabet Statistical Analysis

Author: not given

Source: *Creative Computing* Sep–Oct 75 (1:5) "Alphabet Statistics" p. 25 (25)

In any given piece of text, some letters of the alphabet will occur more frequently than others. This program allows you to check out this phenomenon. It's designed for use by a group of people. Each person counts the numbers of As, Bs, Cs, and Ds that occur in his or her section of the text. The program then combines these results to give an overall percentage by letter. Includes a sample run.

Lines: 32
Version: not given
Hardware: none
Software: none
Non-ANSI: strings, FOR (used as a modifier)

456. Vowel Removing Program

Author: not given

Source: *Interface Age* Aug 76 (1:9) "No Vowels at All" p. 53 (53)

Vowels form an important part of the English language. This program demonstrates just how vital they are. The program removes all the vowels from the words you type in and then prints out the vowelless results. You can use it as a game with one player challenging another to guess what the original words were.

Lines: 14
Version: not given
Hardware: none
Software: none
Non-ANSI: strings

114. Latin/Greek Roots of English Words

Author: Curt Torgerson

Source: *Calculators/Computers Magazine* Nov 77 (1:3) "String BASIC" pp. 29–32 (32)

Many words in the English language derive from Latin and Greek. Remnants of the original roots can still be found in many English words. ROOTZ takes English words and looks for these roots. From the roots that it finds, the program attempts to tell you something about the meanings of the words you give it. Includes a sample run and a list of program variables.

Lines: 52
Version: not given
Hardware: none
Software: none
Non-ANSI: strings, INSTR()

608. Teaching Preschoolers Letter Discrimination

Author: John Victor

Source: *Kilobaud* Feb 78 (14) "Kid Korner" pp. 80–82 (81)

Before children can learn to read—in fact, before they can even name the letters—they must learn to "see" the shapes of the letters. This is a difficult task, because a child must learn to discriminate among slight variations in the shapes of letters. The idea of this program is to have your child match, on the keyboard, a letter or group of letters that the computer displays. The program works on eight different levels. At the lowest level, your child works with just two letters: A and S. As experience is gained, more and more letters are presented. This program, in contrast with other educational media, allows your child to become an active participant in the learning process, and thus to learn faster. Includes a sample run.

Lines: 38
Version: Apple I BASIC
Hardware: none
Software: none
Non-ANSI: HP strings, TAB, extended IF

610. Text Readability Test

Author: Al Gerbens

Source: *Kilobaud* Feb 78 (14) "Read Any Good Books Lately?" pp. 104–106 (104–106)

In these days, most people seem to have lost the ability to write clear and simple English. If you would like to learn the art of writing simply, this program is for you. This program evaluates the readability of a text that is fed to it. The readability of the text is broken down into two categories: (1) ease of understanding, and (2) human interest content. The first is determined by the average number of syllables per word and the average number of words per sentence. The second is based on the number of "personal" words and sentences in the text being analyzed. Using the results of this program as a guide, you should be able to write more clearly and intelligibly. On the other hand, you could use this program to reduce the readability of your works, thus impressing your boss or associates. People always seem to be impressed by what they cannot understand. Includes a sample run.

> *Lines:* 146
> *Version:* DGSS Maxi-BASIC Version 1
> *Hardware:* none
> *Software:* none
> *Non-ANSI:* HP strings, # (used in place of PRINT), extended IF

1132. Sentence Maker Program

> *Author:* Richard Rosner

> *Source:* *ROM* Mar–Apr 78 (1:9)
> "The Pet Talks Hard Copy for the First Time" pp. 32–33 (33)

This program accepts a sequence of numbers at your keyboard and then prints out a sentence based on those numbers. Your challenge is to try to make a logical sentence by rearranging the numbers you have entered. The OPEN, PRINT #, and POKE statements are used for the special requirements of the PET computer; other systems may omit them.

> *Lines:* 65
> *Version:* PET BASIC
> *Hardware:* none
> *Software:* none
> *Non-ANSI:* OPEN, PRINT #, POKE, ASC(), multi-letter variables, AND(), strings

135. Vocabulary Building Game

> *Author:* Linda Schreiber

> *Source:* *Calculators/Computers Magazine* May 78 (2:5)
> "Word Hunters" pp. 48–52 (50–51)

WANTED: BETTER VOCABULARY challenges students to increase their vocabularies. Clues are given to help identify the "wanted" words. Each clue aids in the recognition of the fugitive word by stating the number of syllables, the placement of the accent, and the number of vowels and consonants that make up the word. The program can also give the student clues about the meaning of the word. The student may try to identify a maximum of 10 words per run. At the end of the run the score is tabulated by totaling the number of clues that have been

given and dividing by the number of words that were offered for identification. The lower the score, the better the pupil's command of the vocabulary words given. Includes a sample run.

> *Lines:* 99
> *Version:* Altair BASIC
> *Hardware:* none
> *Software:* none
> *Non-ANSI:* ON ERROR, string, extended IF, ASC( ), (used in place of REM)

973. Spelling Drill

> *Author:* Michael Tulloch

> *Source:* *Personal Computing* Sep 78 (2:9)
> "Spelling Bee for a PET" pp. 56–57 (57)

> *Updates:* correction
> *Personal Computing* Dec 78 (2:12)
> "PET Bee Stings" p. 6 (6)
>
> correction
> *Personal Computing* Sep 79 (3:9)
> "Spelling Bee Changes" p. 9 (9)

Here is a program that can help a young student with spelling. The program quickly flashes a word on the video screen. The child is then asked to spell the word. The computer compares the student's word with the presented word, and prints messages based on the number of letters in the same positions within the two words. The list of words to be presented in each session can be varied to provide spelling practice for a wide variety of words.

> *Lines:* 28
> *Version:* not given
> *Hardware:* video display
> *Software:* none
> *Non-ANSI:* strings, extended IF, CLS(), two-letter variables

654. Spelling Bee Using a Cassette Recorder

> *Author:* David Moody

> *Source:* *Kilobaud* Dec 78 (24)
> "Spelling Bee" pp. 64–66 (65)

> *Updates:* correction
> *Kilobaud Microcomputing* Feb 79 (26)
> "Corrections" p. 155

Here is a unique Computer Assisted Instruction (CAI) Program. This program drills students in spelling. The program is unique in that it uses an ordinary audio cassette recorder to provide voice output. First, the program is used to record words for the spelling drill. The program then plays back the tape, stopping and starting the tape so that the student has a chance to spell out each word. If the student makes a mistake, clues are given for the correct spelling of the word. Includes a sample run.

Lines: 85
Version: TDL 12K BASIC
Hardware: audio cassette recorder
Software: none
Non-ANSI: CLEAR, OUT, strings, extended IF, two-letter variables

312. Speed Reading Drill

Author: Tom Rugg and Phil Feldman

Source: *Creative Computing* Jan 79 (5:1)
"Speed Reading Made Easy . . . Via Your PET" pp. 132–133

Updates: program listing
Creative Computing Mar 79 (5:3)
"Speed Reading Made Easy" p. 104 (104)

A tachistoscope is a device used to help students read faster. The tachistoscope flashes a short phrase on a screen. The student must then say what the phase was. This teaches the student to read whole phrases at a time, instead of reading word by word. This program lets your computer act as a tachistoscope. The program flashes phrases and asks the student to repeat them. The length of time the phrases are displayed is constantly adjusted up or down depending on whether the student is answering correctly or not. Includes a sample run and a list of program variables.

Lines: 73
Version: PET BASIC
Hardware: video terminal
Software: none
Non-ANSI: strings, GET, extended IF

336. Thesaurus Index

Author: Derek Kelly

Source: *Creative Computing* May 79 (5:5)
"Beyond the Text Editor" pp. 32–33 (32)

A thesaurus is a special type of dictionary. The purpose of a thesaurus is to give you synonyms for words. You can use a thesaurus to avoid repetition and add color to your writings. This is a computer-based index to *Roget's Thesaurus*. You type in a word and the computer will tell you if it corresponds to one of the 1,042 categories in *Roget's Thesaurus*. (The data base for this program is *not* supplied.)

Lines: 18
Version: not given
Hardware: none
Software: none
Non-ANSI: HOME, strings

338. Reading and Comprehension Tests

Author: Andrew Nicastro

Source: *Creative Computing* May 79 (5:5)
"Exam Time: Reading and Comprehension Tests for Language Arts" pp. 62–66 (63–65)

Students can use this set of programs to improve their learning and reading comprehension. This system acts as a tachistocope; it flashes a passage, one phrase at a time, on a viewing screen. Each phrase is timed so that the student must scan it quickly before the next phrase is flashed. At the end, questions are presented to gauge how much of the material the student has absorbed. The system records the results so that the teacher can follow the progress of each individual. Includes a sample run.

Lines: 11, 78, 144
Version: DEC MU BASIC-RT
Hardware: video display, sequential file device
Software: none
Non-ANSI: not translatable

347. Spelling Drill Using the TRS-80 Voice Synthesizer

Author: John Rogers

Source: *Creative Computing* Jun 79 (5:6)
"TRS-80 Voice Synthesizer Phonetically Speaking" pp. 96–101 (98–99)

For years, computers have lived in a silent world, unable to either speak or hear. Though low-cost voice recognition is still a ways off, the age of voice synthesis is here today—your computer can speak to you at last! This program (two versions) uses the TRS-80 Voice Synthesizer to say words for a children's spelling drill. The computer speaks a word. The child then types out the correct spelling of the word.

Lines: 90, 60
Version: TRS-80 Level II BASIC
Hardware: TRS-80, TRS-80 Voice Synthesizer
Software: none
Non-ANSI: not translatable

1025. Alphabet Picture Book

Author: Mark Zimmermann

Source: *Personal Computing* Jun 79 (3:6)
" 'G' is for Graphics" pp. 38–41 (40–41)

Updates: correction
Personal Computing Feb 80 (4:2)
" 'G' is for Graphics" p. 8 (8)

Everyone remembers those "A" is for Apple"-type books they had when they were learning how to read. Here is a computerized version of the same thing. This program produces pictures when keys are pressed on the keyboard of your PET. You can change around the pictures if the old ones lose interest. Includes a sample output.

Lines: 58
Version: PET BASIC
Hardware: none
Software: none
Non-ANSI: not translatable

1048. Readability of Text Measurement

Author: Steve Irving and Bill Arnold

Source: *Personal Computing* Sep 79 (3:9)
"Measuring Readability of Text" pp. 34–36 (36)

Not all pieces of text are equally easy to read. Children's books are simple to understand. Adult textbooks are more difficult. Government reports are often all but incomprehensible. The longer the sentences and the more difficult the words, the less understandable the material. This program accepts passages that you type in and analyzes how difficult they are. This information can be translated directly into a measure of the school grade level of the work.

Lines: 15
Version: PET BASIC
Hardware: none
Software: none
Non-ANSI: CLR, GET, strings, multi-letter variables, extended IF, ASC()

FOREIGN LANGUAGES

174. German Vocabulary Tester

Author: Barney Milstein

Source: *Creative Computing* Mar–Apr 75 (1:3)
"A Universal Word Game in BASIC" pp. 48–49 (49)

Updates: correction
Creative Computing Sep–Oct 75 (1:5)
untitled p. 7 (7)

This program is designed to build your vocabulary in English or in a foreign language. As written, the program tests your knowledge of German. The computer gives you sets of German words. You must reply with the appropriate antonyms.

Lines: 180
Version: CALL-OS BASIC
Hardware: none
Software: none
Non-ANSI: strings

141. French Drill

Author: David Bunting

Source: *Calculators/Computers Magazine* Sep–Oct 78 (2:6)
"French Program" pp. 76–77 (77)

This program drills students in French. The student gives the French translation of the English word that the computer prints out. The program introduction is printed out entirely in French. Includes a sample run.

Lines: 46
Version: PDP-11 BASIC
Hardware: none
Software: none
Non-ANSI: strings

GEOGRAPHY

208. Map Making Program

Author: James Cerny

Source: *Creative Computing* Nov–Dec 76 (2:6)
"CMAPS: A Basic Language Program for Choropleth Mapping" pp. 72–74 (73–74)

A choropleth map is a "shading-by-area" map. This is the familiar type of map in which there is a single data value or color for each common observation area (state, county, etc.). CMAPS is a set of two programs that produce choropleth maps on a standard terminal. The first program in the package accepts "scan-lines" which define the areas to be mapped. Up to 20 map areas can be defined. The second program prints out the actual maps. It has provisions for such things as labeling the maps. The maps are not high quality due to the limitations of the terminals available. CMAPS does, however, do a good job of producing working maps for quick proofing of data. Includes sample runs.

Lines: 31, 95
Version: not given
Hardware: sequential file device
Software: none
Non-ANSI: strings, MAT operations, OPEN, CLOSE, GET, PUT

18. Program to Help a Student Learn the States and Their Capitals

Author: Loring White

Source: *Byte* Mar 78 (3:3)
"The Capital of New Mexico is Santa Fe" pp. 170–171 (170)

This is a program to help students learn the states of the United States and their capitals. The program drills students by asking the students what the capital of each state is. The computer tells the student when the answer is right and keeps track of how well the student has done.

Lines: 61
Version: MITS 8K BASIC
Hardware: none
Software: none
Non-ANSI: strings, CLEAR

611. Test Your Knowledge of the States and Their Capitals

Author: Dave Alverson

Source: *Kilobaud* Mar 78 (15)
"State Capitals, A New Education Program for the Kids" pp. 28–30 (28–29)

This game tests your knowledge of the states and their capitals. You have the option of having the program give you the state and ask you the capital of that state, or having the program give you the capital and ask you for the state. You also have the option of filling in the correct choice or selecting from a multiple-choice list. The computer keeps track of your right and wrong answers. Includes a sample run.

Lines: 102
Version: IMSAI Disk BASIC
Hardware: none
Software: none
Non-ANSI: strings, extended IF

55. Computer-Generated Map Projections

Author: William Johnston

Source: *Byte* May 79 (4:5)
"Computer Generated Maps" pp. 10–12, 76–101 (78–100)

Byte Jun 79 (4:6)
"Computer Generated Maps" pp. 100–123 (102–106)

Updates: commentary, supplementary program
Byte Oct 79 (4:10)
"Phone Company Maps" p. 18 (18)

A problem arises when you try to map the Earth's surface. The Earth is a ball. Maps are flat. How do you transfer spherical coordinates onto a flat surface? The answer is that you have to "project" or mathematically distort the coordinates. There are many types of projections that you can use, each having its own advantages and disadvantages. Given here are five subroutines to do five different kinds of map projections. The projections include orthographic polar projection, polar equidistant projection, and rectangular projection. You must supply a data base with the map coordinates to be projected and a main program to do your mapping. Includes lists of program variables.

Lines: 90, 59, 60, 57, 115, 301
Version: not given
Hardware: none
Software: none
Non-ANSI: none

376. GEOGRAPHY: Geography Learning Game

Author: Jonathan Amsterdam

Source: *Creative Computing* Sep 79 (5:9)
"GEOGRAPHY" pp. 136–138 (136–138)

This program plays the game of Geography. You and the computer take turns naming various types of geographical locations. Each location must start with the same letter that ended the previous location. You play until you can no longer think of an appropriately named place. At that point you "challenge." If the computer can think of a place, you lose; otherwise, you win. (The computer can also challenge you.) Includes a sample run.

Lines: 146
Version: PDP 11/70 RSTS/E BASIC
Hardware: none
Software: none
Non-ANSI: strings

80. Outline Map of the U.S. for the Apple II

Author: Joseph P. Garber

Source: Byte Oct 79 (4:10)
"Phone Company Maps" p. 18 (18)

The telephone industry has placed a grid over the U.S. with a system of vertical and horizontal coordinates. These "V & H" coordinates form a convenient system for drawing maps. This program uses the V & H coordinates for the border towns of the U.S. to draw an outline map of this country. Includes a sample output.

Lines: 29
Version: Apple BASIC
Hardware: Apple II
Software: none
Non-ANSI: not translatable

HISTORY

275. Oregon Trail

Author: Bill Heinemann

Source: Creative Computing May–Jun 78 (4:3)
"Oregon Trail" pp. 132–139 (137–139)

Updates: improvement
Dr. Dobb's Journal of Computer Calisthenics &
Orthodontia Jun–Jul 79 (4:6)
"Adding CLK to SWTPC" pp. 48–49 (49)

This program simulates a trip over the Oregon Trail from Independence, Missouri to Oregon City, Oregon in 1847. Your "family" will cover the 2,040-mile Oregon Trail in five to six months—if you make it alive. The program was developed to give students a better feeling of what the journey west was like for the people who attempted it. It does not attempt to exactly replicate a wagon train trip. Instead, the intent is to present students with some of the resources, decisions, and events that faced the pioneers of that day. The student can buy oxen, food, ammunition, clothing, and miscellaneous supplies. He or she must deal with bad weather, attacks, and other hazards. Includes a flowchart, list of program variables, and sample run.

Lines: 680
Version: CDC Cyber BASIC 3.1
Hardware: none
Software: none
Non-ANSI: HP strings, multiple-assignment, CLK()

554. Historical Quiz (CAI Demonstration)

Author: Jim Schreier

Source: Interface Age Oct 79 (4:10)
"SWTPC's New PILOT" pp. 135–137 (136)

This program just asks a couple of historical questions. Its purpose is to demonstrate that the language PILOT is more appropriate than is BASIC for computer-assisted-instruction (CAI) applications.

Lines: 38
Version: SWTPC BASIC
Hardware: none
Software: none
Non-ANSI: LINE, DIGITS, strings

LAW

287. Jury Selection Simulation

Author: Gary Greenberg

Source: Creative Computing Sep–Oct 78 (4:5)
"Jury Selection: A Simulation" ph. 74–77
(75–76)

Jury selection is a key part of criminal trials. Most attorneys feel—probably rightly—that certain types of people will be biased toward or against the defendant in a trial. A case can sometimes be decided by which jurors are selected. In this simulation you are the defense attorney. Your task is to select a jury that will be most sympathetic to your client. You will be presented with several groups of possible jurors and their respective backgrounds. You must use your "challenges" to weed out those jurors who might be biased against your client. After the jury is empaneled, the program prints out the results of the first ballot of the jury and the final verdict. Includes a sample run.

Lines: 164
Version: PET BASIC
Hardware: none
Software: none
Non-ANSI: strings, extended IF

MEASUREMENT

98. MILLIWORM: A Metric Learning Game

Author: Linda Schreiber

Source: Calculators/Computers Magazine May 77 (1:1)
"Games Computers Play" pp. 49–52

program listing
Calculators/Computers Magazine Oct 77 (1:2)
"MILLIWORM" pp. 93–95 (93)

MILLIWORM is a game designed to help you acquire a feeling for length in millimeters. The computer prints a "milliworm" of random length. It then asks you to guess the length of the worm in millimeters. The object is to guess the length of the milliworm to within one-half millimeter. Since the spacing on various computer terminals varies, it may be necessary to adjust the program for your terminal. Includes a sample run.

Lines: 43
Version: Altair Extended BASIC
Hardware: none
Software: none
Non-ANSI: strings, extended IF, ' (used in place of REM)

638. Metric-American Conversion

Author: Mickey Ferguson

Source: *Kilobaud* Sep 78 (21)
"Metric-American Conversion Program" pp. 46–50 (47–50)

Updates: corrections
Kilobaud Microcomputing Jan 79 (25)
"Can America Go Metric?" pp. 20–21 (20)

This is a program to convert measurements between metric units and American units, and vice-versa. The program can handle conversions dealing with length, area, volume, weight, and temperature. Includes a sample run.

Lines: 180
Version: SWTPC 8K BASIC
Hardware: none
Software: none
Non-ANSI: ON . . . GOSUB

544. Acreage Calculations

Author: Jim Schreier

Source: *Interface Age* Aug–Sep 79 (4:8)
"Changing Acres to Rods to Yards to . . ." p. 48 (48)

This program calculates how many acres there are in a given area. You specify the length and width of the area. Your measurements can be in yards, rods, or feet. The program then computes the number of acres in the area. The title of the article notwithstanding, the program does *not* convert acres to other measurements.

Lines: 37
Version: not given
Hardware: none
Software: none
Non-ANSI: LINE, DIGITS, strings, extended IF

727. Metric/English Translator for the TRS-80

Author: Allan S. Joffe

Source: *Kilobaud Microcomputing* Sep 79 (33)
"ON X GOSUB VVVV, TTTT" p. 32 (32)

This program translates metric measures to English and vice-versa. The translation to be performed is selected from a "menu" on the screen of the TRS-80. The program can translate yards/meters, inches/centimeters, and gallons/liters.

Lines: 18 (plus patch)
Version: TRS-80 Level II BASIC
Hardware: TRS-80
Software: none
Non-ANSI: not translatable

MEDICINE

461. Diet Planning

Author: Martin Beattie, M.D.

Source: *Interface Age* Oct 76 (1:11)
"BASIC Diet Planning" pp. 26–32 (30–32)

Perhaps the majority of people in this country are overweight to some degree. Unfortunately, dieting is a difficult task. This program can help in planning a diet. The program uses information you supply to determine your basal metabolic rate, your total daily caloric use, and your caloric intake. From this it can show you how much less you must eat to achieve a specific weight loss. The program allows for the selection of either English or metric units of height and weight.

Lines: 168
Version: MITS 8K BASIC
Hardware: none
Software: none
Non-ANSI: strings, extended IF, two-letter variables

597. Predict Your Life Expectancy

Author: Terrence Lukas

Source: *Kilobaud* Nov 77 (11)
            "Lifetime Program" pp. 34–36 (34–36)

Updates: improvements
            Kilobaud Feb 78 (14)
            "Lifetime Update" pp. 19–20

This program can predict your life expectancy. The program first determines your base life expectancy from your sex and age. You are then presented with questions about your health, diet, exercise, and other factors. After each question, a value is added or subtracted from your previous subtotal. At the end, the program prints out your life expectancy.

       Lines: 268
     Version: MITS 8K 3.1 BASIC
    Hardware: none
    Software: none
    Non-ANSI: strings, two-letter variables, extended IF

1128. Personal Nutritional Analysis

Author: Karen Brothers

Source: *ROM* Dec 77 (1:6)
            "The Micro Diet: Better Health through Electronics" pp. 36–42 (40–41)

Do you know whether or not your diet is balanced? Here is a program that can tell you what your diet is really like. It is a Personal Nutritional Analysis Program. This program accepts data about the kinds and amounts of food you eat and then prints out a table showing what kinds of nutrients are in the food. The program can be used to plan special diets such as low carbohydrate or low sodium diets, or to figure the relative economies of various protein sources. Includes a flowchart, sample run, and a list of program variables.

       Lines: 89
     Version: not given
    Hardware: none
    Software: none
    Non-ANSI: none

625. Computerized Exercise/Fitness Program

Author: Al Gerbens

Source: *Kilobaud* Jun 78 (18)
            "A Strategy for Healthy Living" pp. 32–35 (32–35)

This is a program to monitor a body fitness program. The fitness program is based on the use of your pulse rate as a guide to how hard you should exercise. The program handles several jobs. Among the jobs performed by the computer are: (1) displaying the exercise sequence, (2) calculating your pulse rate, (3) timing each exercise segment, (4) indicating when pulse rate determinations should be made, and (5) interpreting the pulse rate and recommending an increase or decrease in your level of activity. The pulse rate is input to the program by a pushbutton—you must feel your own pulse; no provision is made for automatic pulse-readings. Includes a sample run.

       Lines: 35, 160
     Version: Maxi-BASIC
    Hardware: digital input (pushbutton and interface)
    Software: none
    Non-ANSI: # (used in place of PRINT), extended IF, INP(), EXIT

501. Heart Disease Analysis

Author: Leo Biese, M.D.

Source: *Interface Age* Jul 78 (3:7)
            "Heart Attack: How You Can Predict It and Some Things You Can Do About It" pp. 56–61 (58–61)

This is a program to predict your risk of heart disease. The program calculates your risk of heart attack and shows the improvement that you can achieve by reducing the factors that lead to heart disease. The risk factors taken into account include your age, cholesterol level, blood pressure, whether or not you smoke, and whether or not you have any enlargement of your heart. By studying these factors you may be able to reduce your risk of having a heart attack. The statistical base used for this program is only valid for the ages of 35–65 (45–64 for women) and does not apply to people with a known history of heart disease. Includes a sample run.

       Lines: 139
     Version: MITS 4.0 Disk BASIC
    Hardware: none
    Software: none
    Non-ANSI: not translatable

516. Diabetes Monitoring Program

Author: Mathew Tekulsky and Steve Faber

Source: *Interface Age* Dec 78 (3:12)
            "It's Not a Big Miracle" pp. 70–73 (73)

Updates: commentary
            Interface Age May 79 (4:5)
            "A Diabetic and the PET" p. 8

Diabetes is an inherited disease which prevents the body from using sugar by blocking the production of insulin in the pancreas. This results in a build-up of sugar in the bloodstream, sugar which can harm the body. To combat this, the diabetic must take insulin regularly. But maintaining the proper level of insulin is a difficult task. This program assists the diabetic in maintaining the proper insulin level by allowing him or her to monitor and record sugar level. (The diabetic must take his or her own urine sugar readings—there is no provision for direct computer input of this data.) This program can't cure diabetes, but it can help make life a little more comfortable for those who must live with it. Includes a sample run.

Lines: 95
Version: Micropolis BASIC ver. 3.0
Hardware: 132-column printer
Software: none
Non-ANSI: strings, CHAR$(), ASSIGN, extended IF

309. Medical Audit

Author: Charles Hemminger and Joseph Tarantino

Source: *Creative Computing* Jan 79 (5:1)
"Medical Audit Time!" pp. 92–99 (96–99)

One method being used more and more these days to improve hospital medical care is the medical audit. A medical audit is a special review of selected hospital charts. The audit looks for signs that may indicate above average or below average patient care. A medical audit involves the collecting and tabulating of a great deal of data. That is where the computer comes in. Though the computer cannot do the auditing itself, it can assist in the collecting and summarizing of the data. This program is designed to help collect medical data for audits. The program can be customized easily to collect information for a wide variety of medical audits. Includes a list of program variables.

Lines: 155
Version: TRS-80 Level I BASIC
Hardware: TRS-80
Software: none
Non-ANSI: not translatable

328. PET Reflex Tester

Author: Gregory Yob

Source: *Creative Computing* Apr 79 (5:4)
"Personal Electronic Transactions" pp. 28–32 (29)

Do you have quick relexes? You can test how fast your reflexes are with this reflex tester for PET computer systems. The program flashes a dot. You try to hit a key on the keyboard as fast as you can. The computer then displays how long it took you to respond.

Lines: 18
Version: PET BASIC
Hardware: PET
Software: none
Non-ANSI: not translatable

1017. Personal Health Manager

Author: Keith Jones

Source: *Personal Computing* May 79 (3:5)
"Your Family Health Plan" pp. 20–25 (24)

Updates: correction to flowchart
Personal Computing Jul 79 (3:7)
"Health Plan Remedies" p. 9

One way that your computer can help keep you healthy is by acting as your personal health advisor. A computer can't be a doctor but it can discuss your current state of health and advise you of things you should know. This program is set up to be a demonstration of how such a program might work. This program is designed specifically for a person who has diabetes and is pregnant. Includes a sample run and a flowchart.

Lines: 142
Version: not given
Hardware: none
Software: none
Non-ANSI: none

62. Muscle Action Sensor

Author: Steve Ciarcia

Source: *Byte* Jun 79 (4:6)
"Mind Over Matter" pp. 49–58 (58)

Updates: commentary
Byte Nov 79 (4:11)
"Mind Over Matter Expansion" p. 12

Using biofeedback hardware and sensors described in the article, this program can sense a muscle twitch and perform a command based on it. The computer cycles through a series of lights. When the light corresponding to the action you want is lit, you twitch a muscle. The computer senses this through an electrode and branches to the action selected.

Lines: 64
Version: Micro Com 8K Zapple BASIC
Hardware: homemade sensors and interface hardware
(described in article)
Software: none
Non-ANSI: OUT, INP(), extended IF

1029. Surgical Procedure Retrieval System

Author: William Walker

Source: Personal Computer Jul 79 (3:7)
"Filing Medical Records" pp. 28–31 (30–31)

One of the most important—yet frequently neglected—parts of patient care is the keeping of accurate medical records. Such records can often point out problems that may not otherwise be apparent. The SURGICAL PROCEDURE RETRIEVAL SYSTEM is a program that allows a doctor, dentist, or veterinarian to create a computerized patient data base. This data base records patient names, dates of surgery, and the type of surgery performed. Includes a list of program variables.

Lines: 271
Version: TRS-80 Level II BASIC
Hardware: sequential file device
Software: none
Non-ANSI: CLEAR, strings, two-letter variables, extended IF, INPUT #, PRINT #

731. Adult Caloric Requirements

Author: John R. Cameron

Source: Kilobaud Microcomputing Sep 79 (33)
"Adult Caloric Requirements in Xitan BASIC" pp. 136–137 (137)

Updates: commentary
Kilobaud Microcomputing Feb 80 (38)
"You Are What You Eat" p. 16

It is a reflection on the advanced state of our society that more people in America are worried about getting fat, rather than about getting enough to eat. If you're worried about your weight, then this program may benefit you. You type in information about how active you are, how tall you are, and what your current weight is. The program then figures out what your caloric requirements are. It also shows you how much less you'll have to eat each week to lose a given amount of weight. Includes a sample run.

Lines: 64
Version: Xitan SuperBASIC
Hardware: none
Software: none
Non-ANSI: ? (used in place of PRINT), LINE INPUT, extended IF, ASC(), two-letter variables, strings, PRECISION

558. Pathology Recordkeeper

Author: Jon R. Lindsay

Source: Interface Age Nov 79 (4:11)
"The Pathology Bookkeeper" pp. 61–64 (62–64)

Nowhere is the keeping of accurate records more important than in medicine; often it can be literally a matter of life and death. This program records surgical pathology data. The program keeps information on patient names and addresses, sex, doctor, date of surgery, and other information. The records for any particular patient may be called up and reviewed or corrected with ease. The program can select all the patients whose last names start with a particular character string. You can, for example, list all the patients on file who have names that start with "Be."

Lines: 300
Version: Microsoft BASIC
Hardware: random-access file device, addressable-cursor video display
Software: none
Non-ANSI: not translatable

752. Weight Watcher's Record

Author: Margot Critchfield and Tom Dwyer

Source: Kilobaud Microcomputing Nov 79 (35)
"Weight-Watching Special" pp. 156–157 (156)

If your waistline makes you look like you're trying to hide a pillow under your shirt, you need to go on a diet. This program can help you diet by keeping an accurate record of how much you lose or gain over the course of several weeks. The program notes how much you've lost so far, what your average weekly loss has been, and how much farther you have to go to reach your goal. The program also prints out a graph showing your weight over the span of time. Includes a sample run.

Lines: 92
Version: not given
Hardware: none
Software: none
Non-ANSI: strings

1069. Calorie Counter

Author: Gary Rensberger

Source: Personal Computing Dec 79 (3:12)
"Calorie Counter" pp. 60–62 (61–62)

One way to shed those excess pounds is to go on a calorie-counting diet. The problem with calorie counting is that it's difficult to keep track of how much you've eaten and how many calories are in what kinds of foods. This program takes care of such a diet by doing all the computations involved. You enter what things you've consumed during the day, noting how many ounces, cups, pieces, etc. you've had. The program looks up the calorie counts and prints out the calories for each item, and your total calories for the day. Includes a sample run.

Lines: 168
Version: Microsoft BASIC
Hardware: none
Software: none
Non-ANSI: strings, multi-letter variables, extended IF, ON . . . GOSUB, STR$()

METEOROLOGY

984. Meteorology Program

Author: Glenn Prescott

Source: *Personal Computing* Jan 79 (3:1)
"WEATHERMAN" pp. 23–26 (26)

Maybe you can't do anything about the weather, but this program may be able to help you predict it. WEATHERMAN is a program that performs meteorological calculations. The program can: convert temperatures between any one of four different scales, calculate the temperature humidity index (a measure of how "comfortable" the air is), do wind chill calculations, and compute relative humidity and dew point. Includes a sample run.

Lines: 135
Version: not given
Hardware: none
Software: none
Non-ANSI: CLG(), strings

733. Hurricane Location and Distance Calculator

Author: Bryce Segar

Source: *Kilobaud Microcomputing* Oct 79 (34)
"Hurricane!" pp. 84–86 (84–85)

Updates: commentary
Kilobaud Microcomputing Jan 80 (37)
"Oh-Oh" p. 17

If you live in the southeastern part of the U.S., hurricanes are a fact of life for you. While there's nothing you can do to stop a hurricane from blowing your roof in, you can at least know when it's time to get out of the way. This program tracks hurricanes and makes predictions about when and if they are likely to reach your location. You feed in information about the hurricane's position and direction of travel. The program then computes whether or not the hurricane will reach you, and if so, when. Includes a sample run.

Lines: 135
Version: TRS-80 Level II BASIC
Hardware: TRS-80
Software: none
Non-ANSI: not translatable

PHYSICS

180. Escape Velocity Program

Author: J. Harris

Source: *Creative Computing* May–Jun 75 (1:4)
"ESCAPE" pp. 29–31 (31)

This program is designed to help you investigate how an object travels if it's launched straight up from the earth's surface. You can use it to determine what launch velocity you'd need to reach a given height, your velocity at different heights for a given launch velocity, and your maximum height reached for a given launch velocity. The program can produce both tables and graphs. Includes a sample run.

Lines: 236
Version: not given
Hardware: none
Software: none
Non-ANSI: none

479. Harmonic Analysis of Sound

Author: Timothy O'Shaughnessy

Source: *Interface Age* Oct 77 (2:11)
"Acoustical Analysis: The Effects of Noise on the Environment" pp. 48–54 (54)

This program does a harmonic analysis of the combined effects of signals and noise, and produces a graphic plot of the result. The program can handle five point sources of sound and one noise source. The article discusses noise and sound. No special graphics terminal is required. Sample runs are included.

Lines: 127
Version: not given
Hardware: none
Software: none
Non-ANSI: none

37. Fast Fourier Transforms

Author: William Stanley and Steven Peterson

Source: *Byte* Dec 78 (3:12)
"Fast Fourier Transforms on Your Home Computer" pp. 14–25 (20)

Updates: modification
Byte May 79 (4:5)
"FFT BASIC Problem" p. 205 (205)

commentary
Byte May 79 (4:5)
"Fast Fourier Transforms on Your Home Computer" p. 225

One method of doing signal analysis is through *Fast Fourier Transforms* (FFTs). FFTs break down a signal into its basic power spectrum. This is a program to run FFTs on your computer. You input a series of data points or a function capable of generating the points desired (patches are provided showing how this is done). From this, the program uses FFTs to output the components of the FFT spectrum. The article has a discussion of FFTs and how they are generated. Includes sample runs.

Lines: 103 (plus patches)
Version: Digital Group BASIC
Hardware: none
Software: none
Non-ANSI: strings, extended IF, SQRT()

153. Physics Drill

Author: Frank Bobek

Source: *Calculators/Computers Magazine* Jan–Feb 79 (3:1)
"VATS RIGHT" pp. 41–45 (41–44)

VATS RIGHT is a microcomputer program to drill physics students in motion calculations. The program presents the students with problems in the calculation of velocities, acceleration, and changes in distance and time. The program also requires the student to make and interpret graphs. Includes a sample run.

Lines: 295
Version: PET BASIC
Hardware: none
Software: none
Non-ANSI: ? (used in place of PRINT), strings, GET, extended IF

523. Fast Fourier Transforms and Power Curve Fitting

Author: G. S. Stiles

Source: *Interface Age* Mar 79 (4:3)
"Spectral Music" pp. 56–63 (62–63)

Updates: commentary
Interface Age Jun 79 (4:6)
"Understanding Spectral Music" p. 14

These routines are part of a program to do spectral analysis of music. The main program is provided only in flowchart form. The BASIC routines listed do Fast Fourier Transforms and power curve computations. Includes flowchart.

Lines: 160, 30
Version: not given
Hardware: none
Software: none
Non-ANSI: ' (used in place of REM), strings, multi-letter variables, extended IF

51. Gas Simulation for the PET

Author: Mark Zimmermann

Source: *Byte* Apr 79 (4:4)
"Simulating Physical Systems" pp. 26–41 (34–41)

No, this isn't a program to help your car get better mileage. This program is a simulation of a closed box filled with "ideal" gas molecules. A simulation of this type is used in physics to study the behavior of gas molecules under various conditions. This simulation displays the "gas molecules" in real time on the screen of a PET. The program uses machine language to perform the critical inner-loop operations. Includes a sample output.

Lines: 68
Version: PET BASIC
Hardware: PET
Software: 6502 assembly language routine
Non-ANSI: not translatable

793. Harmonic Analysis for the Apple

Author: Charles Putney

Source: *Micro* Jun 79 (13)
"Harmonic Analysis for the Apple" pp. 5–8 (6–8)

Updates: corrections
Micro Sep 79 (16)
untitled p. 34 (34)

This program performs harmonic analysis of a wave. The program calculates a listing of coefficients of the wave's Fourier series to the fifth harmonic. The output wave and all five harmonics are plotted on the Apple's color display.

Lines: 112
Version: Applesoft II Floating Point BASIC
Hardware: Apple II
Software: none
Non-ANSI: not translatable

409. "Weighted Spring" Model

Author: Gregory Yob

Source: *Creative Computing* Nov 79 (5:11)
"Personal Electronic Transactions" pp. 183–185 (185)

Physical equations can be used to represent the motions of objects. Where these equations are complex, visualizing the resulting motion can be difficult. A good way around this problem is to let your computer demonstrate graphically how an object governed by a particular equation will move. This program shows how a weighted spring moves back and forth. By varying the "mass" of the weight, or by changing the "stiffness" of the spring, you can vary how the weighted spring will move.

Lines: 8 (plus patches)
Version: PET BASIC
Hardware: PET
Software: none
None-ANSI: not translatable

410. One-Dimensional Gravity Model

Author: Gregory Yob

Source: *Creative Computing* Nov 79 (5:11)
"Personal Electronic Transactions" pp. 183–185 (185)

This program models gravity for a collection of objects with various positions and velocities. To simplify the model, only one-dimensional gravity along a line is considered. You specify the positions of the objects. The program then moves the objects back and forth along the line as their "gravitational fields" interact.

Lines: 31
Version: PET BASIC
Hardware: PET
Software: none
Non-ANSI: not translatable

94. Fourier Spectrum Analyzer

Author: F. R. Ruckdeshel

Source: *Byte* Dec 79 (4:12)
"Frequency Analysis of Data Using a Microcomputer" pp. 10–35 (14)

Updates: commentary and corrections
Byte Apr 80 (5:4)
"Disputed Analysis of Frequency" pp. 12–14 (14)

commentary
Byte Apr 80 (5:4)
"A Dead Transformation?" pp. 14–16

This program performs a Fourier Spectrum Analysis for data you specify. You type in the data points corresponding to the wave you wish to analyze. The computer prints out a graph of the data. It then transforms the data and outputs a table of the transformed data, as well as a frequency space plot. Includes a sample run.

Lines: 128 (plus patch)
Version: North Star BASIC, ver. 6, Release 2
Hardware: none
Software: none
Non-ANSI: extended IF, SQRT()

95. Noniterative Digital Solutions of Linear Transfer Functions

Author: Bryan Finlay

Source: *Byte* Dec 79 (4:12)
"Noniterative Digital Solutions of Linear Transfer Functions" pp. 144–166 (155–160)

These two programs implement a technique for precise, noniterative, digital solution of the time-domain response of linear transfer functions with constant coefficients. The program is suitable for solving equations that, in the Laplace domain, exhibit up to ten roots in either the numerator or denominator. (The above is paraphrased from the first paragraph of the article. Frankly, we haven't the foggiest notion of what the author is talking about.)

Lines: 55, 23
Version: Hewlett-Packard 9830A BASIC
Hardware: none
Software: none
Non-ANSI: DISP

PSYCHIATRY

196. DR. Z: Computerized Therapist

Author: Zeddies

Source: *Creative Computing* Jan–Feb 76 (2:1)
"DR. Z" pp. 69, 71 (71)

Feeling low? Tell your troubles to this computerized therapist. You type in English language sentences. The computer responds to your thoughts, trying to give you counsel. It actually does a fairly good job of creating reasonable responses to your questions and statements. Includes a sample run.

```
     Lines:  85
   Version:  not given
  Hardware:  none
  Software:  none
  Non-ANSI:  HP strings, multiple-assignment
```

236. Psychoanalysis by Computer

Author: Steve North

Source: *Creative Computing* Jul–Aug 77 (3:4)
"ELIZA" pp. 100–103 (100–103)

Updates: improvements
Creative Computing Nov–Dec 77 (3:6)
"Shorter and Faster ELIZA" p. 10 (10)

comments
Creative Computing Mar–Apr 78 (4:2)
"ELIZA" p. 8

ELIZA is a program that accepts natural English as input, and carries on a reasonably coherent conversation based on the psychoanalytic techniques of Carl Rogers. The computer, in effect, takes the place of a $75/hour shrink (well, sort of). ELIZA works by finding keywords in the input string. When a keyword is found, the program processes the keyword and the phrases around it. The computer then generates a reply. Because the translation techniques do not fully break down and analyze the input strings, the conversation that the computer generates is sometimes slightly stilted. This trade-off was necessary to keep the processing time down. Within its limitations, however, the program does a surprisngly good job of producing reasonable replies. Includes a sample run and a list of program variables.

```
     Lines:  207
   Version:  MITS 8K BASIC
  Hardware:  none
  Software:  none
  Non-ANSI:  strings, extended IF
```

349. INKBLOT

Author: Scott Costello

Source: *Creative Computing* Jun 79 (5:6)
"INKBLOT" pp. 108–109 (109)

INKBLOT is a program that creates "inkblot" patterns similar to those used in the Rorschach Inkblot Test. The patterns consist of randomly placed ellipses, mirrored from left to right across the display. (A special graphics terminal is not required.) It seems to us that this program could be hooked up to a psychiatry program like ELIZA. The program could administer an inkblot test and then discuss it with the patient! Includes a sample run. (This program was originally printed in the book, *More BASIC Computer Games.*)

```
     Lines:  72
   Version:  not given
  Hardware:  none
  Software:  none
  Non-ANSI:  strings
```

404. TRS-80 Rorschach Patterns

Author: not given

Source: *Creative Computing* Nov 79 (5:11)
"Rorschach II" p. 141 (141)

Rorschach patterns have long been used in psychiatry to help learn what's going on in patients' minds. The patterns are actually almost random, but by getting a patient to talk about a pattern, the doctor can help to discover what is troubling the person. This program produces Rorschach-like patterns on a TRS-80. Includes a sample output. (The program is reprinted from *Micronews,* January 1979.)

```
     Lines:  22
   Version:  TRS-80 Level I BASIC
  Hardware:  TRS-80
  Software:  none
  Non-ANSI:  not translatable
```

PSYCHOLOGY

165. Pattern Recognition Experiment

Author: William Bewley

Source: *Creative Computing* Nov–Dec 74 (1:1)
"Computer-Based Experiments in Cognitive Psychology" pp. 36–42 (41–42)

According to the Pandemonium model of pattern recognition, people recognize things using a level-by-level succession of analyzers or "demons." When you view something, the first group of demons in your brain breaks down the image into a set of simple features. The next set of demons "extract" more complex features from the simpler features. This process continues until your mind has completely analyzed the picture. This program highlights principles about this process. You are given target characters to look for in lists of other characters. The time that it takes you to discover that given letters are present or absent demonstrates theories given in the article. Includes a sample run.

Lines:	254
Version:	Dartmouth BASIC
Hardware:	none
Software:	none
Non-ANSI:	strings, CLK$( ), SEG$( ), DEF . . . FNEND, multiple-assignment

63. Control Theory Demonstrations

Author:	William T. Powers
Source:	*Byte* Jun 79 (4:6) "The Nature of Robots" pp. 132–144 (144)
	Byte Jul 79 (4:7) "The Nature of Robots" pp. 134–152 (134–135)
	Byte Aug 79 (4:8) "The Nature of Robots" pp. 94–116 (110–111)
	Byte Sep 79 (4:9) "The Nature of Robots" pp. 96–112 (98–102)

This series of articles discusses *control theory* and how it can be used to explore and describe behavior. The programs demonstrate various control theory principles. The first three programs require no special hardware or software. The final program requires a video display and joystick (it's given in both North Star and Apple BASIC versions). Includes sample runs.

Lines:	13, 129, 119, 131, 84
Version:	North Star BASIC ver. 6 Release 3, Apple II BASIC
Hardware:	video display, joystick, Apple II required for Apple II program
Software:	8080/Z80 assembly language routine
Non-ANSI:	[North Star BASIC programs] %() (used to format printouts), HP strings, DEF . . . FNEND, extended IF, VAL(), ! (used in place of PRINT), ! # (PRINT #), INPUT1, FILL, ASC(), EXIT, CALL, OUT [Apple II BASIC program] not translatable

1114. Pattern Matching Exercise for the TRS-80

Author:	Don Inman
Source:	*Recreational Computing* Nov–Dec 79 (8:3) "Match Me" pp. 11–13 (12–13)
Updates:	modifications for sound *Recreational Computing* Nov–Dec 79 (8:3) "The Joy of Sound from SOUNDWARE" pp. 16–20 (20)

This program helps young children learn about shapes. The program displays seven different random shapes on the screen, plus a "target" shape. The child is then asked which shape best matches the target shape. When the child makes a guess, the target shape is placed alongside the guessed shape. A message tells whether the choice was correct or not. Includes a sample run and a list of program variables.

Lines:	59
Version:	TRS-80 Level II BASIC
Hardware:	TRS-80
Software:	none
Non-ANSI:	not translatable

SOCIOLOGY

206. Prejudice Analysis

Author:	Mark Gross
Source:	*Creative Computing* Sep–Oct 76 (2:5) "Prejudice Analysis" pp. 67–68 (68)

Are you a foaming-at-the-mouth bigot? Find out what your true feelings are with this prejudice analysis program. The program is based on a personality inventory developed by Dr. George Siegel at the Tufts Medical Center. The program asks you to answer a series of questions. Based on your replies, the computer scores you on how prejudiced you are. The program is set up so that a number of people can take the test, with the program summarizing the group's responses at the end.

Lines:	88
Version:	not given
Hardware:	none
Software:	none
Non-ANSI:	none

321. Social Science Survey Program

Author: James Owens

Source: *Creative Computing* Mar 79 (5:3)
"Teachers! A Social Science Survey
Program!" pp. 68–72 (72)

The best way to find out what people think about a given subject is to conduct a survey; ask people what they think about a given topic and then tabulate the results. This can give you a good idea of which direction public opinion is running. This program assists in the administration of such surveys. Data from a survey you run is stored in DATA statements in the program. Using this information, the program produces tables showing such information as the means, standard deviations, and standard errors. The output is broken down to show differences between males and females, and between those over 30 and those under 30. Includes a sample run.

Lines: 72
Version: Ohio Scientific 8K BASIC
Hardware: none
Software: none
Non-ANSI: extended IF

TEACHING

895. CAI Routines

Author: Franz Frederick

Source: *People's Computers* Jul–Aug 77 (6:1)
"Computer Assisted Instruction in BASIC"
pp. 51–58 (53–58)

With the advent of low-cost microcomputers, Computer Assisted Instruction has become a reality. New techniques are constantly being developed to aid the programmer in designing CAI material. Here are three routines which can be used in constructing CAI programs. The first is a keyword processor. This generalized keyword processor allows a student to input a phrase in response to a question. The computer can then take a variety of actions depending on whether or not it finds certain keywords in the student's answer. The second routine is a phonetic answer processor. It reduces student answers to a special phonetic representation. This reduces the problems of typographic and spelling errors. The third routine keeps records of a student's performance. Such information is useful in helping the student learn and in helping the teacher identify areas of the task that need redesigning.

Lines: 101, 92, 103
Version: not given
Hardware: none
Software: none
Non-ANSI: strings, STR$(), CLEAR, extended IF

378. Student Grade Records Program for the Apple II

Author: Jim Hunter

Source: *Creative Computing* Sep 79 (5:9)
"A Grade Maintenance Program for the
Apple II with Disk Drive" pp. 142–149
(146–149)

Maintaining student grade records is a laborious task. At the same time, it's a task that requires great accuracy (unless you don't mind howls of righteous indignation from students whose records have been messed up). This program takes advantage of the computer's record-keeping abilities to maintain grade records. The program has provisions for weighting marks for various assignments and tests, as well as provisions for entering missing grades and make-up work. The program can output several kinds of reports including individual student records, class averages by students, class averages by assignment, and ranked averages by student. The program might be adaptable to non-Apple systems; but note that it uses Applesoft's peculiar file commands: OPEN, CLOSE, READ, and WRITE are performed by PRINTing a control/d followed by the command. Includes a sample output.

Lines: 35, 452
Version: Applesoft BASIC
Hardware: random-access file device
Software: none
Non-ANSI: not translatable

1051. Examination Administrating Programs

Author: Loyd Bulmer

Source: *Personal Computing* Sep 79 (3:9)
"EXAM" pp. 54–56 (55–56)

These two programs allow a teacher to use a microcomputer to make up and administer examinations. The teacher first uses the programs to create a test. The computer then administers the exam to the students, recording the results. The programs are quite flexible in the types of questions they can ask. If more than one answer is correct for a question, they can accept either answer. They can also accept variations on correct answers. Includes a sample run and a list of a program variables.

Lines: 29, 36
Version: Radio Shack Level-II BASIC
Hardware: sequential file device
Software: none
Non-ANSI: CLEAR, CLS, strings, two-letter variables,
extended IF, PRINT #, INPUT #, VAL(),
STRING$()

553. Student Information and Grade Records for the TRS-80

Author: Richard Lemon and Craig Jones

Source: *Interface Age* Oct 79 (4:10)
"TEACHER: The Classroom Record Keeper" pp. 74–84 (76–84)

This program is designed to help the classroom teacher keep student information and grade records. The program, called TEACHER, consists of several independent segments which CALL each other. The program maintains two kinds of data: personal student information and grade records. The personal information includes names, addresses, phones, and comments. The grade information shows the students' performances on the various tests and assignments. Both kinds of data can be edited and listed on demand. Includes a sample output.

Lines: 16, 45, 171, 145
Version: TRS-80 Level II BASIC
Hardware: TRS-80, random-access file device
Software: none
Non-ANSI: not translatable

400. Test Evaluation Program

Author: Douglas W. Green and Jeffrey Hering

Source: *Creative Computing* Nov 79 (5:11)
"Teacher-Made Tests: Debugging & Evaluating" pp. 104–107 (106–107)

In theory, a teacher should be able to learn as much from his or her own tests as do the students. By analyzing student responses to the questions on the tests, a teacher can find out which questions are effective and which are not. A good question is one that is neither too hard nor too easy for the students involved. Students who understand the subject matter should be able to answer it; those who do not should *not* be able to answer it. This program uses point bisereal coefficients to analyze test questions. Includes a sample output, flowchart, and a list of program variables.

Lines: 139
Version: Wang BASIC
Hardware: none
Software: none
Non-ANSI: strings, STOP [print string], % (used to format PRINT USING), PRINT USING, multiple-assignment, CONVERT, SELECT, ON . . . GOSUB, HEX( )

TYPING

972. Touch Typing Practice

Author: Kevin Stumpf

Source: *Personal Computing* Sep 78 (2:9)
"A Magic Touch" pp. 52–55 (54–55)

To use computers, you have to get programs into the machines. You can hunt and peck at the keyboard, but if you really want to make use of your computer, sooner or later you are going to have to learn touch typing. In touch typing you train your fingers to know the places of the internationally standard typewriter key positions. Using all 10 fingers, and not having to constantly search out characters, you can speed through your typing in one-tenth the time. This program is a drill to help you learn the proper finger-to-key assignments. The computer types out the letter, and you respond with the proper letter at the keyboard. Includes a sample run.

Lines: 115
Version: North Star BASIC
Hardware: none
Software: none
Non-ANSI: HP strings, PRINT #, extended IF

96. Touch Typing Drill

Author: Arthur Armstrong

Source: *Byte* Dec 79 (4:12)
"Thirty Days to a Faster Input" pp. 250–251 (251)

When entering a new program into your computer, how do your fingers move? Do you peck here and there at the keys on your keyboard? If you do, it's high time you learned touch typing. With touch typing you train your fingers to "know" instinctively where the various letters are so that your fingers can fly across the keyboard at lightning speed. This program drills you in touch typing. The program prints out letters which you must repeat without looking at the keyboard. Includes a sample run.

Lines: 42
Version: MITS 3.2 8K BASIC
Hardware: none
Software: none
Non-ANSI: CLEAR, extended IF, two-letter variables, WAIT, INP(), AND(), strings

827. Speed Typing Test for the Apple II

Author: John Broderick

Source: *Micro* Dec 79 (19)
"APPLE II Speed Typing Test With Input Clock" p. 69 (69)

How fast a typist are you? Do you zip along with the speed of a hyperactive jackrabbit, or do you plod along at a more leisurely pace? This typing test can show you how fast you are. The program prints out sentences which you must repeat as fast as you can. After you do, the program displays your typing speed and the number of errors you made.

Lines: 48
Version: Apple BASIC
Hardware: Apple II
Software: none
Non-ANSI: not translatable

MISCELLANEOUS

474. Viking Spacecraft Software

Author: not given

Source: *Interface Age* Aug 77 (2:9)
"Viking Uplink . . . Downlink" pp. 56–93 (78–93)

This program is used to process communications and experimental data for the Viking Mars spaceprobe. The article discusses communication with Viking. This program should be just the thing for those of you planning to launch a mission to Mars in the near future. A flowchart and sample runs are included.

Lines: 2100 (whew!)
Version: HP BASIC
Hardware: Hewlett Packard 9830A, cassette, plotter
Software: none
Non-ANSI: not translatable

106. Routing Worksheets

Author: Mac Oglesby

Source: *Calculators/Computers Magazine* Oct 77 (1:2)
"UPS" pp. 34–37 (34–36)

This program generates worksheets of routing problems. Each page displays *n* locations placed at random on an 8-by-7 map. The user is directed to draw the shortest route which begins and ends at UPS and reaches each location. A coded solution is provided for the teacher. Includes a sample run.

Lines: 270
Version: Dartmouth BASIC
Hardware: none
Software: none
Non-ANSI: strings, STR$( ), RESET, multiple-assignment, ' (used in place of REM)

20. Program to Produce Fertility Figures

Author: Dennis Barbour

Source: *Byte* Apr 78 (3:4)
"User's Report: The SOL-20" pp. 126–130 (129)

This program produces fertility (birth rate) figures from data you input. The output consists of the ratio of births to marriages over the time period you specify. Program output is in both tabular and graphic form. No special graphics terminal is required. A sample run is included.

Lines: 54
Version: SOL BASIC-5
Hardware: none
Software: none
Non-ANSI: none

134. Plug Matching Exercises

Author: Mac Oglesby

Source: *Calculators/Computers Magazine* May 78 (2:5)
"PLUGS" pp. 42–46 (42–43)

This program generates worksheets of electronic plug symmetry problems. Given diagrams of the connecting faces of a plug and four sockets, the student must decide which socket(s) would fit that plug. The two plug faces must match exactly in pin configuration, socket shape, and socket orientation. Extra holes don't matter. At the bottom of the page, the program prints out an answer key. Includes a sample run.

Lines: 312
Version: Dartmouth BASIC
Hardware: none
Software: none
Non-ANSI: MAT operations, STR$( ), strings, ' (used in place of REM), ON . . . GOSUB

1085. Dyslexic Word Timer

Author: John Pollard

Source: *Recreational Computing* May–Jun 79 (7:6)
"Peter Can Now Read" pp. 8–12 (11)

Updates: commentary
Recreational Computing Sep–Oct 79 (8:2)
"Improving Voice Responses" p. 6

commentary and new program for PET
Recreational Computing Jan–Feb 80 (8:4)
"PET Reading Program" pp. 25–28 (28)

Dyslexia is a puzzling ailment. Children who suffer from it are unable to read, even though they may be intelligent, because the disease causes printed words to be "scrambled." For most children, learning to read is a relatively straightfoward process. For the dyslexic child, however, the letters of each word can seem to "float around," turning the words into an indecipherable code. This program can help dyslexic children learn to read. It presents words in a structured fashion for them to recognize. A cassette recorder can be used to provide verbal confirmation of each word. (Reprinted from the Australian magazine *COM-3*.)

Lines: 85
Version: TRS Level I BASIC
Hardware: TRS-80
Software: none
Non-ANSI: not translatable

1088. FLASH Word Recall Drill

Author: Jerry Russell and Theodore Hines

Source: *Recreational Computing* May–Jun 79 (7:6)
"FLASH" pp. 46–47 (46–47)

This is a word recall drill in the form of a game. The player can choose the word difficulty and the length of time that each word will stay on the screen. The computer then flashes words on the display. After each word is flashed, the player is asked to type the word in at the keyboard.

Lines: 153
Version: Processor Technology Extended BASIC
Hardware: addressable-cursor video display
Software: none
Non-ANSI: HP strings, SET, PAUSE, CURSOR, extended IF

77. Analog Data Display for the Apple II

Author: Richard C. Hallgren

Source: *Byte* Sep 79 (4:9)
"A Low-Speed Analog-to-Digital Converter for the Apple II" pp. 70–78 (74–78)

Microcomputers can be very useful for collecting and displaying data. This program uses an Apple II and a homemade analog-to-digital converter to read and display analog signals. (The computer is acting, in effect, as a low speed oscilloscope.) Includes a sample output and flowchart.

Lines: 81
Version: Applesoft floating point BASIC
Hardware: Apple II, homemade analog-to-digital converter
Software: 6502 assembly language routine (supplied)
Non-ANSI: not translatable

92. Spacecraft Design and Flight Simulator

Author: Gary Sivak

Source: *Byte* Nov 79 (4:11)
"A Spacecraft Simulator" pp. 104–111 (104–111)

You may not have the budget of NASA, but now you can still design and "launch" your own multistage rocket. This spaceship simulation comes in two parts: In the first part you specify the design characteristics of your rocket—how many stages it will have, its payload weight, and so on. Then in the second part of the program, the flight of the craft is simulated. As the rocket "takes off," the program prints out the elapsed flight time, the fuel remaining, and other data. The object, of course, is to design a vehicle that can successfully boost its way into orbit. The documenation says that you can plot a picture of your trajectory, but the program code to do this is apparently missing.

Lines: 209
Version: not given
Hardware: none
Software: none
Non-ANSI: none

6
UTILITY

APPLE II, GRAPHICS

For more entries in this category, see specific topics.

771. Apple II Color Display Demos

Author: Richard Suitor

Source: *Micro* Aug–Sep 78 (6)
"Brown and White and Colored All Over"
pp. 33–35 (33–35)

These programs demonstrate principles about the Apple II's color display, as well as "brown" and "1/f" noise.

Lines: 12, 6, 29
Version: Apple BASIC
Hardware: Apple II
Software: none
Non-ANSI: not translatable

775. Apple II High-Resolution Graphics Learning Aid

Author: Andrew Eliason

Source: *Micro* Oct–Nov 78 (7)
"Apple II High Resolution Graphics Memory Organization" pp. 43–44 (43)

The Apple II computer has the ability to do detailed color graphics using its high resolution mode. This program will help you to learn how high-resolution data is stored in memory. The program takes a byte that you specify and loads it into every position in the high-resolution memory so that you can see its effects.

Lines: 14
Version: Apple II BASIC
Hardware: Apple II
Software: none
Non-ANSI: not translatable

781. Apple II Display Demo

Author: M. R. Connolly, Jr.

Source: *Micro* Dec 78–Jan 79 (8)
"An Apple II Page 1 Map" pp. 41–42 (41)

In the Apple II, text can be displayed on the screen by simply storing the characters in the right locations in memory. This program demonstrates this feature by displaying the word "MICRO" surrounded by a block.

Lines: 4
Version: Apple II BASIC
Hardware: Apple II
Software: none
Non-ANSI: not translatable

808. Defining HI-RES Characters for the Apple II

Author: Robert F. Zant

Source: *Micro* Aug 79 (15)
"Define HI-RES Characters for the Apple II" pp. 44–45 (45)

From its library of user-contributed programs, the Apple Computer Company has released a machine language routine for generating characters using the HI-RES features of the Apple II. This program allows you to modify the table that defines what the characters will look like.

Lines: 51
Version: Apple BASIC
Hardware: Apple II
Software: none
Non-ANSI: not translatable

729. Apple II High-Resolution Graphics Demos

Author: Darrell G. Smith

Source: *Kilobaud Microcomputing* Sep 79 (33)
"Apple II High-Resolution Graphics" pp.
104–106 (105–106)

These are three short programs to show how points are
plotted using the Apple II's high-resolution graphics.

    Lines: 4, 7, 17
  Version: Apple BASIC
Hardware: Apple II
 Software: none
Non-ANSI: not translatable

552. Apple II String and Graphics Demos

Author: Don Inman

Source: *Interface Age* Oct 79 (4:10)
"Apples, Computers and Teachers" pp.
68–72 (68–70)

This is a set of short demonstration programs for the
Apple II. The first few programs illustrate the use of
strings. The rest of the programs demonstrate various
Apple II graphics features. Includes a sample output.

    Lines: 13 programs ranging from 3 to 11 lines
  Version: Apple BASIC
Hardware: Apple II
 Software: none
Non-ANSI: not translatable

89. Shape Table Builder for the Apple II

Author: Dave Partyka

Source: *Byte* Nov 79 (4:11)
"Shape Table Conversion for the Apple II"
p. 63 (63)

The Apple II has a unique way of doing graphics. By
defining a "shape table" you can create graphics objects
for positioning on the display. This program allows you to
easily create and store objects in the shape table.

    Lines: 9
  Version: Apple BASIC
Hardware: Apple II
 Software: none
Non-ANSI: not translatable

818. Apple II HIRES Picture Data Compression

Author: Bob Bishop

Source: *Micro* Nov 79 (18)
"Apple II Hires Picture Compression" pp.
17–24 (20–24)

Updates: corrections to assembly language routines
Micro Jan 80 (20)
"Microbes and Miscellanea" pp. 39–40 (40)

This program demonstrates a technique for compressing
the data used to generate pictures on an Apple II using its
high resolution mode. The program divides a picture into
7-by-7 bit squares ("pixels"). It then goes through, looking for squares which are the same or nearly the same as
other squares in the picture. By storing only a list of the
basic pixels and their locations, the program greatly reduces the amount of memory needed to store an image.
This costs some loss of detail in the picture. Includes
sample output.

    Lines: 83
  Version: Apple BASIC
Hardware: Apple II
 Software: 6502 assembly language routines
Non-ANSI: not translable

413. "Walking Bird" Animation for the Apple II

Author: Mitchell Waite

Source: *Creative Computing* Dec 79 (5:12)
"Animation for the Apple" pp. 126–128
(127–128)

An animation is a series of pictures, each slightly different
from the one before it, presented to the viewer at a fast
enough rate to give the impression of smooth movement.
These programs demonstrate the use of animation on an
Apple II. They display a bird walking across the screen.
(These programs were reprinted from the book, *Computer
Graphics Primer*.)

    Lines: 36, 65
  Version: Apple BASIC
Hardware: Apple II
 Software: none
Non-ANSI: not translatable

820. Apple Shape Table Generator/Display

Author: John Figueras

Source: *Micro* Dec 79 (19)
"How to do a Shape Table Easily and
Correctly!" pp. 11–22 (19–22)

In the Apple's high resolution mode, characters and special shapes are generated using a "shape table." This special table defines what each of the characters will look like. But before you can use the shapes, you must create them. This shape table-generating system uses your Apple to assist you in making and maintaining shape tables. The first program in the system set up shape files. The second program displays individual shapes as you create them using keyboard commands. The final program displays the shapes in your table, 36 at a time.

Lines: 30, 137, 55
Version: Applesoft BASIC
Hardware: Apple II
Software: none
Non-ANSI: not translatable

APPLE II, MISCELLANEOUS

For more entries in this category, see specific topics.

327. Apple II EXEC Command Demos

Author: Richard Milewski

Source: *Creative Computing* Apr 79 (5:4)
"Apple-Cart" pp. 22–23 (23)

One of the most overlooked commands in the Apple II system is the EXEC command. This is potentially one of the most useful commands available. The EXEC command executes a set of commands in a file just as though they were being typed in at the keyboard. Five demonstration programs are listed which give examples of how to use this facility.

Lines: 15, 22, 2, 12, 34
Version: Applesoft II BASIC
Hardware: random-access file device
Software: none
Non-ANSI: not translatable

364. Translating Arrays from Two Dimensions to One Dimension in Apple BASIC

Author: Ned W. Rhodes

Source: *Creative Computing* Aug 79 (5:8)
"Translating Two-Dimensional Arrays For Integer BASICs" pp. 106–108 (107–108)

One of the frustrating points about Apple Integer BASIC is that arrays can have only one dimension. You can still use it, however, to run programs that use arrays with more than one dimension. These programs show how this can be done. Two ways of generating the necesssary array coordinates are given: (1) by calculating the coordinates in the program, and (2) by using an assembly language subroutine to do the calcuations.

Lines: 14, 20, 18, 20
Version: Apple Integer BASIC, Applesoft II BASIC
Hardware: 6502-based microcomputer
Software: 6502 assembly language routine
Non-ANSI: not translatable

741. Apple II Lowercase Demos

Author: Don Lancaster

Source: *Kilobaud Microcomputing* Nov 79 (35)
"Lowercase for Your Apple II (Part I)" pp. 30–36 (36)

Kilobaud Microcomputing Dec 79 (36)
"Lowercase for Your Apple II (Part II)" pp. 34–42 (38–41)

For as little as $10, you can modify your Apple II to display lowercase characters. These demo programs test and demonstrate the homemade lowercase modification discussed in the article. The programs vary from a simple display of one line of characters to a full screen editing program with cursor controls. Includes a flowchart.

Lines: 7, 13, 42, 6, 16
Version: Apple Integer BASIC
Hardware: Apple II, homemade lowercase generator
Software: none
Non-ANSI: not translatable

ASSEMBLERS

495. BASIC Cross Assembler for the 8080

Author: Peter Reece

Source: *Interface Age* Feb 78 (3:2)
"BASIC Cross Assembler for the 8080" pp. 76–81 (79–81)

This is a cross assembler for the 8080 written in BASIC. The purpose of a cross assembler is to produce machine code for a computer which does not have an assembler of its own. The cross assembler is run on a larger machine which produces a binary code to be read in by the target computer. This cross assembler produces machine code for the 8080 and for similar microcomputers. It has two passes. On the first pass the cross assembler creates a symbol table. During the second pass it translates the opcodes and outputs the binary machine code. The user can request a listing in either hex or octal. Includes a flowchart and sample run.

Lines: 683
Version: PDP-10 BASIC
Hardware: two sequential file devices
Software: none
Non-ANSI: FILES, INSTR(), VAL(), STR$(), INPUT:, PRINT:, RESTORE:, END(), strings

770. 6502 Assembler/Disassembler

Author: Michael McCann

Source: Micro Aug–Sep 78 (6)
"A Simple 6502 Assembler for the PET" pp. 17–21 (18–21)

Updates: corrections
Micro Nov–Dec 78 (7)
"Microbes" p. 27 (27)

This program acts as both an assembler and disassembler for 6502 machine language. The assembler portion of the program takes assembly language code and translates it into 6502 machine language. The assembler is a simple one and does not permit symbolic addresses or operands. The disassembler portion of the program translates machine language back into assembly language. The program also has facilities for saving object code on tape, loading object code from tape, and starting machine language programs that have been entered. Includes a sample run.

Lines: 201
Version: PET BASIC
Hardware: 6502-based microcomputer, sequential file device
Software: none
Non-ANSI: VAL(), ON . . . GOSUB, two-letter variables, strings, PEEK(), GET, extended IF, OPEN, INPUT #, POKE, CLOSE, SYS, USR(), PRINT #, STR$(), TI()

981. Assembler for the PET

Author: Mark Zimmermann

Source: Personal Computing Dec 78 (2:12)
"Assembler for the PET" pp. 42–45 (43–45)

An assembler translates assembly-language instructions such as "LDA 17" into internal machine language. Why would anyone want to program in assembly language when they have BASIC? The usual reason is speed—assembly language programs can often run 10 to 100 times faster than their BASIC counterparts. This is an assembler for the 6502-based Commodore PET. The assembler is a rather simple one with no symbol table for variables or labels. The output from the assembler is stored on tape. A loader is supplied to read in the assembly language output.

Lines: 122, 5
Version: PET BASIC
Hardware: PET
Software: none
Non-ANSI: strings, two-letter variables, OPEN, CLOSE, GET, PRINT #, ASC(), VAL(), POKE, PEEK(), extended IF

BENCHMARKS

632. Speed Benchmark

Author: Fred Ruckdeschel

Source: Kilobaud Aug 78 (20)
"Mits vs. North Star: Which is Faster?" pp. 44–46 (45)

For most people, any BASIC is fast enough. If all you're going to do is play STAR TREK, the computer is going to be spending most of its time waiting for you to type in input. If you are doing a lot of "number crunching," however, you need the fastest BASIC that you can find. Here is a program that can help you determine which BASIC runs the fastest on your computer. This program is a "benchmark" program; that is, it's a standard reference program used to compare the speeds of various BASICs. The program times how long it takes a BASIC interpreter to complete a set of standard tasks. By comparing how long it takes each interpreter to complete the benchmark, you can tell which interpreter is fastest. Includes a sample run.

Lines: 80
Version: North Star BASIC
Hardware: Canada Systems CL2400 real-time clock
Software: none
Non-ANSI: INP(), SQRT()

46. Speed Benchmark using the Heath H 8 Real Time Clock

Author: J. G. Letwin

Source: Byte Mar 79 (4:3)
"Building the Heath H8 Computer" pp. 12–13, 124–140 (134)

Not all BASICs run at the same speed. This speed benchmark allows you to compare the speeds of various BASICs using the real time clock on a Heath H8 computer. Speed comparisons for three different Heath BASICs are given.

Lines: 10
Version: not given
Hardware: Heath H8 real time clock
Software: none
Non-ANSI: POKE, PEEK()

1138. Speed Benchmarks

Author: Chuck Adams

Source: '68' *Micro Journal* Jul 79 (1:5)
"G2-BASIC" pp. 31–33 (32–33)

How fast is the BASIC on your machine? One way to find out is to run "benchmark" programs. By running these programs on several machines, you can see on which computer they take the least time. These simple benchmark programs were run on a G2 Standard BASIC system (the running times are given).

Lines: 9, 10, 10, 10, 9, 10, 10, 10
Version: G2 Standard BASIC
Hardware: none
Software: none
Non-ANSI: none

COMMUNICATIONS

423. Terminal-to-Terminal Talk Program for MITS Systems

Author: Robert Wilcox

Source: *Dr. Dobb's Journal of Computer Calisthenics & Orthodontia* Oct 76 (1:9)
"A BASIC Terminal Exchange Program" p. 24 (24)

This program adds the ability to talk to another terminal to those versions of MITS BASIC which do not have the CONSOLE command. The terminal change is accomplished by calling a machine language (USR) program which has been loaded into reserved high memory. This program does the loading of the machine language routine. The terminal switch is accomplished by executing a USR(1) function call.

Lines: 18
Version: MITS 8K BASIC ver. 3.2
Hardware: 8080-based microcomputer
Software: none
Non-ANSI: not translatable

813. PET Terminal Program

Author: C. H. Scanlon

Source: *Micro* Oct 79 (17)
"Hooking PET to Ma Bell" pp. 11–13 (11)

How would you like to turn your PET computer into a computer terminal, for peanuts? You can do just that with this terminal program and a homemade interface circuit described in the article. The program uses the interface to make your PET act like a regular "dumb" computer terminal. It has a provision for generating control characters needed by most computer systems. You can use this interface and a modem to dial up a large computer system over the phone lines. The hardware and software can probably be adapted to other 6502-based microcomputers.

Lines: 25
Version: PET BASIC
Hardware: homemade interface, PET
Software: none
Non-ANSI: not translatable

COMPILERS

27. "Tiny" PASCAL Compiler

Author: Kin-Man Chung

Source: *Byte* Sep 78 (3:9)
"A 'Tiny' Pascal Compiler" pp. 58–65, 148–155

Byte Oct 78 (3:10)
"A 'Tiny' Pascal Compiler" pp. 34–52 (36–48)

Byte Nov 78 (3:11)
"A 'Tiny' Pascal Compiler" pp. 182–192

Updates: commentary
Byte Jan 79 (4:1)
"Tiny Pascal" p. 168

commentary
Byte Jul 79 (4:7)
" 'Tiny' Pascal in 8080 Assembly Language" pp. 174–175

supplementary program
Byte Jul 79 (4:7)
"A 'Tiny' Pascal Source Creator" pp. 231–232 (231)

Some people claim that PASCAL is the language of the future for personal computers. This may or may not be true, but PASCAL certainly is a *nice* language. This is a set of programs that allow you to run programs in a subset of PASCAL on your computer. The system is broken down into two parts: a "p-compiler" and a "translator." The p-compiler takes source programs in PASCAL and translates them into an intermediate code called "p-code." The translator translates the p-code into 8080 machine language. The translator is not included; you must mail away for it. Also included are several programs in PASCAL. Includes sample runs.

> *Lines:* 658
> *Version:* North Star BASIC (ver. 6, release 3)
> *Hardware:* sequential file device, 8080-based microcomputer
> *Software:* none
> *Non-ANSI:* HP strings, ! (used in place of PRINT), extended IF, FILL, CHAIN, DEF . . . FNEND, %() (used to format printouts), OPEN, CLOSE, READ #, TYP(), ASC(), VAL()

DATA ENTRY

28. Touch Scanner Applications

> *Author:* Steve Ciarcia

> *Source:* *Byte* Aug 78 (3:8)
> "Let Your Fingers Do the Talking" pp. 156–165 (165)
>
> *Byte* Sep 78 (3:9)
> "Let Your Fingers Do the Talking" pp. 94–100 (96–100)

This is a collection of routines designed to demonstrate the capabilities of a noncontact touch scanner. The scanner consists of 32 pairs of infrared light emitting diode transistors and photo transistor receivers arranged around the perimeter of a picture frame. The frame is set up in front of a video display. When you point at something on the video display, you interrupt the light beams, allowing the computer to sense where you are pointing. The BASIC programs demonstrate some very simple applications for such a scanner. One program outputs the coordinates of the point you are touching on the screen. Another simulates the function of a keyboard; as you point at letters, the program "types" them. Includes a sample output.

> *Lines:* 12, 15, 38, 31, 42, 16
> *Version:* Micro Com 8K Zapple BASIC
> *Hardware:* touch scanner, video display
> *Software:* none
> *Non-ANSI:* strings, OUT, INP(), USR(), extended IF, AND()

647. Scratchpad Input Routine

> *Author:* Bob Lurie

> *Source:* *Kilobaud* Nov 78 (23)
> "Special Function Keys Needed" p. 16 (16)

One limitation of BASIC is that the only things you can INPUT are constants. Sometimes you need to do some figuring before you know what number you want to enter. This means you have to do the calculations on a calculator even though you're sitting in front of a high-powered computer. This special number entry routine allows you to stop, do some calculations at the keyboard, then resume the program. Includes a sample run.

> *Lines:* 19
> *Version:* Processor Technology BASIC
> *Hardware:* none
> *Software:* none
> *Non-ANSI:* HP strings, ASC(), VAL(), extended IF

307. Counterfeit Cursor for the PET

> *Author:* Ralph Wells

> *Source:* *Creative Computing* Jan 79 (5:1)
> "How About A 'Counterfeit Cursor' For Your PET?" pp. 60–61 (60)

This section of BASIC code generates a "counterfeit cursor" for your PET computer system. You can use this special cursor to input data based on the position of the cursor. In this way you can "point" at things on the screen, rather than having to input some numerical position.

> *Lines:* 53
> *Version:* PET BASIC
> *Hardware:* PET
> *Software:* none
> *Non-ANSI:* not translatable

679. Keyboard Interrupt Technique for TRS-80 Level I BASIC

> *Author:* Paul Klinger

> *Source:* *Kilobaud Microcomputing* Mar 79 (27)
> "Keyboard Interrupt for the TRS-80" p. 128 (128)

TRS-80 Level I BASIC lacks a keyboard interrupt, making it difficult for it to interact with moving displays. This program demonstrates a technique that you can use to generate such a break. The idea involves using the cursor to blank out a dot on the screen. The program can then check for the dot using the TRS-80 POINT function. The sample program moves a dot around on the screen in response to keys pressed at the keyboard.

Lines:	31
Version:	TRS-80 Level I BASIC
Hardware:	TRS-80
Software:	none
Non-ANSI:	not translatable

56. Data Tablet Input of Three-Dimensional Objects

Author: Richard Blum

Source: *Byte* May 79 (4:5)
"Representing Three-Dimensional Objects in Your Computer" pp. 14–29 (18)

To manipulate the "image" of a three-dimensional object in your computer, you must find a way to input the dimensions of the object into your system. You could measure the object and compute the coordinates by hand. But this is very time-consuming. In some cases, the object may be so large or oddly shaped that it may not be possible to get all of the needed measurements. A better way to generate the desired information is to use a data tablet. You place a drawing or photo on the data tablet and then trace over it with a special "pen." As you move the pen around, the data tablet records the coordinates of the pen. The problem with this technique is that data tablets can only handle two-dimensional objects. This program uses a variation of the data tablet method. You photograph the object from two different positions. You enter these photos with the tablet. The computer can then use the perspective information in the photographs to compute the three-dimensional coordinates of the object. The program requires a machine language interface for the data tablet (not supplied).

Lines:	92
Version:	not given
Hardware:	data tablet, sequential file device
Software:	none
Non-ANSI:	OPEN, CLOSE, PRINT FILE, CALL, extended IF

700. Direct Access to TRS-80 Keyboard

Author: Greg Perry

Source: *Kilobaud Microcomputing* Jun 79 (30)
"Every Key" p. 23 (23)

PEEK statements can be used to access the TRS-80 keyboard directly. This program checks to see if any of the direction arrow keys are being pressed.

Lines:	6
Version:	TRS-80 Level II BASIC
Hardware:	TRS-80
Software:	none
Non-ANSI:	not translatable

70. Data Entry Routine for the Summagraphics Bit Pad

Author: Stephen P. Smith

Source: *Byte* Jul 79 (4:7)
"Graphic Input of Weather Data" pp. 16–30 (26)

Data tablets are devices for inputting graphic data. A map, picture, graph, or other data is placed on the tablet. A stylus is used to trace out the information desired. The data tablet transmits to the computer the coordinates of the stylus as it moves around. The Summagraphics Bit Pad is a data tablet designed for use with personal computers. This routine allows a BASIC program to record data using a Bit Pad.

Lines:	63
Version:	Microsoft 6502 BASIC
Hardware:	Summagraphics Bit Pad
Software:	none
Non-ANSI:	POKE, PEEK(), WAIT, two-letter variables

1111. Inputting Strings With Commas

Author: John Davidson

Source: *Recreational Computing* Sep–Oct 79 (8:2)
"Getting Around 'Extra Ignored' " p. 63 (63)

On most machines, when you INPUT a string with a comma in it, everything beyond the comma is ignored. In such cases, the comma is treated as a separator for entering more than one string at a time (e.g., INPUT A$,B$). If commas were treated as part of the first string, then the computer would never know where the second string started. But if you *want* commas in your input strings, then you'll have to use a technique such as this program demonstrates.

Lines:	8 (plus patch)
Version:	not given
Hardware:	none
Software:	none
Non-ANSI:	strings, GET

385. Single Character Input for the Sorcerer

Author: Eli Cohen

Source: *Creative Computing* Oct 79 (5:10)
"More Sorcerer Feedback" p. 16 (16)

Many home computers have a feature that makes it easy to program real-time games and other programs that require a quick response from the user. The feature is single character input—when you type a character, the program accepts it immediately without waiting for a RETURN. This program loads a machine language subroutine that gives Sorcerer users this valuable ability. A short demo routine shows how a program can use the subroutine.

Lines: 12, 6
Version: Sorcerer BASIC
Hardware: Z80-based microcomputer
Software: none
Non-ANSI: not translatable

451. Digital Image Processing Using a Diablo Printer

Author: Jay C. Bowden and Anna K. Scharschmidt

Source: *Dr. Dobb's Journal of Computer Calisthenics & Orthodontia* Oct 79 (4:9)
"Producing Pictures on Your Computer with a Diablo Printer" pp. 26–29 (28)

Digital image processing is the conversion of pictures into digital form. Once a picture is in digital form you can use your computer to increase the contrast in the picture, or to enhance or alter the picture in other ways. Usually such processing requires an expensive scan converter camera, but this article shows how it can be done with a phototransistor, an analog-to-digital (A/D) converter, and a Diablo-type printer (one that can move in small vertical or horizontal steps). The programs supplied store a digital image and then print it out again. Also included is a homemade circuit and BASIC subroutine to do A/D conversion. Includes sample runs.

Lines: 35, 24, 12
Version: BASIC-E
Hardware: phototransistor, A/D converter, Diablo printer, sequential file device
Software: none
Non-ANSI: strings, FILE, multi-letter variables, extended IF, PRINT #, CLOSE, READ #, ASC(), OUT, INP()

DATABASE SYSTEMS

508. IDMAS Data Base Management System

Author: Peter Reece

Source: *Interface Age* Aug 78 (3:8)
"Complete Data Base Management System" pp. 108–115 (113–115)

One of the most common uses of computers is the manipulation of large amounts of data. One of the most efficient ways to handle data is to use data collections and systems called "data bases." The idea behind data bases is that by standardizing the storage and manipulation of data collections, systems can be generated that are so easy to use that people with no knowledge of computers can use the data. Interactive Data Base Manipulator and Summarizer is such a system. Using IDMAS you can create and maintain a variety of data bases. With the system you can easily add, delete, search, retrieve, store, scan, summarize, display, or change data in a data base. The system uses a table-driven English language parser, so you can create English-like commands to manipulate the data in your data base. Includes a flowchart.

Lines: 570
Version: PDP-10 BASIC
Hardware: random-access file device
Software: none
Non-ANSI: not translatable

1063. IRIS: Database System for the DEC System-10

Author: David E. Toliver

Source: *Personal Computing* Nov 79 (3:11)
"An Interactive Retrieval Information System" pp. 38–50 (43–50)

One of the most powerful tools for maintaining "on-line" data storage systems is the *database management system* (DBMS). With a DBMS you can store, edit, select, and print data without having to write new computer programs to carry out each task. These programs form IRIS, the Interactive Retrieval Information System, a DBMS for the DEC System-10. With this system you can store and retrieve a wide variety of data. Includes a sample run.

Lines; 76, 65, 57, 674
Version: DEC System-10 Dartmouth BASIC
Hardware: random-access file device
Software: none
Non-ANSI: not translatable

DIAGNOSTICS

30. Memory Tester

Author: Russell Adams

Source: *Byte* Oct 78 (3:10)
"Testing Memory in BASIC" pp. 58–60 (58)

Who says computers remember everything perfectly? Yours won't if your memory boards are defective. Use this memory tester to test them out. This program lays down two different patterns of alternating on-off bits in the sections of memory that you specify. It then checks the patterns to see if they have been accepted correctly. The locations of any bad bytes are listed along with the intended contents and the actual contents. Includes a sample run.

Lines: 44
Version: MITS 8K ver. 4.0 BASIC
Hardware: none
Software: none
Non-ANSI: CLEAR, POKE, PEEK(), strings, STR$(), extended IF, two-letter variables

774. Memory Tester

Author: Michael McCann

Source: *Micro* Oct–Nov 78 (7)
"A Memory Test Program for PET" p. 25 (25)

Got some bugs in your computer's memory? Find out with this memory tester. Though designed for the PET, it should be usable on most systems. The program performs such tests as "write all ones," "write all zeros," and "write consecutive integers." You may specify the locations to be tested.

Lines: 80
Version: PET BASIC
Hardware: none
Software: none
Non-ANSI: POKE, PEEK(), CHR$(), extended IF, two-letter variables

440. Memory Tester

Author: Paul Warme

Source: *Dr. Dobb's Journal of Computer Calisthenics & Orthodontia* Nov–Dec 78 (3:10)
"BASEX: A Fast, Compact Interactive Compiler for Microcomputers" pp. 26–31, 39 (29)

Does your computer have a memory like an elephant's? If it doesn't, maybe it has a bad memory board. This program tests RAM memory boards for correct operation. The program writes every possible 8-bit byte into every memory location within a selected region. It then reads back the bytes to see if they were recorded correctly. The locations and values of faulty bytes are printed out. This program is included in an article on a language called BASEX.

Lines: 10
Version: Altair BASIC, ver. 3.2
Hardware: none
Software: none
Non-ANSI: POKE, PEEK()

662. PET Tape Tracer

Author: Gregory Yob

Source: *Kilobaud Microcomputing* Jan 79 (25)
"PET Techniques Explained" pp. 82–86 (85)

If you have been having trouble reading data from a PET data cassette, this program may be able to locate the source of the trouble for you. The program dumps PET data tapes, giving status information about the tapes as it does so. The data on the tape is dumped directly to the screen of the PET by block. Errors such as "short block," "read error," and "checksum error" are noted as they occur. Includes a sample run.

Lines: 36
Version: PET BASIC
Hardware: PET
Software: none
Non-ANSI: not translatable

690. PET Tape Test

Author: Jim Butterfield

Source: *Kilobaud Microcomputing* May 79 (29)
"PET-Pourri" pp. 6–7 (7)

Updates: correction
Kilobaud Microcomputing Jul 79 (31)
"PET-Pourri" pp. 6–7, 129 (129)

One problem that owners of PET computers seem to run into frequently is poor tape head alignment on their machines' cassette tape drives. If the tape head is not properly aligned on your PET, it may be difficult for you to read tapes. This program can help you align the tape head in your system to give you the best possible performance.

Lines: 36
Version: PET BASIC
Hardware: PET
Software: none
Non-ANSI: not translatable

802. Memory Tester

Author: William L. Taylor

Source: *Micro* Jul 79 (14)
"OSI Memory Test in BASIC" p. 29 (29)

If you're ever going to run programs successfully, your computer's memory must be in flawless operating condition. To make sure that it is, you should run a memory testing program from time to time. This memory tester uses only BASIC, so it can be run on computers that don't allow machine language routines. The program writes all possible combinations of bits into each one of the bytes in the area of memory that you select.

Lines: 18
Version: OSI Challenger MicroSoft BASIC
Hardware: none
Software: none
Non-ANSI: POKE, PEEK(), extended IF

723. Printer Test

Author: Ken Barbier

Source: *Kilobaud Microcomputing* Aug 79 (32)
"The Sorcerer Connection" pp. 84–86 (85)

This program uses the OUT statement to output a test string of characters over and over. This can be used to test the functioning of a printer or teletype. Includes a sample output.

Lines: 18
Version: Sorcerer BASIC
Hardware: none
Software: none
Non-ANSI: OUT

725. Memory Tester

Author: Tom Hayek

Source: *Kilobaud Microcomputing* Aug 79 (32)
"PET Wrap-up" pp. 110–112 (111)

This program checks sections of RAM for correct operation. Though designed specifically to test the operation of

an add-on memory for the PET, slight modifications should allow it to test any section of RAM that you desire.

Lines: 15
Version: not given
Hardware: none
Software: none
Non-ANSI: POKE, PEEK( ), extended IF, strings, STR$( )

805. Apple II RS-232 Interface Test

Author: Donald W. Bixby

Source: *Micro* Aug 79 (15)
"Apple II Serial Output Made Simple" pp. 5–8 (5–8)

Updates: correction to assembly language routine
Micro Sep 79 (16)
untitled p. 34 (34)

This program tests an Apple II RS-232 interface and an assembly language driver described in the article. The driver can be used to get printer output from an Apple II system. The interface used by the program is a homemade one described in the *Apple II Reference Manual*.

Lines: 31
Version: Applesoft BASIC
Hardware: 6502-based microcomputer, RS-232 interface (homemade)
Software: 6502 assembly language routine
Non-ANSI: strings, extended IF, CALL, POKE

DISASSEMBLERS

427. 8080 Disassembler

Author: not given

Source: *Dr. Dobb's Journal of Computer Calisthenics & Orthodontial* Nov–Dec 79 (4:10)
"An 8080 Disassembler Written in MITS 3.2 BASIC" pp. 25–29 (25–29)

Updates: modified program for Heath H-8
Dr. Dobb's Journal of Computer Calisthenics & Orthodontia Nov–Dec 79 (4:10)
"An Interactive Heath H-8 Disassembler" pp. 42–45 (43–45)

Debugging a machine language program is a very frustrating task—especially if you don't have the assembly language source from which the code was generated. To make this task a little easier, a disassembler can be used. A disassembler takes machine language and outputs an assembly language translation. This program is a disassembler for 8080 machine language. Using this program, you can debug programs, make patches in binary copies of programs, and find out how programs work. This disassembler disassembles one address at a time. Typing a carriage return causes the program to disassemble the next address. At any time you can jump to another section of RAM. By typing "J" you can follow branching instructions.

Lines: 315
Version: MITS 3.2 BASIC
Hardware: none
Software: none
Non-ANSI: multi-letter variables, strings, ASC(), extended IF, WAIT, PEEK(), AND()

435. 6502 Disassembler

Author: Stephen Smith

Source: Dr. Dobb's Journal of Computer Calisthenics & Orthodontia Jan 78 (3:1)
"Challenging Challenger's ROMs" p. 6 (6)

Updates: correction
Dr. Dobb's Journal of Computer Calisthenics & Orthodontia Mar 78 (3:3)
"6502 Disassembler Fix" p. 3 (3)

correction
Dr. Dobb's Journal of Computer Calisthenics & Orthodontia Aug 78 (3:7)
"Yet Another 6502 Disassembler Fix" p. 39 (39)

The best way to find out how a system works is to dump it out on your terminal. This program can dump the contents of your 6502 system (Ohio Scientific Challenger, Apple, or PET), and give a translation showing the instruction generated by each word of memory. You type in the starting and ending address to dump. The program then produces a listing, by address, of the section of memory you have specified. Each line of the listing shows an address, an instruction mnemonic, and an argument (if any). Includes a sample run.

Lines: 102
Version: OSI Microsoft BASIC
Hardware: none
Software: none
Non-ANSI: PEEK(), strings

609. 8080 Disassembler and Instruction Searcher

Author: Clint Woeltjen

Source: Kilobaud Feb 78 (14)
"Source Listing the Hard Way" pp. 90–95 (90–91, 94–95)

What do you do if your version of BASIC doesn't have a certain feature that you wish? One way to handle the problem is to rewrite a portion of your BASIC interpreter. Here are two programs to help you accomplish such a feat. The first program is a disassembler for 8080 (or similar) machine code. Feed in a starting and ending address, and the program grinds out (as best it can) an assembly language listing of the area of memory that you have specified. You can use this to find out how your BASIC operates, and where it can be changed. The second program is an instruction searching program. It can help you by finding all the instances of a particular instruction occurring in the area that you specify. The article accompanying the programs deals with how to use the programs to decode your BASIC interpreter. The programs can be useful in decoding any machine language program that you might wish. Includes sample runs and flowcharts.

Lines: 108, 99
Version: MITS BASIC Rev. 3.1
Hardware: none
Software: none
Non-ANSI: strings, PEEK(), extended IF, STR$()

437. Z-80 Disassembler with TDL Mnemonics

Author: not given

Source: Dr. Dobb's Journal of Computer Calisthenics & Orthodontia Jun–Jul 78 (3:6)
"A Z-80 Disassembler in TDL 8K BASIC" pp. 42–44 (42–44)

Debugging machine language can be a difficult task if you don't have the source code. Since this is frequently the case when you receive ready-to-run versions of programs, it's nice to have a disassembler around. A disassembler inputs machine language code and then does its best to reconstruct an assembly language translation. Of course, it can't reconstruct program labels or comments, but a disassembler can go a long way toward demystifying a section of machine language code. This disassembler works on Z-80 code. It outputs the code using TDL mnemonics. The machine codes are printed out along with the mnemonics. Includes a sample run.

Lines: 310
Version: TDL 8K BASIC
Hardware: none
Software: none
Non-ANSI: strings, mutli-letter variables, ASC(), extended IF, AND(), SPC(), PEEK(), INP()

766. 6502 Disassembler

Author: Michael J. McCann

Source: Micro Jun–Jul 78 (5)
"A BASIC 6502 Disassembler for Apple and PET" pp. 25–27 (26–27)

Updates: corrections
Micro Aug–Sep 78 (6)
"Microbes" p. 4 (4)

modifications for OSI BASIC
Micro Oct–Nov 78 (7)
"A Suggestion" p. 27 (27)

A disassembler is a program that reads a computer's internal machine (object) code and translates it into symbolic assembler language. Though a disassembler can't recreate the original labels, it can bring you one step closer to understanding what the code does. This disassembler works on 6502 machine language code (used by such computers as the Apple II and the PET). Includes a sample run.

Lines: 85
Version: Commodore BASIC
Hardware: none
Software: none
Non-ANSI: strings, two-letter variables, PEEK()

375. 6502 Machine Code Disassembler

Author: Anthony T. Scarpelli

Source: *Creative Computing* Sep 79 (5:9)
"A 6502 Disassembler In Microsoft BASIC"
pp. 124–129 (129)

The job of a disassembler is to "look" at the machine code stored in a computer and turn it back into an assembly language listing. This disassembler converts 6502 microcomputer code (for a computer such as an Apple II or a PET) that has been previously brought into RAM. You specify the starting address. The program then translates 17 lines at a time, stopping at the end of each "page" until you prompt it to continue. Includes a flowchart.

Lines: 173
Version: Microsoft BASIC
Hardware: none
Software: none
Non-ANSI: extended IF, strings, PEEK(), two-letter variables, AND(), ? (used in place of PRINT), ASC()

453. Interactive 8080 Machine Code Disassembler

Author: Ronald T. Borochoff

Source: *Dr. Dobb's Journal of Computer Calisthenics & Orthodontia* Nov–Dec 79 (4:10)
"An Interactive Heath H-8 Disassembler"
pp. 42–45 (43–45)

Updates: *Dr. Dobb's Journal of Computer Calisthenics & Orthodontia* Mar 80 (5:3)
"Invisible Programmer's Law" p. 45 (45)

If you want to see what's going on inside your computer, you need a disassembler. A disassembler takes the machine code inside a computer and translates it into assembly language. This disassembler works on 8080 machine code. You can disassemble one address at a time or disassemble a whole section of code with one command. When the disassembler reaches a jump instruction, you have the option of continuing on to the next address or branching to the address specified in the jump. This disassembler prints out the memory contents in octal as well as mnemonic form.

Lines: 325
Version: Heath Benton Harbor Extended BASIC
Hardware: none
Software: none
Non-ANSI: extended IF, strings, ASC(), AND(), PEEK(), PIN(), PAUSE

823. 6502 Disassembler

Author: Jack Swindell

Source: *Micro* Dec 79 (19)
"If You Treat It Nicely It Won't Byte" pp. 31–34 (33–34)

A disassembler is a program that takes the machine language inside a computer and translates it into human-readable assembly language. With assembly language, all of the internal machine codes are printed out as three-letter mnemonics, codes which indicate what the instructions do. This disassembler works on 6502 machine language. It prints out listings of the area of memory that you specify. The program uses Rockwell/Sybex mnemonics. The data is also printed out in octal, decimal, hexadecimal, and ascii format. Includes a sample run.

Lines: 126
Version: not given
Hardware: none
Software: none
Non-ANSI: strings, CLEAR, PEEK(), extended IF, STR$()

FILE INDEXES

297. Computer Program and Cassette Tape Indexes

Author: Rod Hallen

Source: *Creative Computing* Nov–Dec 78 (4:6)
"INDXA—A BASIC Routine File Index"
pp. 116–122 (118–121)

Having trouble remembering where you stored that nifty little game program? Maybe you need the help of these indexing programs. The first program indexes programs on a single tape. You merge the programs you want into a single program. Then you add the indexing section. This creates one large program out of a collection of small programs. To access the individual programs, you use the program index provided in the indexing section. Not only do you now have an index, but you also spend less time loading programs from cassettes. The second program is a variation of the first. It provides an index for your tapes. The last program is used to index articles in magazines. Includes sample runs.

Lines: 47 (plus patches), 69, 51
Version: SOL BASIC
Hardware: sequential file device
Software: none
Non-ANSI: CLEAR, extended IF

790. CASSOS Cassette Tape Catalog

Author: Robert Stein, Jr.

Source: *Micro* Apr 79 (11)
"A Cassette Operating System for the Apple II" pp. 21–23 (22–23)

Updates: corrections to assembly language
Micro May 79 (12)
"Microbes" p. 3 (3)

The CASSOS Operating System is a cassette-oriented loader for Apple II programs. This program lists out the contents of CASSOS format tapes. (The article describes CASSOS and has an assembly language listing of it.)

Lines: 22
Version: Apple Integer BASIC
Hardware: sequential file device, 6502-based microcomputer
Software: 6502 assembly language routine
Non-ANSI: not translatable

794. File System for the PET

Author: William Pytlik

Source: *Micro* Jun 79 (13)
"Case of the Missing Tape Counter" pp. 11–12 (12)

The PET is an excellent computer. Its file system leaves something to be desired, though. The problem is that the PET's cassette drive has no tape counter, making it difficult to use the fast forward control to advance quickly to a file. This program takes care of this problem. It provides both a directory of the files on any particular tape and a means to advance rapidly to a desired file.

Lines: 61
Version: PET BASIC
Hardware: PET
Software: none
Non-ANSI: not translatable

817. Tape Indexing System for the PET

Author: Alan R. Hawthorne

Source: *Micro* Nov 79 (18)
"A Tape Indexing System for the PET" pp. 11–13 (12–13)

Because Commodore chose not to include a tape counter on the PET's cassette recorder, finding files on PET tapes can be difficult. This system solves the problem by setting up a tape indexing system. For a given program on tape, the system computes how long it would take to reach the file using *fast forward*. This information is deposited in a tape directory for future reference. When you want to find the program again, you use a USR call to execute a machine language subroutine that this system stores in memory. You then press the fast forward button. When the subroutine determines that the correct amount of time has elapsed, it stops the tape—right at the program that you want.

Lines: 10, 41
Version: PET BASIC
Hardware: PET
Software: none
Non-ANSI: not translatable

FILES

764. PET Files Demo

Author: Charles Floto

Source: *Micro* Feb–Mar 78 (3)
"The PET Vet Tackles Data Files" pp. 9–10 (10)

If you're to do any serious computing work on your computer, you need to know how to read and write data files. This demonstration program shows how to read and write data files on a PET.

Lines: 35
Version: PET BASIC
Hardware: sequential file device
Software: none
Non-ANSI: strings, two-letter variables, FRE(), OPEN,
              CLOSE, PRINT #, GET #, GET, extended
              IF

325. Apple II Disk Files

Author: Carl Swenson

Source: *Creative Computing* Mar 79 (5:3)
              "Disk Power: How to Use It" pp. 124–127
              (125–126)

This group of programs demonstrates the use of Apple II
disk files. Demonstrations of sequential and random-
access files are given.

Lines: 33, 41, 10, 10
Version: Apple Integer BASIC, Applesoft II BASIC
Hardware: random-access file device
Software: none
Non-ANSI: not translatable

1004. File Dumper for North Star BASIC

Author: Ilona Grochalska

Source: *Personal Computing* Mar 79 (3:3)
              "Two Handy Programs in North Star
              BASIC" pp. 32–34 (34)

Paranoia has finally crept into your thoughts. You wrote
out that important data to a file. But how do know that it
was written correctly? Set your mind at ease with this
North Star BASIC file dumper. It reads files (either
string or numerical) and prints them out on your terminal
for you to verify. You can control how fast the information is dumped. Includes a sample run.

Lines: 21
Version: North Star BASIC
Hardware: sequential file device
Software: none
Non-ANSI: not translatable

361. ELECTRIC PENCIL/SOL BASIC File Converters

Author: Rosann Collins, Theodore C. Hines, and
              George Rowan

Source: *Creative Computing* Aug 79 (5:8)
              "Manipulating Pencil Files" pp. 98–99 (99)

ELECTRIC PENCIL is a highly popular text editor. You
can use it to create mailing lists, write reports, or do any
other task that involves manipulating text. Unfortunately, ELECTRIC PENCIL uses files that are not compatible
with SOL BASIC. These two programs convert files between ELECTRIC PENCIL format and SOL BASIC
format. The programs require a monitor (or some other
program) to copy data directly from memory to files and
back.

Lines: 29, 46
Versions: SOL BASIC
Hardware: sequential file device
Software: monitor (see text)
Non-ANSI: PEEK(), POKE, HP strings, DEF . . .
              FNEND, FILE, READ #, PRINT #, CLOSE
              ASC(), extended IF

545. Indexed Sequential Access Method (ISAM) Files for the TRS-80

Author: Phil Slaughter

Source: *Interface Age* Aug–Sep 79 (4:8)
              "Indexed-Sequential Random Files for the
              TRS-80" pp. 60–64 (64)

Most people are familiar with sequential and random-
access files. Another type of file is the indexed sequential
access method (ISAM) file. This type of file uses keys and
pointers to access the data in the file. This program demonstrates how data can be stored on a TRS-80 disk using
ISAM. The program sorts random numbers and then
retrieves the numbers in sorted order. Includes a sample
run.

Lines: 115
Version: TRS-80 DISK BASIC
Hardware: TRS-80, random-access file device
Software: none
Non-ANSI: not translatable

806. PET Cassette I/O Driver

Author: Ronald Smith

Source: *Micro* Aug 79 (15)
              "PET Cassette I/O" p. 19 (19)

Due to a bug in PET BASIC, some early versions of the
PET computer cannot do cassette input/output correctly.
The problem occurs because the PET is not writing long
enough "inter-block gaps." This program demonstrates a
technique for working around this bug.

Lines: 11
Version: PET BASIC
Hardware: PET
Software: none
Non-ANSI: not translatable

449. String Data Compression Program

Author: Graham K. Jenkins

Source: *Dr. Dobb's Journal of Computer Calisthenics & Orthodontia* Sep 79 (4:8)
"A General Purpose Data Compression Program" pp. 16–18, 14 (18, 14)

Updates: correction to article
Dr. Dobb's Journal of Computer Calisthenics & Orthodontia Nov–Dec 79 (4:10)
"Hair Today, Gone Tommorrow" p. 56

The price of computer memory keeps dropping and dropping. But somehow you always seem to need more memory than you can afford. One way to get the most out of the memory that you do have is to "compress" your data. This program compresses string data files so that they take up less space. The program searches through the files you specify and replaces frequently used groups of characters with special symbols. Since the symbols take up less space than the characters that they replace, the files shrink to a fraction of their former size. Note that files so compressed will no longer be acceptable as input to regular programs unless the programs have been modified to accept the new special characters.

Lines: 118
Version: not given
Hardware: two sequential file devices
Software: none
Non-ANSI: FILES, FILE, strings, DELIMIT, SCRATCH, CHANGE, END #(), RESTORE #, PRINT # . . . USING, PRINT #, INPUT #, : (used to specify format for PRINT USING), SST()

162. PET Disk Operations Demo

Author: Chuck Stuart

Source: *Compute* Fall 79 (1)
"Using Direct Access Files with the Commodore 2040 Dual Drive Disk" pp. 93–96 (95)

Updates: continuation of article into 1980
Compute Jan–Feb 80 (2)
"Using Direct Access Files with the Commodore 2040 Dual Drive Disk" pp. 87–89 (89)

The PET 2040 Disk Operating System version 1 does not have true random-access operation. However, this operation can be simulated. This program demonstrates how records can be randomly read and written on a PET disk.

Lines: 49
Version: PET BASIC
Hardware: random-access file device
Software: PET 2040 Disk Operating System
Non-ANSI: not translatable

549. TDL File Saving

Author: William F. Curran

Source: *Interface Age* Oct 79 (4:10)
"Comments on TDL BASIC" p. 14 (14)

This routine demonstrates a technique for saving data in files from TDL BASIC.

Lines: 23
Version: TDL 12K BASIC
Hardware: sequential file device
Software: none
Non-ANSI: not translatable

732. PET Disk Program Loader

Author: Len Lindsay

Source: *Kilobaud Microcomputing* Oct 79 (34)
"PET-Pourri" pp. 16–20, 190 (18)

This automatic program loader makes it easy to load programs off of a PET disk. The program displays the directory of the disk. You type in a character corresponding to the program that you want. The loader then loads the desired program.

Lines: 114
Version: PET BASIC
Hardware: random-access file device
Software: PET DOS 3.1
Non-ANSI: not translatable

737. North Star Disk File Directory Lister

Author: Edwin Milne

Source: *Kilobaud Microcomputing* Oct 79 (34)
"File Directory Analysis for North Star DOS" pp. 116–118 (117–118)

This directory program prints out the contents of North Star DOS disk file directories. The program lists for each file on the disk: the file name, the file type (both numerical code and alphabetic description), the starting address of the file, and the amount of space allocated to the file. The program also prints out a summary of the disk usage. Includes a sample run and a list of program variables.

Lines: 114
Version: North Star BASIC ver. 6, Release 3
Hardware: random-access file device
Software: none
Non-ANSI: HP strings, LINE, OPEN, READ #, CLOSE, extended IF, PRINT #, %() (used to format printouts), TYP(), ASC()

561. Index Sequential (ISAM) File Operations for Apple II

Author: Robert Zant

Source: Interface Age Nov 79 (4:11)
"Index Sequential File Processing on Microcomputers" pp. 102–112 (108–112)

Most programmers are familiar with random-access and sequential files. There is another type of file known as the "index sequential" file. This type of file allows individual records to be retrieved quickly and allows the file to be updated without copying. At the same time, it generally uses much less space than the typical random-access file. With index sequential files, you maintain a directory separate from the main data. This directory contains pointers into a random-access file. Because pointers are used to specify where each record is, the data can be located quickly. This demonstration program provides a set of index sequential file routines. The program lets you store, delete, and list addresses. The file routines can be used by any program that needs ISAM files. Note that the program uses the Apple's *very* peculiar file operations: OPENing, CLOSEing, READing, and WRITEing are performed by PRINTing a control/d followed by the operation.

Lines: 378
Version: Applesoft BASIC
Hardware: random-access file device
Software: none
Non-ANSI: not translatable

FORMATTING

576. Number Rounding Program

Author: Jack Inman

Source: Kilobaud Apr 77 (4)
"Number Rounding Program" pp. 40–41 (40)

This program demonstrates a method for rounding decimal numbers to a specific number of digits of precision. One of the difficulties that most advanced-computer users have with BASIC is BASIC's lack of formatted output (in those versions of BASIC without PRINT USING). You can, however, do some formatting by limiting the number of decimal places that you print. This program walks you through one method for doing this. The program is mostly PRINT statements. Includes a sample run.

Lines: 64
Version: SWTPC 4K BASIC
Hardware: none
Software: none
Non-ANSI: none

31. Formatting Dollars and Cents

Author: Les Palenik

Source: Byte Oct 78 (3:10)
"Formatting Dollars and Cents" p. 68 (68)

Not all BASICs on the market have the PRINT USING statement. This can make it hard to format output from business programs. This subroutine can help out. It accepts a number and outputs it as a "dollars and cents" string. Includes a sample run.

Lines: 32
Version: PET BASIC
Hardware: none
Software: none
Non-ANSI: strings, STR$(), extended IF

49. Dollars and Cents Formatting Subroutine

Author: James Thebeault, Sr.

Source: Byte Apr 79 (4:4)
"Making Cents" p. 8 (8)

Updates: improvements
Byte Sep 79 (4:9)
"Good Cents" p. 150 (150)

correction to update
Byte Jan 80 (5:1)
"Reformatting Dollars and Cents" p. 199 (199)

Many programs for small businesses need to print out dollars and cents figures. This can be a problem in some BASICs that don't have the PRINT USING statement. Normally, most BASICs chop off zeros to the right of the decimal point. But in business programs, you want two of those zeros to mark the "cents" place in printouts. The subroutine accomplishes this function.

Lines: 12
Version: not given
Hardware: none
Software: none
Non-ANSI: strings, STR$(), extended IF

702. Creative Tabulation

Author: Marc Leavey

Source: *Kilobaud Micrcomputing* Jun 79 (30)
"Creative Tabulation" pp. 54–55 (54–55)

Unlike FORTRAN or COBOL, BASIC has only limited facilities built into it for formatting print output. If your version of BASIC has the PRINT USING statement, then you're in reasonably good shape. But if your BASIC doesn't have that statement, then you may find it difficult to get good-looking printouts. This is a special problem in business printouts where a specific format is needed to display dollar amounts. These three programs demonstrate how BASIC's TAB function can be used creatively to get such things as right-justified columns. Includes sample runs.

Lines: 39, 20, 21
Version: SWTPC BASIC
Hardware: none
Software: none
Non-ANSI: DIGITS, LINE, strings, STR$(), extended IF

1037. Right-Justified Number Formatting

Author: Bill Roch

Source: *Personal Computing* Aug 79 (3:8)
"Formatting Numbers in 8K BASIC" pp. 24–26 (25)

Updates: commentary
Personal Computing Nov 79 (3:11)
"Formatting Numbers" p. 7

Does your BASIC have the PRINT USING statement? If it doesn't, you'll have trouble getting reasonably formatted printouts. One way to handle the problem is to do the formatting in your program. This subroutine can do such formatting. It takes a number and converts the number into a right-justified numerical string. It is included in a demonstration program that accepts a number you type in and prints the number out in right-justified format. Includes a flowchart and sample run.

Lines: 58
Version: not given
Hardware: none
Software: none
Non-ANSI: strings, VAL(), STR$(), extended IF

753. Dollar Edit Routine

Author: Michael Donahue

Source: *Kilobaud Microcomputing* Nov 79 (35)
"A BASIC DOLLAR Edit $ubroutine" pp. 162–163 (163)

Printout formatting is almost mandatory for business applications. You may find it difficult to do, however, unless your BASIC has a PRINT USING statement. If it doesn't, you can use this "dollar" editing subroutine to format dollars and cents figures. A short program demonstrates the use of the subroutine. Includes a sample run.

Lines: 60 (plus patch)
Version: SWTP 8K BASIC
Hardware: none
Software: none
Non-ANSI: strings, STR$(), LINE, extended IF

FUNCTIONS

6. How to Calculate Elementary Math Functions

Author: John Rheinstein

Source: *Byte* Aug 77 (2:8)
"Simple Algorithms for Calculating Elementary Functions" pp. 142–145 (145)

This article describes how to implement various math functions in systems that do not have them. The article describes how to write functions in BASIC that will calculate SIN, COS, TAN, EXP, and LOG, as well as several inverse and hyperbolic functions. The example program given calculates TAN and ARCTAN. Included are flowcharts and a sample run.

Lines: 51
Version: MaxiBASIC
Hardware: none
Software: none
Non-ANSI: none

438. Mathematical Functions

Author: Dennis Allison

Source: *Dr. Dobb's Journal of Computer Calisthenics & Orthodontia* Oct 78 (3:9)
"Quick and Dirty Functions for BASIC" pp. 13–15 (13–15)

Updates: correction
*Dr. Dobb's Journal of Computer Calisthenics &
Orthodontia* Jan 79 (4:1)
"We Blew It!" pp. 43, 41 (41)

Not all versions of BASIC have a complete range of
mathematical functions. If you want to implement a program that needs a math function and your BASIC does
not have it, you will have to write the routine in BASIC.
This is a collection of mathematical functions written in
BASIC. The functions supplied are square root, arctangent, sine, cosine, log base 10, and ten to the *x* power.

Lines: 14, 17, 16, 14, 17
Version: UNIX BASIC
Hardware: none
Software: none
Non-ANSI: extended IF

34. Arctangent

Author: Fred Ruckdeschel

Source: *Byte* Nov 78 (3:11)
"Functional Approximations" pp. 34–46
(44)

Updates: correction
Byte Jan 79 (4:1)
"Functional Bug" p. 53

Not all BASICs have the arctangent function. If you need
it and your BASIC does not have it, this program will be
of interest to you. It demonstrates a method for computing the arctangent of a number. The program is contained in an article which gives a general description of
the problems involved in computing trigonometric functions. Includes a sample run.

Lines: 14
Version: North Star BASIC, ver. 6, release 2
Hardware: none
Software: none
Non-ANSI: SQRT(), extended IF

985. LOG and EXP Functions

Author: Laurence Dishman

Source: *Personal Computing* Jan 79 (3:1)
"Log Functions in BASIC" pp. 41–42 (42)

Log to the base *e* (LOG) and exponentiation (EXP) are
among the most useful of the mathematical functions,

because they can be used to calculate many other functions. If your BASIC doesn't have LOG and EXP built in,
you'll want to program these functions in BASIC. This
program computes LOG and EXP using Maclaurin
series. Includes a sample run and a list of program variables.

Lines: 54
Version: Processor Technology BASIC 5
Hardware: none
Software: none
Non-ANSI: extended IF

519. Arctangent

Author: Alfred Adler

Source: *Interface Age* Feb 79 (4:2)
"The Micro-Mathematician" pp. 41–42 (42)

This program demonstrates a technique for computing
the arctangent function in BASICs which do not already
have it. The algorithm used is the same one that is hard-
wired into the Hewlett-Packard line of pocket calculators.
Includes a sample run.

Lines: 22
Version: PolyMorphic BASIC, ver. A00
Hardware: none
Software: none
Non-ANSI: extended IF

45. Arcsine and Arccosine

Author: Alan Miller

Source: *Byte* Mar 79 (4:3)
"Inverse Trig Functions" p. 92 (92)

Updates: improvements
Byte Jun 79 (4:6)
"A Negative Sine" p. 133 (133)

All but the very smallest BASICs have the arctangent
function (ATN). Very few, however, have arcsine or
arccosine. Fortunately, these functions are very easy to
compute if you have the arctangent function. This short
demonstration program shows how to use arctangent to
compute arcsine or arccosine.

Lines: 8
Version: not given
Hardware: none
Software: none
Non-ANSI: none

525. Factorials and Hyperbolic Functions

Author: Alfred Adler

Source: *Interface Age* Apr 79 (4:4)
"The Micro Mathematician" pp. 40–42 (42)

These are demonstrations of how to compute factorials and hyperbolic functions in BASIC. A factorial is an integer multiplied by all the whole numbers less than it. It is denoted by the number followed by an exclamation point. The demonstration program computes the factorial of any number you give it. Hyperbolic functions are based on the equilateral hyperbola. The hyperbolic functions demonstrated include hyperbolic sine, cosine, and tangent, as well as the corresponding inverse hyperbolic functions. Includes a sample run.

Lines: 47
Version: PolyMorphic BASIC ver. A00
Hardware: none
Software: none
Non-ANSI: HP strings, ! (used in place of PRINT), extended if, SQRT()

57. Sine and Arctangent for Tiny BASIC

Author: David Beard

Source: *Byte* May 79 (4:5)
"Spacewar in Tiny BASIC" pp. 110–115 (112–114)

Just because your BASIC has only integers, don't think that you can't compute trigonometric functions. These programs show how to compute sine and arctangent in an integer-only BASIC.

Lines: 11, 6, 30
Version: Tiny BASIC
Hardware: none
Software: none
Non-ANSI: extended IF

447. Ackermann's Function

Author: James Monagan

Source: *Dr. Dobb's Journal of Computer Calisthenics & Orthodontia* May 79 (4:5)
"Goodbye to Ackermann's Function" pp. 48–49 (49)

Ackermann's function is a very strange function. It is usually defined *recursively* (meaning it is a function that calls itself) as:

PROCEDURE ACKERMANN (M,N);
IF M=0 THEN RETURN (N+1)
ELSE IF N=0 THEN RETURN (ACKERMANN (M−1,1))
ELSE RETURN (ACKERMANN (M−1, ACKER-MANN(M,N−1)));
END;

These two programs demonstrate two ways of computing Ackermann's function. One program computes the function recursively; the other does so iteratively. Includes a sample run.

Lines: 32, 34
Version: not given
Hardware: none
Software: none
Non-ANSI: CLEAR, multi-letter variables, DEFINT, PRINT USING, extended IF, FRE(), ' (used in place of REM)

1136. Arcsine and Arccosine Routines

Author: David Eagle

Source: *'68' Micro Journal* Jun 79 (1:4)
"BASIC Programming Quickies" p. 12 (12)

Most BASICs have sine and cosine functions built in (SIN and COS). But very few have the corresponding inverse functions; arcsine and arccosine. These two short subroutines provide these functions.

Lines: 7, 6
Version: SWTPC BASIC, ver. 2.3
Hardware: none
Software: none
Non-ANSI: extended IF, ATAN()

365. Double Precision Functions

Author: Delmar D. Hinrichs

Source: *Creative Computing* Aug 79 (5:8)
"Double Precision: Does Your BASIC Have It? Now It Can . . ." pp. 110–114 (110–111)

One of the major shortcomings of TRS-80 Level II BASIC is that although it has double precision *variables*, it does not have double precision *functions*. If you use any of the built-in functions, you get only a single precision result. The rest of the significant digits just get filled up with garbage. You can get around this by calculating the functions in your program. That is what this program does. As written, the program gives the result of a function you select for an argument that you type in. The subroutines in the program can, however, be adapted for use in any program (and with any extended-precision BASIC). Functions supplied include: square root, sine, cosine, tangent, arctangent, logarithm (natural and base (10), exponential (natural and base 10), and power (y to the x power). The trigonometric functions are given for both degrees and radians.

Lines: 195
Version: TRS-80 Level II BASIC
Hardware: none
Software: none
Non-ANSI: CLS, ' (used in place of REM), DEFDBL, DEFINT, FIX(), two-letter variables, extended IF

389. Hastings-14 Sine Function Approximation

Author: Project Solo

Source: *Creative Computing* Oct 79 (5:10) "Trigonometric Functions and Tchebychev Approximations" pp. 116–119 (119)

Because sine function values cannot be computed directly, computers use polynomial approximations of the sine function. Many different polynomials can be used to generate approximate values for the sine. This program computes the sine function using a variation on a method developed by the mathematician Hastings. The "Hastings-14" sine values are printed up in a comparison table along with the values generated by your BASIC's built-in SIN function. Includes a sample run.

Lines: 16
Version: not given
Hardware: none
Software: none
Non-ANSI: none

412. Hastings-35 Arcsine Function

Author: Project Solo

Source: *Creative Computing* Dec 79 (5:12) "Inverse Circulator Functions" pp. 118–119 (119)

There are many ways to compute the arcsine of a number. This program uses the Hastings-35 method to compute the arcsine of a series of numbers. For comparison, it also prints out the values obtained by using your computer's built-in arcsine function. Includes a sample run.

Lines: 13
Version: not given
Hardware: none
Software: none
Non-ANSI: SQRT(), ARCSIN()

GRAPHICS

For more entries in this category, see specific topics.

23. Color Graphics for the Compucolor 8051

Author: Thomas Dwyer

Source: *Byte* May 78 (3:5) "Color Graphics on the Compucolor 8051" pp. 32–39 (33–35)

This is a group of six programs that demonstrate the color graphics capabilities of the Compucolor 8051. The article describes the Compucolor 8051. The programs include one that draws a sine wave in seven colors, one that draws a chain of random vectors, and one that draws concentric rectangles. Included are samples of the output.

Lines: 6, 6, 13, 13, 9, 11
Version: Compucolor 8051 BASIC
Hardware: Compucolor 8051
Software: none
Non-ANSI: not translatable

284. Demonstration Display for the Merlin Video Interface

Author: Jim Baker

Source: *Creative Computing* Sep–Oct 78 (4:5) "Merlin Video Interface" pp. 52–54 (54)

There are several video interfaces on the computer market these days. These interfaces enable your computer to display graphics on a video screen. One such interface is the Merlin by MiniTerm. This is a demonstration program for the Merlin. It draws perspective "boxes" on your video display. Includes a sample output. Requires assembly language subroutines (not supplied).

Lines: 140
Version: not given
Hardware: Merlin video interface, Z80-based microcomputer
Software: Z80 assembly language routines (not supplied)
Non-ANSI: CALL, POKE, extended IF

974. KEA GraphicAdd Demo

Author: Howard Johnson and Steve Johnson

Source: *Personal Computing* Sep 78 (2:9)
"KEA GraphicAdd" pp. 93–94 (93)

This program demonstrates the ability of the KEA GraphicAdd module. The program plots a modified sine wave. Includes a sample output.

Lines: 16
Version: North Star BASIC ver. 6, Release 3
Hardware: KEA GraphicAdd and associated graphics hardware
Software: graphics driver routine (not supplied)
Non-ANSI: CALL, HP strings

643. Demo Programs for the Cromemco T.V. Dazzler

Author: Jon Rick

Source: *Kilobaud* Oct 78 (22)
"Dazzler and BASIC" pp. 64–71 (68–71)

Cromemco's TV Dazzler is an interface which allows your computer to output color graphics on a TV. These are three demonstration programs which show off the abilities of the Dazzler. The first program plays tic-tac-toe. The second plots trig functions. The third plots polar equations. The programs use interface routines written in assembly language. These routines are discussed in the article. Includes a sample output.

Lines: 130, 26, 24
Version: Imsai 8K BASIC, Processor Technology 5K BASIC
Hardware: Cromemco T.V. Dazzler, 8080-based microcomputer
Software: 8080 assembly language routines
Non-ANSI: CALL, ARG, POKE, extended IF

441. Graphics for the SWTPC GT-6144 T.V. Graphics Board

Author: Joel Swank

Source: *Dr. Dobb's Journal of Computer Calisthenics & Orthodontia* Nov–Dec 78 (3:10)
"Tiny GRAFIX for Tiny BASIC" pp. 32–33 (33)

Tiny GRAFIX is a graphics system for the SWTPC GT-6144 T.V. graphics board. These two programs use this system to plot things on a television screen. The first program graphs an equation of the form $y = f(x)$. You can select the equation you want graphed. The second program plots computer art patterns. Includes a sample output.

Lines: 34, 16
Version: Tiny BASIC
Hardware: SWTPC GT-6144, 6800-based microcomputer
Software: 6800 assembly language routine
Non-ANSI: USR(), PR, extended IF

648. TVT-II Scan Graphics

Author: David Koh

Source: *Kilobaud* Nov 78 (23)
"Raster Scan Graphics for the 6800" pp. 26–32

Kilobaud Dec 78 (24)
"Raster Scan Graphics for the 6800" pp. 56–60 (58)

These two articles describe a modification to the TVT-II video display unit. The modification allows the TVT-II to display raster scan graphics. The program is a demonstration program that plots Lissajous figures on the TVT-II. The heart of the program is a routine that does general graphing using the scan graphics unit. Includes a sample run.

Lines: 63
Version: SWTP 8K BASIC 2.0
Hardware: scan graphics unit
Software: none
Non-ANSI: PEEK(), POKE, extended IF

311. Cursor Control for the Ohio Scientific Superboard II

Author: Randy Heuer

Source: *Creative Computing* Jan 79 (5:1)
"Ohio Scientific Superboard II and Challenger 1P"
pp. 120–122 (121)

This program demonstrates how graphics characters can be moved around on the screen of an Ohio Scientific Superboard II (or its brother, the Challenger 1P). The program moves a "tank" across the screen.

Lines: 28
Version: Ohio Scientific Superboard II BASIC
Hardware: Ohio Scientific Superboard II
Software: none
Non-ANSI: not translatable

1014. Graphing With the TAB Function

Author: R. Tickell

Source: *Personal Computing* Apr 79 (3:4)
"How to Add Graphs to Your Computer Output" pp. 44–48 (44–48)

Just because you don't have a graphics display screen on your computer, don't think that you can't do graphics. You can use BASIC's TAB function to create a surprisingly varied array of graphics. This set of programs shows how you can use the TAB function to produce art, plot mathematical functions, and produce other kinds of displays. Includes sample runs.

Lines: 15, 46, 15, 10, 19
Version: Sperry Univac Series 1100 BASIC
Hardware: none
Software: none
Non-ANSI: MOD(), strings, LINES, FOR (used as a modifier)

343. HIPLOT Digital Plotter Demo

Author: Randy Heuer

Source: *Creative Computing* Jun 79 (5:6)
"HIPLOT Digital Plotter" pp. 28–30 (30)

This program demonstrates the abilities of the HIPLOT digital plotter. The program draws two axes and a sine curve. Includes a sample run.

Lines: 208
Version: not given
Hardware: HIPLOT digital plotter
Software: none
Non-ANSI: strings, multi-letter variables, LPRINT

705. Elimination of "Skip" in Graphics Displays

Author: Wendell Brown

Source: *Kilobaud Microcomputing* Jun 79 (30)
"Vector Graphing Techniques (North Star with Merlin)" pp. 64–66 (64–66)

In graphics displays, *skip* occurs when dots are used to draw continuous curves. Because the dots usually don't cover every point on the curve, there are "gaps" in the line which are referred to as skip. These routines demonstrate

ways to reduce skip. The routines to do the actual plotting are not provided. Includes a sample output.

Lines: 9, 9, 19, 27
Version: North Star BASIC ver. 6.3
Hardware: graphics device
Software: none
Non-ANSI: none

804. OSI Fast Screen Erase

Author: William Taylor

Source: *Micro* Jul 79 (14)
"OSI Fast Screen Erase under BASIC" p. 53 (53)

Clearing the screen of an Ohio Scientific Instruments system by POKEing blanks is a slow process. This program shows how screen clearing can be done quickly using a machine language routine (stored in DATA statements).

Lines: 13
Version: OSI Microsoft BASIC
Hardware: 6502-based microcomputer, OSI display board
Software: none
Non-ANSI: POKE, USR(), extended IF

1106. Atari Color Graphics Demos

Author: Herb Moore

Source: *Recreational Computing* Sep–Oct 79 (8:2)
"See What You Hear & Hear What You See" pp. 32–36 (33–36)

These programs draw various simple patterns to show off the color graphics capabilities of the Atari home computer.

Lines: 6, 4, 4, 5, 4, 6, 9 (plus patches), 10, 10 (plus patch), 11 (plus patches)
Version: Atari BASIC
Hardware: Atari computer
Software: none
Non-ANSI: not translatable

83. LED Graphics Display Demos

Author: Steve Ciarcia

Source: *Byte* Oct 79 (4:10)
"Self-Refreshing LED Graphics Display" pp. 58–69 (68–69)

Updates: corrections to circuits
           Byte Dec 79 (4:12)
           "Some Refreshing Bugs" p. 102

           commentary
           Byte Jun 80 (5:6)
           "Ask Byte" p. 86

One way to display information is to build an array of light-emitting diodes (LEDs). Patterns in the lights can then be used to display various kinds of data. These programs demonstrate the abilities of the homemade LED display discussed in the article. One program flashes the LEDs in sequence. Another displays the word "GO" followed by an arrow. The third program moves the letter "A" across the display. Includes a sample output.

Lines:	26, 13, 32
Version:	not given
Hardware:	LED display (homemade)
Software:	none
Non-ANSI:	OUT, extended IF

734. Direct-Memory-Access (DMA) Video Display/Interface Demo

Author: Dewey Holten and Jerry Boehme

Source: *Kilobaud Microcomputing* Oct 79 (34)
          "Video DMA Interface for SWTP Systems"
          pp. 88–92 (92)

This demonstration program shows how data can be displayed using a direct-memory-access (DMA) video interface; in this case, one designed for use with a Southwest Technical Products Corporation CT-64 terminal and a 6800 computer system. The demo program draws a line curve and axes.

Lines:	52
Version:	not given
Hardware:	direct-memory-access video display
Software:	none
Non-ANSI:	strings, POKE, ASC()

1118. Texas Instruments 99/4 Graphics Demo

Author: Don Inman

Source: *Recreational Computing* Nov–Dec 79 (8:3)
          "Texas Instruments Graphics & Animation"
          pp. 40–43 (43)

With the Texas Instruments 99/4 computer system you can create graphics by defining your own characters. This program demonstrates this procedure by drawing a picture of a "little person."

Lines:	7
Version:	TI BASIC
Hardware:	TI 99/4
Software:	none
Non-ANSI:	not translatable

759. Graphics Scissoring Program

Author: Leonard Kilian

Source: *Kilobaud Microcomputing* Dec 79 (36)
          "The BASICs of Computer Art" pp. 122–126 (124–125)

When you draw something on a video display or plotter, not all of the object may be visible within the "viewing" area. Before the picture can be drawn, those portions of the picture that cross out of the display area must be removed. This process is known as "scissoring." This program scissors an arbitrarily sized display field. The sections of the program that do the actual drawing are not given; you must write them to suit your own system.

Lines:	112
Version:	not given
Hardware:	graphics display or plotter
Software:	none
Non-ANSI:	DIGITS, extended IF

760. Polygon Shading Program

Author: Leonard Kilian

Source: *Kilobaud Microcomputing* Dec 79 (36)
          "The BASICs of Computer Art" pp. 122–126 (124–125)

When drawing a display, you can represent "solid" areas by drawing lines across the areas. If the picture is broken up into small polygons, with the polygons having their lines drawn at differing angles, the effect can be quite dramatic. This program does such shading. The sections of the program that do the actual plotting are not included; you must write them to suit your own system. Includes a sample output. (Note that the program incorporates within it a smaller program from the same article.)

Lines:	182
Version:	not given
Hardware:	graphics display or plotter
Software:	none
Non-ANSI:	DIGITS, extended IF

822. Numeric Display for the Superboard II

Author: Jack Swindell

Source: *Micro* Dec 79 (19)
"If You Treat It Nicely It Won't Byte"
pp. 31–34 (32)

This short routine enables you to display a numerical variable on your Superboard II video monitor while your software is busy generating graphics. A second routine uses the first. The second routine displays numerical variables at any angle that you select.

Lines: 3, 8
Version: not given
Hardware: Superboard II
Software: none
Non-ANSI: strings, POKE, STR$()

826. OSI Challenger C1P Number Graphics Demo

Author: William Taylor

Source: *Micro* Dec 79 (19)
"Graphics and the Challenger 1P" pp. 61–65 (63–65)

This program demonstrates how the OSI Challenger C1P's character generator ROM can be used to display numbers on the C1P's screen. The program displays random numbers.

Lines: 132
Version: Microsoft OSI BASIC
Hardware: OSI Challenger C1P
Software: none
Non-ANSI: POKE, USR(), extended IF

GRAPHICS, THREE-DIMENSIONAL

595. 3-D Computer Graphics

Author: Bruce Artwick

Source: *Kilobaud* Oct 77 (10)
"3D Computer Graphics" pp. 50–56 (55–56)

This is a program to generate 3-D graphics. As written, the program maps 3-dimensional points into a 2-di-

mensional coordinate system. The input is a set of 3-dimensional points. The output is a list of the corresponding 2-dimensional equivalents, ready for plotting. The program can, however, be modified for direct output of the points (and lines generated from the points) to a graphics device such as the Dazzler. The accompanying article describes the problems of generating 3-dimensional graphics. It discusses such topics as transformation, clipping, and projection. This program is a smaller version of a much larger graphics system available from the Sublogic Company. Includes a sample output, a flowchart, and a list of program variables.

Lines: 234
Version: SWTPC 4K BASIC
Hardware: none
Software: none
Non-ANSI: extended IF

22. True 3-Dimensional Displays

Author: Timothy Walters and William Harris

Source: *Byte* May 78 (3:5)
"Graphics in Depth" pp. 16–18, 116–130 (123–128)

These are two programs to produce 3-dimensional images. The article is about a hardware and software system to create true 3-D images. The two sample programs draw a "square spiral" and a "house." Both programs are heavily dependent on the hardware and software discussed in the article. Samples of the program runs are provided.

Lines: 33, 146
Version: MaxiBASIC
Hardware: special graphics hardware, Z-80 microcomputer
Software: Z-80 assembly language routines
Non-ANSI: CALL, HP strings, EXAM, FILL, FREE( ), # (used in place of PRINT), SQRT( ), extended IF

29. 3-D Drawing of a Cup

Author: Joel Hungerford

Source: *Byte* Sep 78 (3:9)
"Graphic Manipulations Using Matrices" pp. 156–165 (164–165)

One interesting application of computer graphics is the drawing of 2-dimensional representations of 3-dimensional objects. The article covers this topic. The program demonstrates 3-D techniques by drawing a cup on a Tektronix 4051 graphics computer with 4662 plotter. The mathematical coordinates generated by the program can be used to generate pictures on whatever graphics device you have available. The sample output given is from a similar but more complicated program.

Lines: 131
Version: Tektronix 4051 BASIC
Hardware: graphics device
Software: none
Non-ANSI: DELETE, PRINT @, MPY( )

357. 3-D Graphics Demo for the Apple II

Author: Richard A. Milewski

Source: *Creative Computing* Jul 79 (5:7)
"Apple-Cart" pp. 116–117

program listing
Creative Computing Sep 79 (5:9)
"Apple Cart 3-D Graphics" p. 17 (17)

Updates: commentary
Creative Computing Sep 79 (5:9)
"Apple 3-D Graphics" p. 14

Remember those old 3-D comic books—the kind that you viewed through cardboard-framed glasses with lenses made of red and green plastic film? Now you can use the same sort of process to create 3-D images using your Apple II. This program produces a demonstration 3-D scene using this technique.

Lines: 37
Version: Apple BASIC
Hardware: Apple II
Software: none
Non-ANSI: not translatable

809. 3-Dimensional Graphics on the PET

Author: John Sherburne

Source: *Micro* Sep 79 (16)
"Plotting A Revolution" pp. 5–10 (5–9)

One of the most impressive (and difficult to program) forms of computer graphics is "3-dimensional" plotting. Trying to display a 3-dimensional function on a computer display can be a very frustrating task. These demonstration programs show off an assembly language routine for the PET computer system. The assembly language routine permits you to do 3-dimensional plotting easily from a BASIC program. The routine even has a provision for removing "hidden" lines in your plots. Includes a sample output.

Lines: 21, 23, 22, 22, 22
Version: PET BASIC
Hardware: PET
Software: 6502 assembly language routine
Non-ANSI: not translatable

84. Plotting Stereoscopic 3-D Images

Author: William T. Powers

Source: *Byte* Oct 79 (4:10)
"The XYZ Phenomenon" pp. 140–149
(144–146)

The stereopticon is an old device used to view "3-dimensional" pictures. The 3-D effect is achieved by viewing two pictures through two different lenses. The two pictures are the same scene photographed from slightly different angles, so when they are viewed together, your brain perceives a 3-dimensional image. This program uses the same effect to create 3-dimensional computer plots. The computer uses a pen plotter to draw line drawings as they would appear from two different viewpoints. You can then view these through lenses (or by crossing your eyes) to see the 3-dimensional figure. As written, the program draws 3-dimensional Lissajous figures. Includes a sample output.

Lines: 97
Version: North Star BASIC
Hardware: plotter
Software: none
Non-ANSI: HP strings, %() (used to format printouts), OUT, extended IF, ASC()

1060. Drawing 3-Dimensional Objects

Author: John W. Ross

Source: *Personal Computing* Nov 79 (3:11)
"Drawing Three-Dimensional Objects" pp. 22–26 (26)

Personal Computing Dec 79 (3:12)
"Drawing Three-Dimensional Objects" pp. 40–47 (46–47)

One of the most fascinating (and frustrating) applications of computer graphics is the drawing of perspective views of 3-D objects. This program makes the creation of such drawings quick and easy. You input a list of vertex coordinates for the object to be drawn. You then specify which vertexes belong on which faces of the object. Finally, you specify a "place" from which to view the object. The computer uses this information to draw a perspective line drawing of your object. A second version of the program adds "hidden line" removal. With this addition, the program can eliminate lines on the back sides of the object where they would not be seen in a real, solid object (the technique used works only for simple, convex objects). Includes sample runs.

Lines: 115, 140
Version: Tektronix 4051 BASIC
Hardware: graphics display
Software: none
Non-ANSI: VIEWPORT, WINDOW, PAGE, DELETE, DRAW, MOVE, strings, MIN(), MAX()

INTERPRETERS

843. PILOT 73 Interpreter

Author: Gregory Yob

Source: *People's Computer Company* Apr 73 (1:4)
"PILOT 73" pp. 11–17 (15–16)

PILOT is an easy-to-learn computer language. It is simple, yet powerful. This PILOT interpreter is written in BASIC. When you run it, your BASIC system becomes a PILOT system, allowing you to edit and run PILOT programs. Because the program is large, it has been broken into three sections: PILOT1, PILOT2, and PILOT3. (PILOT3 is not needed to run the system and is not supplied.) The system CHAINs between the various sections. If you have enough RAM, the sections can be combined into one large program. Includes sample runs.

Lines: 610, 600
Version: HP 2000E BASIC
Hardware: random-access file device
Software: none
Non-ANSI: HP strings, CHAIN, FILES, READ #, PRINT #, END(), MAT operations, multiple-assignment, COM

898. Tiny-PILOT Interpreter in HP-3000 BASIC

Author: Charles Shapiro

Source: *People's Computers* Sep–Oct 77 (6:2)
"A BASIC PILOT" pp. 56–60 (58–60)

BASIC is not the only computer language that's good for beginners—many places use PILOT instead. Here is an interpreter that will enable you to run Tiny-PILOT (a subset of the full PILOT language) using your BASIC system. The program has editing facilities similar to those in BASIC, so you can type in programs in PILOT and run them immediately. Includes a sample run and a list of program variables.

Lines: 157
Version: HP-3000 BASIC
Hardware: none
Software: none
Non-ANSI: HP strings, MAT operations, multiple-assignment, LIN(), ELSE

379. Tiny BASIC Interpreter Written in BASIC

Author: Philip Tubb

Source: *Creative Computing* Sep 79 (5:9)
"Q and A" pp. 162–176 (166–176)

Updates: commentary
Creative Computing Jan 80 (6:1)
"From An 'Interpreter Author'" p. 10

Tiny BASIC is a very limited BASIC which has only a few statements. This is an interpreter written in BASIC which executes Tiny BASIC programs. If you already have regular BASIC, why would you want a Tiny BASIC interpreter? By studying how this program works, you can get an idea of how a regular BASIC interpreter written in machine language works. This interpreter does the things that a machine language interpreter does, but because it's written in BASIC, it's easier to understand.

Lines: 112
Version: Applesoft BASIC
Hardware: none
Software: none
Non-ANSI: multi-letter variables, strings, extended IF, ASC(), NOT(), POP, ON . . . GOSUB

1104. PILOT Interpreter for the Apple II

Author: Arthur Wells, Jr.

Source: *Recreational Computing* Sep–Oct 79 (8:2)
"An Apple PILOT Interpreter" pp. 24–27 (26–27)

PILOT is an easy-to-use computer language. This program allows you to run PILOT programs on your Apple II. The system includes both an editor to help you write and store PILOT programs, and an interpreter section that runs the programs. The program uses Apple BASIC's peculiar way of doing monitor calls by PRINTing control/d followed by the command desired.

Lines: 267
Version: Apple BASIC
Hardware: Apple II
Software: none
Non-ANSI: not translatable

INTERFACING

672. Analog-to-Digital and Digital-to-Analog Conversion

Author: Rod Hallen

Source: *Kilobaud Microcomputing* Mar 79 (27)
"Learn with Me: Analog and Digital Interfaces" pp. 40–44 (42–43)

Most signals in the "real" world are analog; they can vary up and down in a smooth, continuous fashion. Your computer is basically digital; it uses signals that move up or down in discrete steps. Thus, to connect your computer to the real world, you'll need analog-to-digital (A/D) and digital-to-analog (D/A) converters. This article describes the circuits to perform these conversions. Two programs demonstrate two different methods (ramp and successive-approximation) of A/D conversion. A third program demonstrates D/A conversion.

Lines: 10, 17, 12
Version: Processor Technology Extended Cassette BASIC
Hardware: A/D and D/A circuits (homemade)
Software: none
Non-ANSI: OUT, INP(), extended IF

673. PET User Port Demos

Author: Gregory Yob

Source: *Kilobaud Microcomputing* Mar 79 (27)
"PET User Port Cookbook" pp. 62–73 (63–73)

The Commodore PET 2001 computer system has a special user port that you can use to interface your machine with the outside world. This is a collection of programs designed to demonstrate how to use the user port. Among the demonstration programs are ones to do simple input from the port and output to the port, as well as a simple tone generator and a routine to allow you to hook up a keyboard to the port.

Lines: 14 programs ranging from 5 to 63 lines
Version: PET BASIC
Hardware: PET
Software: none
Non-ANSI: not translatable

692. Analog and Digital Interface Demos

Author: Rod Hallen

Source: *Kilobaud Microcomputing* May 79 (29)
"Learn with Me: Analog and Digital Interfaces" pp. 58–64 (58–64)

Computers are basically digital devices. That is, most of their internal signals are restricted to being either "on" or "off." In the outside world, however, most signals are analog. By analog we mean that the signals can vary up or down across a wide range. An example of an analog device is a light with a dimmer switch. The light can be set to be bright, dim, or anything in between. To interface your computer to analog signals, you will need analog-to-digital and digital-to-analog converters. This group of demonstration programs show how your computer can work with analog devices.

Lines: 3, 18, 16, 16, 13, 16, 5, 13
Version: SOL BASIC
Hardware: various homemade electronic circuits
Software: none
Non-ANSI: SET, INP(), PAUSE, extended IF, OUT, CHR()

452. Analog-to-Digital (A/D) Converter

Author: Jay C. Bowden and Anna K. Scharschmidt

Source: *Dr. Dobb's Journal of Computer Calisthenics & Orthodontia* Oct 79 (4:9)
"Producing Pictures on Your Computer with a Diablo Printer" pp. 26–29 (28)

Analog signals are ones that can vary smoothly up and down, such as the voltages in a wall socket. Computers want digital signals; that is, ones that vary up and down in discrete steps. (An analog signal is to a digital signal as a driveway is to a set of steps.) This subroutine drives a homemade analog-to-digital (A/D) converter circuit. With it, you can read in analog signals and convert them to digital form for processing by your computer.

Lines: 12
Version: BASIC-E
Hardware: A/D circuit (homemade)
Software: none
Non-ANSI: OUT, INP()

MACHINE LANGUAGE

869. Machine Language Subroutine Linkage for Altair 8K BASIC

Author: not given

Source: *People's Computer Company* Sep 75 (4:2)
"Altair BASIC" pp. 19–22 (22)

When you require a program which for some reason (speed or special bit handling) must be written in assembly language, you face the task of interfacing such code to your BASIC program. Altair 8K BASIC has a relatively straightforward means built into it for doing such interfacing. This program demonstrates linkage techniques for Altair 8K BASIC. To use machine language, you first use a routine in BASIC to store the assembly language code in memory. You then access the code using a USR function call.

Lines: 35
Version: Altair 8K BASIC
Hardware: none
Software: none
Non-ANSI: POKE, USR()

463. Relative Address Backstepper

Author: J. Huffman

Source: *Interface Age* Dec 76 (2:1)
"Relative Address Backstepper in Micro-Basic" p. 80 (80)

This program is a utility to assist in the writing of assembly language programs. The program takes the number of back-steps that have to be made in a relative address and converts these to hexadecimal form. Includes a sample run and a flowchart.

Lines: 56
Version: SWTPC MicroBASIC
Hardware: none
Software: none
Non-ANSI: extended IF

786. Machine Language Debugger

Author: Jim Zuber

Source: *Micro* Mar 79 (10)
"Using Tiny BASIC to Debug Machine Language Programs" pp. 25–30 (26–27)

Debugging machine language code can be a very frustrating affair. Sometimes the program goes into an endless loop. You sit at the keyboard waiting hopefully for output that never comes. This program can help you debug machine language programs by giving you the ability to trace and modify machine code as it operates. You can have the debugger print out each address that executes, print only those addresses that match a predefined value, or print at specific intervals. Includes a sample run.

Lines: 193
Version: Tiny BASIC
Hardware: none
Software: none
Non-ANSI: extended IF, USR(), PR, GOSUB [computed line number]

538. Program Relocator for Machine Language Code

Author: Alfred Adler

Source: *Interface Age* Jul 79 (4:7)
"The Micro-Mathematician" pp. 24–25 (25)

This program, called RELOCAT, moves machine language code around in memory. Suppose you have a section of machine language code that you'd like to move to somewhere else in memory. If you have a loader or an assembler you could just reload the code. But suppose you don't. This program can copy the program into its new location, saving you a lot of error-prone rekeying. RELOCAT does *not* modify the addressing in the bytes moved, so if the program has any location-dependent addressing, you'll have to change the addressing by hand. Even so, this is still faster than typing in the whole thing again. Includes a sample run.

Lines: 57
Version: PolyMorphic BASIC, ver. A00
Hardware: none
Software: none
Non-ANSI: HP strings, PEEK(), POKE, ! (used in place of PRINT), multiple-assignment, ASC(), extended IF

MEMORY DUMPS/LOADERS

433. Memory Dumper

Author: John Palmer

Source: *Dr. Dobb's Journal of Computer Calisthenics & Orthodontia* Sep 77 (2:8)
"BASIC-Coded Memory Dumper" p. 41 (41)

From time to time, most programmers need to make a quick check of what is in some part of memory. This program can do the job. It prints out the contents of a specified section of RAM. The left-hand margin of the printout gives the addresses in octal, followed by octal data from eight consecutive bytes of memory. The right-hand margin gives the ASCII characters for the same eight memory locations. Non-ASCII values show up as a ".". Carriage returns and line feeds are displayed as "CR" and "LF," respectively. The letters "P," "I," and "O" indicate jump, input, or output instructions. The program also gives you the option of printing out a decimal-format dump of memory.

Lines: 93
Version: MITS 8K BASIC
Hardware: none
Software: none
Non-ANSI: strings, multi-letter variables, STR$( ),
PEEK( ), SPC( ), extended IF

436. Disk and Memory Searcher/Patcher

Author: James Monagan

Source: *Dr. Dobb's Journal of Computer Calisthenics &
Orthodontia* Feb 78 (3:2)
"BASIC Searcher/Patcher" pp. 8–9 (8)

When used in conjunction with a machine language disassembler, this program can help you make patches in machine-language programs. This program can make searches, patches, or perform bootstraps. The searches and patches can be made on either memory or disk. The searches are made by specifying a section to search and a search string. The search string can be either a character string or a hex-format binary string. The search returns the locations of all occurrences of the search string in the area specified. The patch function allows you to make changes in the memory or disk. The patches can be made on successive locations in ASCII, decimal, or hex. The bootstrap function allows you to start execution at any location in memory. Includes a sample run.

Lines: 144
Version: MITS BASIC
Hardware: random-access file device
Software: none
Non-ANSI: not translatable

941. Loading Machine Language from BASIC

Author: John Palmer

Source: *Personal Computing* Mar 78 (2:3)
"Machine Language" pp. 46–47 (47)

Updates: *Personal Computing* Jul 78 (2:7)
"Oops!" p. 8 (8)

BASIC is fine for playing STAR TREK, but if you want to really get into programming, sooner or later you're going to need to use machine language. Many special devices need machine language routines to activate them. Don't fret. You don't need an assembler to load machine language. You can load machine language directly from BASIC. This article and sample programs demonstrate how it can be done. The sample programs operate the interrupt light on an ALTAIR 8800 front panel.

Lines: 24, 8
Version: MITS 8K ALTAIR BASIC REV. 4.3
Hardware: 8080-based microcomputer
Software: 8080 machine language routine
Non-ANSI: strings, VAL(), POKE, USR(), ASC(),
extended IF

773. Machine Language Load and Save for the PET

Author: Gary Creighton

Source: *Micro* Oct–Nov 78 (7)
"PET Update" pp. 13–15 (13–15)

Programming in machine language is a drag. Sometimes, though, you have no choice. In such cases a good compromise is to write your main program in BASIC and then use machine language for the critical functions. These programs enable you to load (and save) machine language in your PET. The first program stores machine language code in RAM (patches to the program allow you to make the code a USR function). The second program is actually machine language stored in DATA statements (to be loaded by the first program). The second program SAVEs machine language on cassette. The third program loads machine language off of cassette.

Lines: 26 (plus patches), 74, 11
Version: PET BASIC
Hardware: PET
Software: none
Non-ANSI: not translatable

1083. POKE Routines for Apple BASIC

Author: Chuck Carpenter and Bob Sander-Cederlof

Source: *Recreational Computing* Mar–Apr 79 (7:5)
"Easy POKEing with Applesoft BASIC" pp.
46–47 (46–47)

It's not always possible to use BASIC to do your programming. Sometimes you have no choice but to use machine language for at least part of a job. These routines can be used to store machine language code in memory for later use. Includes a sample run.

Lines: 21, 18, 23
Version: Applesoft BASIC, Apple Integer BASIC
Hardware: none
Software: none
Non-ANSI: multi-letter variables, strings, ASC(),
extended IF, POKE, CALL, HOME

791. PET Hex Memory Dump

Author: Joseph Donato

Source: *Micro* May 79 (12)
"A PET Hex Dump Program" pp. 13–15
(13–15)

Have you ever wondered what's inside your PET's Read Only Memory (ROM)? Find out with this memory dumping program. It prints out (in hexadecimal format) the contents of PET's ROM memory area. With it you should be able to locate all sorts of interesting tidbits of information about how the PET operates. As written, the program sends its output to a printer. However, a quick patch will allow the program to work on a "bare bones" PET. By changing the starting address, any section of memory can be dumped. Includes a sample run.

Lines: 100 (plus patch)
Version: PET BASIC
Hardware: 6502-based microcomputer
Software: none
Non-ANSI: not translatable

67. Hexadecimal POKE

Author: M. Parris

Source: *Byte* Jun 79 (4:6)
"A Peek at Poke" pp. 212–213 (212)

BASIC is flexible and easy to use. Machine language is fast and efficient. One way you can get the benefits of both is to write your main program in BASIC, but use machine language for the few "critical" parts of the program. This program helps you store machine language into memory. The program accepts bytes in hexadecimal format and stores them. Includes a sample run.

Lines: 21
Version: TRS-80 Level II BASIC
Hardware: none
Software: none
Non-ANSI: CLS, strings, POKE, extended IF, INKEY$(), ASC()

701. Assembly Language Monitor

Author: Rod Hallen

Source: *Kilobaud Microcomputing* Jun 79 (30)
" 'Monitor' " pp. 26–30 (26)

Updates: improvement
Kilobaud Microcomputing Sep 79 (33)
"From 1710 to 1810" p. 21 (21)

BASIC is fine for most computing jobs, but sometimes you may wish (for reasons of speed or flexibility) to use machine language. When running machine code, a virtually indispensable aid is a monitor. A monitor will allow you to load, dump, and execute machine code quickly and easily. With this monitor you can print out desired blocks of memory, enter machine code into memory, execute a routine or program, save a program on cassette tape, or load it back. The monitor is patterned after Processor Technology's SOLOS monitor. Includes a sample run.

Lines: 104
Version: TRS-80 Level II BASIC
Hardware: sequential file device
Software: none
Non-ANSI: strings, CLS, PEEK(), POKE, USR(), extended IF, PRINT #, INPUT #

1041. Hex or Octal Machine Language Loader

Author: Rod Hallen

Source: *Personal Computing* Aug 79 (3:8)
"Let's Have a BALL" pp. 44–49 (47–48)

What happens when you have a machine language routine written in octal that you want to load into your computer? If you have a monitor that accepts octal notation, then you're in luck. But if you don't have a monitor, or if your monitor only accepts hex notation, then what do you do? You could enter the routine using this machine language loader. It accepts machine code in either octal or hex and stores the code in memory. To prevent the code being stored from messing up the BASIC interpreter, the program gives you the option of storing the machine code in one location, and then later moving it to another using a short assembly language routine. Includes a sample run.

Lines: 66
Version: Processor Technology Extended Cassette BASIC
Hardware: 8080-based microcomputer
Software: none
Non-ANSI: CHR(), HP strings, extended IF, POKE, CALL()

1042. Decimal Machine Language Reader/Lister

Author: Rod Hallen

Source: *Personal Computing* Aug 79 (3:8)
"Let's Have a BALL" pp. 44–49 (49)

Machine language routines can be stored in DATA statements in a BASIC program. These routines can then be loaded and used by the program. However, the data in DATA statements must be stored in decimal. So to get the machine language routine into your BASIC program you must first read it from memory and then print it out in decimal form. That is what this program does. Includes a sample run.

Lines: 14
Version: Processor Technology Extended Cassette BASIC
Hardware: none
Software: none
Non-ANSI: SET, PEEK()

450. Memory Dump for 6502 Microcomputers

Author: Gary Ratliff

Source: *Dr. Dobb's Journal of Computer Calisthenics & Orthodontia* Oct 79 (4:9)
"Just Poking Around with my PET" pp. 22–23 (23)

If you want to know what the machine language in your computer looks like, you can dump it out using the PEEK function. Another way to dump memory is to use a machine language subroutine, as this program does. When you run the program you have to type in the decimal values corresponding to the bytes of a machine language subroutine (these are given in the article). The program dumps out memory a "page" at a time.

Lines: 7
Version: PET BASIC
Hardware: 6502-based microcomputer
Software: 6502 machine language subroutine
Non-ANSI: GET, strings, SYS(), POKE

761. Machine Language Monitor for the PET

Author: D. David

Source: *Kilobaud Microcomputing* Dec 79 (36)
"PET's Machine Language Monitor" pp. 134–140 (135–140)

BASIC is fine for most programs, but sometimes you need to add on machine language subroutines to perform special-purpose functions. This monitor for the PET can help you load, debug, and store machine language routines. Includes a sample run.

Lines: 184
Version: PET BASIC
Hardware: 6502-based microcomputer, sequential file device
Software: 6502 assembly language routines
Non-ANSI: not translatable

PET, GRAPHICS

For more entries in this category, see specific topics.

901. PET Uppercase Graphic Characters

Author: Edna Wells

Source: *People's Computers* Jan–Feb 78 (6:4)
untitled p. 7 (7)

The Commodore PET computer uses a special set of graphics characters to do the displays for its video screen. This program prints out a list of those characters and their numerical equivalents.

Lines: 22
Version: PET 8K BASIC
Hardware: PET
Software: none
Non-ANSI: not translatable

156. Simple Animation Program for the PET

Author: Bob Albrecht and Karl Albrecht

Source: *Calculators/Computers Magazine* Jan–Feb 79 (3:1)
"PET BASIC for Parents and Teachers" pp. 54–55 (54–55)

This is a simple animation program for the PET computer system. The program clears the screen of the PET, draws a stretch of "ground," plants a "tree" (the club's symbol), and walks a "dog" (the symbol for *pi*) over to it.

Lines: 33
Version: PET BASIC
Hardware: PET
Software: none
Non-ANSI: not translatable

664. PET Graphics Demo

Author: Len Lindsay

Source: *Kilobaud Microcomputing* Feb 79 (26)
"PET-Pourri" pp. 9–10, 21 (10)

This program demonstrates the PET's graphics capabilities by displaying a "ball" which moves around the screen in response to keys being pressed at the keyboard. A short patch adds sound to the program.

Lines: 68 (plus patch)
Version: PET BASIC
Hardware: PET
Software: none
Non-ANSI: not translatable

342. PET High-Resolution Graphics

Author: Gregory Yob

Source: *Creative Computing* May 79 (5:5)
"Personal Electronic Transactions" pp. 122–127 (123–126)

High-resolution graphics can be done on the PET using its special character set. These programs demonstrate the special uses of the PET's character set.

Lines: 3, 6 (plus patches), 17, 34, 9 (plus patch)
Version: PET BASIC
Hardware: PET
Software: none
Non-ANSI: not translatable

1097. LIST Mode "Ping Pong" Display for the PET

Author: Len Lindsay

Source: *Recreational Computing* Jul–Aug 79 (8:1)
"PET Fun Without Games" pp. 24–26 (26)

One peculiar feature of Commodore's PET computer is that it is possible to use the PET to create displays when you LIST a program. This program demonstrates this feature by displaying a "ping pong" ball (an "*" that moves back and forth across the screen) when the program is LISTed. Patches are provided for 16K/32K PETs.

Lines: 65 (plus patches)
Version: PET 8K BASIC
Hardware: PET
Software: none
Non-ANSI: not translatable

408. Graphics Gizmos for the PET

Author: Gregory Yob, Jack Rossum, Alex Breed, K. Palmistrol

Source: *Creative Computing* Nov 79 (5:11)
"Personal Electronic Transactions" pp. 183–185 (183–185)

This is a collection of short programs which perform neat graphics tricks on a PET. Included are programs that: draw "Navajo rugs," create "wallpaper" patterns, wiggle "worms" around the screen, shower "snow," and draw "icicles."

Lines: various
Version: PET BASIC
Hardware: PET
Software: none
Non-ANSI: not translatable

PET, MISCELLANEOUS

For more entries in this category, see specific topics.

917. Decimal-to-PET Internal Format Number Conversion

Author: Mark Zimmermann

Source: *People's Computers* Sep–Oct 78 (7:2)
"Snooping With Your PET" pp. 16–19 (17)

PET computers store numbers in a special internal format. These are two programs to display and convert PET format numbers. One program converts from decimal to PET format. The other converts back.

Lines: 9, 23
Version: PET BASIC
Hardware: none
Software: none
Non-ANSI: extended IF

660. PET Character Set Demo

Author: Don Ketchum

Source: *Kilobaud Microcomputing* Jan 79 (25)
"Display Your PET!" p. 53 (53)

Commodore's PET 2001 computer system can display 316 different characters in any of 1,000 positions on the display screen. Sixty of the characters can be switched between the standard character set and an extended character set by POKEing a location in memory. This program demonstrates these capabilities.

Lines: 17
Version: PET BASIC
Hardware: PET
Software: none
Non-ANSI: not translatable

671. Automatic PET Line-Erasing Program

Author: Len Lindsay

Source: *Kilobaud Microcomputing* Mar 79 (27)
"PET-Pourri" pp. 9–14 (12)

Do you have a program that you want to run on your PET that almost—but not quite—fits into memory? You might be able to squeeze the program in if you could erase some of the remarks and introductory statements at the start of the program before you declare your arrays. This routine demonstrates how to do this dynamic line erasing. Two versions of the routine are given: a bare-bones version and a version with lots of remarks explaining what's going on.

Lines: 9, 68
Version: PET BASIC
Hardware: none
Software: none
Non-ANSI: not translatable

680. PET Routines to Prevent Line Listing

Author: Len Lindsay

Source: *Kilobaud Microcomputing* Apr 79 (28)
"PET-Pourri" pp. 8–10 (9)

Suppose you have a program on your PET that you would like to be able to loan out to others. You're afraid, however, that they might copy it. How do you loan out the program without losing its secrecy? Curiously enough, there is a way to make PET programs unlistable. These routines and a sample program demonstrate how this can be done. Programs that use this technique can be run, but cannot be listed. It is even possible to make only selected lines "invisible."

Lines: 5, 6, 27
Version: PET BASIC
Hardware: PET
Software: none
Non-ANSI: not translatable

697. PET Line Hider

Author: Len Lindsay

Source: *Kilobaud Microcomputing* Jun 79 (30)
"PET-Pourri" pp. 6–12, 25 (12)

Suppose you have a PET program you want others to be able to RUN, but not to LIST. How do you arrange this? One way is to insert characters into the listing that will cover the program as it is listed. This program lets you place "cover-up" characters into programs.

Lines: 5
Version: PET BASIC
Hardware: PET
Software: none
Non-ANSI: not translatable

699. STOP Key Disable for the PET

Author: Len Lindsay

Source: *Kilobaud Microcomputing* Jun 79 (30)
"PET-Pourri" pp. 6–12, 25 (12)

When running on the PET, it is possible to stop the program by pressing the STOP key. There are times when it is advisable to prevent a user from doing this. This routine, when inserted into your program, will allow you to lock out (and then later reactivate) the STOP key on your PET.

Lines: 6
Version: PET BASIC
Hardware: PET
Software: none
Non-ANSI: not translatable

358. PET "Add-A-Line-To-A-Running-Program" Demos

Author: Gregory Yob

Source: *Creative Computing* Jul 79 (5:7)
"Personal Electronic Transactions" pp. 118–122 (120–122)

With Commodore's PET computer it is possible to enter lines while a program is running by forcing the system to "copy" the lines off of the display screen. This set of demonstration programs shows how this is done. Includes sample runs.

Lines: 28, 17, 16, 13, 5, 9, 8
Version: PET BASIC
Hardware: PET
Software: none
Non-ANSI: not translatable

159. Token Lister for the PET

Author: Harvey B. Herman

Source: *Compute* Fall 79 (1)
"Tokens Aren't Just for Subways—A Convenient Method to List Microsoft BASIC Tokens" pp. 29–30 (29–30)

Most BASIC interpreters do not execute your BASIC programs as soon as you type them in. Usually, an interpreter will convert the keywords (like PRINT, GOTO, etc.) into *tokens*. These tokens are one-byte codes which can be stored more efficiently and executed more quickly than the original ASCII code. This program lists the tokens used in PET BASIC. Includes a sample run.

Lines: 82
Version: PET BASIC
Hardware: none
Software: none
Non-ANSI: not translatable

738. Moving the PET Monitor to High Memory

Author: Kendal T. Rogers

Source: *Kilobaud Microcomputing* Oct 79 (34)
"Beefing Up PET" p. 122 (122)

The PET's monitor is very useful for developing machine language programs. A problem with the monitor is that it normally resides where BASIC code is stored. This means that you can't have both a BASIC program and monitor in memory at the same time. This program solves this problem by moving the monitor to high memory.

Lines: 18
Version: PET 8K BASIC
Hardware: 6502-based microcomputer
Software: PET monitor, 6502 machine language routine
Non-ANSI: not translatable

821. "Shifted" PET Program Saver

Author: not given

Source: *Micro* Dec 79 (19)
"Relocating PET BASIC Programs" pp. 25–27 (27)

By changing various internal pointers, it's possible to store PET programs in other than the usual areas of memory. This article discusses such "shifted" programs. The short program given is used to save the shifted programs on tape. (The program is reprinted from the *Commodore PET Users Newsletter*, Volume 1, Issues 4 and 5.)

Lines: 6
Version: PET BASIC
Hardware: sequential file device
Software: none
Non-ANSI: not translatable

PRINTING

767. Listing Program for the PET

Author: Charles R. Husbands

Source: *Micro* Aug–Sep 78 (6)
"Design of a PET/TTY Interface" pp. 5–9 (7–8)

Updates: corrections to assembly language
Micro Dec 78–Jan 79 (8)
"Microbes" p. 4 (4)

This program allows you to print out a listing of your PET program on a printer attached to your PET with an interface described in the article. The program stores a machine language routine in the PET's second cassette buffer. You use a USR call to activate the routine to do the listing. Includes a flowchart.

Lines: 207
Version: PET BASIC
Hardware: PET
Software: none
Non-ANSI: not translatable

801. Screen Dump to Printer for the Apple II

Author: R. M. Mottola

Source: *Micro* Jul 79 (14)
"Screen Dump to Printer for the Apple II" pp. 27–28 (28)

Updates: modification
Micro Jan 80 (20)
"Microbes and Miscellanea" pp. 39–40 (39)

A very useful feature in a program is an optional screen dump. Such a routine allows you to scan text on the screen. Then, when you find something that interests you, it allows you to dump the material onto your printer. This program demonstrates a routine that allows you to dump whatever is displayed on the screen of your Apple II onto your printer. The subroutine that does the dumping can be removed and used in whatever program you want.

> *Lines:* 48
> *Version:* Apple II Applesoft BASIC
> *Hardware:* Apple II
> *Software:* none
> *Non-ANSI:* not translatable

359. PET Printer Demo

> *Author:* Sol Friedman

> *Source:* *Creative Computing* Aug 79 (5:8)
> "A Printer For Your PET—For Under $300!" pp. 32–35 (34)

The Southwest Technical Products PR-40 printer can be interfaced to a PET to give the PET low-cost hardcopy capability. This program demonstrates how the printer can be used. It prints a copy of itself and a listing of the PR-40 character set on the printer. Includes a sample run.

> *Lines:* 17
> *Version:* PET BASIC
> *Hardware:* none
> *Software:* none
> *Non-ANSI:* not translatable

160. Screen Print Program for the PET

> *Author:* David Malmberg

> *Source:* *Compute* Fall 79 (1)
> "Screen Print Routine" p. 78 (78)

This program is a general utility to print the contents of a PET display screen. The program can handle both upper- and lowercase, as well as graphics and reverse fields. It also takes care of converting the screen printing format to the PET printer format. It can be appended to a program as a subroutine or used as a stand-alone routine.

> *Lines:* 28
> *Version:* PET BASIC
> *Hardware:* PET
> *Software:* none
> *Non-ANSI:* not translatable

91. PET Display Printer

> *Author:* P. K. Govind

> *Source:* *Byte* Nov 79 (4:11)
> "Interfacing the PET to a Line Printer" pp. 98–102 (100)

PRINTSCREEN is a program which takes whatever is displayed on the screen of a PET and outputs it to a printer. The program assumes that a printer has been interfaced to the PET using the 8-bit user port. Includes a flowchart.

> *Lines:* 46
> *Version:* PET BASIC
> *Hardware:* PET
> *Software:* none
> *Non-ANSI:* not translatable

754. Commodore 2022/2023 Printer Demo

> *Author:* Len Lindsay

> *Source:* *Kilobaud Microcomputing* Dec 79 (36)
> "PET-Pourri" pp. 12–16 (12)

Commodore's model 2022 and 2023 printers have impressive arrays of features. They can print boldface, print user-defined characters, and do local editing. This program demonstrates these capabilities. Includes a sample run.

> *Lines:* 33
> *Version:* PET BASIC
> *Hardware:* Commodore 2022/2023 printer
> *Software:* none
> *Non-ANSI:* strings, OPEN, CLOSE, PRINT #, two-letter variables

PROGRAM DEVELOPMENT AIDS

779. Expression-Variable-Keyword Searcher for the PET

> *Author:* Jim Butterfield

> *Source:* *Micro* Dec 78–Jan 79 (8)
> "Inside PET Basic" pp. 39–41 (40)

Updates: corrections
Micro Feb 79 (9)
untitled p. 34 (34)

modifications
Micro Jul 79 (14)
untitled p. 15–16 (15)

Need to search for an expression, variable, or keyword in a PET program? This program can do the job. You load this PET searcher program into memory behind the program that you wish to search (how this is done is described in the article). The searcher program then looks for all occurrences of the "target" in your program.

Lines: 8
Version: PET BASIC
Hardware: none
Software: none
Non-ANSI: not translatable

678. BASIC Variables List

Author: Robert Goff

Source: *Kilobaud Microcomputing* Mar 79 (27)
"Too Many Variables?" pp. 104–105 (104)

One of the problems with BASIC is that in standard BASIC, variable names can be, at most, one letter and one number. Because the variables names are not very descriptive, it can be hard to keep track of what variable does what. This program can help straighten things out. It prints out a check-off list of all the variables that can be used by BASIC—in this case, North Star BASIC. Includes a sample run.

Lines: 45 (plus patch)
Version: North Star BASIC
Hardware: none
Software: none
Non-ANSI: LINE, PRINT #, HP strings

788. Variable and Character String Searcher for Apple Integer BASIC

Author: Alan Hill

Source: *Micro* Apr 79 (11)
"An Apple II Program Edit Aid" pp. 5–7 (5–7)

When working with a large program, you sometimes lose track of things. It's very frustrating to make a change in a variable, only to later find that you forgot about one occurrence of the variable. This program can help you by printing out a list of all occurrences of a variable or character string in your program. To run this searcher, you load it into memory and "hide" it (the article describes how). You then load your own program and run the searcher.

Lines: 14
Version: Apple Integer BASIC
Hardware: 6502-based microcomputer
Software: 6502 assembly language routine
Non-ANSI: not translatable

707. Automatic Generation of DATA Statements

Author: John Stanton

Source: *Kilobaud Microcomputing* Jun 79 (30)
"Data Files for Processor Tech 5K BASIC" pp. 92–94 (92–93)

BASIC's facilities for storing data are extremely limited. You can store data in DATA statements, but these statements must generally be typed in by hand. Now there is a way to automatically generate DATA statements (at least for Processor Technology BASIC). This program takes data and turns it into DATA statements. These statements are then recorded onto cassette. From there, the statements can be added onto another program. Includes a sample run.

Lines: 30
Version: Processor Tech 5K BASIC
Hardware: 8080-based microcomputer, sequential file device
Software: 8080 assembly language routine
Non-ANSI: not translatable

74. "Tiny" Pascal Source Creator

Author: Thomas W. Phillips, M.D.

Source: *Byte* Jul 79 (4:7)
"A 'Tiny' Pascal Source Creator" pp. 231–232 (231)

In the September, October, and November 1978 issues of *Byte*, a compiler for "Tiny" Pascal was printed. This is a very simple-minded editor to create the Pascal source programs for that compiler. The Pascal code is stored in DATA statements in the program. When your Pascal program is completed, the editor writes it out into a file and then CHAINs to the Pascal compiler. Includes a sample run.

Lines: 21
Version: North Star BASIC
Hardware: sequential file device
Software: none
Non-ANSI: HP strings, OPEN, CLOSE, READ #,
WRITE, NOENDMARK(), CHAIN

711. PEEK and POKE Finder for PET BASIC

Author: Len Lindsay

Source: *Kilobaud Microcomputing* Jul 79 (31)
"PET-Pourri" pp. 6–7, 129 (6)

To get the greatest use out of your computer, you sometimes have to make use of those special "bells and whistles" the manufacturers build into their software. In the PET computer system you can do many neat things by PEEKing and POKEing around in memory. The problem comes when you try to move a program with PEEKs and POKEs in it to another system. You find that—phooey—the memory locations in the new system are different from those in the old one. Your bells and whistles sound a sour note. The purpose of this program is to list the line numbers of all the PEEKs and POKEs in a PET BASIC program. Using this program you can (we hope) make the changes necessary to switch your programs between systems.

Lines: 57
Version: PET BASIC
Hardware: PET
Software: none
Non-ANSI: not translatable

548. Flowchart Writer for Zapple BASIC

Author: Alfred S. Baker

Source: *Interface Age* Aug–Sep 79 (4:8)
"Making the Computer Work for You" pp.
121–136 (128–136)

Flowcharts are an excellent aid for helping you to understand the internal logic of a program. But drawing flowcharts is a laborious task, so few nonprofessional programmers bother with them. This program eases the task of drawing a flowchart by letting the computer do the drawing. You specify which boxes are to go where and how they should be interconnected. The computer then prints out the finished flowchart. Includes a sample run.

Lines: 474
Version: Xitan Zapple BASIC
Hardware: Z80-based microcompuer, two sequential
file devices
Software: Zapple monitor, FDOS, Z80 assembly
language routine
Non-ANSI: not translatable

718. Automatic Line-Numbering Aid for the PET

Author: Len Lindsay

Source: *Kilobaud Microcomputing* Aug 79 (32)
"PET-Pourri" pp. 6–12 (12)

You can speed up the entering of BASIC programs on your PET by using this automatic line-numbering program. It automatically provides the line numbers for you as you type.

Lines: 8
Version: PET BASIC
Hardware: PET
Software: none
Non-ANSI: not translatable

815. Available Variable Names List

Author: Henri Reiher

Source: *Micro* Oct 79 (17)
untitled p. 56 (56)

One very annoying feature of BASIC is its very limited number of available variable names. One letter plus one optional digit just doesn't give you much flexibility. This program eases the problem slightly by printing out a list of available variable names, so you can at least keep track of which ones you have already used.

Lines: 17
Version: Kim BASIC
Hardware: none
Software: none
Non-ANSI: strings, CHR(), NUM()

755. PET Program Initializer

Author: Len Lindsay

Source: *Kilbaud Microcomputing* Dec 79 (36)
"PET-Pourri" pp. 12–16 (14)

This PET program can be added on to the start of any program to insure that all proper initiation is done. It does such things as set the PET to either graphics or lowercase mode, clear the screen, and seed the random number generator.

Lines: 37 (plus patches)
Version: PET BASIC
Hardware: none
Software: none
Non-ANSI: not translatable

819. Data Statement Generator for Applesoft BASIC

Author: Virginia Lee Brady

Source: *Micro* Dec 79 (19)
"Data Statement Generator" pp. 5–7 (6)

One flaw in BASIC is the way that it provides for storing data within a program; those DATA statements are cumbersome to enter. One way to get around this problem is to have your program generate its own DATA statements. These statements can then become a permanent part of the program. This program demonstrates a technique for generating DATA statements in Applesoft BASIC.

Lines: 28
Version: Applesoft BASIC
Hardware: none
Software: none
Non-ANSI: not translatable

RENUMBERERS

780. RESEQUENCE for the PET

Author: Jim Butterfield

Source: *Micro* Dec 78–Jan 79 (8)
"Inside PET BASIC" pp. 39–41 (40–41)

Updates: corrections
Micro Feb 79 (9)
untitled p. 34 (34)

modifications
Micro Jul 79 (14)
untitled pp. 15–16 (15)

One problem with BASIC is the "fixed" line numbers that are attached to each line. If you run out of space between two lines when adding code, you have no choice but to retype some of the lines. This usually entails changing GOTO and GOSUB statements in other parts of the program. A better way to shift around lines in a BASIC program is to use an automatic line resequencer. RESEQUENCE is such a program. Its job is to move lines around in a program, changing GOTO and GOSUB references as it does so. This program is used by adding it into memory after your program to be resequenced (how this is done is described in the article).

Lines: 26
Version: PET BASIC
Hardware: none
Software: none
Non-ANSI: not translatable

1001. Line Renumbering for the PET

Author: Mark Zimmermann

Source: *Personal Computing* Mar 79 (3:3)
"Line Renumbering on the PET" pp. 24–29 (27)

Updates: corrections
Personal Computing Jun 79 (3:6)
"Line Renumbering Renumbered" p. 7 (7)

commentary
Personal Computing Jul 79 (3:7)
"Merging on the Challenger" p. 8

modifications for OSI C2 4P
Personal Computing Jul 79 (3:7)
"Line Renumbering on the OSI" p. 9 (9)

commentary, modifications for TRS-80
Personal Computing Nov 79 (3:11)
"TRS-80 Line Renumbering" p. 8

commentary
Personal Computing Jan 80 (4:1)
"POKEing Your PET" p. 6

What could be more frustrating? You've just finished your latest whiz-bang program. Then you find a small error that can be corrected by placing a new line between lines 37 and 38 in your program. It suddenly dawns on you that there is no such line number as "37.5." What do you do? Retype large sections of your code to make room for the patch? No. There's a better way to handle the situation. Use a renumbering program to shift around the lines to make room for the new statement. This program renumbers PET BASIC programs. It keeps track of jumps such as GOTOs and GOSUBs and redirects them to the proper line numbers in the updated program. Includes a flowchart. Also provided is an assembly language version of the same program.

Lines: 30
Version: PET BASIC
Hardware: none
Software: none
Non-ANSI: not translatable

542. TRS-80 Line Renumbering Program

Author: Arlan Dabling

Source: *Interface Age* Aug–Sep 79 (4:8)
"The Column" pp. 14–17 (14–17)

What happens when you want to place a new line between lines 56 and 57 of your BASIC program? Are you forced to retype some of the lines in your program to make room for the new line? This program can "shuffle" around the program lines automatically. As it does so, it keeps track of the GOTOs and GOSUBs and makes the appropriate changes so that the branches will continue to jump to the correct lines. Though designed for use with the TRS-80 disk drive, the program uses only sequential files.

Lines: 31
Version: TRS-80 BASIC
Hardware: two sequential file devices, TRS-80
Software: none
Non-ANSI: not translatable

720. BASIC Renumberer

Author: Adrian R. Thornton

Source: *Kilobaud Microcomputing* Aug 79 (32)
"The BASIC BASIC Renumberer" pp. 58–60 (58–59)

This program renumbers the lines in BASIC programs. It keeps track of all the GOTOs and GOSUBs so that all the branches will come out right in the final program. This renumbering program is designed to work on files in regular "uncompressed" ASCII format. If your computer reduces all of the BASIC keywords to tokens, you won't be able to use this program. Includes a list of program variables and a sample run.

Lines: 134
Version: Heath H8 Extended Cassette BASIC
Hardware: two sequential file devices
Software: none
Non-ANSI: LINE INPUT, strings, CLOSE, MATCH, extended IF, CHAIN, LINE INPUT #, STR$(), PRINT #

810. Applesoft Renumbering Program

Author: J. D. Childress

Source: *Micro* Sep 79 (16)
"Applesoft Renumbering" pp. 15–16 (16)

This is a relatively primitive line renumbering program for Apple II Applesoft BASIC. The program can renumber lines in the range you specify to give you more room to work. Unfortunately, it requires that you make some changes by hand. That's still probably better than doing the whole job by hand.

Lines: 37
Version: Applesoft BASIC
Hardware: none
Software: none
Non-ANSI: not translatable

1057. BASIC Renumbering Program

Author: Charles K. Ballinger

Source: *Personal Computing* Oct 79 (3:10)
"BASIC Renumbering" pp. 44–48 (45–47)

This program renumbers BASIC programs to give you more "space" to add new lines between existing lines. This BASIC renumbering program does not support multiple statements per line. It does not renumber ON . . . GOTO statements (but it does flag them so that you can make the changes by hand). The BASIC programs to be renumbered must be in ASCII and not in the compressed token format that some BASICs such as PET BASIC use. Includes a flowchart.

Lines: 178
Version: Heath HDOS BASIC
Hardware: two sequential file devices
Software: none
Non-ANSI: LINE INPUT, strings, OPEN, CIN(), INPUT #, VAL(), CLOSE, LINE INPUT #, STR$(), MATCH(), PRINT #

SORTING

846. Sorting by Linked-List Insertion

Author: Marc LeBrun

Source: *People's Computer Company* May 73 (1:5)
"The Programmer's Toolbox" p. 22 (22)

One way to sort a list of numbers is to build a linked list. This program demonstrates this sorting method. The program starts with one number. It then takes a larger number and sets a pointer from the smaller number to the larger one. After this, the program takes each number to be sorted and inserts it into the proper place in the list. When all the numbers have been inserted in the list, the numbers are sorted.

Lines: 48
Version: not given
Hardware: none
Software: none
Non-ANSI: none

209. HEAPSORT

Author: Geoffrey Chase

Source: *Creative Computing* Nov–Dec 76 (2:6)
"HEAPSORT" p. 75 (75)

This program demonstrates one of the fastest sorting routines available, Heapsort. This program uses the heapsorting algorithm to sort either numbers or character strings. Heapsort is fairly long compared to other kinds of sorting routines, but it is extremely fast. It is certainly the sort routine of choice for long data lists. Includes a sample run.

Lines: 95
Version: not given
Hardware: none
Software: none
Non-ANSI: strings, ! (used in place of REM), extended IF

210. Comparison of the Bubble, Delayed Replacement, and Shell-Metzner Sorts

Author: John Grillo

Source: *Creative Computing* Nov–Dec 76 (2:6)
"A Comparison of Sorts" pp. 76–80 (79)

One of the standard problems given to students in computer programming classes is, "Sort a group of numbers." Unfortunately, the algorithm usually given is about the worst one available, the infamous bubble sort. This is too bad, since there are many other kinds of sorts that are only slightly more difficult to program, but which are orders of magnitude more efficient. This program and article compare three kinds of sorting algorithms: the bubble sort, the delayed replacement sort (slightly better than the bubble sort), and the Shell-Metzner sort (far superior to the bubble sort). The program tests each of these sorting algorithms for speed. A sort that would take 2.5 hours using the bubble sort takes the Shell-Metzner sort only one minute! Includes flowcharts and a sample run.

Lines: 190
Version: not given
Hardware: sequential file device
Software: none
Non-ANSI: HP strings, multiple-assignment, TIM(), ' (used in place of REM), FILE, SCRATCH, PRINT #

258. Woodrum Sort

Author: Richard Hart

Source: *Creative Computing* Jan–Feb 78 (4:1)
"A New Fast Sorting Algorithm" pp. 96–101 (100–101)

Updates: comments
Creative Computing Sep–Oct 78 (4:5)
"Publish or Perish" pp. 10–12

The speed and efficiency of an internal sorting algorithm is directly related to the number and complexity of the programming steps which are used in its execution. By making certain intelligent comparisons, it is possible to reduce to a minimum the number of comparisons needed. The Woodrum Sort uses this premise to generate a super-fast sorting algorithm. The program presented is one of the fastest sorting algorithms available; it's even faster than the Shell Sort. The article accompanying the BASIC program is written as an allegory about a mouse, a spider, and a forest of binary trees.

Lines: 93
Version: not given
Hardware: none
Software: none
Non-ANSI: multiple-assignment, ! (used in place of REM)

21. Short Sorting Routines

Author: Rene Pittet

Source: *Byte* Apr 78 (3:4)
"Basic Sorts" p. 148 (148)

Updates: bubble sort replaced with insertion sort
Byte Jul 78 (3:7)
"Word of a Better Sort" p. 121 (121)

Computers are frequently used to sort lists of numbers or other forms of data. Here are two simple sorting programs. Both use modified bubble sorts. The first program sorts numbers. The second program sorts character strings into alphabetical order. Includes sample runs.

Lines: 24, 24
Version: SWTPC 8K BASIC
Hardware: none
Software: none
Non-ANSI: strings

623. Name Sort Programs

Author: Richard Roth

Source: *Kilobaud* May 78 (17)
"Strings and Things" pp. 94–98 (97–98)

Updates: improvements, new listing
Kilobaud Aug 78 (20)
"A Better Mailing-List Routine" p. 18 (18)

These are two programs to sort lists of names by last name and first name. They are included in an article describing the differences between HP-type strings and DEC-type strings. The two programs are the same except for the type of string manipulations used. Includes a sample run.

Lines: 56, 44
Version: North Star BASIC Release 2, BASIC-E
Hardware: none
Software: none
Non-ANSI: strings (DEC and HP), extended IF, DEF . . . FNEND

624. Ripple Sort, Bubble Sort, Modified Bubble Sort, and Shell-Metzner Sort

Author: Thomas Doyle

Source: *Kilobaud* May 78 (17)
"5 Minutes or 5 Hours?" pp. 100–102 (101–102)

Updates: correction
Kilobaud Oct 78 (22)
"4220's OK, but . . ." pp. 22–24 (24)

From time to time, most people using computers find that they need to sort some data. The traditional "quickie" method for sorting numbers is the Bubble sort. The problem with the Bubble sort is that for large amounts of data it is very slow. There are many other sorting methods that are much faster. This article compares four types of sorting methods. The programs used are the Ripple sort, the Bubble sort, the Modified Bubble sort, and the Shell-Metzner sort. The SM sort is by far the fastest. Code is also supplied to incorporate each of these methods into the Do-All Program (*Kilobaud*, August 1977). Includes a flowchart and speed comparison.

Lines: 25, 27, 29, 31
Version: MITS 8K BASIC (ver. 3.2)
Hardware: none
Software: none
Non-ANSI: two-letter variables, strings

960. Shell Sort

Author: Robert Irving

Source: *Personal Computing* Jun 78 (2:6)
"Relocatable Routines" pp. 76–77 (76)

Updates: correction
Personal Computing Sep 78 (2:9)
"No-Sort Shell Sort?" p. 6 (6)

improvements
Personal Computing Oct 78 (2:10)
"More Shell Sort" pp. 8–10 (8)

The Shell sort is a fast sorting routine. This version is presented in an article on relocatable routines; that is, routines which may be moved anywhere in a program without renumbering the branch (GOTO) instructions in the program. A version of the routine in "relocatable" form is provided, as well as one in regular BASIC. The sorting routine is stripped down and has no provisions for printing out the sorted numbers.

Lines: 26
Version: not given
Hardware: none
Software: none
Non-ANSI: none

308. Bubble Sort

Author: John Nevison

Source: *Creative Computing* Jan 79 (5:1)
"How to Hide Your BASIC Program" pp. 80–82 (80–82)

Updates: modifications, commentary
Creative Computing May 79 (5:5)
"How to Hide Your BASIC Program Round 2" pp. 72–74 (72–74)

This is a quick and dirty routine to sort a list of numbers into ascending order. The process used is the bubble sort method. The same program is coded seven different ways to show how various styling techniques affect the readability of a program.

Lines: 44, 35, 28, 22, 22, 22, 23
Version: not given
Hardware: none
Software: none
Non-ANSI: none

445. QUICKSORT

Author: Sylvan Rubin

Source: *Dr. Dobb's Journal of Computer Calisthenics & Orthodontia* Mar 79 (4:3)
"Label BASIC" pp. 40, 42 (42)

QUICKSORT is a very fast sorting algorithm. This version of the program is contained in an article on a BASIC preprocessor.

> *Lines:* 26
> *Version:* LABEL-BASIC
> *Hardware:* none
> *Software:* none
> *Non-ANSI:* extended IF

685. Quickie Alphabetization Program

> *Author:* Charles Thomas
>
> *Source:* *Kilobaud Microcomputing* Apr 79 (28)
> "Let's Have Some Order" p. 94 (94)

From time to time you may need a quickie program to alphabetize a list. This program alphabetizes a list that you enter and then prints it out. The program uses the bubble sort method of sorting. Includes a sample run.

> *Lines:* 27 (plus patch)
> *Version:* SWTP 8K BASIC
> *Hardware:* none
> *Software:* none
> *Non-ANSI:* strings, extended IF

686. Shell Sort and Hoare's Quicksort

> *Author:* Steven Harrington
>
> *Source:* *Kilobaud Microcomputing* Apr 79 (28)
> "Quicksort!" pp. 96–98 (96–97)

There are many different ways to sort a list of numbers into numerical order. Each method has its strong points and its weaknesses. Two of the fastest methods are the shell sort and quicksort methods of sorting. Two programs are provided to demonstrate these two ways of sorting. The article discusses the operation of each of these types of sorts.

> *Lines:* 25, 46
> *Version:* not given
> *Hardware:* none
> *Software:* none
> *Non-ANSI:* extended IF

1010. Quicksort Sorting Using Recursion

> *Author:* Herbert Dershem
>
> *Source:* *Personal Computing* Apr 79 (3:4)
> "Recursive Programming in BASIC" pp. 16–18 (18)

Quicksort is a very fast algorithm for sorting a list of numbers. The basic algorithm chooses an arbitrary value from the list of numbers to be sorted. It then rearranges the list so that all the values smaller than the selected number are ahead of it and all the numbers which are larger are behind it. The middle of the list is thus sorted. After this, the upper and lower sections of the list are broken down in the same way until the list is completely sorted. This subroutine demonstrates how quicksort can be implemented using recursion (i.e., the subroutine calls itself).

> *Lines:* 15
> *Version:* Radio Shack Level I BASIC
> *Hardware:* none
> *Software:* none
> *Non-ANSI:* extended IF

796. Shell-Metzner Sort (BASIC and 6502 Assembly Language Versions)

> *Author:* Gary Foote
>
> *Source:* *Micro* Jun 79 (13)
> "Sorting with the APPLE II" pp. 21–26 (22–26)
>
> *Updates:* corrections
> *Micro* Sep 79 (16)
> untitled p. 34 (34)

One of the fastest types of sorting algorithms around is the Shell-Metzner sort. As written, this program uses the Shell-Metzner sort to sort random character strings. Of course, you can separate out the sorting routine and transfer it to your own program. Also provided is a patch that calls an assembly language version of the sort. The assembly language version is much faster than the BASIC version, if less portable.

> *Lines:* 59 (plus patch)
> *Version:* Apple Integer BASIC
> *Hardware:* 6502-based microcomputer
> *Software:* 6502 assembly language routine
> *Non-ANSI:* CALL, HP strings, multiple-assignment, PEEK(), POKE, ASC(), extended IF, multi-letter variables

352. String Sorting Using Sort Keys

> *Author:* Bill Roch
>
> *Source:* *Creative Computing* Jul 79 (5:7)
> "Sorting Simplified: A Keyed String Technique" pp. 78–79 (78)

Updates: corrected listing
Creative Computing Sep 79 (5:9)
"Problems With 'Sorting Simplified' " p. 14
(14)

When sorting records, it's not necessary to sort entire records. Usually it's possible to pick out a subsection of each record (the "sorting key") and just sort using that. At the same time, the subscripts of the records are sorted in the same order as the keys. After the keys have been sorted, the records can be outputted in order according to the subscripts. This program does just that. You type in the records and the specifications for the sorting keys. The program then outputs the records sorted in order, according to the keys. Includes a sample run and a list of program variables.

Lines: 58
Version: not given
Hardware: none
Software; none
Non-ANSI: strings

803. Sorting Subroutine Demonstration

Author: Alan G. Hill

Source: *Micro* Jul 79 (14)
"AMPERSORT" pp. 39–52 (40–49)

Updates: corrections
Micro Sep 79 (16)
"Microbes" p. 34 (34)

modifications and corrections
Micro Nov 79 (18)
"AMPERSORT" p. 45 (45)

It's possible to write a sorting subroutine in BASIC, but such routines are usually agonizingly slow. A faster way to sort the elements in an array is to call a machine language subroutine to do the job. This demonstration program shows off a 6502 assembly language routine that does sorting. The sorting subroutine can sort integer, floating point, or character arrays. Includes a sample run.

Lines: 81
Version: Applesoft BASIC
Hardware: 6502-based microcomputer
Software: 6502 assembly language routine
Non-ANSI: not translatable

1033. List Alphabetizer

Author: Lon Poole and Mary Borchers

Source: *Personal Computing* Jul 79 (3:7)
"Three Practical Programs" pp. 46–50 (49)

This program takes a list of names, phrases, or what have you, and sorts it into alphabetical order. Includes a sample run. (This program is reprinted from *Some Common BASIC Programs.*)

Lines: 38
Version: not given
Hardware: none
Software: none
Non-ANSI: strings

158. Selection, Bubble, and Shell Sorts

Author: Belinda Hulon and Rick Hulon

Source: *Compute* Fall 79 (1)
"Sorting Sorts: A Programming Notebook"
pp. 7–8 (7)

Updates: more sorts
Compute Jan–Feb 80 (2)
"Sorting Sorts: Part 2" pp. 11–16 (12–16)

Sorting lists of things is one of the most common activities that computers are used for. Because sorting takes up so much computer time, it's of more than passing interest to know which types of sorting algorithms are the fastest. This article gives three different sorting algorithms and compares their speeds. The sorts described are the selection sort, the bubble sort, and the shell sort. Includes a list of program variables.

Lines: 9, 12, 16
Version: CBM (PET) BASIC
Hardware: Commodore CBM (PET)
Software: none
Non-ANSI: two-letter variables

STRINGS

1101. Removing Characters From Strings

Author: Bob Albrecht

Source: *Recreational Computing* Jul–Aug 79 (8:1)
"The Programmer's Toolbox" pp. 30–31
(30–31)

From time to time you may want to "squash" certain characters from a string. These two programs remove unwanted characters from input strings. (The subroutines that do removing should be easy to move to your own program.) The first program removes unwanted spaces from strings. The second program removes characters which are not uppercase letters of the alphabet. The listings for these two programs seem to have gotten switched.

> Lines: 15, 13
> Version: not given
> Hardware: none
> Software: none
> Non-ANSI: CLS, strings, multi-letter variables, extended IF, ASC( )

76. String Similarity Comparator

> Author: T. C. O'Haver

> Source: *Byte* Sep 79 (4:9)
> "A Similarity Comparator for Strings" pp. 58–60 (58)

> Updates: version for North Star BASIC
> *Byte* Feb 80 (5:2)
> "String Comparator for Horizon" p. 86 (86)

When you type in answers to your computer, wouldn't it be nice if your computer could accept answers that were *close*, even if they weren't exactly on target? This string comparator program shows how it can be done. The program takes an input string and compares it with a target string. It then prints out a number that indicates how "close" the input string is to the target string. Includes a sample run.

> Lines: 35
> Version: Ohio Scientific Instructions 8K BASIC, ver. 1
> Hardware: none
> Software: none
> Non-ANSI: strings, extended IF

372. Fast String Initialization

> Author: Reginald Gates

> Source: *Creative Computing* Sep 79 (5:9)
> "Helpful Hint for BASIC" p. 6 (6)

This routine demonstrates a fast way to initialize a large string to spaces (or some other character) by concatenating the string with itself repeatedly.

> Lines: 5, 5
> Version: not given
> Hardware: none
> Software: none
> Non-ANSI: HP strings

1110. Remove All But Selected Characters From a String

> Author: Bob Albrecht

> Source: *Recreational Computing* Sep–Oct 79 (8:2)
> "Another String Squeeze" pp. 62–63 (62)

This program demonstrates a subroutine that "squeezes out" all the characters from a string except those characters listed in a master string. The subroutine can be used in other programs. Includes a sample run.

> Lines: 23
> Version: TRS-80 BASIC
> Hardware: none
> Software: none
> Non-ANSI: CLS, multi-letter variables, strings, extended IF

1141. Lowercase to Uppercase Subroutine

> Author: Geoffrey A. Gass

> Source: *'68' Micro Journal* Sep 79 (1:7)
> "BASIC (Not So Quickie)" pp. 29–30 (30)

Suppose you wish to compare two strings to see if they are the same. A regular IF . . . THEN statement is all you need if you can guarantee that both strings will be all uppercase or all lowercase. However, if the characters might be mixed upper- and lowercase you must change the strings to the same case before you can compare them properly. This subroutine takes a string and converts any lowercase characters in it to uppercase so the string can be used in comparisons.

> Lines: 10
> Version: not given
> Hardware: none
> Software: none
> Non-ANSI: strings, ASC(), extended IF

TEXT EDITORS

See *BUSINESS: Word Processing*.

TRACERS

784. Extended TRACE Function for Apple Integer BASIC

> Author: Alan Hill

> Source: *Micro* Mar 79 (10)
> "Apple II Trace List Utility" pp. 9–14 (11–14)

Apple Integer BASIC has a very useful debugging feature known as TRACE. When you run with the TRACE function on, the line numbers of the lines executed are printed out. This allows you to follow the flow of the program as it works. This utility extends the TRACE function by printing out not just the line numbers, but the complete statements. This prevents your having to refer back to the program listing to figure out what's going on. A second version of the utility saves the last 100 lines executed, so you can review the operation of a program after it has stopped. Includes a sample run.

Lines: 19, 12
Version: Apple Integer BASIC
Hardware: Apple II
Software: 6502 assembly language routine
Non-ANSI: not translatable

698. Trace Routine for the PET

Author: Brett Butler

Source: *Kilobaud Microcomputing* Jun 79 (30)
"PET-Pourri" pp. 6–12, 25 (12)

The "trace" feature is a very powerful tool for helping you get those last bugs out of your program. This tracing routine is designed to run on a PET. As a BASIC program is executing, this routine continually lists the line number and command that the PET is executing. In normal mode, the BASIC program runs slow enough for you to watch what's happening. In "fast" mode, the program executes quickly so that you can jump over sections that don't interest you.

Lines: 48
Version: PET BASIC
Hardware: PET
Software: none
Non-ANSI: not translatable

161. Program Tracer for the PET

Author: Brett Butler

Source: *Compute* Fall 79 (1)
"Trace for the PET" pp. 84–85 (84–85)

So you say your program got stuck in a GOTO loop and you sat staring hopefully at the display screen for an hour and a half before you figured out that something was wrong? Can't understand why your new whiz-bang program keeps saying that two and two is five? One way to find out what's going on is to use a program tracer. This program loads a machine language tracer into your PET. The tracer can display each line of your programs as it executes. Two versions of the tracer program are provided: one for 4/8K PETs and one for 16/32K PETs.

Lines: 72, 71
Version: PET BASIC
Hardware: PET
Software: none
Non-ANSI: not translatable

TRANSLATORS

420. Expression Translator

Author: Bill Thompson

Source: *Dr. Dobb's Journal of Computer Calisthenics & Orthodontia* Jun–Jul 76 (1:6)
"An Exercise for Novice Translator Implementors" pp. 11–12 (11–12)

Computers use an internal language all their own. The language that they use, machine language, is not very easy for humans to use. Because of this, easier-to-use "high-level" languages such as BASIC have been created. In order for the computer to run programs written in high-level languages, the programs must first be translated or "compiled" into machine language. This program is a very simple translator to translate arithmetic expressions. It serves as a good exercise for those of you who would like to learn how to write compilers and interpreters. The interpreter that you create is a table-driven one. It can accept assignment statements and arithmetic expressions, including variables. The interpreter can print out the results of expressions on demand. Includes a sample run.

Lines: 135
Version: not given
Hardware: none
Software: none
Non-ANSI: HP strings, DISP, POS(), VAL()

424. BTRANS: Arithmetic Expression Translator

Author: Bill Thompson, modified by Jim Abshire

Source: *Dr. Dobb's Journal of Computer Calisthenics & Orthodontia* Nov–Dec 76 (1:10)
"Arithmetic Expression Evaluator Mod" pp. 52–53 (52–53)

Computers execute machine language. To use high-level languages such as BASIC, a translator is needed. The June–July 1976 issue of *Dr. Dobb's Journal* contains a translator exercise. This is a modification of that program. This program contains improved stack handling and uses DEC strings. Includes a sample run.

Lines: 216
Version: PDP-11 BASIC
Hardware: none
Software: none
Non-ANSI: strings, SEG$(), POS(), VAL(), STR$()

1131. BASIC-to-BASIC Internal Code Translator

Author: Gordon Morrison

Source: *ROM* Feb 78 (1:8)
"Translate!" pp. 84–88 (86–87)

Ever try to switch your programs from one BASIC to another? It can be a frustrating experience. Even if the BASIC that you want to translate to has all the language features you need, you may still have problems. In order to save space and time, most BASIC interpreters condense keywords (such as PRINT and INPUT) into one or two byte tokens. Unfortunately, the tokens are not standardized even within one manufacturer. The token which means PRINT in one BASIC may mean GOTO in another. If you try to read in a program written in BASIC with another interpreter, you may get garbage. This program takes care of this problem by doing token-to-token translations. As written, the program translates MITS 8K BASIC to MITS 8K Extended Disk BASIC. It can, however, be modified for other translations. Includes a flowchart.

Lines: 79
Version: MITS Disk Extended BASIC
Hardware: two sequential file devices
Software: none
Non-ANSI: CLEAR, LINE INPUT, strings, INSTR(), OPEN, CLOSE, LINE INPUT #, PRINT #, EOF(), extended IF

799. Structured BASIC Editor and Pre-Processor

Author: Robert Abrahamson

Source: *Micro* Jul 79 (14)
"Structured BASIC Editor and Pre-processor" pp. 7–14 (8–12)

If BASIC is the only language you've ever programmed in, you're probably not aware of how truly impoverished BASIC is when it comes to control structures. One way to overcome BASIC's limitations is write your program in an extended format and then use a pre-processor to convert

your program back into regular BASIC. This program is a combined line editor and pre-processor for BASIC. It allows you to write programs using such extended statements as DO WHILE, SUBROUTINE, and CASE. You then type the command BASIC and the pre-processor converts your program into regular BASIC statements. Includes a flowchart and sample run.

Lines: 375
Version: Microsoft BASIC
Hardware: sequential file device
Software: none
Non-ANSI: strings, two-letter variables, ASC(), VAL(), STR$(), extended IF

1145. Algebraic-to-Polish Expression Translators

Author: Jack Bryant

Source: '68' *Micro Journal* Nov–Dec 79 (1:9)
"Crunchers Corner" pp. 8–9 (9)

Updates: corrections
'68' *Micro Journal* Mar 80 (2:3)
untitled p. 33 (33)

Most people are familiar with algebraic notation. Algebraic notation uses operators between operands (e.g., $A+B$). Polish notation places operators behind operands (e.g., $AB+$). This program takes algebraic notation expressions and translates them into Polish notation. Two versions of the program are given: one which uses DEC strings and the other which uses HP strings. Includes a flowchart and sample runs.

Lines: 14, 55
Version: TRS-80 Level II BASIC, HP 9830 BASIC
Hardware: none
Software: none
Non-ANSI: [TRS version] CLEAR, DEFINT, strings, extended IF
[HP version] HP strings, multiple-assignment, DISP

TRS-80, GRAPHICS

For more entries in this category, see specific topics.

716. Circle and Spiral Generators

Author: Allan Joffe

Source: *Kilobaud Microcomputing* Jul 79 (31)
"A Circular Handle on Graphics" pp. 76–77 (77)

Two of the basic elements in computer graphics are the circle and the spiral. These programs demonstrate how to create these figures. Includes a sample output.

    Lines: 12, 13 (plus patches)
    Version: TRS-80 Level II BASIC
    Hardware: TRS-80
    Software: none
    Non-ANSI: not translatable

1095. TRS-80 Graphic Figure Creator

    Author: Clyde Farrell

    Source: *Recreational Computing* Jul–Aug 79 (8:1)
                "Don't SET Your Graphics; PRINT Them"
                pp. 16–17 (17)

Graphics displays can be created on the TRS-80 using SET and RESET. But this is a slow process. A faster way to make up a picture is to store the appropriate characters in strings and then PRINT the strings. This program helps you make up such character strings. If you want, you can save on tape the character strings you create. The program can also print out DATA statements containing the values that a program would need to store the figures.

    Lines: 33
    Version: TRS-80 Level II BASIC
    Hardware: TRS-80
    Software: none
    Non-ANSI: not translatable

397. Microsoft TRS-80 Level III BASIC Graphics Demo

    Author: not given
    Source: *Creative Computing* Nov 79 (5:11)
                "TRS-80 Level III BASIC" pp. 42–44 (44)

This demo program shows off Microsoft TRS-80 Level III BASIC's graphics features. It displays a "rocket ship" on the screen of a TRS-80 and makes the rocket ship move across the screen. (Program is reprinted from the Level III Instruction Booklet.)

    Lines: 14
    Version: Microsoft TRS-80 Level III BASIC
    Hardware: TRS-80
    Software: none
    Non-ANSI: not translatable

407. TRS-80 Graphics Character Graphics

    Author: Stephen B. Gray

    Source: *Creative Computing* Nov 79 (5:11)
                "TRS-80 Strings" pp. 178–181 (178–179)

The TRS-80 can display 63 special graphics characters using the ASCII codes 129 through 191. These codes break down a character "cell" into six smaller cells, allowing more detail in a picture. This set of programs demonstrate the uses of these characters. Includes a sample output.

    Lines: 5 (plus patches), 5, 9, 7 (plus patches), 21
                (plus patch)
    Version: TRS-80 Level II BASIC
    Hardware: TRS-80
    Software: none
    Non-ANSI: not translatable

566. TRS-80 High-Resolution Graphics Demo

    Author: Woody Pope

    Source: *Interface Age* Dec 79 (4:12)
                "Using TRS-80 Graphic Codes" pp. 140–141
                (140)

It is possible to display high-resolution graphics on a TRS-80 by PRINTing any of a list of special graphics codes. This program demonstrates a technique for generating and using these codes. The program displays a "robot's" head on the TRS-80's screen.

    Lines: 14
    Version: TRS-80 Level II BASIC
    Hardware: TRS-80
    Software: none
    Non-ANSI: not translatable

TRS-80, MISCELLANEOUS

For more entries in this category, see specific topics.

417. TRS-80 "Key Repeat" Program

    Author: Tahl Milburn

    Source: *Creative Computing* Dec 79 (5:12)
                "TRS-80 Strings" pp. 154–161 (160)

This program causes any key you type to be printed over and over again.

    Lines: 6
    Version: TRS-80 BASIC
    Hardware: TRS-80
    Software: none
    Non-ANSI: not translatable

MISCELLANEOUS

977. Scrolling Text Readout

Author: Karen Wolfe

Source: *Personal Computing* Oct 78 (2:10)
"Scrolling with an Unseen Hand" p. 62 (62)

This program demonstrates how the scrolling rate of your terminal can be adjusted by adding delays to your program. The program prints out a short message.

Lines: 24
Version: North Star BASIC
Hardware: none
Software: none
Non-ANSI: HP strings

517. Suppressing Print Output on an Altair 680

Author: Douglas Jones

Source: *Interface Age* Dec 78 (3:12)
"PEEK and POKE a Total" p. 129 (129)

It is sometimes desirable to suppress print output. This subroutine does the job for Altair 680 BASIC by replacing the BASIC print routine call with NOPs. The subroutine is part of a very short demo program that adds two numbers and prints the total. The numbers are not echoed as they are typed in.

Lines: 15
Version: Altair 680 BASIC
Hardware: 6800-based microcomputer
Software: none
Non-ANSI: not translatable

442. CHAOS Timesharing Demo (Averaging a List of Numbers)

Author: Jeff Levinsky

Source: *Dr. Dobb's Journal of Computer Calisthenics & Orthodontia* Jan 79 (4:1)
"CHAOS" pp. 6–13 (7)

These short programs average a list of numbers. They are included in an article describing the CHAOS timesharing system. Includes sample runs.

Lines: 15, 16
Version: MITS BASIC ver. 4.1
Hardware: sequential file device
Software: CHAOS timesharing system
Non-ANSI: not translatable

313. Character Displays for the PET and SOL Computers

Author: Rod Hallen

Source: *Creative Computing* Feb 79 (5:2)
"PEEKing and POKEing" pp. 34–38 (36–38)

Updates: correction to article
Creative Computing Apr 79 (5:4)
"Octal Code Conversion" p. 11 (11)

corrections
Creative Computing Jul 79 (5:7)
"Picking at 'Peeking and Pokeing' " p. 12 (12)

This is a collection of programs to display characters on the screens of PET and SOL computers. Some of the programs print characters that you specify; others randomly select characters.

Lines: 7, 7, 10, 11, 12, 21
Version: PET BASIC, Processor Technology Extended BASIC
Hardware: PET, SOL
Software: none
Non-ANSI: not translatable

326. Program Condenser

Author: Andrew Nicastro and Daniel Kerns

Source: *Creative Computing* Mar 79 (5:3)
"The Space Saver" pp. 132–147 (136–146)

Updates: correction to article
Creative Computing Jul 79 (5:7)
"Space Saver" p. 12

What do you do when you have a program that you want to run, but don't have enough memory to run it in? Do without? Spend $200 on new memory boards? You may be able to get away with the memory you already have if you have this two-stage program packer. PACKER and PACK2 form a system that condenses programs so they take up less memory. The system removes REMs, squeezes out spaces, and combines multiple statements in a single line. The programs that are produced run exactly like the originals, but take up less room. Includes a sample run and a list of program variables.

Lines: 280, 229
Version: DEC MU BASIC/RT-11
Hardware: sequential file device
Software: none
Non-ANSI: COMMON, OPEN, CLOSE, INPUT #, PRINT #, strings, POS(), SEG$(), TRM$(), VAL(), END #(), CHAIN, extended IF

787. OSI Flasher

Author: Robert Jones

Source: *Micro* Mar 79 (10)
"The OSI Flasher: BASIC-Machine Code Interfacing" pp. 41–42 (41)

This program causes an Ohio Scientific Challenger II to flash a screenful of random characters. It is used as a demonstration of how to access machine code from BASIC.

Lines: 21 (plus patch)
Version: OSI MICROSOFT 8K BASIC
Hardware: Ohio Scientific Challenger II
Software: none
Non-ANSI: POKE, USR()

1003. Program APPENDer for North Star BASIC

Author: Ilona Grochalska

Source: *Personal Computing* Mar 79 (3:3)
"Two Handy Programs in North Star BASIC" pp. 32–34 (33)

One of BASIC's biggest flaws is that it has no provision for loading independent subroutines. You can sidestep this problem by storing subroutines separately from main programs. Then, when you need a copy of a subroutine, use the APPEND command to add the subroutine to your main program. Many BASICs, unfortunately, do not have an APPEND command—or any other facility—for merging two sections of code. This program performs the APPEND function for North Star BASIC. (To complete the appending process, you will need a monitor and a sequential file device.) Includes a sample run.

Lines: 74
Version: North Star BASIC
Hardware: none
Software: none
Non-ANSI: not translatable

1006. Test for Recursive Ability

Author: Herbert Dershem

Source: *Personal Computing* Apr 79 (3:4)
"Recursive Programming in BASIC" pp. 16–18 (16)

A process is recursive if it is defined in terms of itself. In programming, a subroutine is recursive if it calls itself. Recursive subroutines can be used to solve many problems in a simple and elegant fashion. Unfortunately, not all BASICs allow subroutines to call themselves. This program tests BASICs to see if they support recursive subroutine calls.

Lines: 18
Version: Radio Shack Level I BASIC
Hardware: none
Software: none
Non-ANSI: none

73. Manipulating Bits in BASIC

Author: Ralph Owens

Source: *Byte* Jul 79 (4:7)
"BASIC Bit Twiddling" p. 192 (192)

This article and two short demonstration programs show how to manipulate bits and nybbles (groups of four bits) using BASIC. Functions to set or read various combinations of bits in a variable are given.

Lines: 5, 6
Version: not given
Hardware: none
Software: none
Non-ANSI: PEEK(), POKE

717. Hiding Program Author Credit Lines

Author: John Warren

Source: *Kilobaud Microcomputing* Jul 79 (31)
"Red-Handed Credit Grabber" p. 82 (82)

Don't let someone copy your programs and then claim them as his or her own by deleting the credit lines. These short programs demonstrate how to hide your name in your programs.

Lines: 10, 6, 7
Version: not given
Hardware: none
Software: none
Non-ANSI: CLS, strings, ASC()

547. Using the Zapple Monitor from Zapple BASIC

Author: Alfred S. Baker

Source: *Interface Age* Aug–Sep 79 (4:8)
"Making the Computer Work for You" pp. 121–136 (127–133)

These three programs demonstrate some techniques for using the Zapple Monitor from Zapple BASIC. One program shows how multiple disk files can be allocated. Another shows how an assembly language program can be loaded and executed from BASIC. The third uses an assembly language routine to allow printouts wider than the width of the available paper (multiple passes are made through the program with the resulting listings being pasted together to get the needed width).

Lines: 20, 28, 8
Version: Xitan Zapple BASIC
Hardware: Z80-based microcomputer, random-access file device
Software: Z80 assembly language routine, Zapple monitor, FDOS
Non-ANSI: not translatable

812. Screen Wraparound Preventer Routine

Author: Rick Connolly

Source: *Micro* Oct 79 (17)
"Nicer Writer" pp. 5–6 (5–6)

What happens when the text you're printing can't fit on one line? In most computer systems, the end of the text gets cut off and pushed down onto the next line. This can be very annoying if the computer arbitrarily chops some word in half. A better way to handle line "overflows" is to divide the line at some logical point such as between two words. That's what this subroutine does. Instead of splitting up the text at the end of the line, it makes the split at some fairly reasonable place. Includes a list of program variables.

Lines: 32
Version: Apple BASIC
Hardware: none
Software: none
Non-ANSI: strings, HOME, extended IF, HTAB, two-letter variables

816. Real-Time Clock for Disk-Based OSI Systems

Author: Robert T. Kintz

Source: *Micro* Oct 79 (17)
"A Real-Time Clock for OSI Disk Systems" pp. 59–60 (60)

This program uses a quirk in the design of the Ohio Scientific Challenger 470 disk controller to implement a real-time clock function for OSI systems. The article describes how to modify the disk controller to set up the clock interrupts. The program loads a machine language routine that services the clock.

Lines: 49
Version: not given
Hardware: Ohio Scientific Challenger, OSI 470 disk controller (plus homemade modifications)
Software; none
Non-ANSI: POKE, multi-letter variables, strings

402. Double Subscript-to-Single Subscript Translation

Author: James Garon

Source: *Creative Computing* Nov 79 (5:11)
"Double Subscripts Become Single" p. 140 (140)

If your version of BASIC allows only single subscripts, you may be wondering how you can run programs that require double subscripts. These two short programs demonstrate a technique for simulating double subscripts. Includes sample runs.

Lines: 8, 9
Version: not given
Hardware: none
Software: none
Non-ANSI: none

557. SOROC 120 Cursor Addressing Demo

Author: Jon Lindsay

Source: *Interface Age* Nov 79 (4:11)
"The Pathology Bookkeeper" pp. 61–64 (62)

This short program demonstrates the use of cursor addressing on a SOROC 120 terminal.

Lines: 10
Version: Microsoft MBASIC
Hardware: SOROC 120
Software: none
Non-ANSI: CHR$(), extended IF

415. Data "Scrunching" Examples

Author: Gregory Yob

Source: *Creative Computing* Dec 79 (5:12)
"Personal Electronic Transactions" pp.
146–149 (148)

These two programs demonstrate two ways that data can be stored in less space than usual. The first program stores dollars-and-cents amounts using integers, by multiplying the values by 100. The second program uses numerical "weights" to combine several numbers into a single value.

Lines: 17, 13
Version: PET BASIC
Hardware: none
Software: none
Non-ANSI: strings, extended IF

7

APPENDIXES

APPENDIX A

BASIC STATEMENTS AND FUNCTIONS

Below is a listing of BASIC statements, functions, and a few miscellaneous features. The language elements described are: (1) ANSI Minimal BASIC, (2) the "extended" statements and functions found in most advanced BASICs, (3) abbreviations of common BASIC statements, and (4) those features listed in the Non-ANSI sections of the reviews in this book. Functions have been listed separate from other language features.

This is by no means a complete listing of all the statements and functions found in all versions of BASIC. However, it should give you a running start toward determining the meanings of those statements and functions you're not sure about.

Versions of BASIC come and go. Manufacturers add and delete features at will. Some manufacturers are not above even changing the way a statement is used. A statement or function that means one thing in one versions of BASIC may mean something entirely different in another. (Or worse, it may have some *subtle* difference.) It's possible that a statement or function may have a meaning unknown to us. Where we know of more than one meaning, we've listed the possibilities. You'll have to check the program listing to see which definition applies.

STATEMENTS AND SPECIAL FEATURES

Statement or Feature *Probable Meaning(s)*

ARG	Pass an argument to a CALLed subroutine
BASE	Specify whether array numbering starts with zero or one
CALL	Call a subroutine (usually this is a jump to a machine language address)
CHAIN	Load and start another program
CHANGE	(1) Convert a string into an array of ASCII values, or (2) convert a number in string form into a numerical value, or vice-versa

CLEAR	Set all variables to zero
CLICK	Sound a click at the keyboard
CLOAD	(1) Load a program from cassette, or (2) load data from cassette
CLOSE	Close a file
CLR	Set all variables to zero
CLRS	Clear screen
CLS	Clear screen
CMD	Allows output to more than one device
CNTRL	Jump to indicated line when indicated control character is typed at keyboard
COM	Save specified variables in "common" memory when CHAINing
COMMON	Same as COM
CONSOLE	Change primary input/output device
CONVERT	Convert a number in string form to a numerical value, or vice-versa
COPY	Copy screen to printer
CSAVE	(1) Save a program on cassette, or (2) save data on cassette
CURSOR	Move screen cursor to indicated position
D.	Same as DATA
DAT	Same as DATA
DATA	Data storage statement
DEF	Function definition
DEFDBL	Define double-precision variables
DEF . . . FNEND	Multi-statement function
DEFINE FILE	Open a file
DEFINT	Define integer variables
DEFUSR	Define entry address of a machine language subroutine
DELIMIT	Set line delimiter in file
DIGITS	Specify format for printing numbers
DIM	Array definition
DIM #	Set up a file as a "virtual" array
DISP	Display on screen
E.	Same as END
ELSE	Alternate statement to execute when condition of an IF . . . THEN statement is not met
END	Stop execution
ENTER	Timed INPUT statement

ERASE	(1) Delete a file, or (2) delete an array	LET	Assignment (keyword is usually optional)
extended IF	IF statement not in ANSI Minimal BASIC standard form	LIBRARY	Define external library for CALLs
EXIT	Exit from a FOR . . . NEXT loop	LINE	Specify page width
F.	Same as FOR	LINE INPUT	Input an entire line as a single string (even if it has commas in it)
FDEL	Delete a file	LINE INPUT #	LINE INPUT from a file
FILE	Open a file	LINES	Specify number of lines per page
FILES	Open a file	LINPUT	Input an entire line as a single string (even if it has commas in it)
FILL	Store a byte in memory		
FIXED	Specify format for printing numbers	LIST (used as a program statement)	List program statements
FLASH	Flash screen		
FNEND	End of multi-statement DEF	LOAD	(1) Load data from file, or (2) load program
FNRETURN	Return from multi-statement DEF		
FOR (used as a modifier	Execute a statement several times	LOCK	Lock a file to prevent its use by others
FORMAT	Specify printout format	LPRINT	PRINT to a printer
FOR . . . TO . . . STEP	Execution loop	LPRINT USING	Formatted PRINT to a printer
		LWIDTH	Specify page width
G.	Same as GOSUB	MARGIN	Specify page width
GET	(1) Get a character from keyboard, or (2) get a record from a file	MAT INPUT	Input a matrix
		MAT operations	Matrix (MAT) operations
GETSEEK	Locate a record in a random-access file	MAT PRINT	Print a matrix
		MAT READ	Read a matrix from DATA statements
GOS	Same as GOSUB		
GOS.	Same as GOSUB	multi-letter variables	Variable names with more than two characters
GOSUB	Branch to subroutine		
GOSUB [computed line number]	GOSUB to a computed line number	multiple-assignment	Assignment statement which assigns a value to more than one variable
GO SUB	Same as GOSUB	N.	Same as NEXT
GOSUB . . . OF	Same as ON . . . GOSUB	NEX	Same as NEXT
GOT	Same as GOTO	NEXT	End of FOR loop
GOTO	Branch to new statement	NODATA	Go to specified line when data in DATA statements is exhausted
GOTO [computed line number]	GOTO to a computed line number		
GO TO	Same as GOTO	nonstandard strings	Nonstandard strings (strings which are neither HP nor DEC format)
GOTO . . . OF	Same as ON . . . GOTO		
HOME	Clear screen	NULL	Specify number of nulls (ASCII 0) to output after each carriage return
HP strings	Hewlett-Packard format strings		
HTAB	Horizontal tab		
IF END	Specify where to branch when end-of-file is reached	ON END	Specify where to branch when end-of-file is detected
IF . . . G.	Same as IF . . . GOTO	ON ERROR	Used to branch to an error routine when a program error occurs
IF . . . GOT	Same as IF . . . GOTO		
IF . . . GOTO	Conditional branch	ON . . . G.	Same as ON . . . GOTO
IF . . . T.	Same as IF . . . THEN	ON . . . GOSUB	Computed GOSUB
IF . . . THE	Same as IF . . . THEN	ON . . . GOT	Same as ON . . . GOTO
IF . . . THEN	Conditional branch	On . . . GOTO	Computed GOTO
IMAGE	Specify printout format	On . . . THEN GOSUB	Same as ON . . . GOSUB
IN	Same as INPUT		
IN.	Same as INPUT	ON . . . THEN GOTO	Same as ON . . . GOTO
INIT	Initiate system		
INP	Same as INPUT	OPEN	Open a file
INPUT	Input from terminal	OPTION	Set an option
INPUT #	Input from a file	OPTION BASE	Specify whether array numbering starts with zero or one
INPUT:	Input from a file		
INPUT1	INPUT without echoing carriage return (continue on same line after INPUT)	OUT	Output a byte to a port
		P.	Same as PRINT
KILL	Delete a file	P.A.	Same as PRINT AT
L.	Same as LET	PAGE	Clear screen

PAUSE	Temporarily suspend execution
PLOT	Plot a point
POKE	Store a byte in memory
POP	"Forget" last GOSUB
PORT	Set output device for printing
POSITION	Position for file read/write
PR	Same as PRINT
PRECISION	Specify format for printing numbers
PRI	Same as PRINT
PRINT	Output to terminal
PRINT AT	Print starting at specified point on display
PRINT FILE	Print to a file
PRINT statements without the keyword PRINT	Just what it says
PRINT USING	Formatted PRINT
PRINT @	(1) Print starting at specified point on screen, or (2) print to a file
PRINT @ . . . USING	same as PRINT #. . . USING
PRINT #	Print to a file
PRINT # . . . USING	PRINT USING to a file
PRINT:	Print to a file
PUT	Output a record to a file
RAN	Same as RANDOMIZE
RANDOM	Same as RANDOMIZE
RANDOMIZE	Randomize RND function output
REA	Same as READ
REA.	Same as READ
READ	Read data from DATA statements
READ #	Read a record from a file
RECALL	Input data from a file
REM	Remark
REMARK	Remark
RENAME	Rename a file
RES	Same as RESTORE
RESET	(1) Turn off a point on a display, or (2) same as RESTORE, or (3) set file pointer
REST.	Same as RESTORE
RESTOR	Same as RESTORE
RESTORE	Reset READ pointer to first DATA statement
RESTORE [line number]	RESTORE starting at DATA statement on line indicated
RESTORE #	Reset to start of file
RESTORE:	Reset to start of file
RESUME	Resume program after an ON ERROR interruption
RET	Same as RETURN
RET.	Same as RETURN
RETURN	Return from a subroutine
RUN (used as a program statement)	(1) Restart execution at indicated line, or (2) start another program
SAVE (used as a program statement)	Save a copy of the program
SCRATCH	Delete a file

SEARCH	Search a string for occurrences of another string
SELECT	Specify an output device
SET	(1) Plot a point on a display, (2) set a pointer into a file, (3) set display speed, or (4) specify output device
SIGNIFICANCE	Specify format for printing numbers
SLEEP	Temporarily suspend execution
ST.	Same as STOP
STO	Same as STOP
STOP	Stop execution
STOP [print string]	Print a string, then stop execution
STORE	Store data in a file
STRING	Set maximum string length
strings	Digital Equipment Corporation (DEC) format strings
STRSIZ	Set maximum string length
SUB	Define a subroutine
SWAP	Swap contents of two variables
SWITCH	Change to "batch mode" (take input from file instead of from keyboard)
TAB	Space over to column specified
TRACE	Trace execution
two-letter variables	Variable names composed of two alphabetic characters
UNLOCK	Undo a LOCK statement
UPDATE	Change a record in a random-access file
VTAB	Space down from top of screen
WAIT	(1) Temporarily suspend execution, or (2) wait for specified byte to appear at a port
WIDTH	Specify page width
WRITE	(1) Write a record to a file, or (2) formatted print
!	(1) Same as PRINT, or (2) same as REM
'	Same as REM
#	Same as PRINT
:	(1) Same as REM, or (2) specify format for PRINT USING
&	Same as PRINT
;	Same as PRINT
*	Same as REM
?	Same as PRINT

Functions

Function	Probable Meaning(s)
ABS(X)	Absolute value
ACOS(X)	Arccosine
ACS(X)	Arccosine
X AND Y	Logical AND of X and Y
ARG(X)	Pass an argument to a subroutine
ASC(X)	ASCII value of first character in X$
ASCII(X$)	Same as ASC(X$)
ASIN(X)	Arcsine
ASN(X)	Arcsine
ATAN(X)	Same as ATN(X)
ATN(X)	Arctangent
BINAND(X,Y)	Logical AND of X and Y

BINNOT(X)	Logical NOT of X
BINOR(X,Y)	Logical OR of X and Y
BINXOR(X,Y)	Logical exclusive OR (XOR) of X and Y
BRK(X)	Enable/disable "break" key interruptions
CALL(X)	Call user-defined subroutine
CAT(X$,Y$)	Concatenation (joining) of X$ and Y$
CATS(X$,Y$)	Concatenation (joining) of X$ and Y$
CHAR(X)	Same as CHR$(X)
CHAR$(X)	Same as CHR$(X)
CHR(X)	Same as CHR$(X)
CHR$(X)	ASCII character corresponding to X
CIN(X)	Single character input
CLG(X)	Common (base 10) logarithm
CLK(X)	(1) Time of day, or (2) elapsed time
CLK$	Time of day
CLS	Clear screen
COS(X)	Cosine
DATE(X)	Date
END	Write end-of-file mark
END OF	Detect end-of-file
END #X	Detect end-of-file
EOF(X)	Detect end-of-file
EXAM(X)	Contents of memory location X
EXP(X)	Exponential (*e* to the X power)
FIX(X)	Same as INT(X), except negative numbers are rounded up instead of down
FMT(X,Y$)	Output a formatted number
FRE(X$)	Amount of unused string storage space
FREE(X)	Amount of remaining free memory
HEX(X)	Output a byte whose hexadecimal value is X
HEX$(X)	String representation of number whose hexadecimal value is X
INCHAR$(X)	Single character input
INKEY$	Single character input
INP(X)	(1) Input a byte from a port, or (2) same as INT(X)
INSTR(X,Y$,Z$)	Finds first occurrence of Z$ in Y$, starting the search at the Xth character of Y$
INT(X)	Integer (whole number) part of X
LEFT(X$,Y)	Same as LEFT$(X$,Y)
LEFT$(X$,Y)	Left Y characters of X$
LEN(X$)	Length of X$
LIN(X)	Skip X lines
LOG(X)	Natural logarithm
LOG10(X)	Common (base 10) logarithm
LST(X$,Y)	Same as LEFT$(X$,Y)
MATCH(X$,Y$,Z)	Finds first occurrence of Y$ and X$, starting the search at the Zth character of X$
MAT . . . CON	Matrix of all ones
MAT . . . IDN	Identity matrix
MAT . . . INV(X)	Inverse of a matrix
MAT . . . TRN(X)	Transposition of a matrix
MAT . . . ZER	Matrix of all zeros
X MAX Y	The greater of X and Y

MID(X$,Y,Z)	Same as MID$(X$,Y,Z)
MID$(X$,Y,Z)	Part of X$ starting at Yth character, and Z characters long
X MIN Y	The lesser of X and Y
X MOD Y	The remainder of X divided by Y
X MPY Y	Matrix multiply
NDX(X$,Y$)	Finds first occurrence of Y$ in X$
NOENDMARK	Causes end-of-file mark to be omitted when writing a record
NOT X	Logical NOT of X
NUM(X)	Same as STR$(X)
NUM$(X)	Same as STR$(X)
X OR Y	Logical OR of X and Y
PDL(X)	Get control paddle setting
PEEK(X)	Contents of memory location X
PI	The value *pi* (3.14159 . . .)
PIN(X)	Single byte input from a port
POS(X)	Current printing position
POS(X$,Y$,Z)	Finds the first occurrence of Y$ in X$, starting the search at the Zth character of X$
PRC(X)	Print X spaces
RAD(X)	Converts degrees to radians
RIGHT(X$,Y)	Right-hand part of X$, starting with the Yth character (not the same as RIGHT$(X$,Y)!)
RIGHT$(X$,Y)	Right Y characters of X$
RND	Returns a random number
RND(X)	Returns a random number
SEG$(X$,Y,Z)	Portion of X$ from the Yth character (not the same as MID$(X$,Y,Z)!)
SGN(X)	Sign of X
SIN(X)	Sine
SKP(X)	Skip X lines
SPA(X)	Space over X spaces
SPACE$(X)	Returns X spaces
SPC(X)	Space over X spaces
SQR(X)	Square root
SQRT(X)	Same as SQR(X)
SST(X$,Y,Z)	Same as MID$(X$,Y,Z)
STR(X)	Same as STR$(X)
STR$(X)	String representation of X
STRING$(X,Y)	Produces a string X long of ASCII character Y
STRING$(X,Y$)	Produces a string of Y$ repeated X times
SUB(X$,Y)	Yth character of X$
SUBSTR(X$,Y,Z)	Same as MID$(X$,Y,Z)
SYS(X)	Call a system function
T.(X)	Same as TAB(X)
TAB(X)	Space to column X
TAN(X)	Tangent
TI	Elapsed time
TI$	Time of day
TIM	Elapsed time
TIME(X)	Elapsed time
TIME$	Time of day
TRM$(X$)	Trims off trailing blanks
TYP(X)	Data type of data in next file record (0=end-of-file)
TYP(X,Y$)	Status of file

UPS$(X$)	Convert lowercase characters in X$ to uppercase
USER(X)	Call user-defined function (usually this is a jump to a machine language address)
USR(X)	Call user-defined function (usually this is a jump to a machine language address)
VAL(X$)	Numerical value of a number in string form
%X.Y	Specify format for printing numbers

APPENDIX B

PERIODICALS REVIEWED

The following personal computer magazines were used in compiling this book. Except where indicated, we have reviewed every issue of each magazine from the time the magazine started publishing until December of 1979 (updates are current through June, 1980). The number of pages given is the size of a typical issue (but note that a magazine will vary in size from issue to issue). The prices given are as of mid-1980. For current prices, contact the individual magazines.

Magazines which actively market back issues (they run ads describing what back issues are available and how much they are) are noted. Most magazines keep a stock of old copies (usually going back about two to three years from the current issue). Even those magazines that don't run ads for their back issues will usually send you the issue you desire if you send them the current cover price of the magazine.

Magazines which are available in microform (microfilm and microfiche) are indicated. University Microfilms is the national microfilming service which provides these to libraries and to the public (see "Where Can I Get These Programs?"). Prices are usually substantially *less* than the original cover price of the magazine. For a nominal charge, University Microfilms will photocopy an article or an entire issue for you. For more information, contact University Microfilms.

All of the magazines reviewed contain articles on a wide variety of topics. Some of the magazines, however, have a special emphasis on one particular segment of microcomputing. Where this is so, it has been noted.

Byte

70 Main Street
Peterborough, NH 03458
monthly, 288 pages
$18/year, $2.50/issue

Started in 1975, *Byte* has the largest circulation of any of the personal computing magazines. Its emphasis is on articles for the more advanced microcomputer user. *Byte* activity markets back issues. *Byte* is available in microform from University Microfilms.

Calculators/Computers Magazine

No longer published.

Compute

P.O. Box 5119
Greensboro, NC 27403
bimonthly, 113 pages
$9/year, $2/issue

Compute is the successor to *The PET Gazette*. *Compute* is devoted to computers based on 6502-class microprocessors (computers such as the PET, Apple II, etc.).

Creative Computing

P.O. Box 789-M
Morristown, NJ 07960
monthly, 192 pages
15/year, $2.50/issue

Creative Computing is about the fourth largest of the personal computing magazines in circulation. Its emphasis is on software and general programming articles for beginning and intermediate level users. *Creative Computing* actively markets back issues. The magazine is available in microform from University Microfilms. Some of the early articles and programs are available in Volumes 1 and 2 of *The Best of Creative Computing*.

Dr. Dobb's Journal of Computer Calisthenics & Orthodontia

P.O. Box E
Menlo Park, CA 94025
10 issues/year, 58 pages
$15/year, $2.50/issue

Dr. Dobb's Journal is oriented toward users who like to use machine language. The magazine runs little or no advertising. *Dr. Dobb's Journal* actively markets back issues. The magazine is available in microform from University Microfilms. The complete contents of the first three volumes of the magazines are available in book form.

Interface Age

16704 Marquardt Avenue
Cerritos, CA 90701
monthly, 144 pages
$18/year, $2.50/issue

Interface Age has the third largest circulation of the microcomputer magazines. Its emphasis is on information for business and trade users of microcomputers. *Interface Age* started with issue number 9 as a spin-off from the club newsletter, *SCCS Interface. Interface Age* actively markets back issues. The magazine is available in microform from University Microfilms.

Kilobaud

Now *Kilobaud Microcomputing.*

Kilobaud Microcomputing

80 Pine Street
Peterborough, NH 03458
monthly, 258 pages
$25/year, $2.95/issue

Number two in the field of home computer magazines, *Kilobaud Microcomputing* gets our vote for the best all-around microcomputing magazine. It has a great many articles about both hardware and software. It has articles geared for both beginners and for more sophisticated users. Until 1979 it was called *Kilobaud. Kilobaud Microcomputing* actively markets back issues. The magazine is available in microform from University Microfilms.

Micro

P.O. Box 6502
Chelmsford, MA 01824
monthly, 80 pages
$15/year, $2/issue

Micro is devoted to computers based on 6502-class microprocessors (computers such as the PET, Apple II, etc.). *Micro* actively markets back issues. The books, *The Best of Micro* (Volumes 1 and 2) contain everything in the first two years of *Micro* except the advertising. *All of Micro* (Volume 2) contains everything from the second year of *Micro.*

People's Computer Company

Now *Recreational Computing.*

People's Computers

Now *Recreational Computing.*

Personal Computing

1050 Commonwealth Avenue
Boston MA 02215
monthly, 112 pages
$14/year, $2/issue

Personal Computing is geared to general computer topics and software. Each issue has a large section on game-playing programs for such sophisticated games as chess, checkers, and bridge. *Personal Computing* actively markets back issues. Some of the early articles and programs are available in the book, *The Best of Personal Computing.*

Recreational Computing

P.O. Box E
Menlo Park, CA 94025
bimonthly, 50 pages
$10/year, $2.50/issue

The granddaddy of all home computer magazines, *Recreational Computing* began publication back in 1972 as a newspaper called *People's Computer Company.* Changing to a magazine, it was renamed *People's Computers* and later was given its present title. The magazine contains little advertising. *Recreational Computing* actively markets back issues. The magazine is available in microform from University Microfilms.

ROM

No longer published. (Many issues are still available from *Creative Computing.*)

'68' Micro Journal

P.O. Box 849
Hixson, TN 37343
monthly, 48 pages
$14.50/year, $2.50/issue

'68' Micro Journal is devoted to computers based on 6800-class microprocessors.

GLOSSARY

absolute value. The value of a number, ignoring its plus or minus sign.

acoustic coupler. A device which converts data into sound so that it can be transmitted over telephone lines.

A/D converter. See *analog-to-digital converter*.

address. A location in a computer's memory.

addressable-cursor video display. A display in which the cursor can be moved directly to any point on the screen.

algorithm. A procedure for solving a problem or accomplishing a task.

alphanumeric. Having both alphabetic (A–Z) and numerical (0–9) characters.

American National Standards Institute (ANSI). An organization devoted to developing national standards.

analog. Representation of a quantity by a continuously variable value (as opposed to *digital*).

analog-to-digital (A/D) converter. A device that translates an analog voltage into a number proportional to the voltage.

AND. A logic operator. X AND Y is TRUE if both X and Y are TRUE; otherwise it's FALSE.

ANSI. See *American National Standards Institute*.

APL. An acronym for A Programming Language, a computer language characterized by its large set of operators.

append. To add new statements to a program.

application. A problem or task for which a computer is to be used.

argument. A value or variable to be passed to a subroutine, function, or operator.

array. A set of variables referred to by a single subscripted variable name.

ASCII. An acronym for American Standard Code for Information Interchange, a standardized code for transmitting and storing character data.

assembler. A program that translates symbolic instructions into machine language.

assembly language. A "low-level" computer language in which instruction symbols are translated directly into machine language.

assignment. The copying of a value into a variable.

assignment statement. A statement (LET in BASIC) which copies a value from an expression (or variable) into a variable.

base. See *number base*.

BASIC. An acronym for Beginner's All-purpose Symbolic Instruction Code, a computer language designed to be easy to learn.

baud. A data transmission rate equivalent to *bits-per-second*.

Baudot. A five-bit character code. (Has been superseded by ASCII.)

benchmark. A program designed to test the performance (usually the speed) of hardware or software.

binary. Pertaining to the base-2 number system.

bit. The smallest possible unit of information. A bit can have only one of two possible values which can be represented as true/false, on/off, 0/1, etc.

bits-per-second (BPS). A rate of data transmission.

bootstrap. The technique of using a short program to load a larger one.

BPS. See *bits-per-second*.

branch. A transfer of control to another section of a program.

bug. A program flaw.

bus. A circuit that provides a path for transmitting data between devices.

byte. A unit of data composed of eight bits. Frequently used to hold exactly one alphanumeric character.

CAI. See *computer assisted instruction*.

call. See *subroutine call*.

cassette. A type of self-contained packaging for magnetic tape on which data can be stored.

cathode-ray tube (CRT). A television-like display.

central processing unit (CPU). The "main" part of the computer where instructions are executed.

chain. To load and start one program from another (usually by executing a CHAIN statement).

character. A letter, number, or symbol.

character set. A group of characters encoded in a similar manner.

characters-per-second (CPS). A data transmission rate.

character string. See *string*.

chip. See *integrated circuit*.

clock. A device that provides electronic timing signals.

close. To terminate the use of an external file and per-

267

form any "housekeeping" tasks necessary to return the file to an inactive state.

COBOL. An acronym for Common Business Oriented Language, a computer language designed to fit the needs of business users.

comment. See *remark*.

compiler. A program that translates a computer program written in a "high-level" language such as FORTRAN into machine language instructions.

computer assisted instruction (CAI). The use of computers to assist in the teaching of students.

computer language. A language designed to express the steps needed to accomplish a task using a computer.

computer program. A set of instructions telling a computer how to perform a particular task.

computer system. (1) A computer along with its related equipment and software. (2) A collection of programs which form a unified package.

concatenation. The joining of two or more character strings.

constant. A value that does not change during the execution of a program.

control character. (1) A character that causes a special action to occur. (2) Any one of ASCII characters 1 to 26.

controller. A device that controls the operation of a piece of peripheral equipment.

core. (1) A type of random-access memory in which data is stored in tiny doughnut-like ferrite "cores." (2) The main operating memory of a computer.

CP/M. An operating system (produced by Digital Research Corp.) designed for use on microcomputers.

CPS. See *characters-per-second*.

CPU. See *central processing unit*.

cross assembler. An assembler that runs on one type of computer, but outputs machine code for another.

cross compiler. A compiler that runs on one type of computer, but outputs machine code for another.

CRT. See *cathode-ray tube*.

current loop. A type of serial data transmission line.

cursor. A position indicator used to show where the next character is to be placed on a display screen.

D/A converter. See *digital-to-analog converter*.

database. A collection of data stored in a computer in such a way as to provide convenient access.

data processing. (1) The handling of data by electronic means. (2) The business use of computers.

data tablet. A device for inputting data to a computer by "drawing" on a special pad.

debug. To remove the flaws from a program.

decimal. Pertaining to the base-10 number system.

DEC strings. See *Digital Equipment Corporation strings*.

demo. See *demonstration program*.

demonstration program. A program designed to demonstrate how a program works, what a piece of hardware can do, etc.

diagnostic. See *diagnostic program*.

diagnostic program. A program used to detect and diagnose malfunctions in a computer system.

digital. Representation of a quantity by discrete values. As opposed to *analog*.

Digital Equipment Corporation strings. A system of representing character strings in which substrings are extracted from a string by functions such as RIGHT$, LEFT$, and MID$.

digital-to-analog (D/A) converter. A device that translates a number into a voltage proportional to the number.

direct memory access (DMA). A data transfer system in which blocks of data are transmitted directly between a peripheral and memory.

directory. A machine-readable index showing where files are located on a peripheral device such as a disk.

disassembler. A program that translates machine code into assembly language.

disc. See *disk*.

disk. A storage device in which data is stored on magnetic disks. Also used to refer to the magnetic disks themselves.

diskette. See *floppy disk*.

disk file. A data file stored on disk.

disk operating system (DOS). A type of operating system used to load and run programs on a computer system with a disk.

documentation. The documents associated with a computer program which explain what the program does and how to use it.

DOS. See *disk operating system*.

double-precision. A way of storing numbers that allows them to have more significant digits than with normal "single-precision."

DP. See *data processing*.

driver. A set of instructions telling the computer how to reformat data for transfer to or from a peripheral device and how to accomplish that transfer.

dump. (1) A program to output the contents of a file or area of memory. (2) A listing of the contents of a file or area of memory.

EBCDIC. An acronym for Extended Binary Coded Decimal Interchange Code, an eight-bit character code used primarily by International Business Machines (IBM) equipment.

editor. See *text editor*.

8080-based microcomputer. A computer which uses the Intel 8080 microprocessor chip (or similar) as its CPU.

emulator. A program that allows a computer to mimic the instruction set of another.

end-of-file (EOF). A condition signifying that all of the data in an input file has already been read.

end-of-file mark. A character used to mark the end of data in a file.

EOF. See *end-of-file*.

exclusive-OR (XOR). A logic operator. X XOR Y is TRUE if X is TRUE or Y is TRUE, but not if both are TRUE at the same time; otherwise it's FALSE.

execute. To cause a program to start running.

external file. See *file*.

external storage. Data storage separate from, but accessible to, a computer.

FALSE. A logic condition.

file. A group of data treated as a unit.

filename. The name used to refer to a file by a computer system.

firmware. Operating instructions built into a computer using read-only memory.

floppy disk. A storage device in which data is stored on flexible magnetic disks. Also used to refer to the magnetic disks themselves.

flowchart. A formalized diagram representing the flow of logic of a program.

FORTRAN. An acronym for FORmula TRANslator, one of the earliest "high-level" languages.

front panel. A computer control panel.

full-duplex. Transmission in which data can move in both directions simultaneously through a communications line.

function. A special type of subroutine that can be used in place of a variable to provide a single-valued result.

GIGO. Garbage-In-Garbage-Out. An expression meaning, "What you get out of a computer is no better than the data you put into it."

graphics. The use of a computer peripheral such as a CRT or plotter to create drawings or pictures.

graphics display. A peripheral device that can display drawings or figures on its screen.

half-duplex. Transmission in which data can only move in one direction at a time through a communications line.

hardcopy. Printed output from a computer system.

hardware. Electronic and mechanical equipment.

Hewlett-Packard strings. A system of representing character strings in which substrings are denoted by a special bracket construct.

hex. See *hexadecimal.*

hexadecimal. Pertaining to the base-16 number system.

high-level language. A computer language that is designed to be easier for humans to use, at the expense of being harder for the computer to translate into its own internal instruction code.

homebrew. Homemade; as opposed to being professionally manufactured.

home computer. See *personal computer.*

HP strings. See *Hewlett-Packard strings.*

input. (1) Data that is fed into a computer. (2) To enter data into a computer.

input device. A piece of equipment that supplies data to a computer.

input-output. The transmitting of data between a computer and its peripheral devices.

instruction. An electronically encoded command telling a computer to perform a specific operation.

instruction set. The set of elementary operations that a computer can perform.

integer. A "whole number" (number that cannot have a fractional part).

integrated circuit. A small, solid-state electronic circuit mounted in a special case.

interactive. A mode of operation in which a computer responds immediately to commands typed at a keyboard.

interface. A circuit which allows a computer to be connected electronically to another device.

interpreter. A program which reads and immediately executes previously stored instructions.

interrupt. A signal or condition which causes a computer to temporarily stop what it's doing and start another operation.

I/O. See *input-output.*

iteration. The repeated execution of an operation or group of operations.

joystick. An input device that uses a movable stick to select input values.

jump. The transferring of control to another part of a program.

K. See *kilo-.*

keyboard. A console for typing in character data.

keypunch. A device that punches data holes into punch cards.

keyword. A word or symbol that has a special meaning in a computer language.

kilo-. Prefix meaning 1,000. In computing, frequently used to mean 2 raised to the 10th power (1,024).

LED. See *light-emitting diode.*

library. A collection of computer programs.

light pen. A sensor that can be aimed at a display screen to "point out" data on the screen to the computer.

light-emitting diode. A semiconductor device that emits light.

line printer. A printer that prints an entire line of characters at a time.

lines-per-minute (LPM). A rate used to describe the speed of a line printer.

linkage editor. A program that "connects" a set of independent routines into a complete computer program.

linking loader. A program which "connects" a set of independent routines into a complete program and then loads that program into memory.

list. (1) An ordered set of data. (2) To print a listing of a program.

listing. See *program listing.*

load. To transfer a program from external storage to a computer's main memory.

loader. A program which loads other programs into memory.

logic operator. An operator that takes TRUE/FALSE values as arguments and produces a TRUE/FALSE value as a result.

loop. An operation or group of operations that are executed repeatedly.

low-level language. A computer language in which the instructions are very close in meaning to the basic machine language instructions of the computer used.

M. See *mega-.*

machine code. See *machine language.*

machine language. The binary electrical code used to represent elementary computer operations.

machine-readable. In a form readily usable by a computer (such as coded on disk or tape).

macro-assembler. An assembler in which the user may define generalized symbols to represent the machine code to be generated.

magtape. See *tape*.

mass storage. See *external storage*.

matrix (plural matrices). A set of numbers arranged in rows and columns. In BASIC, matrices are represented by arrays.

matrix arithmetic. A system of arithmetic used to manipulate matrices.

mega-. Prefix denoting 1,000,000. In computing, frequently used to mean 2 raised to the 20th power (1,048,576).

memory. The part of the computer used to store data. Normally this term is used to refer specifically to a computer's main internal memory (and not to the computer's external memory, such as disk).

memory-mapped video display. A display in which data is taken directly from memory and displayed; any changes in the memory area are immediately reflected in the display.

microcomputer. A small computer which uses a single integrated circuit or small group of circuits as its CPU. Often used to refer to the computer chip itself.

microprocessor. A CPU on a single integrated circuit.

minicomputer. A "medium-sized" computer or computer system.

minifloppy. A floppy disk that uses disks smaller than eight inches.

mnemonic. A symbolic representation of a machine language instruction.

modem. A device used to allow a computer to communicate with a terminal or with another computer over telephone lines.

monitor. (1) A computer program that assists in the loading and running of other programs. (2) A type of video display.

Murphy's Law. A "law" which states, "If anything can go wrong, it will." Long-term use of computers will give you a deeper understanding of the significance of this law.

NOT. A logic operator. NOT X is TRUE if X is FALSE; otherwise it's FALSE.

number base. The number of symbols used to represent values in a number system. The decimal system is called the "base-10" system because it uses 10 symbols (0–9) to represent values.

nybble. Four bits.

object code. Machine code generated by an assembler or compiler.

octal. Pertaining to the base-8 number system.

off-line. Not actively connected to a computer system.

on-line. Actively connected to a computer system.

open. To prepare a file for input-output.

operand. A value that an operator processes.

operating system. A program or group of programs that assist in the loading and running of other programs.

operator. A symbol used to indicate a particular operation such as addition or string concatenation.

OR. A logic operator. X OR Y is TRUE if X is TRUE, or Y is TRUE, or both are TRUE; otherwise it's FALSE.

output. (1) Data, displays, or printouts that come out of a computer system. (2) To transfer data out of a computer.

output device. A piece of equipment which accepts data from a computer.

papertape. Strips of paper into which holes are punched to represent data.

parallel. A type of operation in which data is transmitted simultaneously in several channels at once.

parity. A computer error-checking method in which a bit is added to each piece of data. The bit is set so that the binary sum of all the data bits is either always even or always odd.

Pascal. An advanced computer language which lends itself well to structured programming.

patch. A correction or modification to a program.

peripheral. See *peripheral device*.

peripheral device. A device electronically attached to, but separate from, a computer.

personal computer. A computer designed for personal use.

PILOT. A computer language designed for use in computer assisted instruction (CAI) applications.

plot. (1) To draw or display. (2) A drawing or graphics display.

plotter. A device used to draw pictures or diagrams.

pointer. An indicator that shows where another piece of data is.

port. A place for input-output from a computer.

precision. The degree of discrimination possible in a number. For example, a two-digit number can distinguish 100 different possibilities.

printer. A device used to print characters or symbols.

printout. The printed output from a computer system.

processor. See *central processing unit*.

program. See *computer program*.

program listing. A listing of the statements in a computer program.

programming language. See *computer language*.

program statement. See *statement*.

program variable. See *variable*.

punch card. A paper card into which holes are punched to represent data.

RAM. See *random-access memory*.

random-access. The characteristic of being able to access data in any sequence without regard to the order in which the data is stored.

random-access file device. A device in which data in files can be accessed in random order (for example, a disk).

random-access memory (RAM). Memory in which the data can be accessed in random order. Generally used to refer specifically to the main computer memory and not to such forms of external storage as disk.

random number generator. A function that outputs a randomly selected number each time it is called.

read. The operation of inputting data from a peripheral device.

read-only memory (ROM). A memory that you can read from, but not write to.

real. A type of number that can have a fractional part.

real-time. Operation fast enough to keep up with "real world" events.

real-time clock. A clock used to synchronize real-time operations.

record. A set of data handled as a single unit.

recursion. A process which allows an operation to be defined in terms of itself.

recursive subroutine. A subroutine that can call itself.

remark. A comment in a program. It is not part of the program itself, but is there merely to explain how the program works.

renumber. To change the numbering of the lines in a BASIC program.

resequence. See *renumber*.

resolution. How small a dot a graphics device can display. The higher the resolution, the more dots can be displayed in a given area on the screen.

ROM. See *read-only memory*.

ROM cartridge. A cartridge which holds ROM memory and can be plugged into a computer.

routine. (1) A procedure to perform a task. (2) A subroutine.

RS-232C. A type of serial data transmission line.

run. (1) To execute a program. (2) The output from an execution of a program.

scrolling. The ability of a video display terminal to shift the text on its screen up automatically to allow new text to be entered at the bottom.

sequential. The characteristic of being able to access data only in the order in which it is stored.

sequential file device. A device in which data in files can be accessed only sequentially (for example, a tape drive).

serial. A type of operation in which data is transmitted sequentially over a single communications line.

significant digit. A digit in a number that can take a value other than zero.

simulation. A program that models a process or system.

single-precision. The "normal" way of storing numbers that is more compact than "double-precision," but allows fewer significant digits.

6800-based microcomputer. A computer which uses the Motorola 6800 microprocessor chip (or similar) as its CPU.

6502-based microcomputer. A computer which uses the MOS Technology 6502 microprocessor chip (or similar) as its CPU.

software. Computer programs or routines.

sort. A program or routine that sorts data into a specified order.

source. See *source code*.

source code. A program that is to be translated into machine usable form by a compiler or assembler.

statement. One step in a high-level language program.

string. A series of characters treated as a single unit.

structured programming. A method of writing programs designed to clarify their meanings and aid in their production.

subroutine. A routine or set of program statements to which control can be temporarily passed from a "main" program.

subroutine call. A transfer of control to a subroutine.

subscript. A number used to indicate a particular element in an array.

substring. A section of a string.

symbol. A character or series of characters used to represent an operation, variable, etc.

system. See *computer system*.

systems program. A program used as a basic part of a computer system to develop and use other programs.

table. An organized collection of data in which a datum can be accessed according to its position.

tape. A type of data storage in which data is stored on magnetic tape.

terminal. A device used to communicate data between a person and a computer.

text editor. A program designed to help create and modify documents and other character data.

timesharing. A system which allows several people to use a computer at one time.

token. A datum used to represent an operation or variable.

trace. A program that allows a user to trace which statements are executing in a program.

translator. A program that translates other programs from one form to another.

TRUE. A logic condition.

utility. See *utility program*.

utility program. A computer program intended to help a person use a computer system.

variable. A symbol and/or storage location for a particular piece of data.

variable name. The name used to refer to a variable.

VDM. See *video display module*.

video display module (VDM). See *video terminal interface*.

video terminal interface (VTI). An interface that allows a video display to get its display information directly from a computer's memory.

VTI. See *video terminal interface*.

word. A unit of data composed of one or more bytes.

word processing. The manipulation of documents or files of text.

write. The operation of outputting data to a peripheral device.

XOR. See *exclusive-OR*.

Z80-based microcomputer. A computer which uses the Zilog Z80 microprocessor chip (or similar) as its CPU.